FOR ORGANS, PIANOS & ELECTRONIC KEYBOARDS

E·Z PLAY® TODAY

359

100 Years of Song
1900-1999

ISBN 0-634-00991-5

HAL·LEONARD®
CORPORATION

7777 W. BLUEMOUND RD. P.O. BOX 13819 MILWAUKEE, WI 53213

Visit Hal Leonard Online at
www.halleonard.com

100 Years of Song

Chronological Listing

100 Years of Song

Alphabetical Listing

Note: In many cases a song's popularity hit its peak in a year (or years, occasionally) after it was written.

WHEN YOU WERE SWEET SIXTEEN
1900

Words and Music by James Thornton. One day James Thornton's wife asked him if he still loved her. He replied, "I love you like I did when you were sweet sixteen." His wife pointed out that there was a song in that statement and Thornton went to work. The song sold over a million copies of sheet music during the early years of the century, appearing later in such films as *Little Miss Broadway* (1938), *The Strawberry Blond* (1941), and *The Jolson Story* (1946). When Perry Como revived the song in 1947, his recording sold over a million copies. It remains a favorite of barbershop quartets.

STARS AND STRIPES FOREVER
1901

Music by John Philip Sousa. Sousa, America's March King, wrote the vast majority of this country's most memorable patriotic tunes. Of the many Sousa marches that remain favorites of professional and school bands throughout the country, none is so familiar as "Stars and Stripes Forever." Written in 1896, Sousa's own recording of the piece went to number 1 in the fledgling gramophone market in 1901. For many years the trio section of the march was used by circus bands to warn circus personnel of a disaster, since it was a piece that all of the musicians knew well enough to play at a moment's notice.

BILL BAILEY, WON'T YOU PLEASE COME HOME
1902

Words and Music Hughie Cannon. It has been said that imitation is the sincerest form of flattery. If that is true, the spate of Bill Bailey songs that followed the success of "Bill Bailey, Won't You Please Come Home," attests to the song's popularity. Follow-ups included "I Wonder Why Bill Bailey Don't Come Home" and "Since Bill Bailey Came Back Home." Although the song is said to be based on a real-life story of musician William Godfrey Bailey, song-writer Hughie Cannon always insisted that the song's plot was pure fiction. It was recorded by Kid Ory, Jimmy Durante, Eddie Jackson, becoming a million-seller for Bobby Darin in 1960. Danny Kaye and Louis Armstrong performed it in *The Five Pennies* (1959). It's the most central song in the Dixieland repertoire.

IDA, SWEET AS APPLE CIDER
1903

Words by Eddie Leonard, Music by Eddie Munson. Best known as the theme song of Eddie Cantor, who sang it as a tribute to his wife Ida, this song is said to have saved lyricist Eddie Leonard's job. In 1903 he was performing with the Primrose and West minstrel company and about to lose his contract, when the company manager allowed him to introduce the song. The song was an instant, enormous success. It not only saved Leonard's job, but also brought him fame on Broadway, where he sang it in the musical *Roly Boly Eyes* (1919), a show written for him.

SWEET ADELINE
1904

Words by Richard H. Gerard (Richard Gerard Husch), Music by Henry Armstrong. Before "Sweet Adeline" became the anthem of barbershop quartets, it was known as one of the most successful echo songs of the early 1900s. Armstrong wrote this melody as an instrumental piece, entitled "Down Home in New England," in 1896. Gerard, asked to write the lyric, first came up with "You're the Flower of My Heart, Sweet Rosalie." When the song was turned down by several publishers, he went looking for a more suitable name. Spotting posters for opera singer Adelina Patti's farewell concert, he landed on the more American name Adeline. In 1906 John F. "Honey" Fitzpatrick adopted the song as his campaign theme song in a Boston mayoral race. Oscar Hammerstein II and Jerome Kern borrowed the title to name a 1929 musical comedy with an original score.

IN THE SHADE OF THE OLD APPLE TREE
1905

Words by Harry H. Williams, Music by Egbert Van Alstyne. Egbert Van Alstyne liked to say that he was inspired to write "In the Shade of the Old Apple Tree" after a visit to New York City's Central Park. There were, however, no apple trees in Central Park. Williams and Van Alstyne had toured the country as a vaudeville act before they came to New York in 1900. Williams and Van Alstyne were working as Tin Pan Alley song-pluggers when they hit the big time with this song.

WAIT 'TIL THE SUN SHINES NELLIE
1906

Words by Andrew B. Sterling, Music by Harry Von Tilzer. This ballad was first introduced in vaudeville, where it quickly became a standard. Several stars brought it to the motion picture screen, including Bing Crosby and Mary Martin in *Birth of the Blues* (1941), Gale Storm and Robert Lowey in *Rhythm Parade* (1942), Judy Garland and Van Johnson in *In the Good Old Summertime* (1949). It's another barbershop era standard.

SCHOOL DAYS
(When We Were a Couple of Kids)
1907

Words by Will D. Cobb, Music by Gus Edwards. This was the title song of Gus Edward's vaudeville act, which produced quite a few hit songs. Edward's act featured a line-up of child stars including George Jessel, Eddie Cantor, Groucho Marx, and others. "School Days" was Edwards' greatest hit, selling over three million copies of sheet music. A recording by Byron G. Harlan is one of the best-selling recordings of all time. Bing Crosby sang the song in *The Star Maker* (1939), a film based on Edwards' life. Gale Storm and Phil Regan sang it in *Sunbonnet Sue* (1945).

TAKE ME OUT TO THE BALL GAME
1908

Words by Jack Norworth, Music by Albert von Tilzer. "Take Me Out to the Ball Game" is the most often repeated sing-along song in America, popping up during the seventh-inning stretch of nearly every major league game. Amazingly, it was twenty years after the song's success before its composer, Albert von Tilzer, saw his first baseball game. Von Tilzer introduced the tune himself in vaudeville, winning a coveted contract to tour the Orpheum circuit on the basis of its success. The "unofficial anthem of baseball" has appeared in numerous films as underscoring to baseball scenes. It was the title song of a 1949 movie musical that starred Gene Kelly, Frank Sinatra and Esther Williams.

SHINE ON, HARVEST MOON
1909

Words by Jack Norworth, Music by Nora Bayes and Jack Norworth. Nora Bayes introduced what became her trademark number in the *Ziegfeld Follies of 1908*. Jack Norworth also made the song centerpiece of his vaudeville act for the rest of his life. "Shine On, Harvest Moon" reappeared in the *Ziegfeld Follies of 1931*, sung by Ruth Etting. In 1944 it served as the title song for a film starring Ann Sheridan and Dennis Morgan. Songwriters Nora Bayes and Jack Norworth sang it themselves in *A Slight Case of Murder* (1936). It was also heard in such films as *Ever Since Eve* (1937), *Nancy Goes to Rio* (1950), and *The Eddy Duchin Story* (1956).

7

LET ME CALL YOU SWEETHEART

1910

Words and Music by Beth Slater Whitson and Leo Friedman. This perennial sing-along favorite was a best-selling record for The Peerless Quartet. It was been sung by Betty Grable in *Coney Island* (1943), Gene Kelly in *Thousands Cheer* (1943), and Beatrice Kay in *Diamond Horseshoe* (1945). It was also heard in *The Rose* (1979), sung by Bette Midler.

ALEXANDER'S RAGTIME BAND

1911

Words and Music by Irving Berlin. Although this is the song that began the American ragtime craze, it's a rag in title only. "Rag" refers to ragged rhythm, or syncopation. The only true syncopation occurs in the chorus on the word "just." The song began as "Alexander and His Clarinet" in 1910. Berlin was not happy with it and set it aside. A year later he fisted it from his famous trunk, adapting the lyric to a melody he had written sometime earlier. Most sources tell us that the song became a hit when Emma Carus introduced it in vaudeville, but there are stories of Berlin's having introduced it himself. Alice Faye sang it in the 1938 film of the same name. In the 1954 film *There's No Business Like Show Business* the song was turned into an elaborate, multi-national production number. "Alexander's Ragtime Band" was also heard in the 1997 blockbuster *Titanic*.

DOWN BY THE OLD MILL STREAM

1912

Words and Music by Tell Taylor. Although Tell Taylor usually receives credit for this favorite sing-along song, there is evidence to suggest that this late classic of the barbershop era was co-authored by Earl K. Smith. Smith claimed to have written the title and the chorus. Some years later Taylor opened a golf course, which he named the Old Mill Stream Golf Course. It was a leading hit of the day, selling over two million copies of sheet music.

DANNY BOY

1913

Words and Music by Frederick Edward Weatherly. This famous melody, with or without words, rarely fails to wring tears from an audience. Weatherly took the traditional Irish melody "Londonderry Air," which had been written in 1855, and made an adaptation that included new lyrics. Operatic contralto Ernestine Schumann-Heink was among the first to perform and record the song. Among artists who later recorded it were Glenn Miller and his Orchestra, Conway Twitty, Andy Williams, Patti LaBelle and The Blue Belles, Ray Price and Judy Garland. It's the kind of song that's probably being sung somewhere in the world right now as you read this sentence.

ST. LOUIS BLUES

1914

Words and Music by W.C. Handy. This is easily the most familiar, successful commercial blues song of all time. Handy wrote the song to capitalize on the previous success of his hit "The Memphis Blues." He had sold that song for a mere $50 to a publisher who made a fortune with it. While searching for an idea for a follow-up song, Handy recalled the days when he had been down on his luck in St. Louis. Learning from the past, he formed his own publishing company to handle the song and reap the profits. Handy brought his own African-American blues tradition into the American pop music mainstream with this song. It was later heard in numerous films, such as *Is Everybody Happy?* (1929), *The Birth of the Blues* (1941), *Jam Session* (1944), *Glory Alley* (1952), and *St. Louis Blues* (1958), the film biography of Handy.

IT'S A LONG, LONG WAY TO TIPPERARY

1915

Words and Music by Jack Judge and Harry H. Williams. One of the anthems of America's involvement in World War I – unlikely, considering the lyrics – this song tells the story of an Irish man in London, whose sweetheart is back in County Tipperary in the south of Ireland. The song first appeared on stage in *Chin Chin* (1914) and *Dancing Around* (1914). It was heard in such films as *Cavalcade* (1933), *The Story of Vernon and Irene Castle* (1939), *For Me and My Gal* (1942), *Presenting Lily Mars* (1943), *Oh! What a Lovely War* (1969), and *Darling Lili* (1970).

PRETTY BABY

1916

Words by Gus Kahn, Music by Tony Jackson and Egbert Van Alstyne. Also known as "the party-pooper song," "Pretty Baby" was introduced to theater audiences by Dolly Hackett in *The Passing Show of 1916*. It appeared in several films such as *Rose of Washington Square* (1939), *Is Everybody Happy?* (1943), *Shine On, Harvest Moon* (1944), *April Showers* (1948), *Jolson Sings Again* (1949), *The I Don't Care Girl* (1953), *The Eddie Cantor Story* (1953), and the Gus Kahn film biography *I'll See You in My Dreams* (1951).

OVER THERE

1917

Words and Music by George M. Cohan. "Over There" is the song most identified with World War I. George M. Cohan was at home on April 6, 1917, when he read in the newspaper that America was at war with Germany. He began humming to himself, quickly coming up with a song, borrowing the title of an 1886 popular song "Johnny, Get Your Gun" as his first line. Charles King introduced "Over There" at a Red Cross Benefit at the Hippodrome Theatre in New York later that year. When Nora Bayes recorded it and featured it in her vaudeville act, it became a national hit. Enrico Caruso recorded it as well. The song became relevant and popular once again when America entered World War II, and was featured in live performances and several films at that time.

SMILES

1918

Words by J. Will Callahan, Music by Lee S. Roberts. Lee S. Roberts attended a convention of music dealers, where he sat through a lecture on the value of smiling while doing business. According to legend, he wrote the song that day on the back of a package of cigarettes. He sent the song to Callahan with a note about writing lyrics about smiles. Callahan wrote the lyrics in less than an hour. When several Tin Pan Alley publishers rejected it, Callahan and Roberts formed a publishing company to publish the song themselves. Within six months of publication, it had sold more than two million copies of sheet music.

A PRETTY GIRL IS LIKE A MELODY

1919

Words and Music by Irving Berlin. An international favorite for fashion shows and beauty pageants, this song was introduced in the *Ziegfeld Follies of 1919*. It quickly became the theme song of the *Follies*, which glorified the female form. The lyric of the song represents girls as different classical compositions. It appeared as a huge production number in *The Great Ziegfeld* (1936), and was also in *Alexander's Ragtime Band* (1938), *The Powers Girl* (1943), *Blue Skies* (1946), and *There's No Business Like Show Business* (1954).

SWANEE

1920

Words by Irving Caesar, Music by George Gershwin. Gershwin and Caesar met for lunch one day to discuss song ideas. After eating they rode the bus together to Gershwin's apartment, discussing a new song on the way. When they arrived at the apartment they went right to the piano and put the song together lickity-split. Songs about the South were a convention for songwriters of the time, regardless of whether or not they had ever set foot below the Mason Dixon Line. Gershwin and Caesar borrowed Stephen Foster's mythical Swanee River locale (it's actually the Sewanee River), selling over two million records and one million copies of sheet music in a year. This was Gershwin's first and greatest commercial song success, and made him famous at the age of 21.

AIN'T WE GOT FUN?

1921

Words and Music by Richard A. Whiting, Raymond B. Egan and Gus Kahn. After it was introduced in the revue *Satires of 1920*, the song was picked up and popularized by Ruth Roye. "Ain't We Got Fun" was interpolated into several film musicals, including *On Moonlight Bay* (1951), *By the Light of the Silvery Moon* (1953), *The Eddie Cantor Story* (1954), and *I'll See You in My Dreams* (1951), the film biography of songwriter Gus Kahn.

CAROLINA IN THE MORNING

1922

Words by Gus Kahn, Music by Walter Donaldson. Brooklyn born Walter Donaldson had never seen either of the Carolinas when he wrote this hit song. Like many other New York songwriters of the early years of the 20th century, he wrote several other songs about a south he had never seen, capitalizing on the public's appetite for the genre. Donaldson and Kahn were a formidable team, producing several other hits, including "Love Me or Leave Me," "My Buddy," "Yes Sir, That's My Baby," and "Makin' Whoopee!" "Carolina in the Morning" was introduced in the Broadway revue *The Passing Show of 1922*. It was later heard in such films as *The Dolly Sisters* (1945), *April Showers* (1948), *Jolson Sings Again* (1949), and the Gus Kahn film biography, *I'll See You in My Dreams* (1951).

YES! WE HAVE NO BANANAS

1923

Words and Music by Frank Silver and Irving Cohn. This is one of the most successful of the novelty songs that were popular in the 1920s. The songwriters introduced it in a New York restaurant to a luke-warm response. Eddie Cantor saw a copy of the sheet music and decided to interpolate it in the revue *Make It Snappy*, which was then playing in Philadelphia. The audience loved it, making Cantor sing the chorus over and over. It stopped the show in its tracks for more than fifteen minutes. Cantor kept the song in his act for years and made a best-selling recording of it as well. Thanks to radio and recordings, the entire country was soon singing "Yes! We Have No Bananas."

SOMEBODY LOVES ME

1924

Words by Ballard MacDonald and B.G. DeSylva, Music by George Gershwin. This was one of George Gershwin's last songs before the period when he began working almost exclusively with his lyricist brother Ira. "Somebody Loves Me" was heard in *George White's Scandals of 1924*. Lena Horne sang it in the film *Broadway Rhythm* (1943), Oscar Levant and Tom Patricola performed it in *Rhapsody in Blue* (1945). It was also heard in the films *Lullaby of Broadway* (1951), *Somebody Loves Me* (1952), and *Pete Kelly's Blues* (1955).

ALWAYS

1925

Words and Music by Irving Berlin. Of all the songs Irving Berlin added to American popular culture, "Always" was one of his favorites. His list of favorites also included "Easter Parade," "God Bless America," "Show Business," and "White Christmas." "Always" was written for the Marx Brothers' stage musical, *The Cocoanuts* (1925). Although dropped from the show, it became a huge hit soon after it was published. Berlin made a gift of the song and its copyright to his bride, Ellin Mackay.

BYE BYE BLACKBIRD

1926

Words by Mort Dixon, Music by Ray Henderson. Although this song became the theme song of vaudeville performer Georgie Price, it was first popularized by Eddie Cantor. The song appeared in several films, including *Rainbow Round My Shoulder* (1952), *River of No Return* (1954), *The Eddie Cantor Story* (1954), and *Pete Kelly's Blues* (1955). Jason Robards, playing Howard Hughes, sang it memorably in the 1980 film *Melvin and Howard*.

MY BLUE HEAVEN

1927

Words by George Whiting, Music by Walter Donaldson. Known to most people from its regular play on the television series *M*A*S*H*, this melody was written one day in 1924, as Walter Donaldson waited for a pool table at the New York Friars Club. George Whiting heard the tune and offered to write lyrics for it. He then introduced it in his act, but with little success. The song was forgotten until radio singer Tommy Lyman took it as his theme song. The Gene Austin recording that followed is said to have sold 12 million discs.

CAN'T HELP LOVIN' DAT MAN

1928

Words by Oscar Hammerstein II, Music by Jerome Kern. Written for the musical *Show Boat*, this dialect song was part of one of the most important productions in American musical theater history. The musical, the second collaboration of Hammerstein and Kern, was certainly the most important musical of the '20s. The show opened in December of 1927, and the song became a big hit in 1928. Turning away from the loosely woven revues popular at the time, *Show Boat* raised the bar for musical theater by combining music, a serious plot, dance and spectacular scenery into an integrated whole. This song is sung in the show by the mulatto character Julie, foreshadowing the revelation of her parentage. It was sung as a slow, sentimental number in the 1951 film version. The 1994 Broadway revival returned it to the up-tempo interpretation of the original production.

AIN'T MISBEHAVIN'

1929

Words by Andy Razaf, Music by Thomas "Fats" Waller and Harry Brooks. Louis Armstrong credited this song with making him internationally famous. It was introduced in the all-African-American revue, *Hot Chocolates*, in 1929. Armstrong joined the company shortly after the show opened and played the song on trumpet during intermissions. Fats Waller made a best-selling recording of the song, adopting it as his theme song. This was the title song for films in 1955 and 1978. Hank Williams Jr. reached number 1 on the country charts in 1986 with this song. It was, of course, the title song for the 1978 Broadway Fats Waller revue.

BODY AND SOUL
1930

Words by Edward Heyman, Robert Sour and Frank Eyton, Music by John Green. Before it was heard in the U.S., this song was became a hit in England. Gertrude Lawrence, for whom it was written, introduced it on the BBC. Then bandleader Bert Ambrose recorded it. When American theatrical producer Max Gordon heard it he quickly secured the rights and included it in the Broadway revue *Three's a Crowd* (1930). Its sophisticated melody and harmonies have elevated it to the status of one of the great jazz standards.

STAR DUST
1931

Words by Mitchell Parish, Music by Hoagy Carmichael. One of the biggest songs of the century, "Star Dust" started out as an up tempo rag. Don Redman and his orchestra introduced it to a luke-warm response. Arranger Jimmy Dale heard it and suggested to Carmichael that it might work better as a slow, sentimental tune. Carmichael asked Mitchell Parish to write the lyrics. The sung, slower version was introduced at the Cotton Club in 1929. Isham Jones' recording of the song charted in 1931, followed by more than 500 other recordings, making this one of the most recorded songs of the twentieth century.

APRIL IN PARIS
1932

Words by E.Y. Harburg, Music by Vernon Duke. Anyone who has been to Paris in April will tell you that this song is a case of false advertising. The city's rainy, unreliable weather is nothing to sing about. But E.Y. "Yip" Harburg of *Wizard of Oz* fame, and the fabulously talented, but only moderately successful Vernon Duke captured romantic imaginations with "April in Paris." Succumbing to the romance of the title, countless tourists have flocked to Paris in April, where the disappointment of dreary weather inevitably awaits them.

STORMY WEATHER
1933

Words by Ted Koehler, Music by Harold Arlen. "Stormy Weather (Keeps Rainin' All the Time)" was written for Cab Calloway. At the time, Arlen and Koehler were writing songs for Cotton Club revues. However, Calloway was not appearing at the Cotton Club in 1933, so the song was tossed aside. It was first introduced, informally, at a party. Arlen and Koehler decided that song would fare best if sung by a woman. In the meantime, a recording of Arlen singing the song with the Leo Reisman Orchestra became a hit. Eventually Ethel Waters sang the great torch song, later calling it "a turning point in my life." "Stormy Weather" also became closely associated with Lena Horne.

MOONGLOW
1934

Words and Music by Will Hudson, Eddie DeLange and Irving Mills. This song, which has had a long life as a jazz standard, is still a favorite over sixty years after it was written. It was recorded by Guy Lombardo, Cab Calloway, Benny Goodman, Art Tatum, Ethel Waters, Art Mooney and a host of others. The song appeared in two important 1956 films: *Picnic*, which starred Kim Novak and William Holden, and *The Benny Goodman Story*.

CHEEK TO CHEEK
1935

Words and Music by Irving Berlin. One of Berlin's most commercially successful songs, this number has always been associated with the inimitable team of Fred Astaire and Ginger Rogers. Astaire, seeking out the very best songwriters, created a remarkable series of elegant film musicals in the 1930s with Rogers. They were built around charming, light-hearted plots and filled with stylish sets and costumes. Astaire's straightforward song deliveries, and the team's magical dancing, helped to make these escapist films the tonic a depression-weary country needed. Fred and Ginger performed "Cheek to Cheek" in *Top Hat* (1935).

PENNIES FROM HEAVEN
1936

Words by Johnny Burke, Music by Arthur Johnston. Nominated for an Academy Award, this was one of the most popular sentimental songs of the Depression era. It was introduced by Bing Crosby in the film of the same name. It was also heard in such films as *Cruisin' Down the River* (1953), and *Pepe* (1960). It appeared again in 1980 in the Steve Martin film *Pennies from Heaven*.

STOMPIN' AT THE SAVOY
1937

Words by Andy Razaf, Music by Benny Goodman, Chick Webb and Edgar Sampson. Although the Big Band era left an indelible mark on popular music, it actually spanned just a few years. One of the most memorable numbers to come out of this style, "Stompin' at the Savoy" was first introduced as an instrumental by Chick Webb and his Orchestra. But it was Benny Goodman's band that made the song a hit. Goodman also recorded it with his quartet. Jimmy Dorsey, Art Tatum and Woody Herman also had notable recordings.

HEART AND SOUL
1938

Words by Frank Loesser, Music by Hoagy Carmichael. This is possibly the most often-played – to say nothing of badly-played – duet in the history of the piano. While countless people can pound out one or the other of the parts, few can tell you the name of the tune. "Heart and Soul" was introduced in the 1938 film short, *A Song Is Born*. It caught the public's attention following Gene Krupa's performance of it in the 1939 film *Some Like It Hot*.

ALL THE THINGS YOU ARE
1939

Words by Oscar Hammerstein II, Music by Jerome Kern. Although the show for which "All the Things You Are" was written, *Very Warm for May* (1939), lasted less than eight weeks on Broadway, the song found a life of its own. It's remembered as one of Kern's best ballads. Ironically, Kern was convinced the song would never become popular. It eventually became one of his best-selling songs in both sheet music and records, and is a perennial favorite among jazz musicians.

IN THE MOOD
1940

Words by Andy Razaf, Music by Joe Garland. We remember Glenn Miller's band by its smooth sounds and romantic melodies. What most people don't remember is that the first two years of the band's existence were a horrible struggle. "In the Mood" was Glenn Miller's first success as a bandleader and his biggest-selling recording. Wherever the band played, people would scream for "In the Mood," and Miller and his musicians would make a great show of getting ready to play it. The song was originally given to Artie Shaw, who played it quite frequently. But it was Miller's arrangement of the piece that caught the ear of the public, and when people hear the name Glenn Miller, they think of "In the Mood."

BEWITCHED
1941

Words by Lorenz Hart, Music by Richard Rodgers. A classic from the team of Rodgers and Hart, this song was written for the musical *Pal Joey* (1940). Hart's original lyrics are naughty and funny, including lines like, "Horizontally speaking, he's at his very best." They were toned down to be a straight love song for public consumption. Though a huge hit in theater circles, and also in Paris, in 1941, a dispute between ASCAP (The American Society of Composers, Authors and Publishers) and the networks prevented it from being heard on the air. It became popular in the U.S. in the late '40s, becoming a radio hit in 1950.

A STRING OF PEARLS
1942

Words by Eddie DeLange, Music by Jerry Gray. Jerry Gray was Glenn Miller's arranger. "A String of Pearls" is one of the quintessential big band numbers. It became a hit for the Miller band in 1941 as an instrumental. A year later it was a number 1 hit for clarinetist Benny Goodman and his band. The hit came for Goodman, known as the "King of Swing," as he was struggling with effects of the World War II draft on his band. This song was featured in the 1954 film, *The Glenn Miller Story*.

I'VE HEARD THAT SONG BEFORE
1943

Words by Sammy Cahn, Music by Jule Styne. Nominated for an Academy Award, this song was introduced in the film musical *Youth on Parade* (1942). It was the first collaboration of Cahn and Styne, beginning a long-standing, highly successful partnership. Trumpeter Harry James' distinctive recording of "I've Heard That Song Before" in 1943, with vocal by Helen Forrest, sold over a million copies.

I'LL BE SEEING YOU
1944

Words by Irving Kahal, Music by Sammy Fain. Although written for a Broadway show called *Right This Way* (1938), "I'll Be Seeing You" didn't make an impression until it was revived five years later. By then, well into World War II, most everyone in the country had sent a friend or family member overseas. The ballad captured the sorrow of missing a loved one. It was popularized through a recording by Frank Sinatra, which appeared on the Hit Parade 24 weeks in 1944.

SENTIMENTAL JOURNEY
1945

Words by Bud Green, Music by Les Brown and Ben Homer. World War II was over in 1945, and our side had won. Americans, still basking in the glow of patriotism and victory, were welcoming home fathers, brothers and sons. This light-hearted, sentimental song captured the tone of the times. Doris Day, one of the biggest stars to come out of the big band era, was discovered at age 17 by Les Brown. She popularized this song in a 1945 recording with Brown and his orchestra.

COME RAIN OR COME SHINE
1946

Words by Johnny Mercer, Music by Harold Arlen. This great song, with no introduction and an ending that lands in a different key than the one in which it the song began, is an anomaly in the world of pop songs. It's thrown more than one Saturday night musician for a loop. It was introduced in the Broadway musical *St. Louis Woman* (1946), which was a box-office failure. Arlen and Mercer's other hits include "That Old Black Magic," "Ac-cent-tchu-ate the Positive," and "Hit the Road to Dreamland."

OLD DEVIL MOON
1947

Words by E.Y. Harburg, Music by Burton Lane. "Old Devil Moon" was introduced in the musical *Finian's Rainbow* (1947), Burton Lane's greatest Broadway success. The musical, an Irish folkloric fantasy, was actually an astute commentary on social and racial issues in the U.S., particularly in the South. While this was one of the biggest hits of the show, this swing tune had little to do with the plot or weighty themes.

NATURE BOY
1948

Words and Music by Eden Ahbez. Ahbez left this song at the stage door of a club where Nat "King" Cole was performing. Cole, finding it highly original, decided to record it. Within a month of its release it had sold over 500,000 copies. By the end of the year it had topped one million. Cole's recording was timely. He managed to get the song wrapped up just before a temporary ban on recording was instituted by the American Federation of Musicians.

SOME ENCHANTED EVENING
1949

Words by Oscar Hammerstein II, Music by Richard Rodgers. Rodgers and Hammerstein are the two names most associated with the Broadway musical. The pair wrote this song for the musical *South Pacific* (1949). They penned this number not with a Broadway singer in mind, but with the voice of opera star Ezio Pinza, who had recently retired from the opera stage and wanted to start doing musicals. Pinza had a successful recording of the song, as did Perry Como. In the 1958 film version, the song was sung by opera great Giorgio Tozzi, dubbing for Rossano Brazzi.

TENNESSEE WALTZ
1950

Words and Music by Redd Stewart and Pee Wee King. This hugely popular song was a hit for Patti Page, a recording that featured her in an over-dubbed duet with herself. More than three million copies of the recording sold by 1951. Cowboy Copas had a hit record at the same time. In 1965 the State of Tennessee adopted the "Tennessee Waltz" as the official state song.

HOW HIGH THE MOON
1951

Words by Nancy Hamilton, Music by Morgan Lewis. This song was written in 1940 and introduced that year as a ballad, in the Broadway revue *Two for the Show*. Helen Forrest made a best-selling recording of it with Benny Goodman and his orchestra. But it wasn't until Les Paul and Mary Ford picked up the tune, and the tempo, a decade later that it became a million seller. Their insouciant, swingin' arrangement made it a completely different song. Ella Fitzgerald recorded the number twice, once in a fast, scat rendition and once as a ballad.

WHEN I FALL IN LOVE
1952

Words by Edward Heyman, Music by Victor Young. It was first heard in the film *One Minute to Zero*. Doris Day made it into the Top Twenty with "When I Fall in Love" in 1952, but it was Nat "King" Cole's recording that was the biggest hit. The Lettermen revived it in 1962. The song found a third life when it was included prominently in the 1993 film *Sleepless in Seattle*; the recording by Celine Dion and Clive Griffin became a radio hit forty years after the classic was written.

THAT'S AMORÉ
1953

Words by Jack Brooks, Music by Harry Warren. This novelty song became popular largely due the casual, insouciant performance by film star Dean Martin. He introduced the song in the 1953 film *The Caddy*. It was nominated for an Academy Award that year. Martin's hit record sold a million copies.

THREE COINS IN THE FOUNTAIN
1954

Words by Sammy Cahn, Music by Jule Styne. This was the title song of 1954 film starring Rossano Brazzi, Clifton Webb, Louis Jourdan and Dorothy McGuire. Sung under the title credits by Frank Sinatra, it won an Academy Award. The lyrics and film's script were loosely based on the legend of the Fountain of Trevi in Rome. While the legend states that anyone who throws a coin into the fountain must return to Rome, the song and film turned it into a wish for true love. The hit tune and movie made the Fountain of Trevi a major tourist destination for many years.

ROCK AROUND THE CLOCK
1955

Words and Music by Max Freedman and Jimmy De Knight (pseudonym for publisher James E. Myers). This is the song credited with beginning the rock 'n' roll era. Bill Haley and His Comets first released a recording of the song in 1954. But it wasn't until it was included in the soundtrack of the film *The Blackboard Jungle* that the song became a hit. It was the first significant mainstream radio hit in a rock 'n' roll style, selling over twenty-five million records in over 30 languages around the world. Haley and his band performed the song in the 1956 film *Rock Around the Clock* and *Don't Knock Rock* (1957). It also appeared in *American Graffiti* (1973) and *Superman* (1978).

DON'T BE CRUEL
1956

Words and Music by Otis Blackwell and Elvis Presley. Elvis Presley was not a performer so much as a phenomenon. He exploded onto the scene in 1956, capturing and holding public attention like no one before or since. Otis Blackwell wrote this song, with Presley tweaking it to fit his style. It was released on a single with "Hound Dog" on the flip side. Both songs became number 1 hits as the disc sold over seven million copies. The song hit the country charts again in 1987, in a recording by The Judds. It was also a hit single in 1988 for Cheap Trick.

THAT'LL BE THE DAY
1957

Words and Music by Jerry Allison, Buddy Holly and Norman Petty. This was Buddy Holly's first hit record, recorded with his band The Crickets. Holly, who began playing hillbilly music in Texas, is remembered for shaping the early rock 'n' roll style, and as a great rock guitarist. He died at age 22 in a plane crash in Clear Lake, Iowa. Flying with him were the Big Bopper and Ritchie Valens. In 1986 Holly was honored as one of the first inductees into the Rock and Roll Hall of Fame.

WITCHCRAFT
1958

Words by Carolyn Leigh, Music by Cy Coleman. During the late '50s, the pop charts were flooded with rock 'n' roll runes, as the new adolescent demographic made its power felt. But there was still room for swing standards, particularly when sung by Frank Sinatra. One of the great moments of Sinatra's swing years, the recording reached number 6 on the pop charts in 1958, and still sounds fresh forty years later.

THE SOUND OF MUSIC
1959

Words by Oscar Hammerstein II, Music by Richard Rodgers. Mary Martin introduced this song to theater audiences in the musical of the same name. Some years earlier she had secured the rights to the story and asked Rodgers and Hammerstein to write a couple of songs for a play about a nun who marries an Austrian widower with seven musical children. They read the story and immediately decided they wanted to write an entire original score, not just a few songs. The show would prove to be the last collaboration for the creative team. Hammerstein died in 1960, not long after the 1959 opening of the Broadway musical. In 1965 Julie Andrews took the role of Maria to the screen, helping to turn *The Sound of Music* into the most popular movie musical of the century.

GEORGIA ON MY MIND
1960

Words by Stuart Gorrell, Music by Hoagy Carmichael. This song is a good example of the fact that a good song has a staying power that transcends time. "Georgia on My Mind" was first recorded in 1930 by its composer, Hoagy Carmichael. Ray Charles revived the song in 1959 in a distinctive arrangement, turning it into a million-seller and winning a Grammy for Best Male Vocal. Carmichael, who performed the song throughout his career, recorded it again in 1960. In 1978 Willie Nelson won a Grammy for Best Male Country Vocal with this song.

MOON RIVER
1961

Words by Johnny Mercer, Music by Henry Mancini. Audrey Hepburn, who was often dubbed in her singing roles, sang this song herself to a simple guitar accompaniment in the non-musical film *Breakfast at Tiffany's*. Andy Williams' recording sold over a million copies. He then adopted it as the theme song for his television show. It has been recorded over 100 times, winning Grammy Awards in 1961 for Best Song and Best Recording (Henry Mancini), and the Academy Award for Best Song. Its deceptive simplicity and Mercer's philosophical lyric has given "Moon River" a long-standing appeal.

THE TWIST
1962

Words and Music by Hank Ballard. It was first released by Hank Ballard as the B-side of the single "Teardrops on My Letter." In 1960 he re-released it as the A-side of a single and it began to catch on. But it wasn't until Chubby Checker covered "The Twist" that it really took off. His version became a number 1 hit in the U.S. and spawned a new dance craze. Checker's record hit the number 1 spot a second time over a year later. "The Twist" and Bing Crosby's recording of "White Christmas" are the only records to have hit the number 1 spot on the chart twice.

MORE
1963

Words and Music by Norman Newell, Riz Ortolani and N. Oliviero. This song is also known as the "Theme from *Mondo Cane*." The 1961 Italian film is a documentary featuring sequences of odd, violent behavior. When the lyric is added, ironically, "More" becomes a love song. It was nominated for an Academy Award.

I WANT TO HOLD YOUR HAND
1964

Words and Music by John Lennon and Paul McCartney. February 19, 1964 was the beginning of what is now known as "the British invasion." Ed Sullivan introduced American audiences to The Beatles that evening, starting an absolute frenzy of "Beatlemania" in the U.S., a phenomenon that had begun in Britain the previous October. Although this was not the first U.S. release for the Fab Four, it was their first U.S. hit. With it the floodgates were opened. British rock songs poured onto the U.S. market, with The Beatles leading the way. Over the next five years the band enjoyed unprecedented, unparalleled success.

DOWNTOWN
1965

Words and Music by Tony Hatch. To most people, the British invasion of the American music scene is a reference to The Beatles and the various other British-import bands that became wildly popular almost overnight. But there were solo artists in the invasion as well, and Petula Clark was certainly one of the more memorable ones. Clark's recording of this song hit the charts late in 1964, staying there for 15 weeks into 1965. An American comic-singer, Mrs. Miller, whose deliberately bad recordings brought her fame, also hit the charts with this song.

CALIFORNIA DREAMIN'
1966

Words and Music by John E.A. Phillips and Michelle G. Phillips. A hit for the Mamas and Papas, this song conjures images of the '60s counter-culture revolution and its California roots. Young people flocked to the west coast to find a freedom that life in the rest of the country didn't seem to offer. By the time the Beach Boys re-released the song in 1986, its counter-culture edge was long gone.

ALL YOU NEED IS LOVE
1967

Words and Music by John Lennon and Paul McCartney. 1967 was the year of the Summer of Love. Young people, proudly calling themselves hippies, gathered in San Francisco's Haight-Ashbury district, in a peaceful rebellion against a mainstream culture that included the Vietnam War, race riots and repressive social and political structures. Tourists and gawkers also gathered, making the Summer of Love rather short lived. Some say it was actually just the month of April. Lennon and McCartney, not for the only time, seemed to perfectly capture the spirit of the time in a song. "All You Need Is Love" was included on the soundtrack of The Beatles' 1968 animated film *Yellow Submarine*.

I HEARD IT THROUGH THE GRAPEVINE
1968

Words and Music by Norman Whitfield and Barrett Strong. Long before it became the theme song for California raisins, this song was a number 1 hit for Marvin Gaye. But the year before he scored his 1968 hit with "I Heard It Through the Grapevine," Gladys Knight and the Pips made it into the Top 10 with it. The song was featured prominently in the 1983 film *The Big Chill*.

LEAVING ON A JET PLANE
1969

Words and Music by John Denver. By the late '60s, folk-rock had found an audience. Performers like Joan Baez, Joni Mitchell, and the duo of Simon and Garfunkel epitomized this soft-edged style of music. Although John Denver wrote this song and recorded it himself, it is most associated with the folk-rock sound of Peter, Paul and Mary, who popularized it.

(THEY LONG TO BE) CLOSE TO YOU
1970

Words by Hal David, Music by Burt Bacharach. While most of Bacharach and David's breezy tunes are associated with singer Dionne Warwick, for whom they were written, this song is forever connected to Karen and Richard Carpenter. The soft-edged sounds of the brother/sister duo took it to number 1 on the charts in 1970, making stars of The Carpenters. Like many of Bacharach and David's tunes, this apparently simple melody is much more complex than it first appears.

YOU'VE GOT A FRIEND
1971

Words and Music by Carole King. Carole King was one of the great songwriters to come out of the famous tune-factory known as the Brill Building in the early 1960s. After years of writing songs for others, she turned her attention to an album performing her own material. And what an album! *Tapestry* helped establish the notion of singer/songwriters. James Taylor, who played guitar on King's recording, took the song to number 1 on his own that same year.

AMERICAN PIE
1972

Words and Music by Don McLean. This cryptic, lengthy song – at 8 and 1/2 minutes long it was one of the longest singles ever to become a hit – mesmerized audiences. Inspired by the death of rock musician Buddy Holly, the song's lyrics were cloaked in double meanings and imagery. Radio stations around the country devoted whole programs to deciphering the meaning of the lyrics. Although this was an enormous hit for McLean, it obscured his career as a folksinger. For years after its success he refused to perform "American Pie," hoping to put his other songs in the spotlight.

YOU ARE THE SUNSHINE OF MY LIFE
1973

Words and Music by Stevie Wonder. Writing his own music and playing all of the instruments used in his recordings, Stevie Wonder created a seamless blend of pop and soul. Also savvy in business, Wonder produced many of his own recordings. At the age of 21 he negotiated a contract with Motown that gave him complete artistic control. He was the first artist to win such control. First known as "Little Stevie Wonder," by the late '60s he had emerged as one of the biggest pop talents around, writing cheerful, sophisticated songs, usually with a bit of a jazz influence not too far beneath the surface.

THE WAY WE WERE
1974

Words by Marilyn Bergman and Alan Bergman, Music by Marvin Hamlisch. The title song of a popular 1973 film starring Robert Redford and Barbra Streisand, this song was an enormous hit for Streisand. The original lyric was actually "The Way We Weren't." Though Barbra Streisand had been a highly visible singer and movie star for years, this was her first number 1 record. It won both an Academy Award for Best Song in 1973 and a Grammy for Song of the Year in 1974. This film, which was part of the nostalgia wave of the mid-70s, was panned by some critics, though a favorite with audiences.

JIVE TALKIN'
1975

Words and Music by Barry Gibb, Maurice Gibb and Robin Gibb. The Bee Gees' distinctive sound is the epitome of the disco era. The trio of Gibb brothers had a number 1, gold record with the song, one of the first hits in the new disco style. The Bee Gees fashioned a remarkable career that spanned three decades, by picking up successful trends and incorporating those trends into their act. In the mid-1970s, the group was securely onboard the disco wagon, sporting long, flowing hair, tight pants and unbuttoned shirts. They went on to immortalize disco music forever in the songs for the 1977 film *Saturday Night Fever.*

I WRITE THE SONGS
1976

Words and Music by Bruce Johnston. The Captain and Tennille released this song in 1975. Teen idol David Cassidy took a turn at it, releasing it in Great Britain. But it was Barry Manilow who made it a hit, from his album *Tryin' to Get the Feeling.* His recording went number 1 on the pop charts, scoring one of the biggest hits of its time, and winning a Grammy for Song of the Year. Manilow continued to be king of pop for the rest of the '70s.

YOU LIGHT UP MY LIFE
1977

Words and Music by Joseph Brooks. This song was introduced in the fairly minor 1977 film of the same name. On the soundtrack it was sung by Kasey Cisyk, dubbing for actress Didi Conn. Debby Boone took this song to number 1 on the pop charts, keeping it there for ten weeks and making it the number 1 single of the entire year. LeAnn Rimes did a remake in 1998.

JUST THE WAY YOU ARE
1978

Words and Music by Billy Joel. This song went gold for singer/songwriter/pianist Billy Joel. It also won him Grammy Awards for both Song of the Year and Record of the Year. It's a great example of Joel's well-crafted, interesting pop/rock music. His energetic performances of his own music have kept him an audience favorite for over twenty years. "Just the Way You Are," with its sophisticated melody and harmony, is one of the few songs of the rock era to enter the jazz repertoire.

I WILL SURVIVE
1979

Words and Music by Dino Fekaris and Freddie Perren. A great disco torch song, "I Will Survive" was originally the B-side of one of Gloria Gaynor's singles. The lyric, which tells the story of a woman becoming independent after leaving a relationship with a self-absorbed lover, struck a chord with listeners. It charted at number 1 and went platinum. It still stands up as one of the most irresistible songs of its era.

ANOTHER ONE BITES THE DUST
1980

Words and Music by John Deacon. The British band Queen had a string of hits for nearly a decade, and "Another One Bites the Dust" came right in the middle of their wave of success. Leaders of the so-called "pomp rock" genre, Queen delivered slickly produced recordings which featured many layers of over-dubbing. Lead singer Freddie Mercury, whose voice and flamboyant persona were the focal point of the group, died in 1991. In 1992 the group found itself back on the charts in a re-release of the hit "Bohemian Rhapsody," which found a second life in the film *Wayne's World.*

ENDLESS LOVE
1981

Words and Music by Lionel Richie. Who would have guessed that this pure American pop love ballad would come from a Franco Zeffirelli movie? Lionel Richie and Diana Ross took this song to number 1 on the pop charts, where it remained for nine weeks. Their recording was one of the most successful duets of all time. The song was nominated for an Academy Award. Richie and Ross won two Grammy Awards with it for Song of the Year and Record of the Year. Mariah Carey and Luther Vandross had a hit with it in 1994, getting to number 2 on the chart.

UP WHERE WE BELONG
1982

Words and Music by Will Jennings, Jack Nitzsche and Buffy Sainte-Marie. It is hard to hear this song without picturing Richard Gere carrying Debra Winger away from her dead-end factory job and into the land of happily-ever-after. Vocalists Joe Cocker and Jennifer Warnes took the Academy Award-winning song to number 1 on the pop charts. Cocker's raspy style gave this rock ballad an edge it wouldn't have had otherwise.

14

EVERY BREATH YOU TAKE
1983

Words and Music by Sting (a.k.a. Gordon Sumner). This song was the biggest hit for the hugely successful British rock trio, The Police. For all their output and success, The Police was a relatively short-lived group. The video of "Every Breath You Take" is one of the only true classics of the genre, taped in black and white, focusing on Sting playing his upright bass. The song won a Grammy for Song of the Year. This song was heard on the platinum album *Synchronicity*.

FOOTLOOSE
1984

Words by Dean Pitchford, Music by Kenny Loggins. Loggins scored a number 1 hit with the title song from this enormously successful movie musical, which starred Kevin Bacon and Lori Singer. The soundtrack is one of the best-selling albums of all time. *Footloose* was adapted for the Broadway stage and opened there in 1999.

CARELESS WHISPER
1985

Words and Music by George Michael and Andrew Ridgeley. This song went to number 1 on the pop charts in a recording by the Michael and Ridgeley duo Wham. The group, which was built around the voice of singer George Michael, produced some of the most successful singles of the '80s. "Careless Whisper" first appeared on Wham's 1984 album, *Make It Big*.

SOMEWHERE OUT THERE
1986

Words and Music by James Horner, Barry Mann and Cynthia Weil. This song was written for the animated film *An American Tail* (1986). Vocalists Linda Ronstadt and James Ingram popularized the sweeping, glamorous duet. Kenny Loggins also recorded it. *An American Tail* was an expensive, fully animated feature about a family of Russian mice who immigrate to the United States. The song received an Academy Award nomination.

(I'VE HAD) THE TIME OF MY LIFE
1987

Words and Music by John DeNicola, Donald Markowitz and Franke Previte. This song became a hit thanks to actor/dancer Patrick Swayze, who had absolutely nothing to do with writing or recording the song. He did, however, dance to it in the 1987 film *Dirty Dancing*, a film young women flocked to see – again and again. Vocalists Bill Medley, former baritone of the Righteous Brothers, and Jennifer Warnes took the recording to number 1 on the pop charts.

ALL I ASK OF YOU
1988

Words by Charles Hart and Richard Stilgoe, Music by Andrew Lloyd Webber. This love anthem of the 1980s appears in Andrew Lloyd Webber's musical adaptation of the Gaston Leroux's novel *The Phantom of the Opera*. The British composer's name was firmly entrenched in musical theater by the time the lavish *Phantom* opened in London in 1986. It came to Broadway in 1988. The show has become the most financially successful musical ever. At one time there were 17 companies playing in the world. More than ten years after it first hit, *Phantom* still sells out. This song, which is heard as a duet between characters Christine and Raoul in the musical, was written with the soprano voice of the composer's former wife, Sarah Brightman, in mind.

DON'T KNOW MUCH
1989

Words and Music by Barry Mann, Thomas R. Snow and Cynthia Weil. This song was a hit for Linda Ronstadt and Aaron Neville, and was nominated for a Grammy for Song of the Year. The songwriting team of Mann and Weil are responsible for a number of hits, including "On Broadway" with Jerry Leiber and Mike Stoller, and "We Gotta Get Outta This Place." With Phil Spector they created "You've Lost That Lovin' Feeling," which BMI had labeled the most-played song in history.

FROM A DISTANCE
1990

Words and Music by Julie Gold. Bette Midler reached number 2 on the pop charts and number 1 on the Adult Contemporary charts with this philosophical, sentimental ballad. Nanci Griffith also had a successful recording of the song that year. With lyrics like "God is watching us from a distance," the song was adopted as an anthem by some religious groups and condemned as blasphemous by others.

BEAUTY AND THE BEAST
1991

Words by Howard Ashman, Music by Alan Menken. The 1991 animated film *Beauty and the Beast* was a return to the fine form of Disney's earlier animated classics. The film was the second Menken-Ashman collaboration for Disney, preceded by the 1989 release *The Little Mermaid*. *Beauty and the Beast* is the only feature-length animated movie nominated for the Academy Award for Best Picture. Menken's work on this film won Academy Awards for Best Score and, with Ashman, Best Song for the title song. Among the songs in the running for the award was another number from this movie, "Belle." *Beauty and the Beast* was adapted for the stage, with additional lyrics by Tim Rice, and opened on Broadway in 1994.

TEARS IN HEAVEN
1992

Words and Music by Eric Clapton and Will Jennings. This heart-rending, autobiographical song was written by Clapton following the tragic, accidental death of his young son. It was featured in the film *Rush*. The song appeared on Clapton's *Unplugged* album, a collection of new and older material performed on acoustic instruments. The success of *Eric Clapton Unplugged* began a spate of "unplugged" albums by other artists.

A WHOLE NEW WORLD
1993

Words by Tim Rice, Music by Alan Menken. After their successes with *The Little Mermaid* and *Beauty and the Beast*, Alan Menken and Howard Ashman teamed up once again to work on *Aladdin*. Their partnership was ended by Ashman's untimely death. The pair had completed only three songs for the film. Lyricist Tim Rice, collaborator with Andrew Lloyd Webber's *Evita* and *Jesus Christ Superstar*, stepped in. Rice and Menken won an Academy Award for "A Whole New World." Menken also took home the Oscar for Best Score. The song was a number 1 hit, recorded by Peabo Bryson and Regina Belle.

THE POWER OF LOVE
1994

Words and Music by Gunther Mende, Candy DeRouge, Jennifer Rush and Mary Susan Applegate. French-Canadian singer Celine Dion scored her first number 1 hit in the U.S. with "The Power of Love." It appeared on a debut album entitled *The Color of My Love*, catapulting her to superstardom by selling more than 15 million copies. The song is also heard on British singer/actor Michael Crawford's (the original Broadway Phantom) album *A Touch of Music in the Night.*

ONE SWEET DAY
1995

Words and Music by Nathan B. Morris, Walter Afanasieff, Patrick Shawn Stockman, Mariah Carey, Michael S. McCary and Wanya Jermaine Morris. Nearly all of Mariah Carey's singles have gone to the top of the charts. "One Sweet Day," a memorial song for departed friends, was no different. It spent 27 weeks on the charts, reaching the number 1 spot in December of 1995. In 1998 she included this song on an album entitled *#1's*, which contained her previous chart-topping hits.

I BELIEVE IN YOU AND ME
1996

Words and Music by David Wolfert and Sandy Linzer. "I Believe in You and Me" was a mediocre success for The Four Tops in 1983, reaching number 40 on the pop charts. Its success was assured when it was chosen to be the featured single sung by Whitney Houston in the 1996 movie *The Preacher's Wife*, which also starred Denzel Washington. A remake of the 1947 Cary Grant film *The Bishop's Wife*, the movie is a light, Christmas-season comedy/drama that soars to life when Houston sings, especially in the rousing gospel numbers. "I Believe in You and Me" is sung in a jazz club in the context of the film's story, with a cameo appearance by Lionel Richie as the pianist.

CANDLE IN THE WIND
1997

Words and Music by Elton John and Bernie Taupin. John and Taupin wrote this song in 1973 about the short life and tragic death of Marilyn Monroe. When Elton John's dear friend, Diana, the Princess of Wales, died in a tragic auto accident in 1997, the song was quickly reworked. John performed it in the new version at her funeral, which was televised throughout the world to billions of people. Gone were such lyrics as "Goodbye Norma Jean..." Instead he sang, "Goodbye, England's rose..." Proceeds from post-funeral sales of the recording were donated to Diana's charities. John has vowed to retire the song forever from live performance in honor of Diana's memory.

MY HEART WILL GO ON
(Love Theme from 'Titanic')
1998

Words by Will Jennings, Music by James Horner. *Titanic*, the biggest movie success in history, spawned an enormous hit with "My Heart Will Go On." It was another in a string of hits for Celine Dion. The Academy Award for Best Song was just one of eleven Academy Awards bestowed on the film that evening. Horner and Jennings also won an ASCAP award for the Most Performed Song for Motion Pictures.

ANGEL
1999

Words and Music by Sarah McLachlan. Hit songs in the rock era are songs about romantic love of some kind a good 99% of the time. Once in a great while, a philosophical song comes along and scores a success, and "Angel" is one of them. In a poetic way it captures the restless angst of the fin-de-siècle. Sarah McLachlan has emerged as the one of the most important personalities in rock. Beyond her successful career as a singer and songwriter, she organized an ambitious tour, Lilith Fair. Termed "A Celebration of Women in Music" the hugely successful tour showcased established stars, and also embraced a mission of featuring emerging artists.

1900

When You Were Sweet Sixteen

Registration 10
Rhythm: 8 Beat

Words and Music by
James Thornton

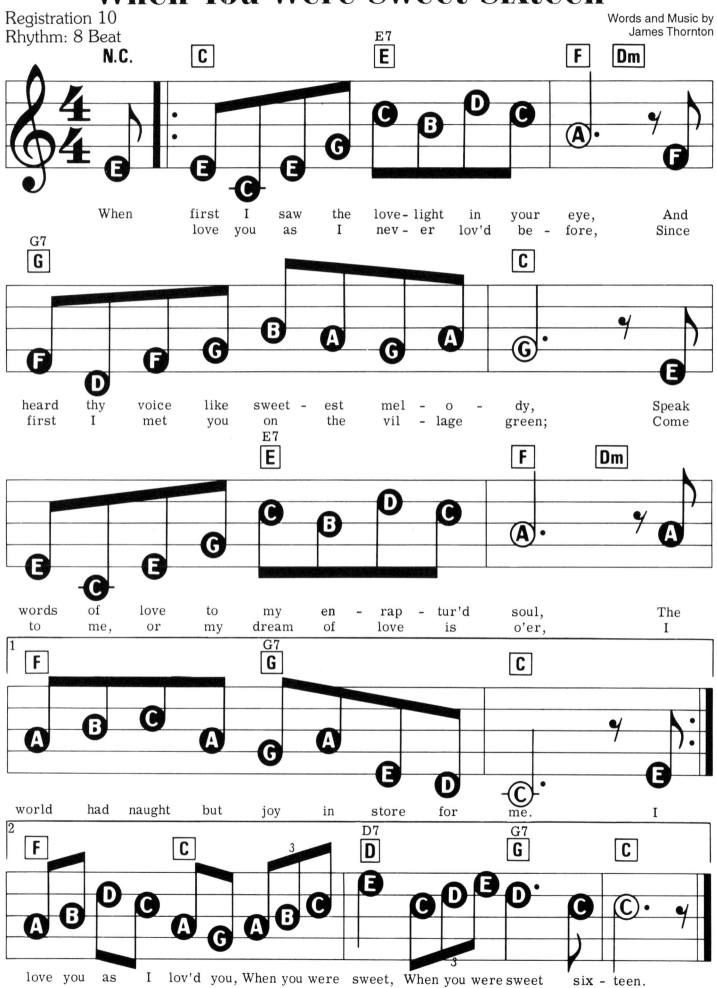

1901
Stars and Stripes Forever

Registration 2
Rhythm: March

By John Philip Sousa

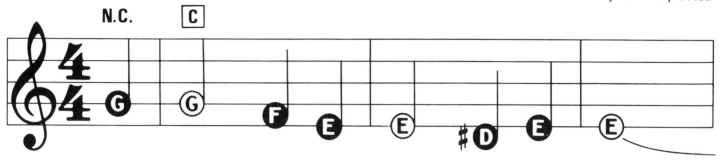

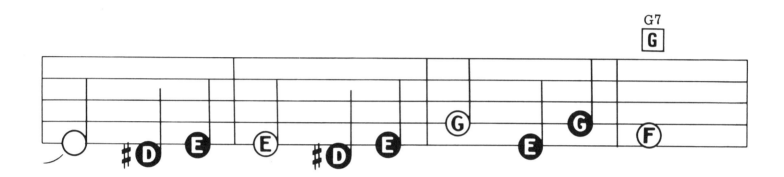

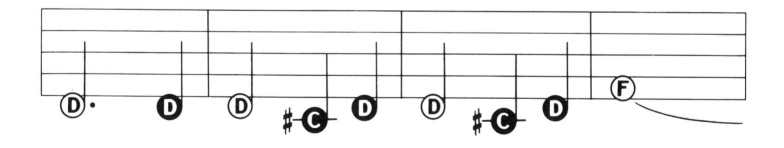

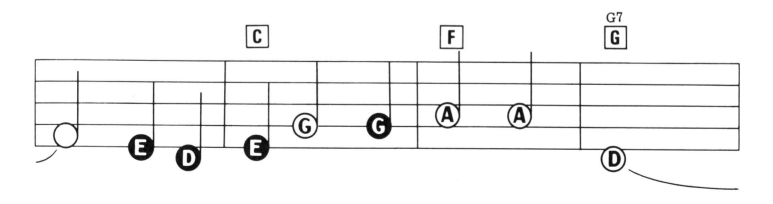

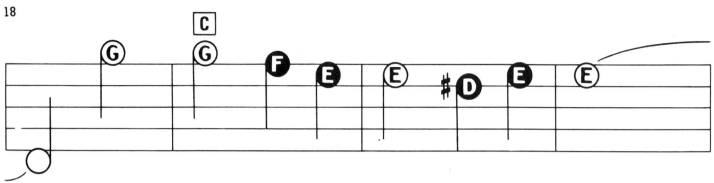

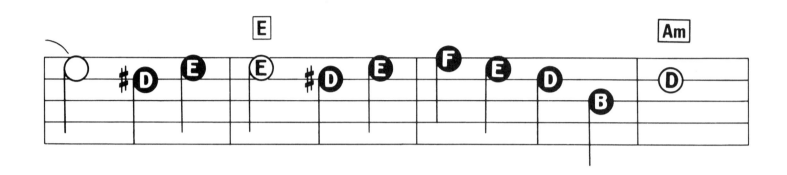

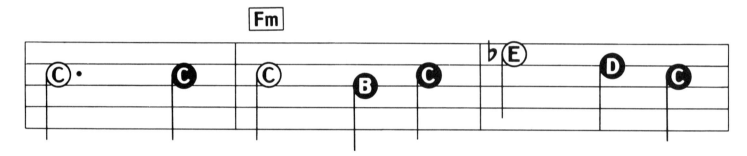

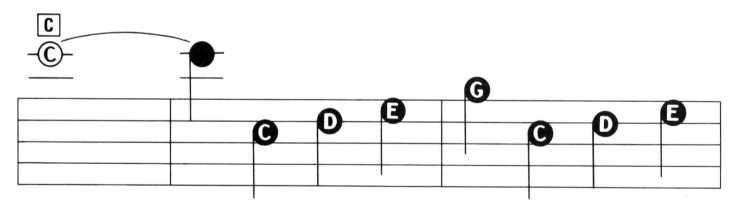

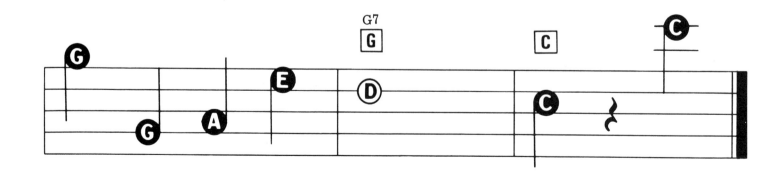

1902
Bill Bailey, Won't You Please Come Home

Registration 7
Rhythm: Swing

Words and Music by
Hughie Cannon

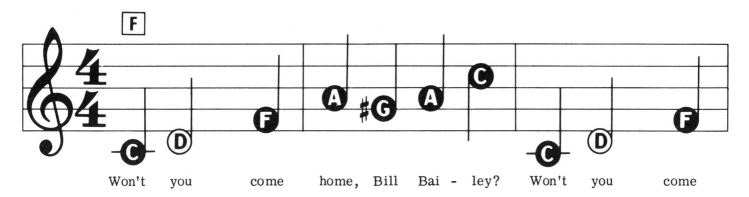

Won't you come home, Bill Bai - ley? Won't you come

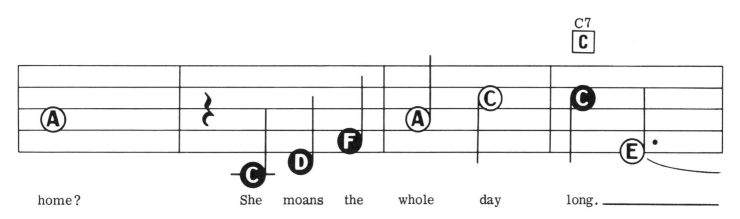

home? She moans the whole day long. _____

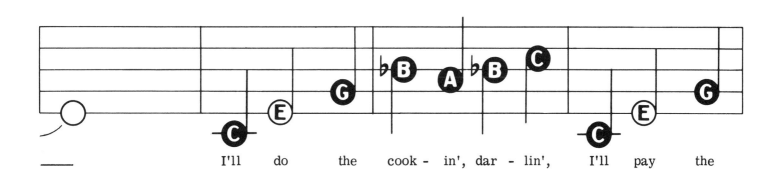

_____ I'll do the cook - in', dar - lin', I'll pay the

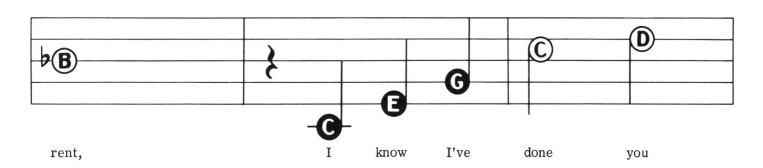

rent, I know I've done you

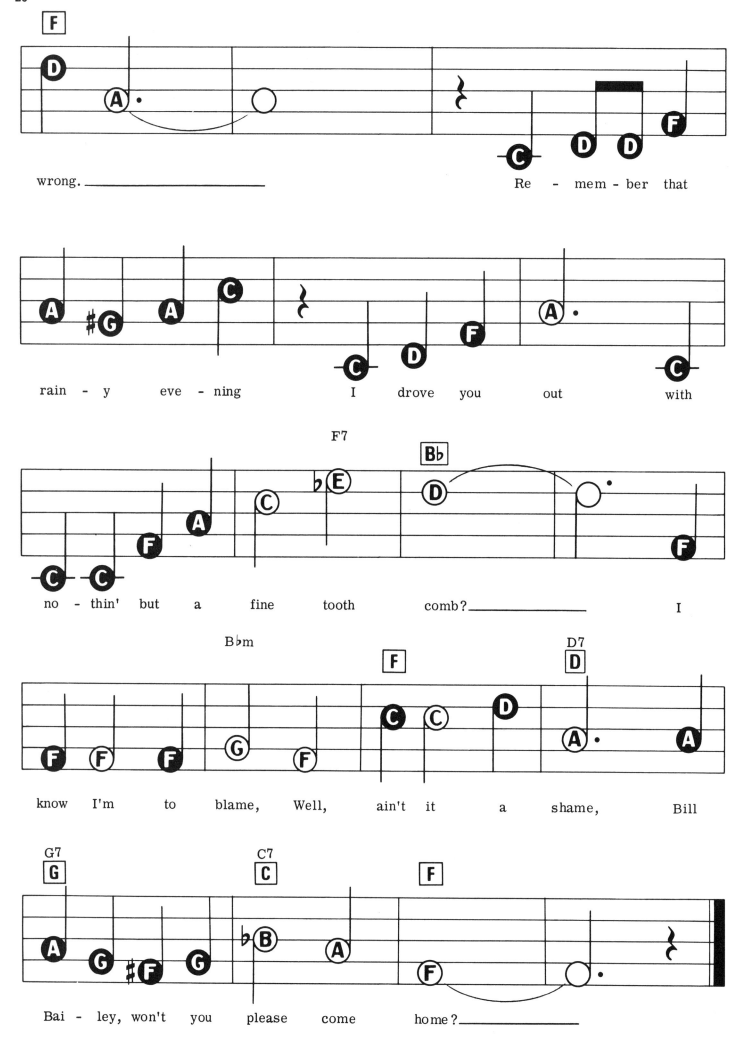

1903

Ida, Sweet as Apple Cider

Words by Eddie Leonard
Music by Eddie Munson

Registration 3
Rhythm: Fox Trot or Swing

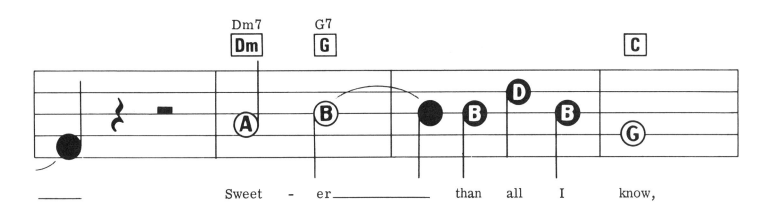

I - da! sweet as ap - ple ci - der,

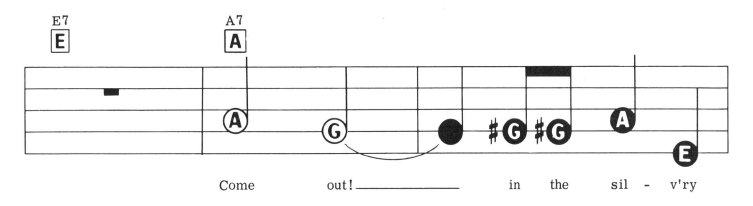

Sweet - er than all I know,

Come out! in the sil - v'ry

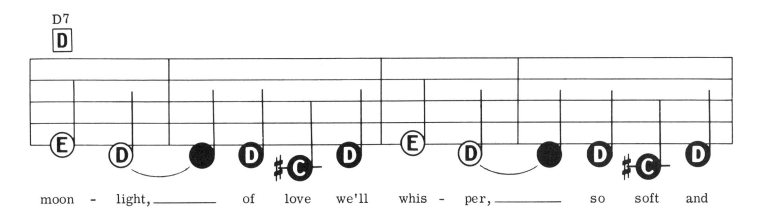

moon - light, of love we'll whis - per, so soft and

22

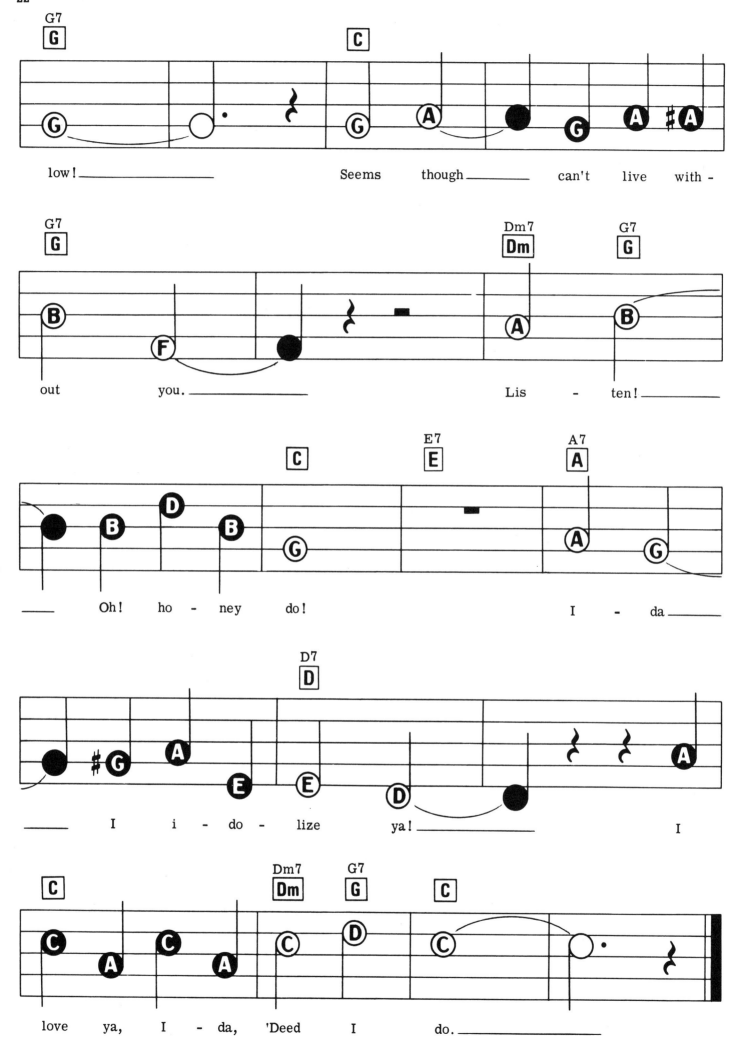

1904

Sweet Adeline
(You're the Flower of My Heart, Sweet Adeline)

Registration 4
Rhythm: Fox Trot or Shuffle

Words and Music by Richard H. Gerard
and Henry W. Armstrong

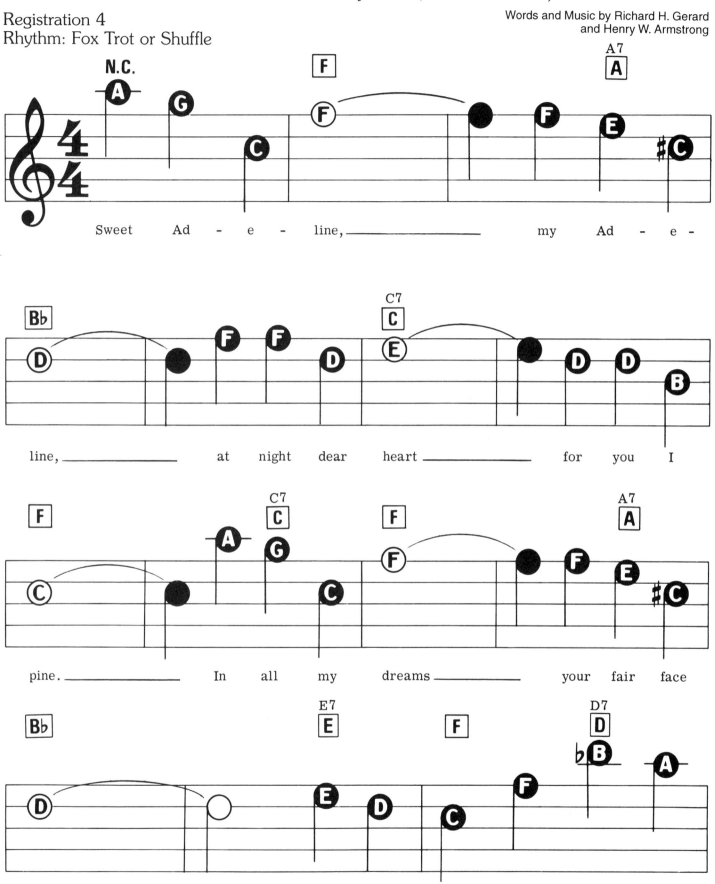

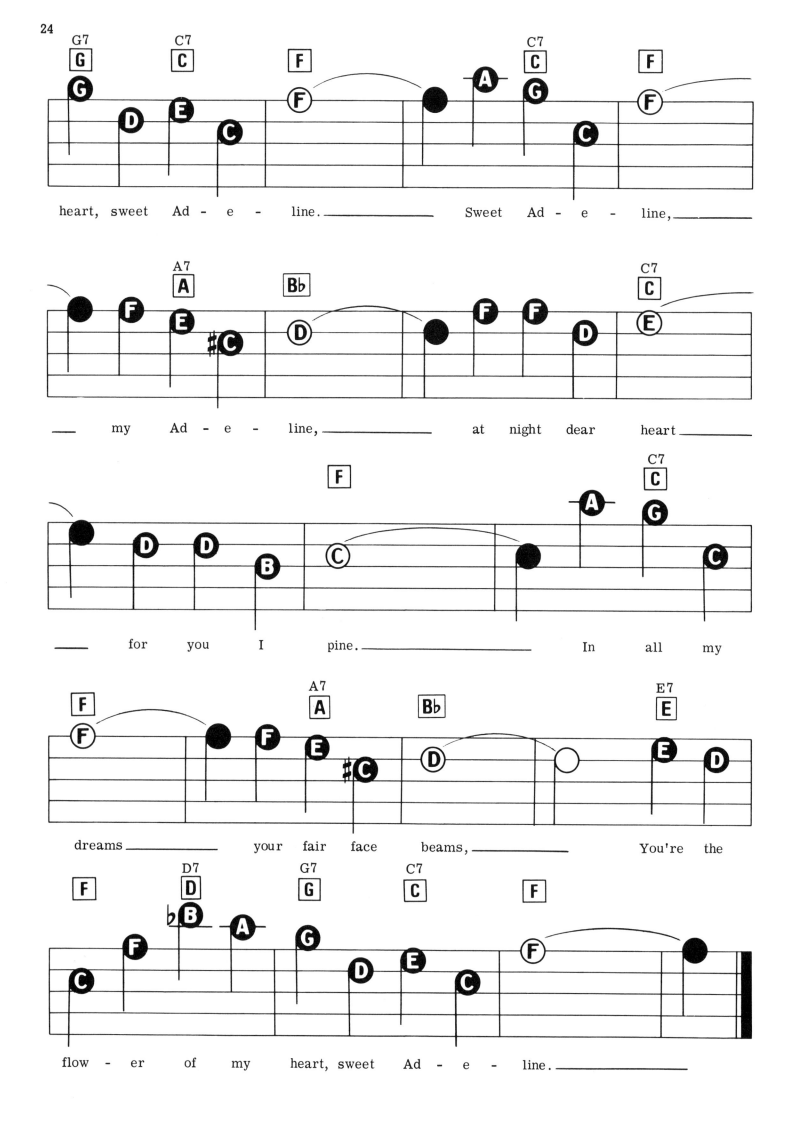

1905
In the Shade of the Old Apple Tree

Registration 3
Rhythm: Waltz

Words by Harry H. Williams
Music by Egbert Van Alstyne

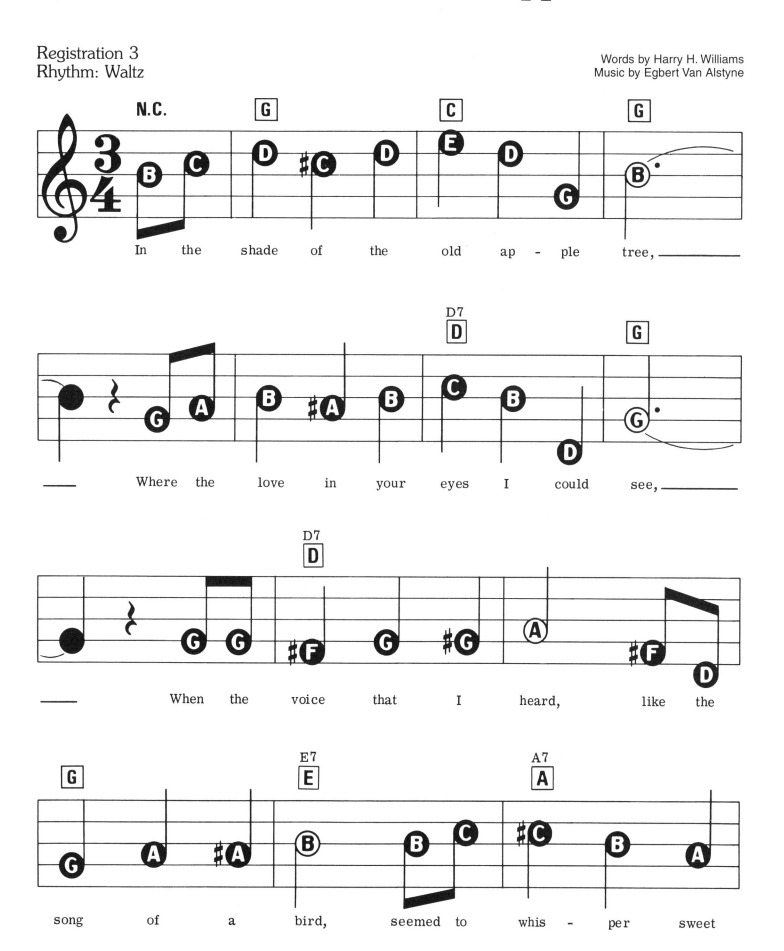

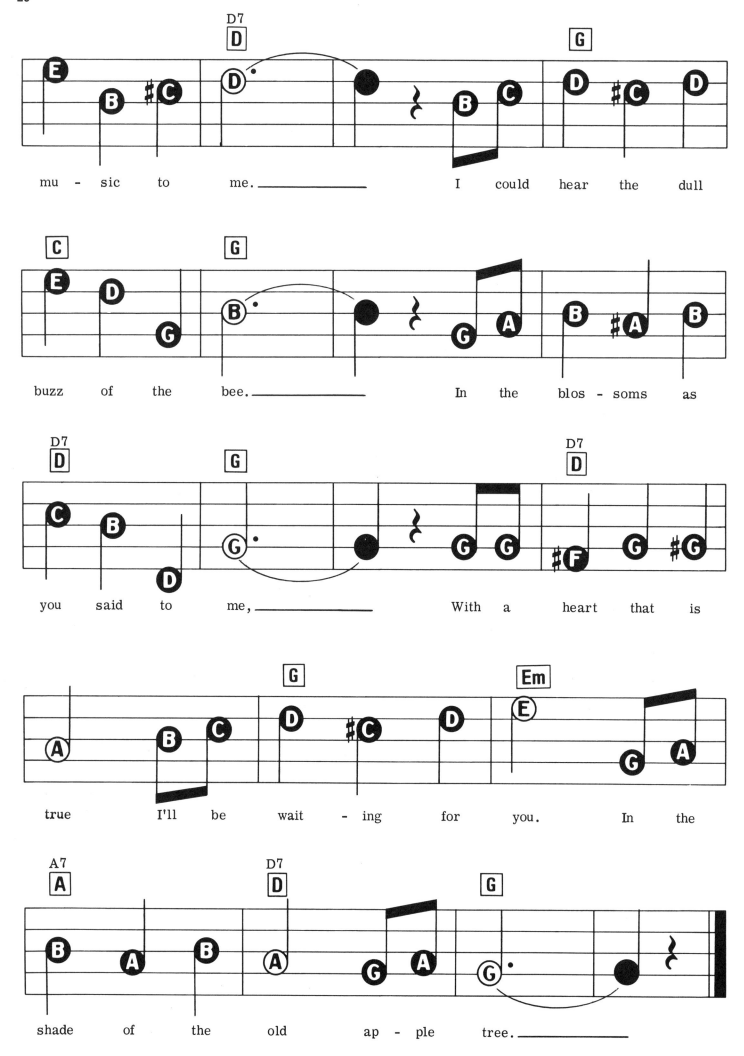

1906
Wait 'til the Sun Shines, Nellie

Words by Andrew B. Sterling
Music by Harry von Tilzer

Registration 2
Rhythm: March or Polka

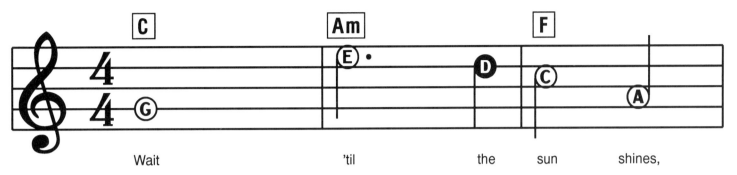

Wait   'til   the   sun   shines,

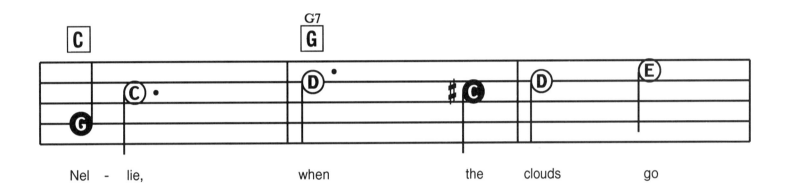

Nel - lie,   when   the   clouds   go

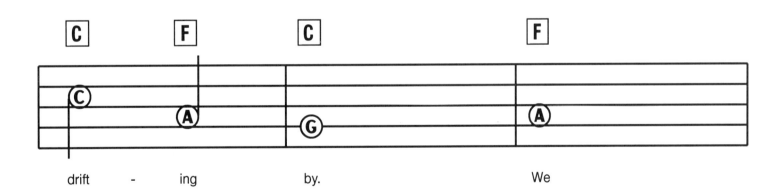

drift - ing   by.   We

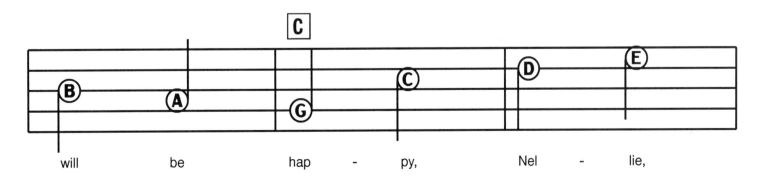

will   be   hap - py,   Nel - lie,

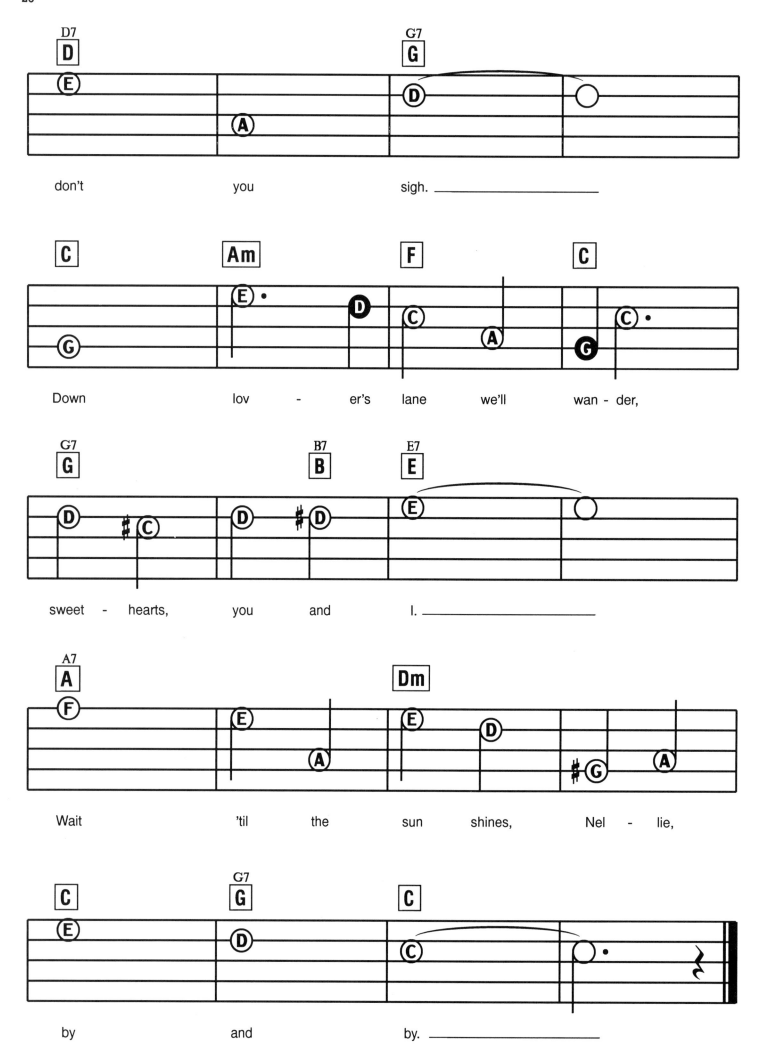

1907
School Days
(When We Were a Couple of Kids)

Registration 2
Rhythm: Waltz

Words by Will D. Cobb
Music by Gus Edwards

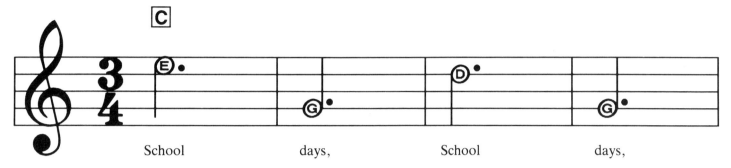

School   days,   School   days,

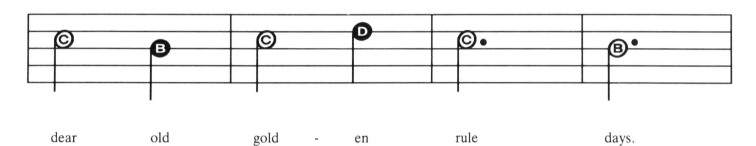

dear   old   gold - en   rule   days.

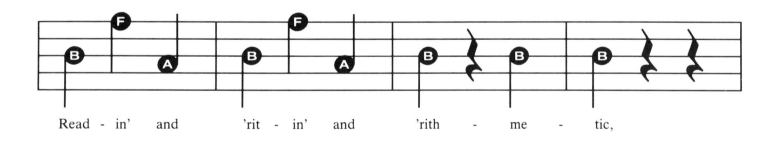

Read - in' and   'rit - in' and   'rith - me - tic,

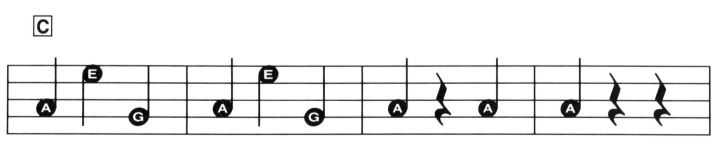

Taught   to   the   tune   of   a   hick - 'ry   stick.

You were my queen in cal - i - co,

I was your bash - ful bare - foot beau. And you

wrote on my slate, "I love you, Joe," When

we were a cou - ple of kids. _____

1908
Take Me Out to the Ball Game

Registration 4
Rhythm: Waltz

Words by Jack Norworth
Music by Albert von Tilzer

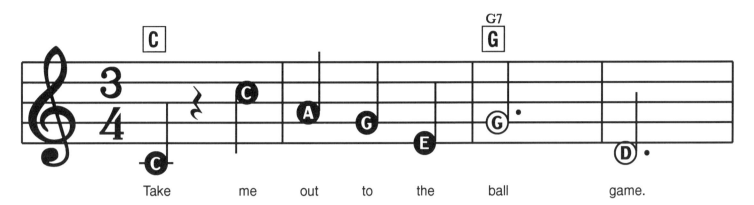

Take me out to the ball game.

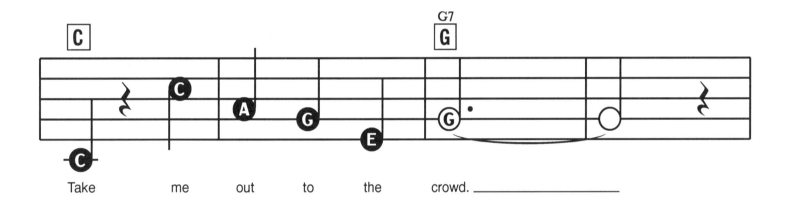

Take me out to the crowd. _____

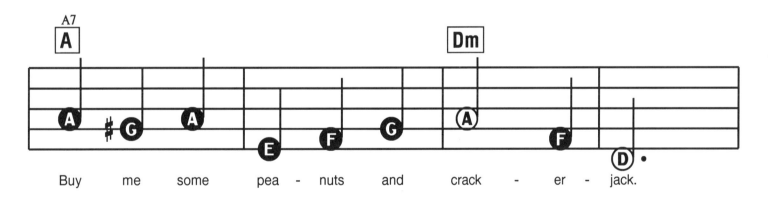

Buy me some pea - nuts and crack - er - jack.

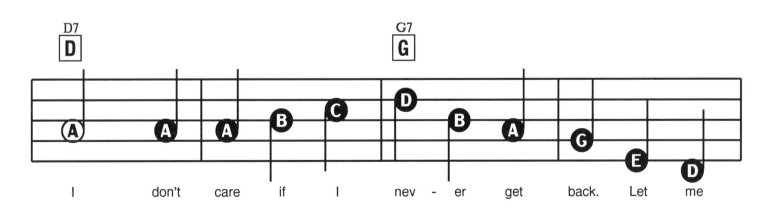

I don't care if I nev - er get back. Let me

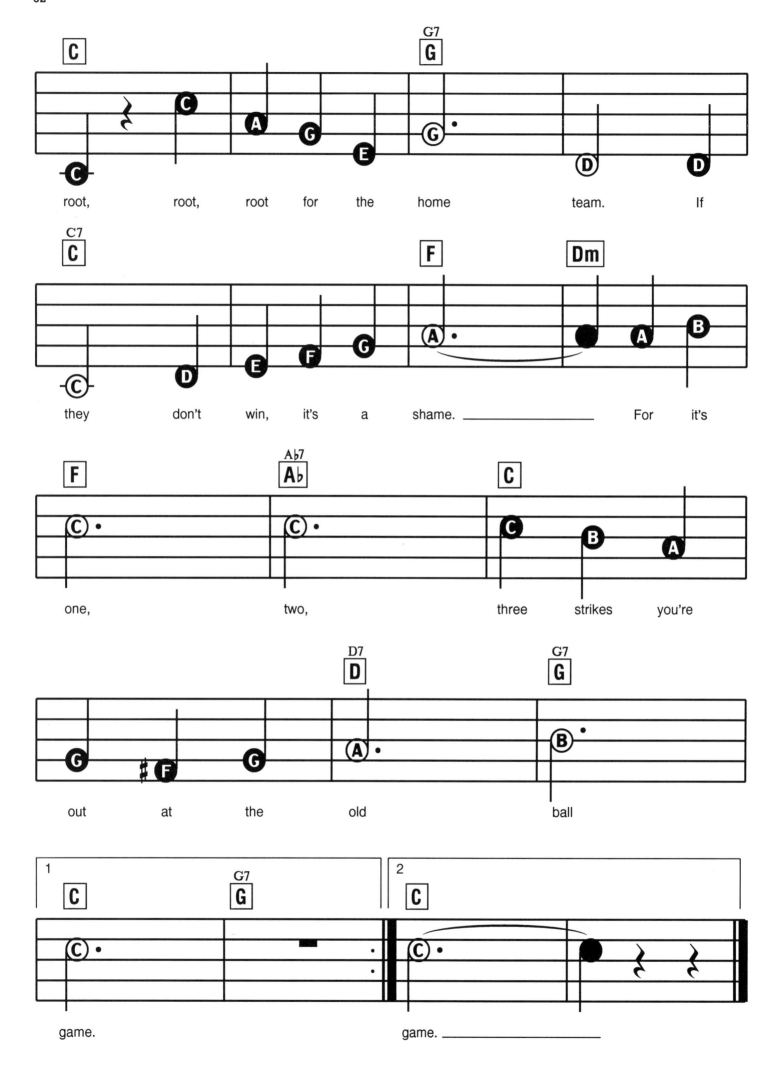

1909
Shine on, Harvest Moon

Registration 9
Rhythm: Fox Trot or Swing

Words by Jack Norworth
Music by Nora Bayes and Jack Norworth

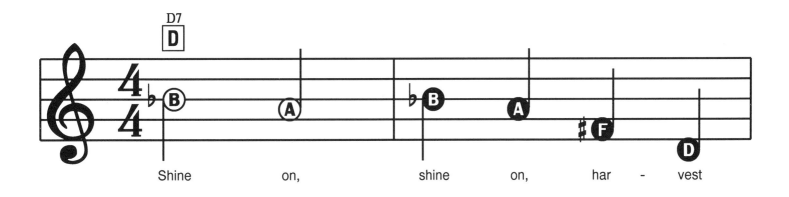

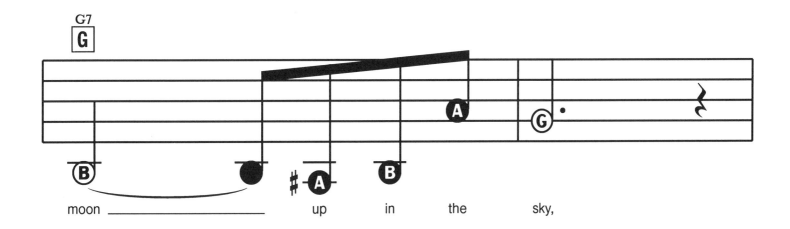

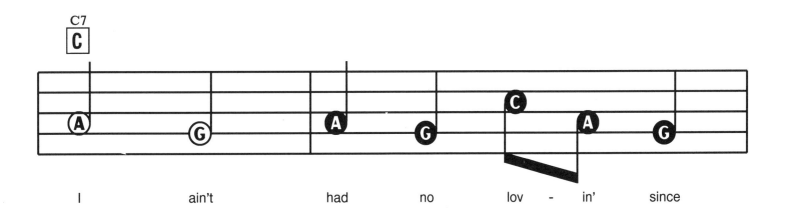

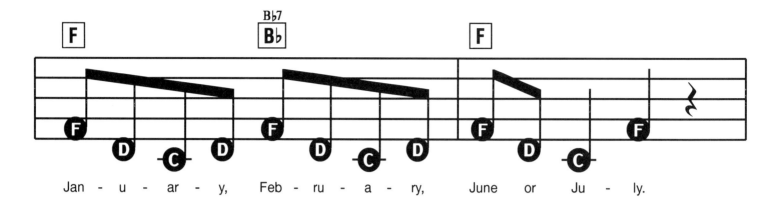

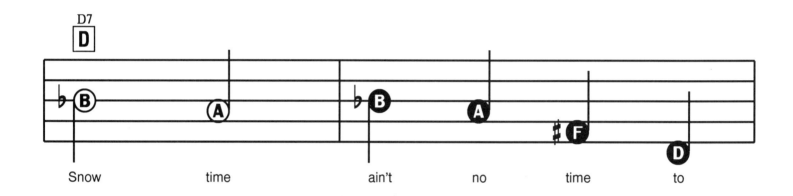

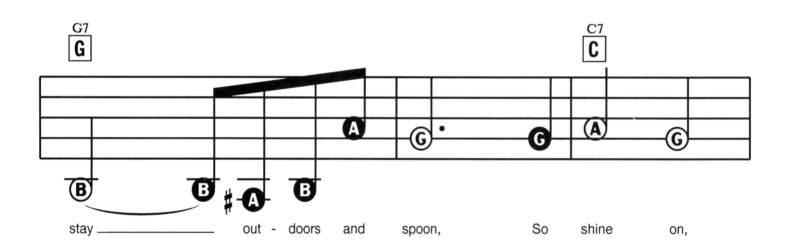

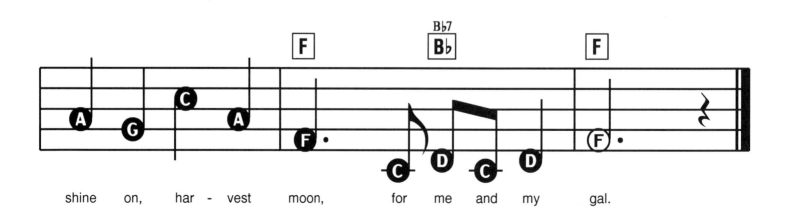

1910
Let Me Call You Sweetheart

Registration 3
Rhythm: Waltz

Words by Beth Slater Whitson
Music by Leo Friedman

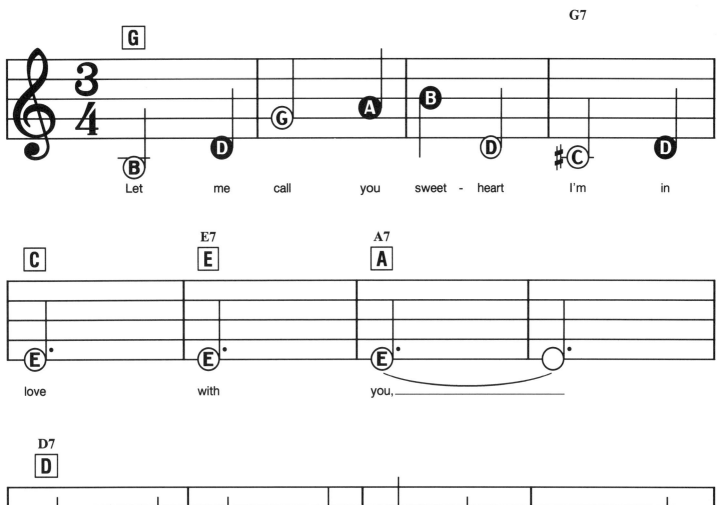

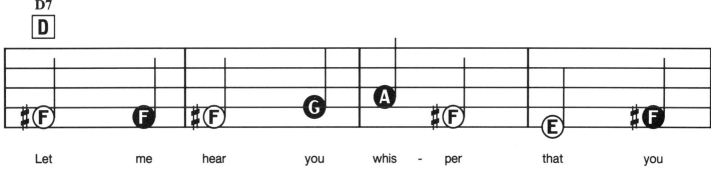

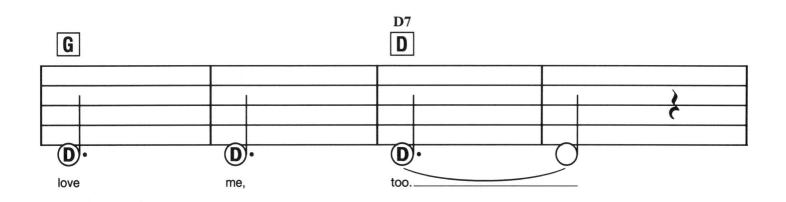

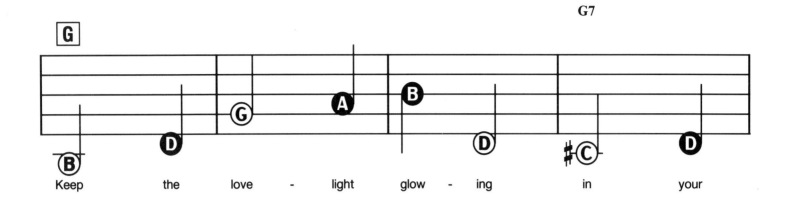

Keep the love - light glow - ing in your

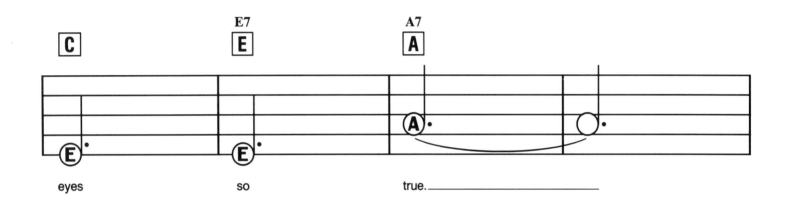

eyes so true.____

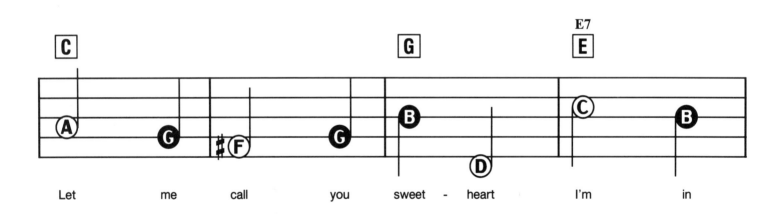

Let me call you sweet - heart I'm in

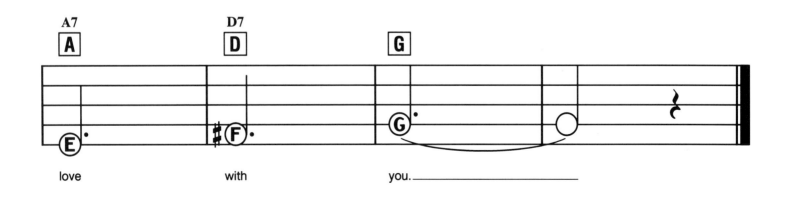

love with you.____

1911
Alexander's Ragtime Band
from ALEXANDER'S RAGTIME BAND

Registration 5
Rhythm: Fox Trot or Swing

Words and Music by
Irving Berlin

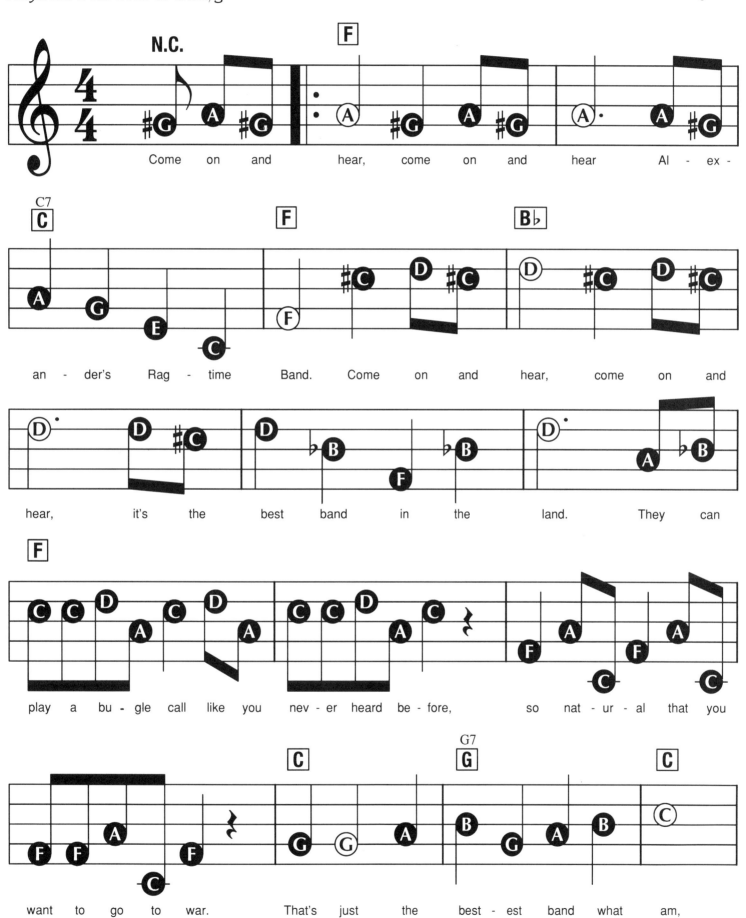

38

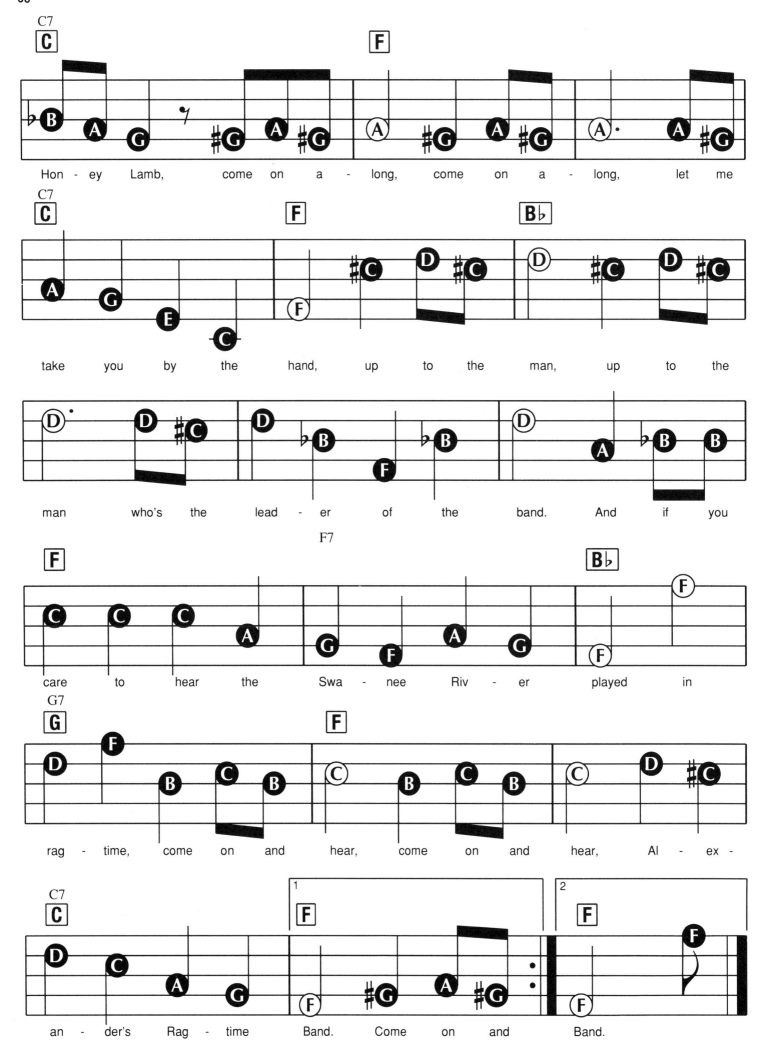

1912
Down by the Old Mill Stream

Registration 3
Rhythm: Waltz

Words and Music by
Tell Taylor

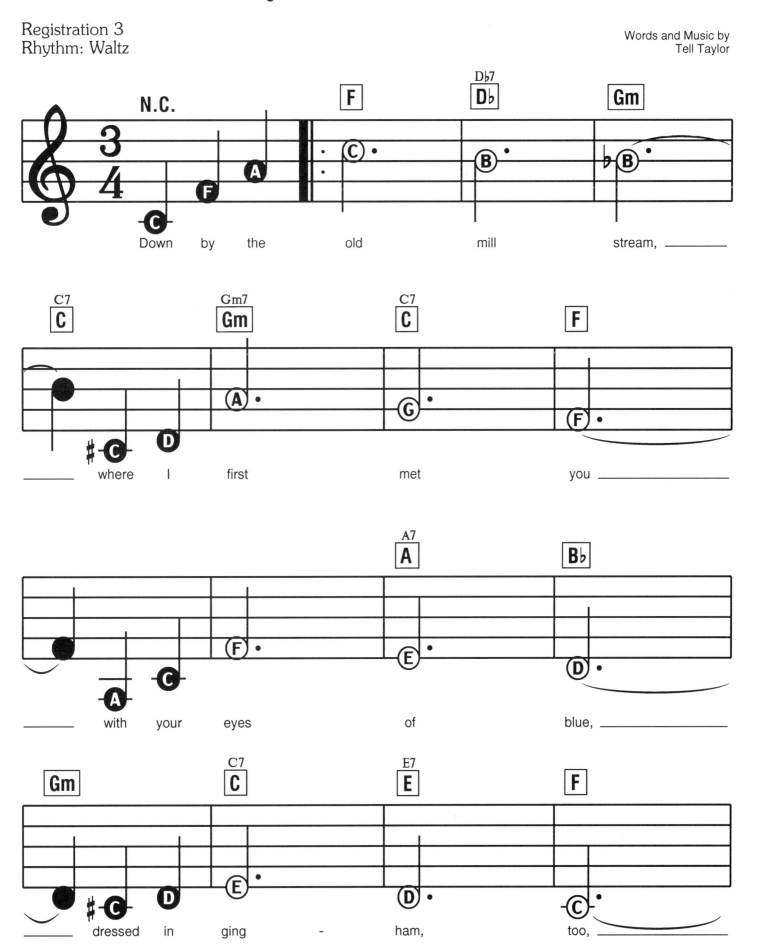

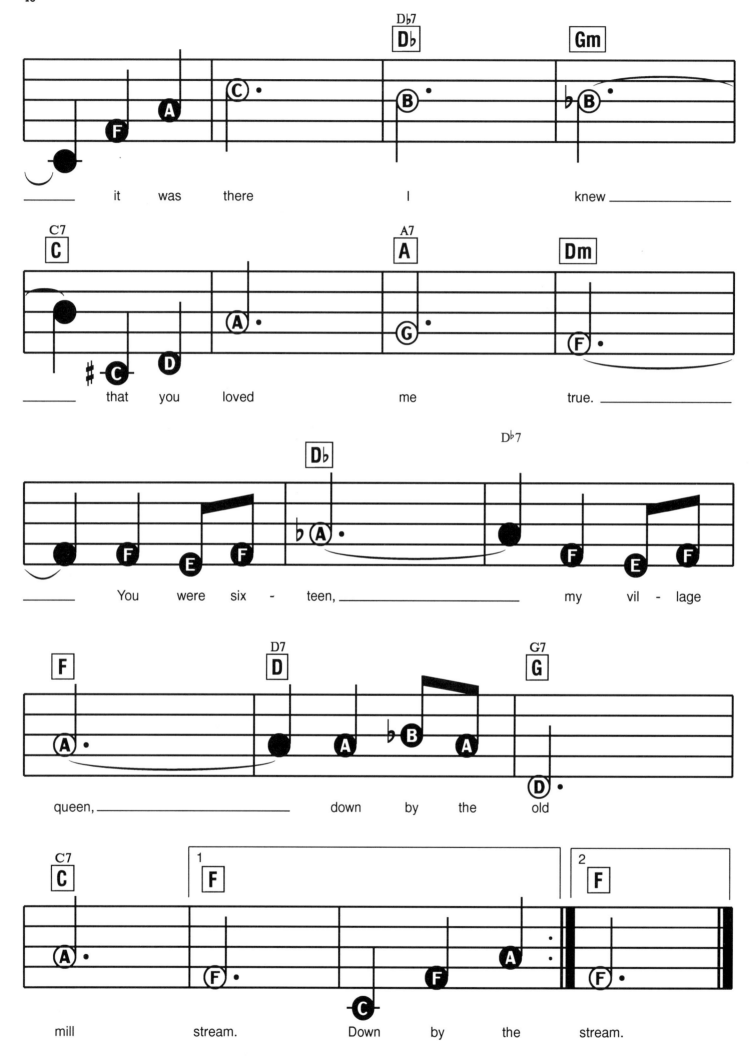

1913

Danny Boy
(Londonderry Air)

Registration 10
Rhythm: 8 Beat or Pops

Words by Frederick Edward Weatherly
Traditional Irish Folk Melody

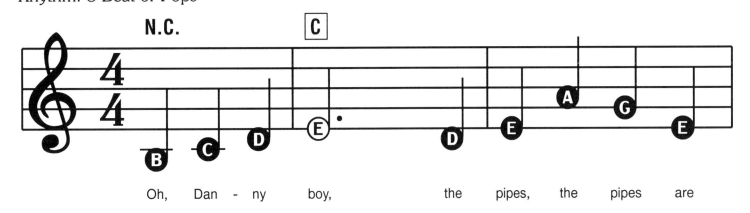

Oh, Dan - ny boy, the pipes, the pipes are

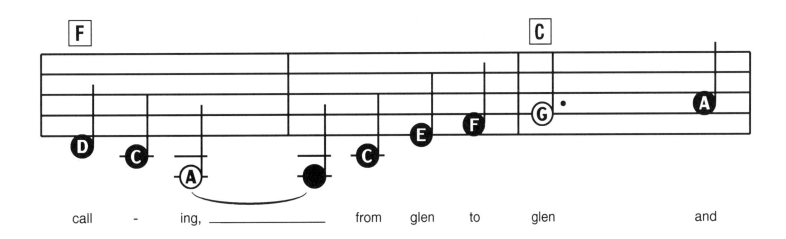

call - ing, _____ from glen to glen and

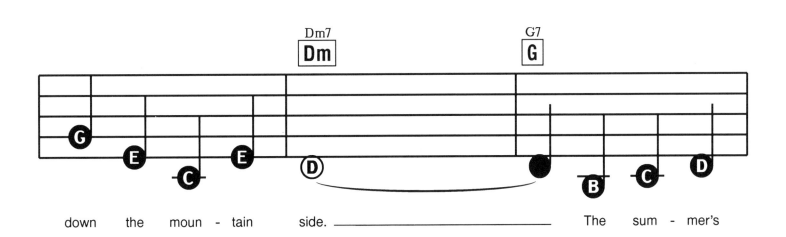

down the moun - tain side. _____ The sum - mer's

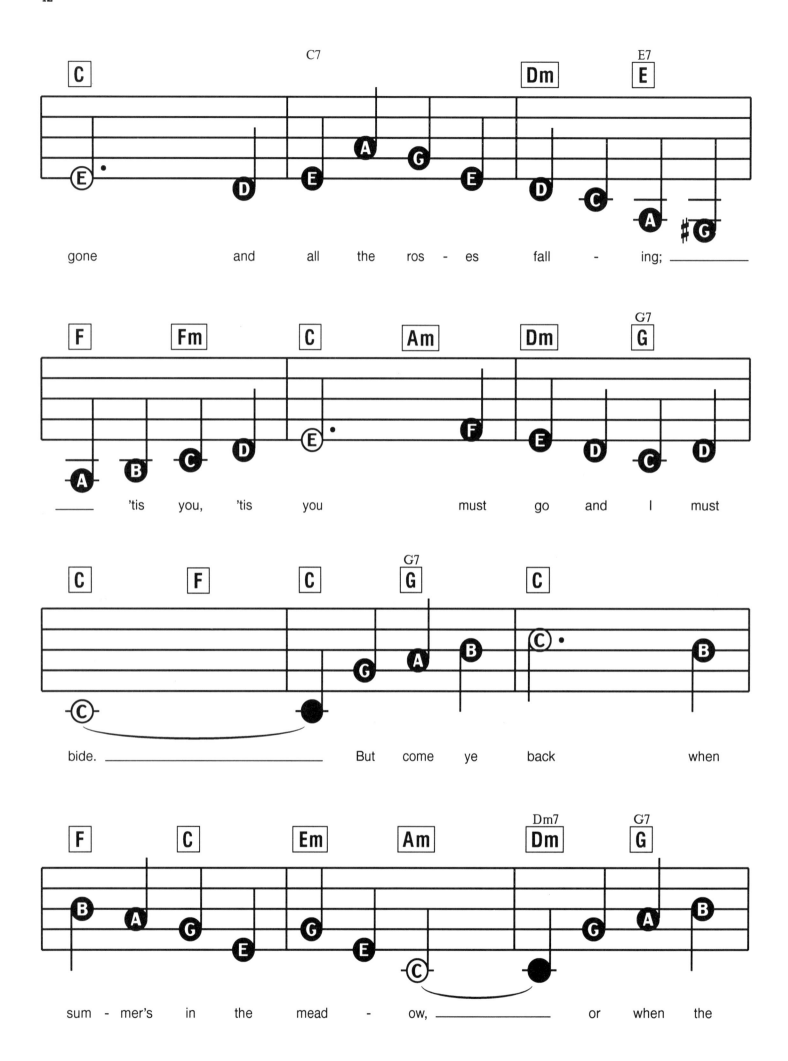

43

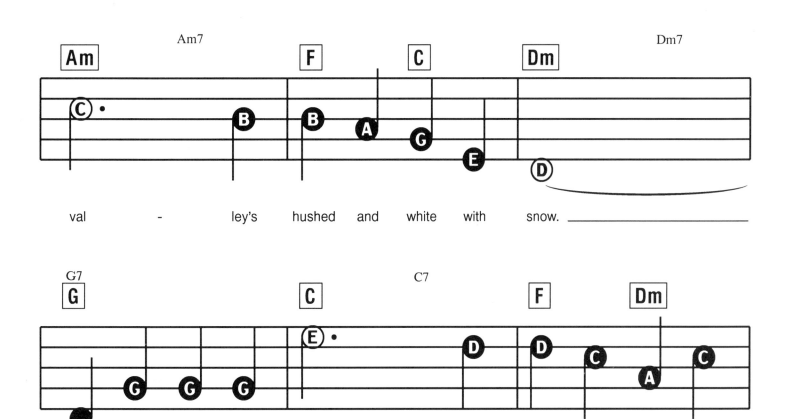

val - ley's hushed and white with snow. _____

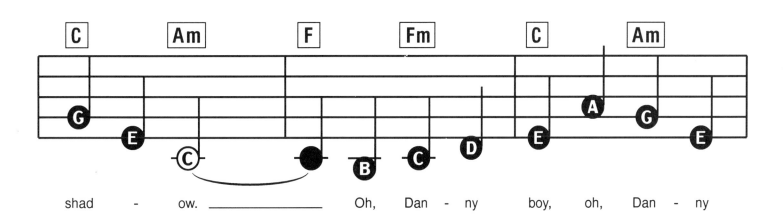

___ 'Tis I'll be there in sun - shine or in

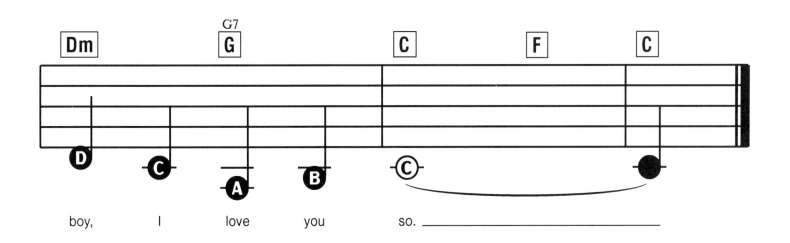

shad - ow. _____ Oh, Dan - ny boy, oh, Dan - ny

boy, I love you so. _____

1914
St. Louis Blues
from BIRTH OF THE BLUES

Registration 7
Rhythm: Swing

Words and Music by
W.C. Handy

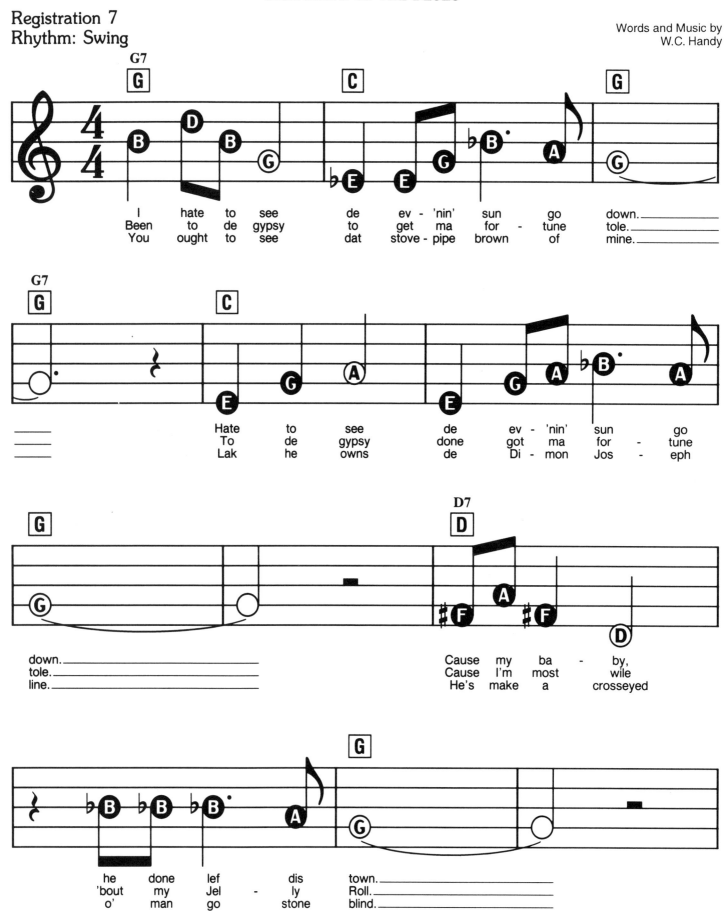

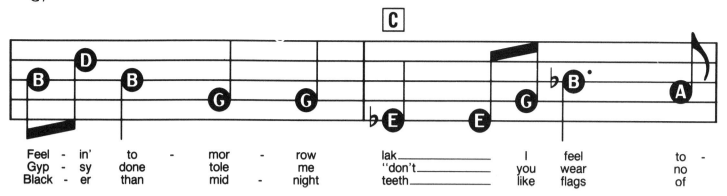

Feel - in' to - mor - row lak_____ I feel to -
Gyp - sy done tole me "don't_____ you wear no
Black - er than mid - night teeth_____ like wear flags of

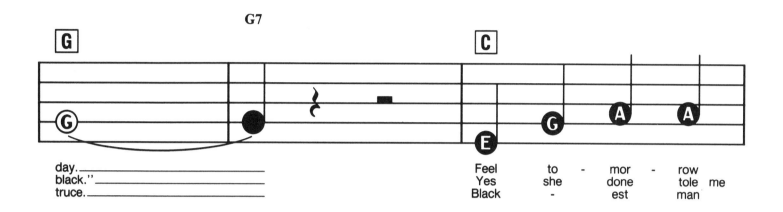

day._____ Feel to - mor - row
black."_____ Yes she done tole me
truce._____ Black - est man

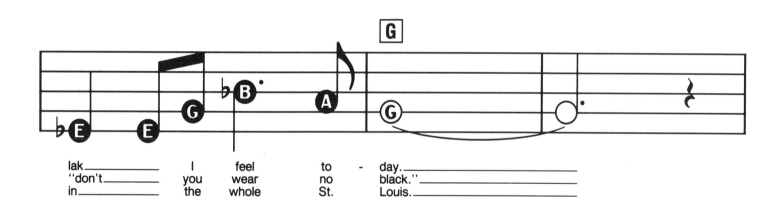

lak_____ I feel to - day._____
"don't_____ you wear no black."_____
in_____ the whole St. Louis._____

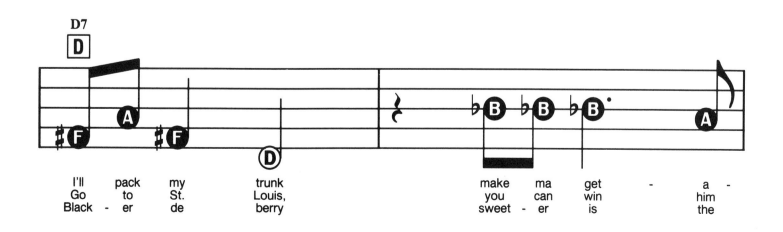

I'll pack my trunk make ma get - a -
Go to St. Louis, you can win him
Black - er de berry sweet - er is the

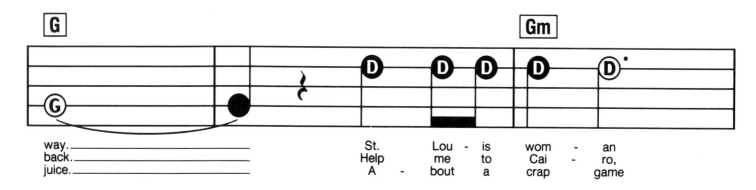

way. _____
back. _____
juice. _____

St. Lou - is wom - an
Help me to Cai - ro,
A - bout a crap game

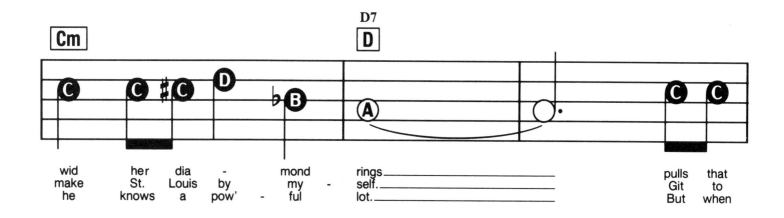

wid her dia - mond rings _____ pulls that
make St. Louis by my - self. _____ Git to
he knows a pow' - ful lot. _____ But when

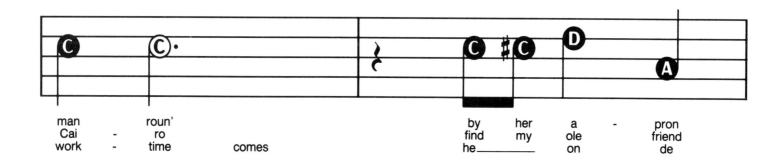

man roun' by her a - pron
Cai - ro find her my ole friend
work - time comes he _____ on de

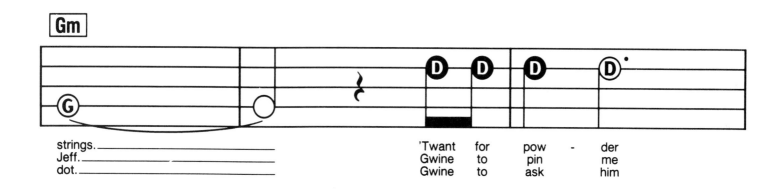

strings. _____ 'Twant for pow - der
Jeff. _____ Gwine to pin me
dot. _____ Gwine to ask him

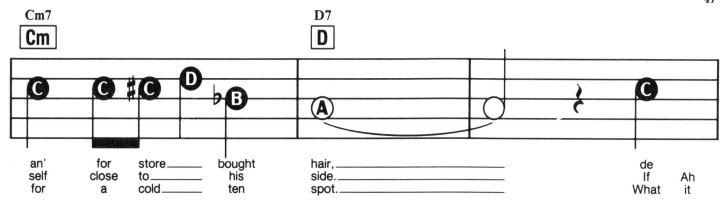

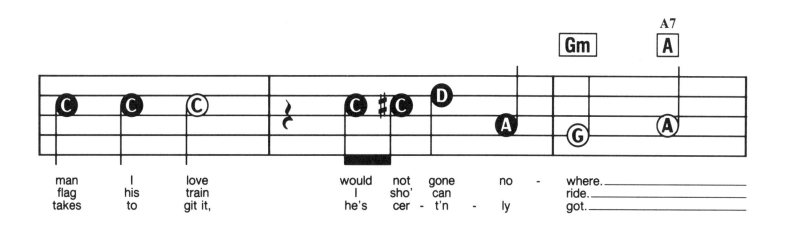

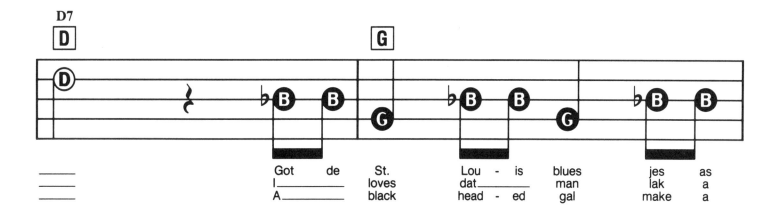

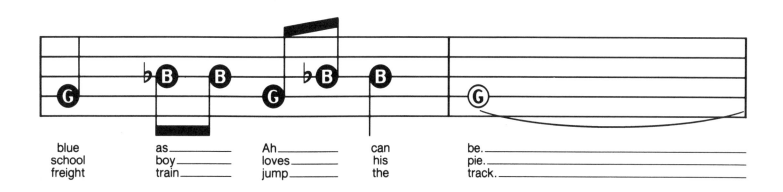

48

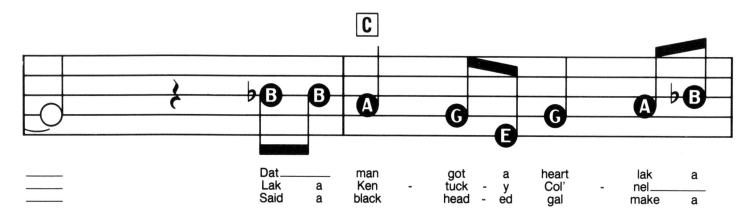

Dat_____ man   got   a   heart   lak   a
Lak   a   Ken - tuck - y   Col' - nel_____
Said a   black head - ed   gal   make a

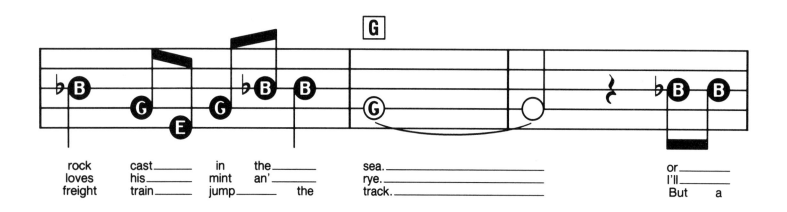

rock   cast_____ in   the_____   sea._____   or_____
loves   his_____ mint an'_____   rye._____   I'll_____
freight train_____ jump_____ the track._____   But   a

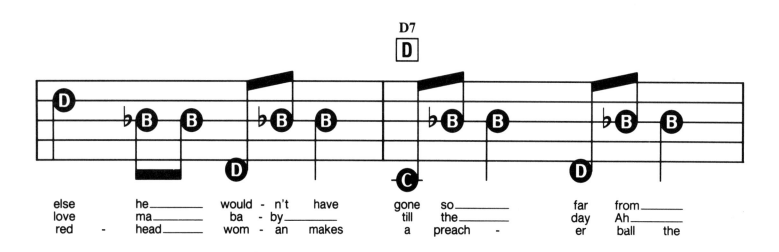

else   he_____   would - n't have   gone   so_____   far   from_____
love   ma_____   ba - by_____   till   the_____   day   Ah_____
red - head_____   wom - an   makes   a   preach -   er   ball   the

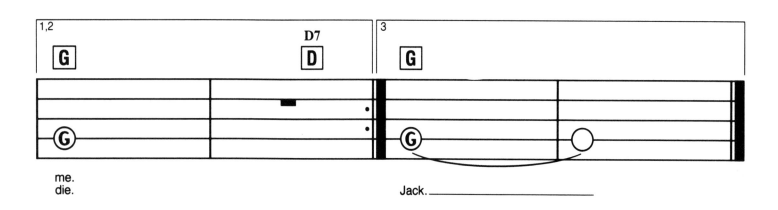

me.
die.   Jack._____

1915

It's a Long, Long Way to Tipperary

Registration 8
Rhythm: March

Words and Music by Jack Judge
and Harry Williams

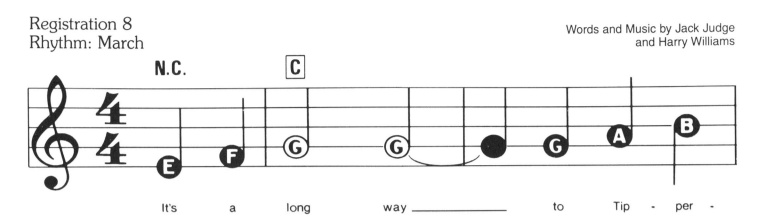

It's a long way _____ to Tip - per -

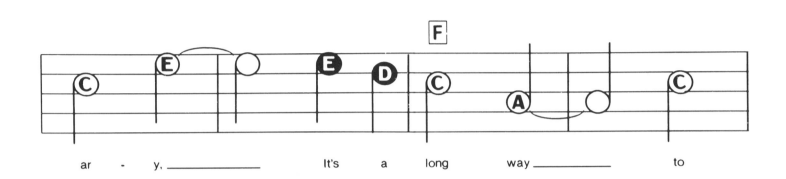

ar - y, _____ It's a long way _____ to

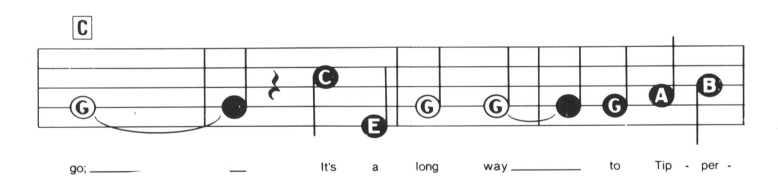

go; _____ It's a long way _____ to Tip - per -

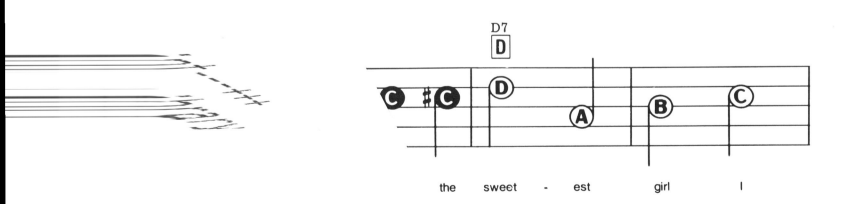

the sweet - est girl I

50

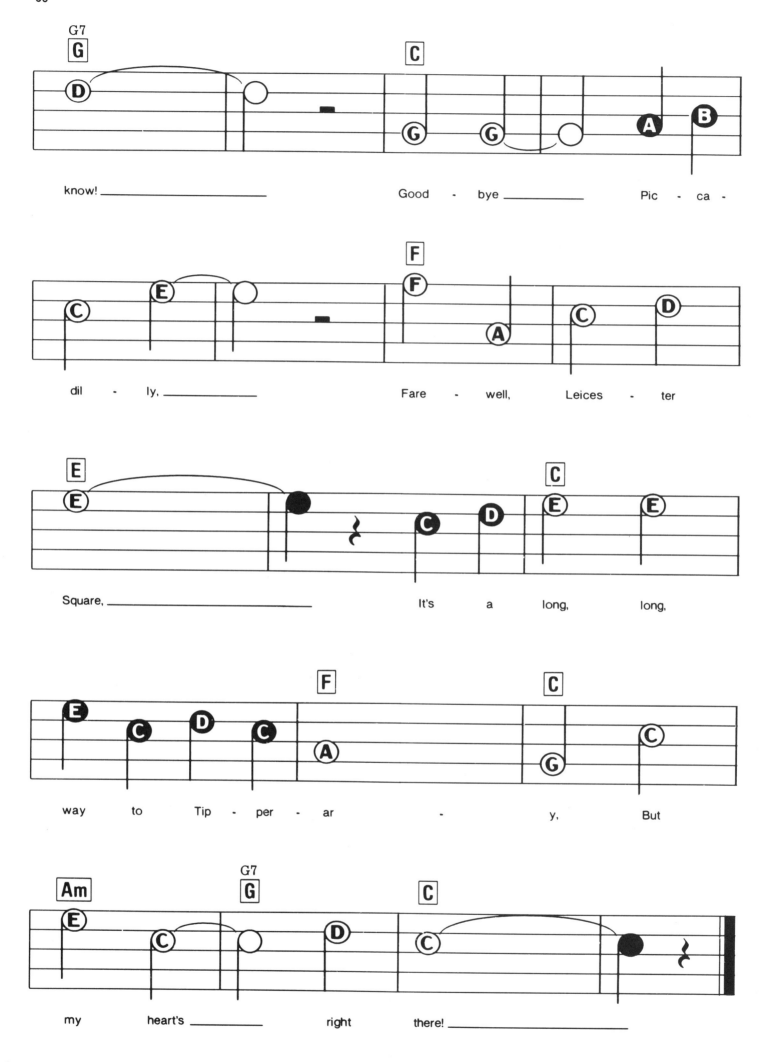

1916
Pretty Baby

Registration 2
Rhythm: Swing

Words by Gus Kahn
Music by Egbert Van Alstyne and Tony Jackson

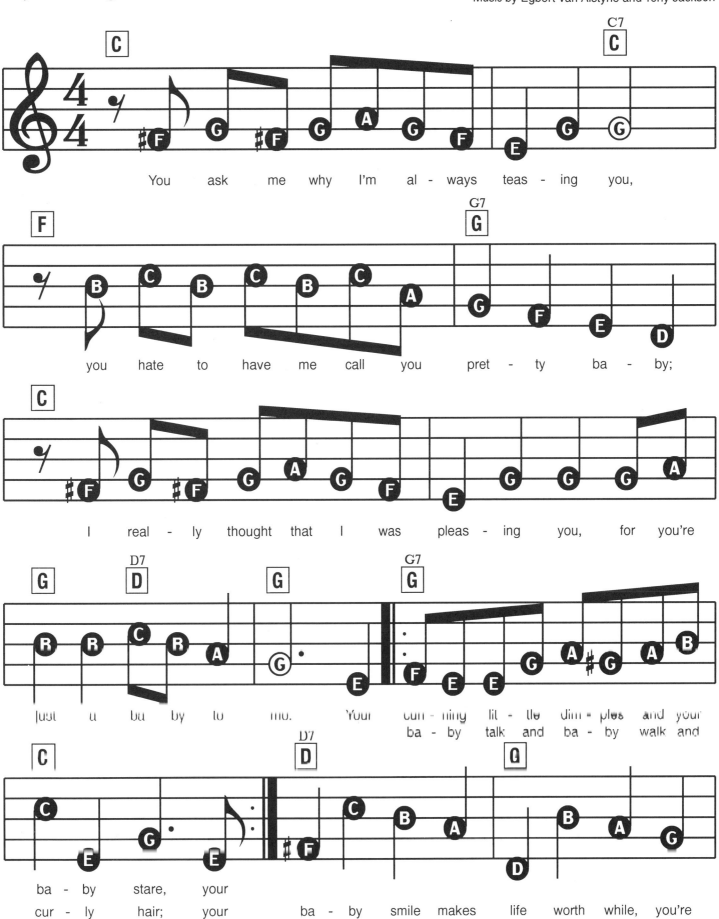

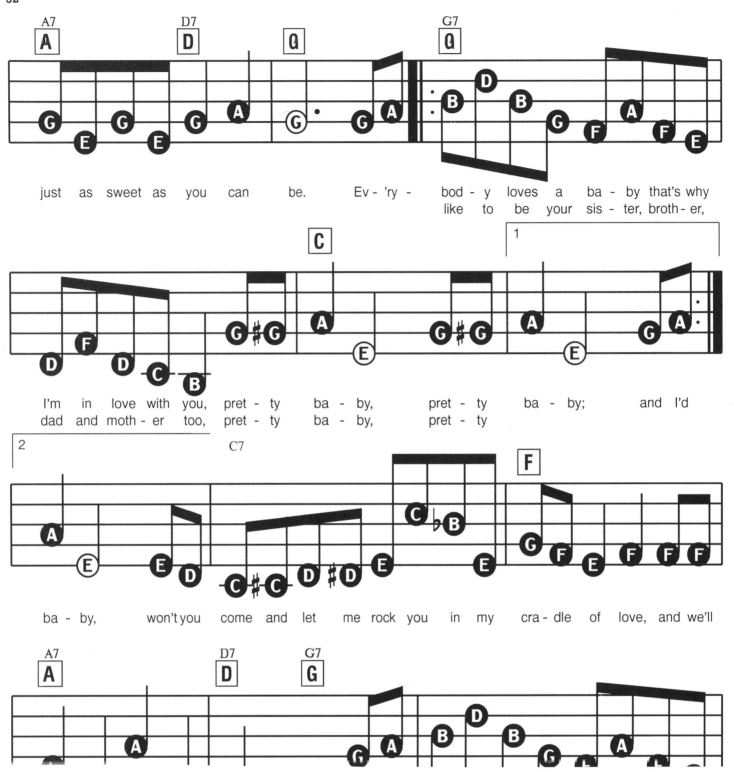

just as sweet as you can be. Ev - 'ry - bod - y loves a ba - by that's why
like to be your sis - ter, broth - er,

I'm in love with you, pret - ty ba - by, pret - ty ba - by; and I'd
dad and moth - er too, pret - ty ba - by, pret - ty

ba - by, won't you come and let me rock you in my cra - dle of love, and we'll

1917

Over There

Registration 9
Rhythm: March

Words and Music by
George M. Cohan

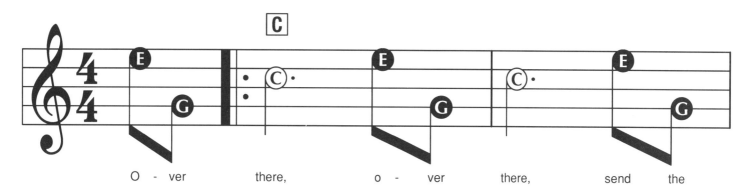

O - ver there, o - ver there, send the

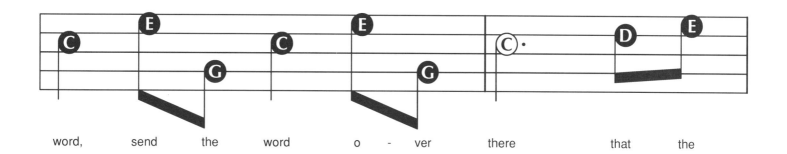

word, send the word o - ver there that the

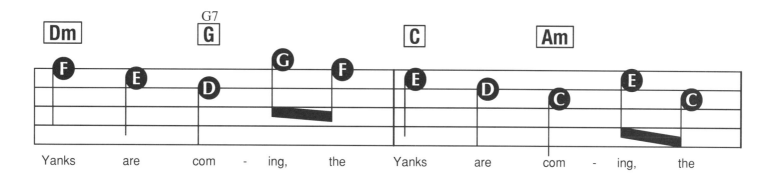

Yanks are com - ing, the Yanks are com - ing, the

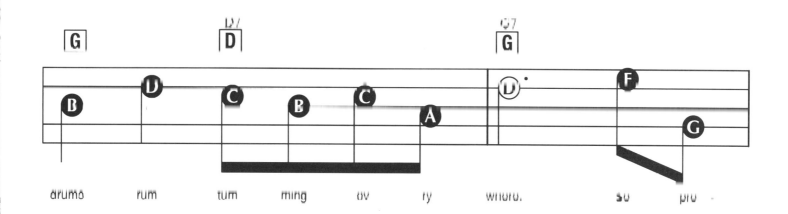

drums rum tum ming ev ry where. So pro -

54

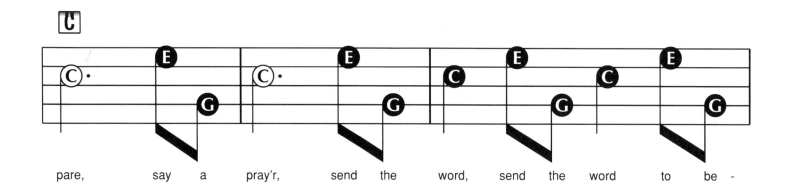

pare, say a pray'r, send the word, send the word to be -

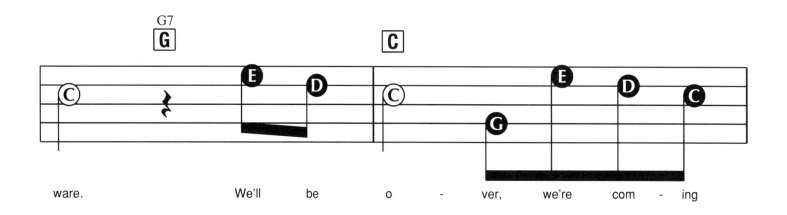

ware. We'll be o - ver, we're com - ing

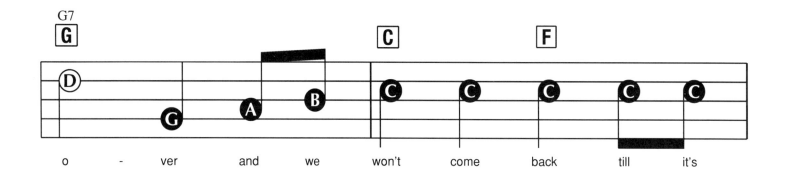

o - ver and we won't come back till it's

1918
Smiles

Registration 5
Rhythm: Fox Trot or Swing

Words by J. Will Callahan
Music by Lee S. Roberts

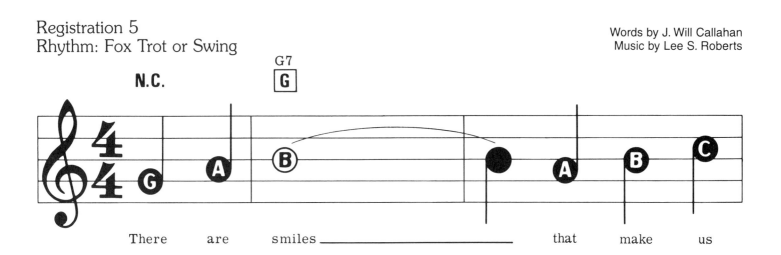

There are smiles _____ that make us

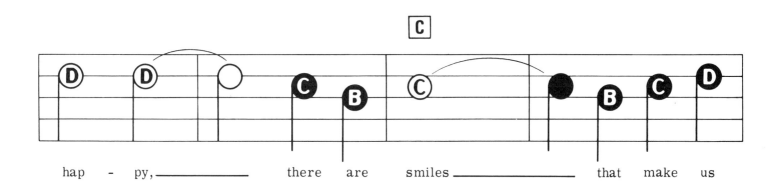

hap - py, _____ there are smiles _____ that make us

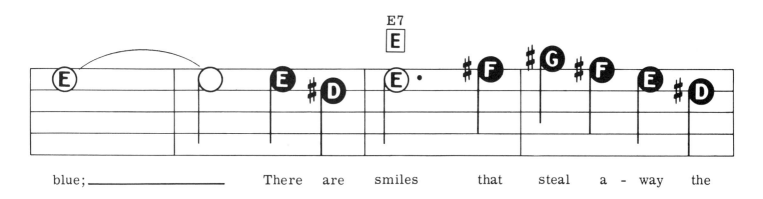

blue; _____ There are smiles that steal a - way the

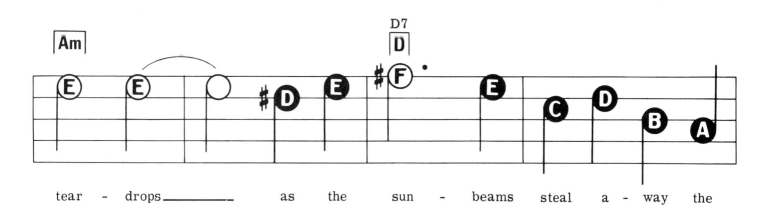

tear - drops _____ as the sun - beams steal a - way the

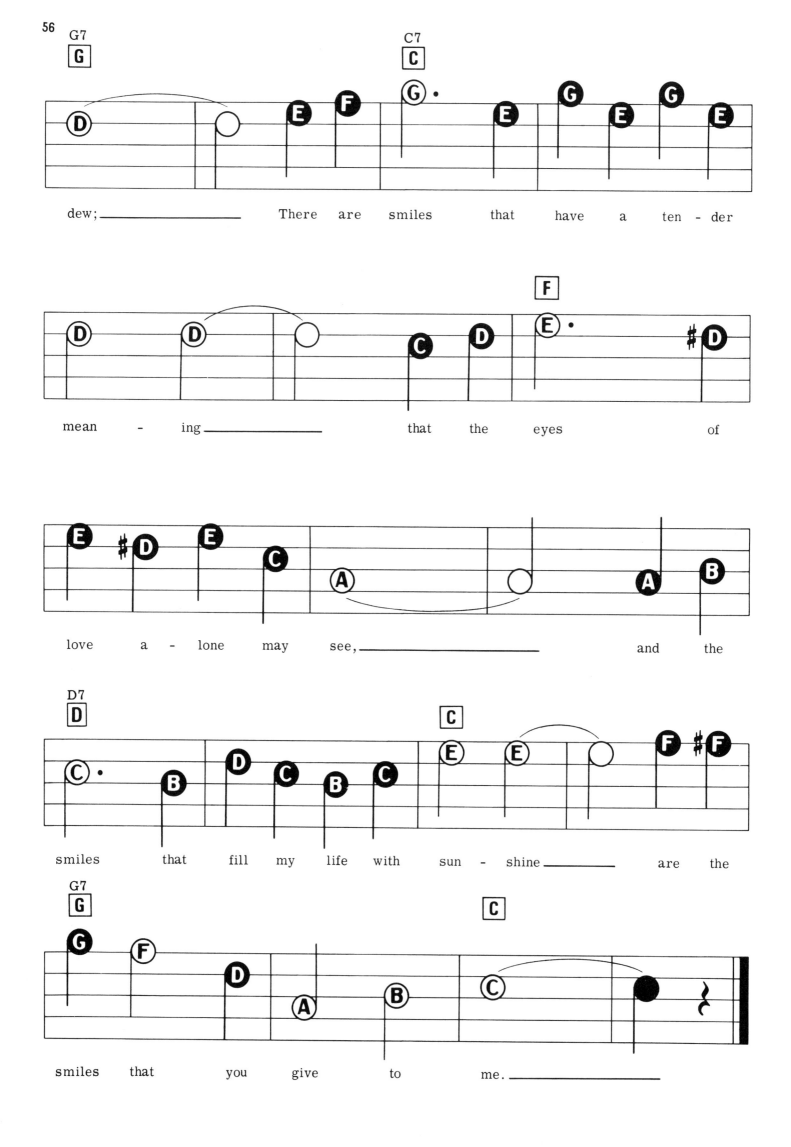

1919
A Pretty Girl Is Like a Melody
from the 1919 Stage Production ZIEGFELD FOLLIES

Registration 8
Rhythm: Fox Trot or Ballad

Words and Music by
Irving Berlin

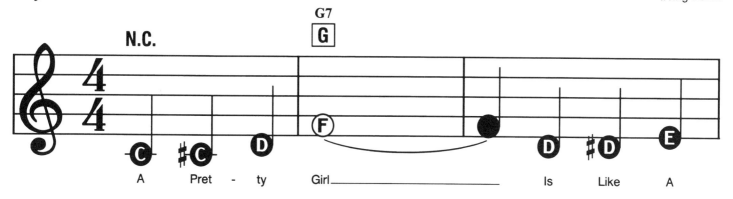

A Pret - ty Girl_____ Is Like A

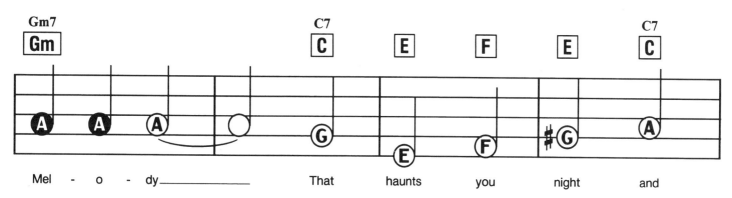

Mel - o - dy_____ That haunts you night and

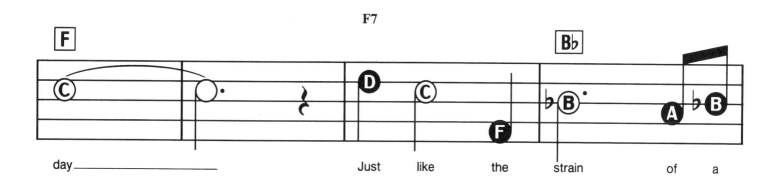

day_____ Just like the strain of a

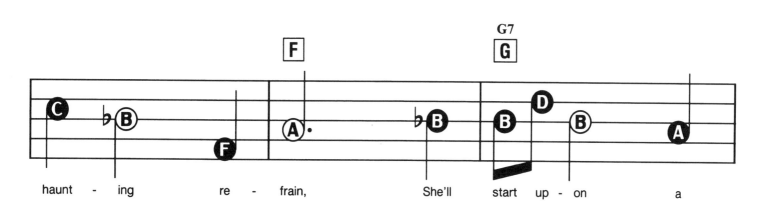

haunt - ing re - frain, She'll start up - on a

58

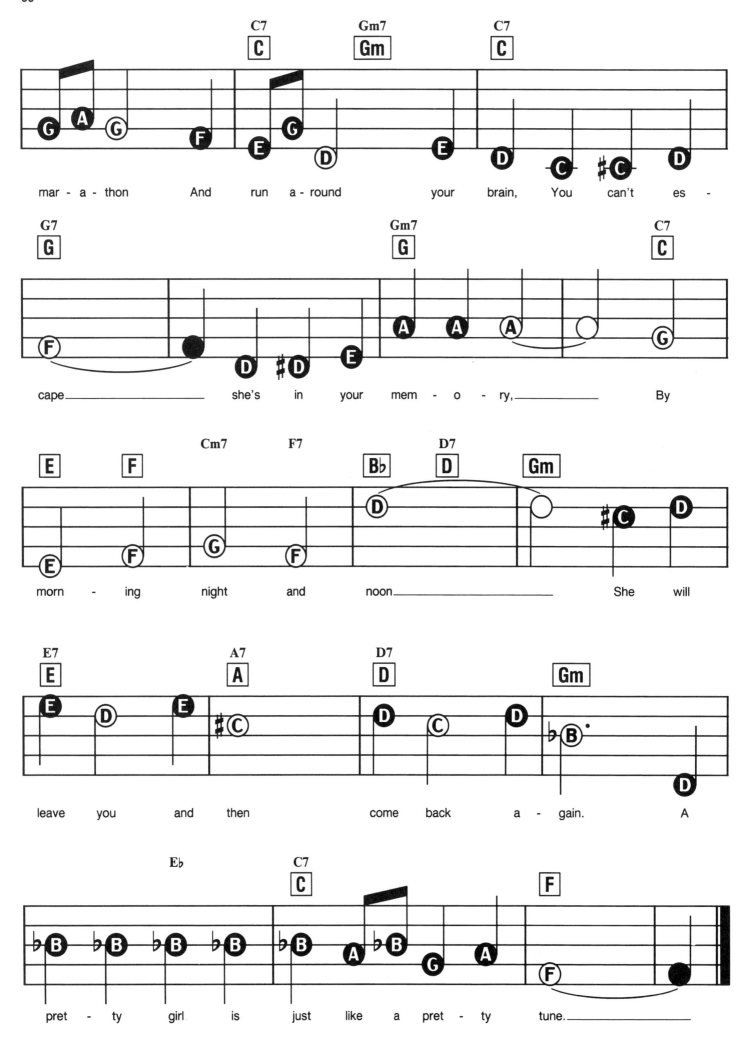

1920
Swanee

Registration 9
Rhythm: Fox Trot or Swing

Words by Irving Caesar
Music by George Gershwin

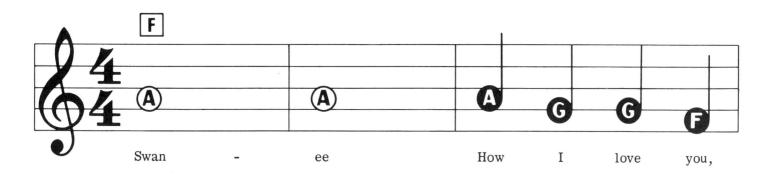

Swan - ee   How   I   love you,

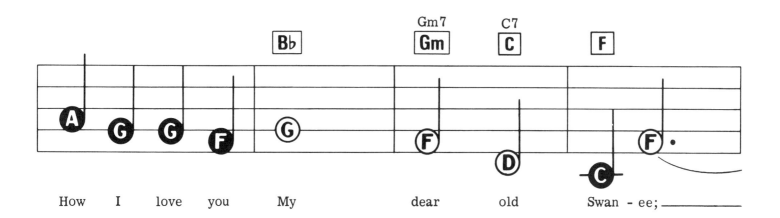

How I love you My   dear   old   Swan - ee;____

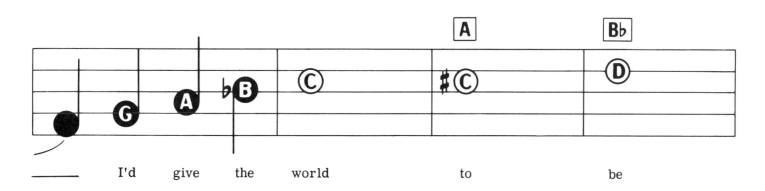

____ I'd give the world   to   be

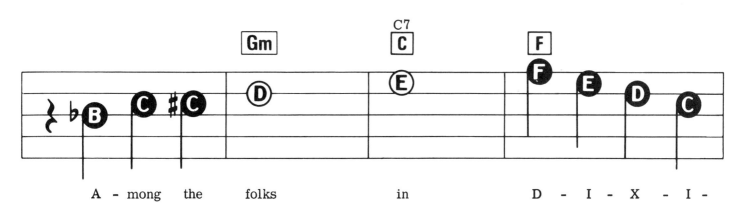

A - mong the folks   in   D - I - X - I -

60

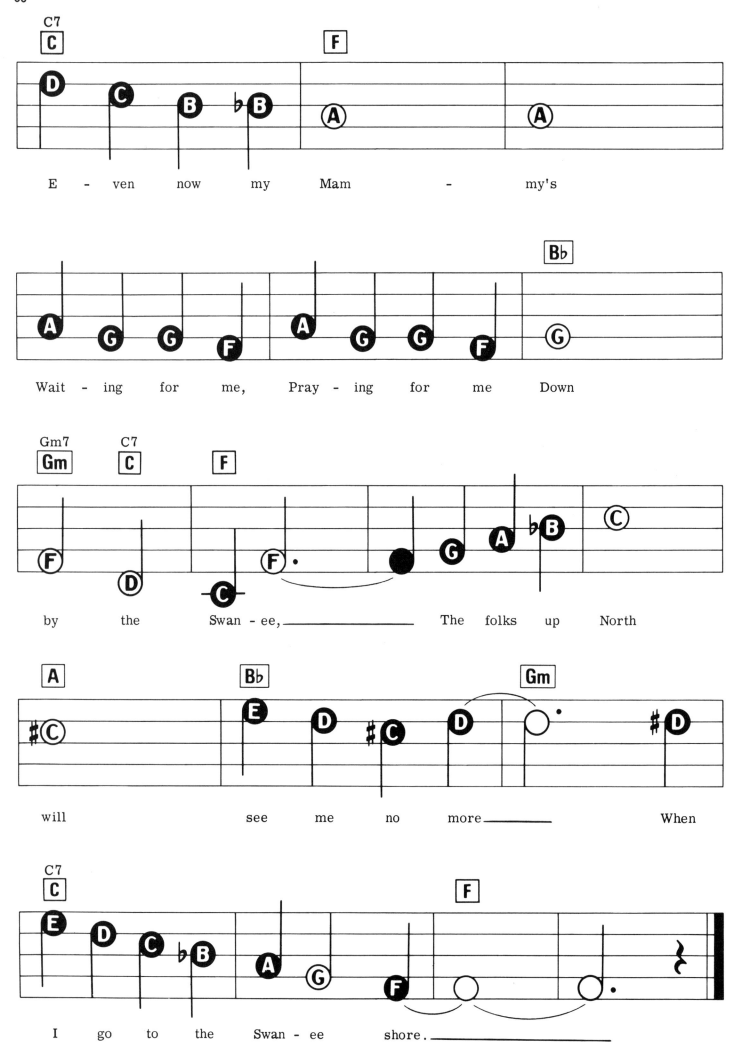

1921

Ain't We Got Fun?

from BY THE LIGHT OF THE SILVERY MOON

Words by Gus Kahn and Raymond B. Egan
Music by Richard A. Whiting

Registration 5
Rhythm: Fox Trot or Swing

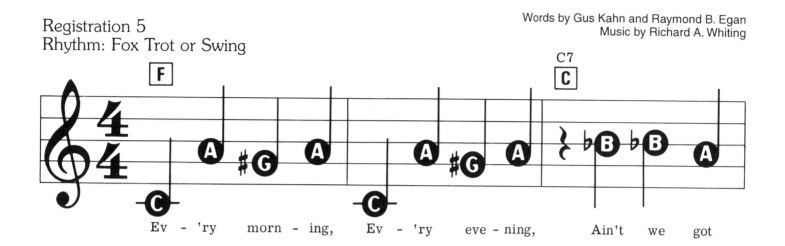

Ev - 'ry morn - ing, Ev - 'ry eve - ning, Ain't we got

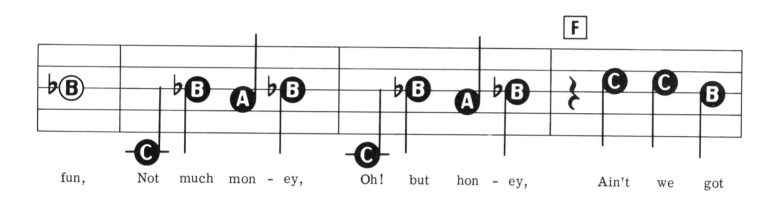

fun, Not much mon - ey, Oh! but hon - ey, Ain't we got

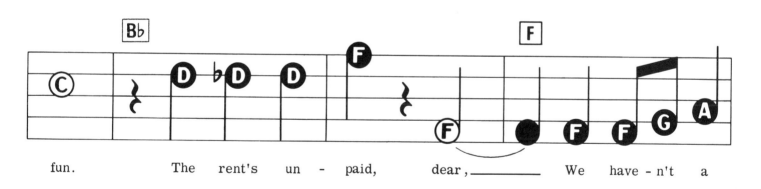

fun. The rent's un - paid, dear,_____ We have - n't a

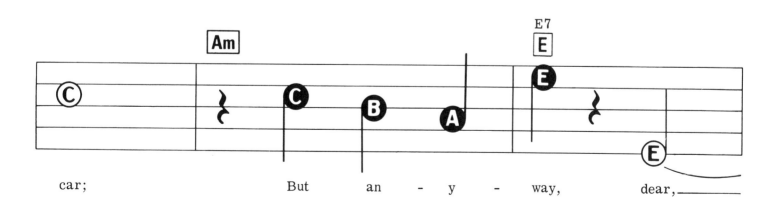

car; But an - y - way, dear,_____

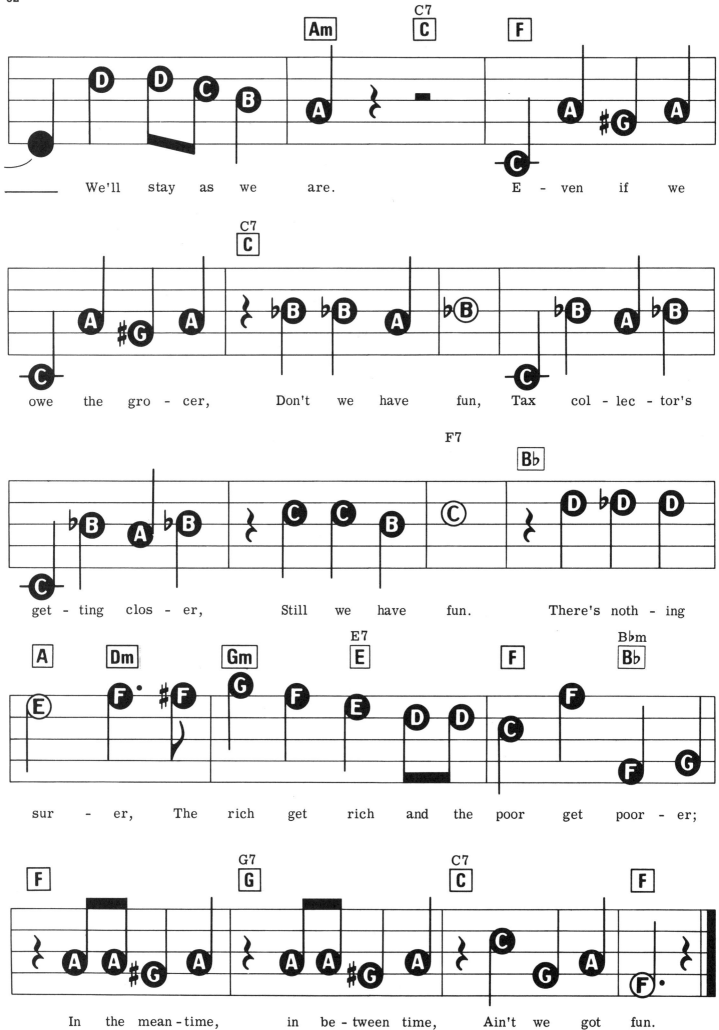

1922
Carolina in the Morning

Registration 5
Rhythm: Swing or Jazz

Lyrics by Gus Kahn
Music by Walter Donaldson

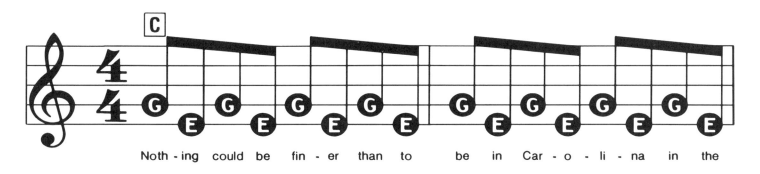

Noth - ing could be fin - er than to be in Car - o - li - na in the

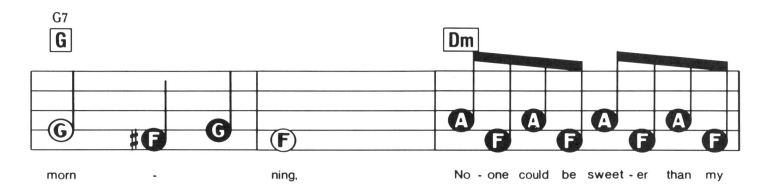

morn - ning, No - one could be sweet - er than my

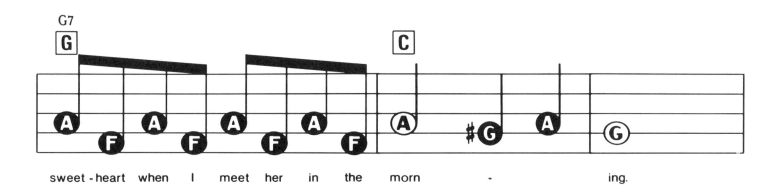

sweet - heart when I meet her in the morn - ing.

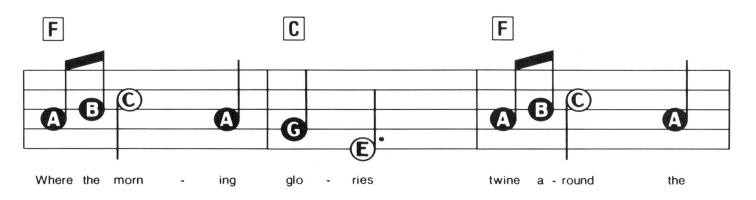

Where the morn - ing glo - ries twine a - round the

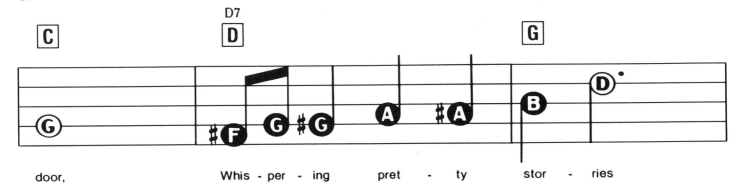

door,   Whis - per - ing   pret - ty   stor - ries

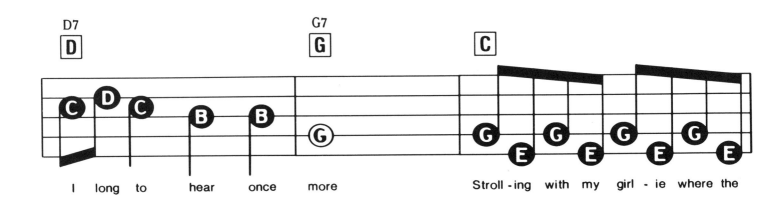

I   long   to   hear   once   more   Stroll -ing with my girl - ie where the

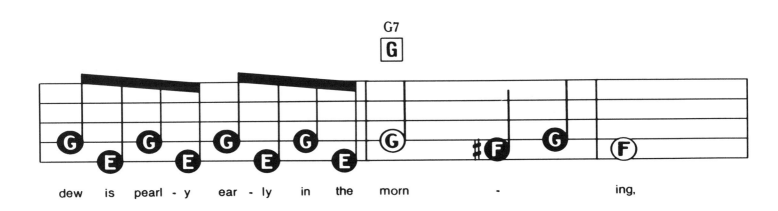

dew   is   pearl - y   ear - ly   in   the   morn   -   ing,

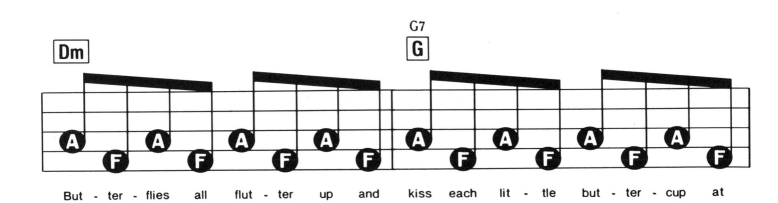

But - ter - flies all flut - ter up and kiss each lit - tle but - ter - cup at

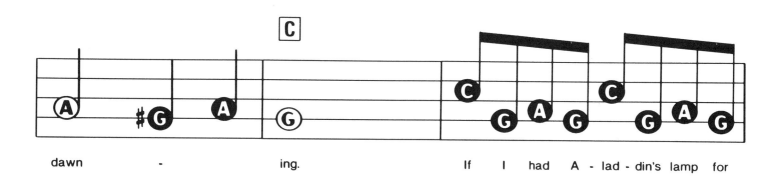

dawn - ing. If I had A - lad - din's lamp for

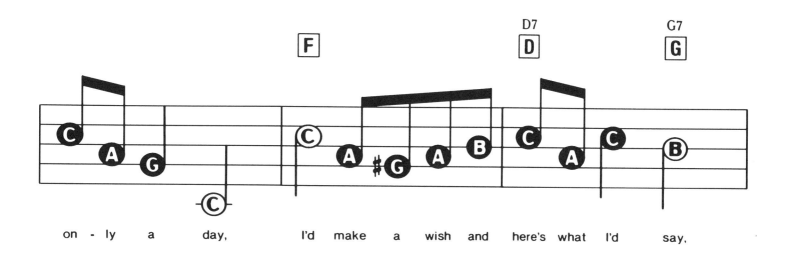

on - ly a day, I'd make a wish and here's what I'd say,

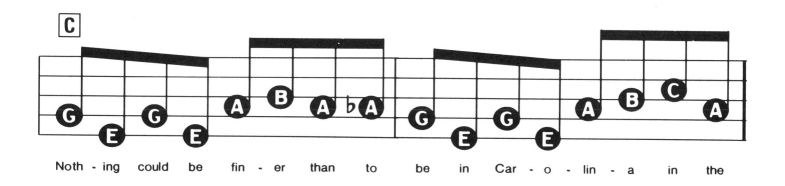

Noth - ing could be fin - er than to be in Car - o - lin - a in the

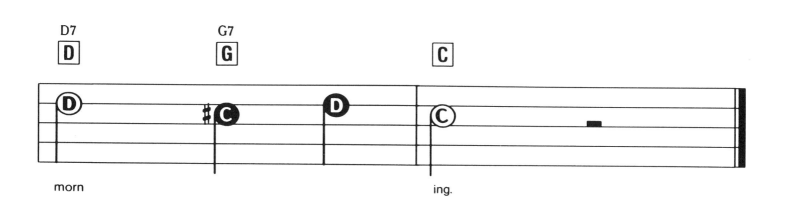

morn ing.

1923

Yes! We Have No Bananas

Registration 5
Rhythm: March or Polka

By Frank Silver
and Irving Conn

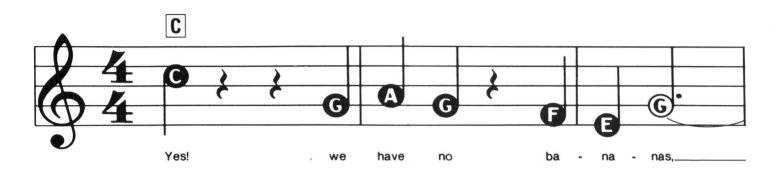

Yes! we have no ba - na - nas,_____

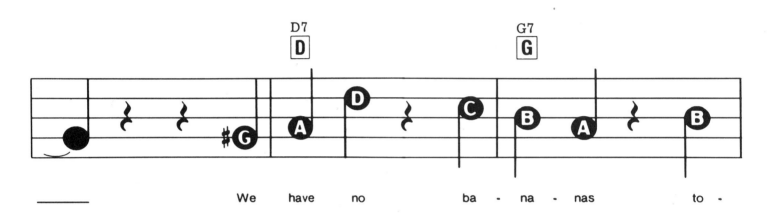

_____ We have no ba - na - nas to -

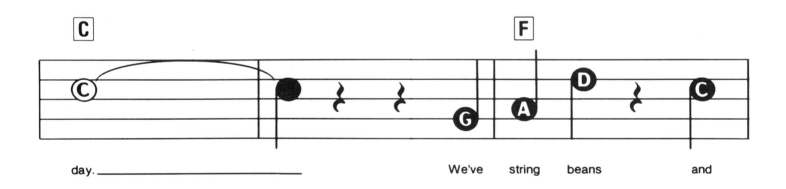

day._____ We've string beans and

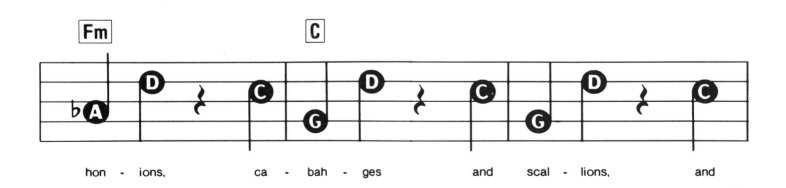

hon - ions, ca - bah - ges and scal - lions, and

67

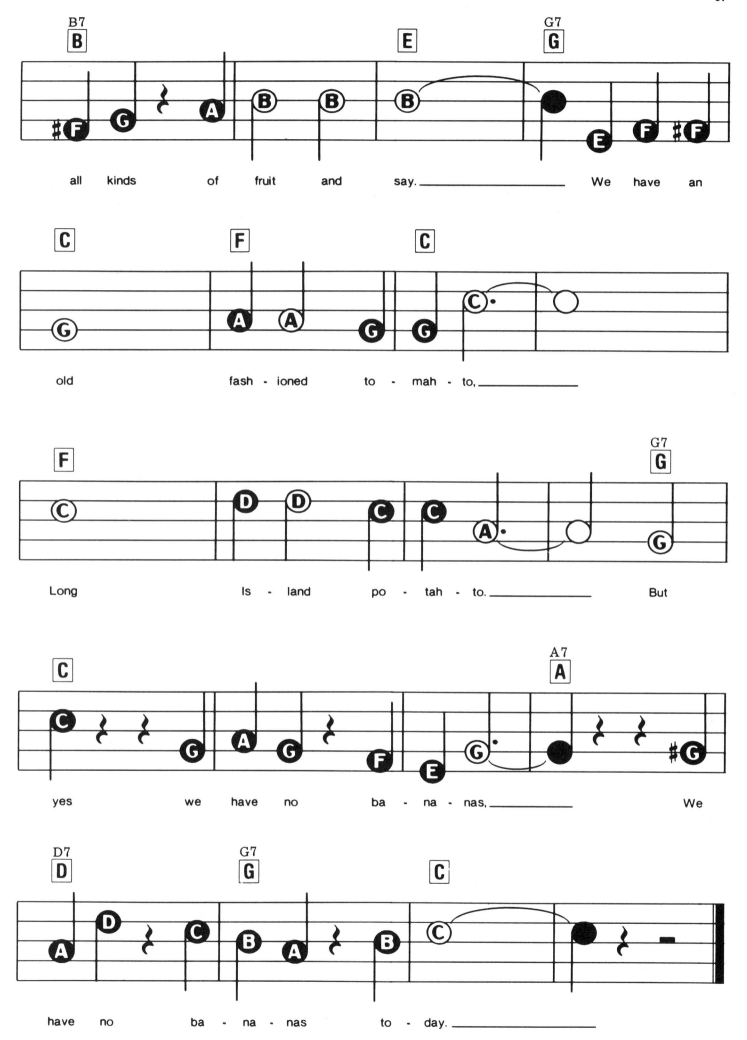

1924
Somebody Loves Me
from SHE LOVES ME

Registration 4
Rhythm: Fox Trot or Swing

Words by B.G. DeSylva and Ballard MacDonald
Music by George Gershwin
French Version by Emelia Renaud

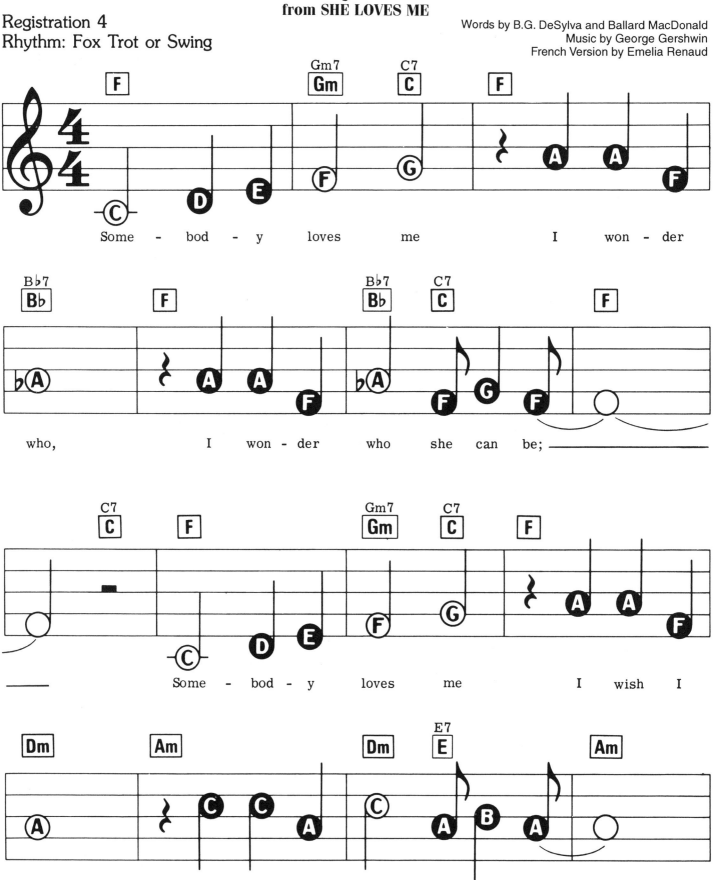

69

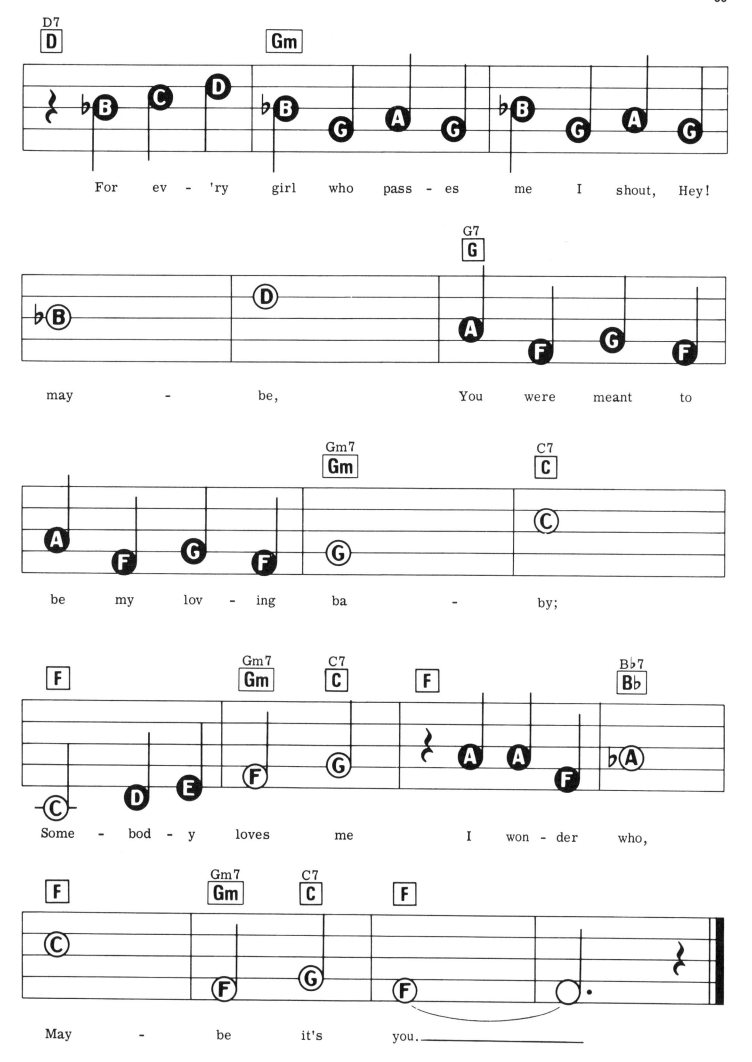

1925

Always

Registration 2
Rhythm: Waltz

Words and Music by
Irving Berlin

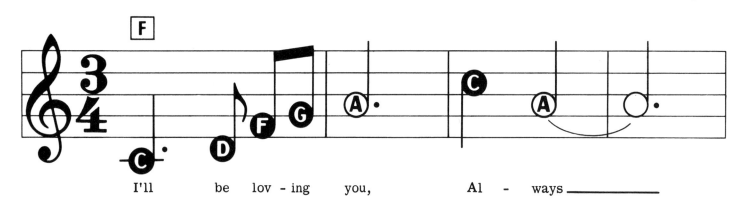

I'll be lov - ing you, Al - ways _____

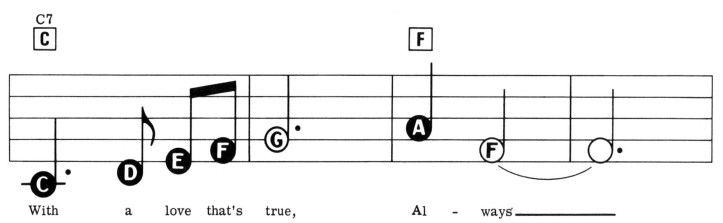

With a love that's true, Al - ways _____

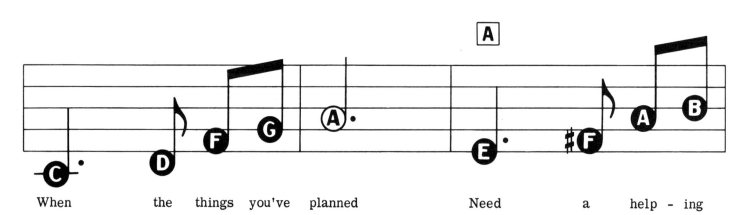

When the things you've planned Need a help - ing

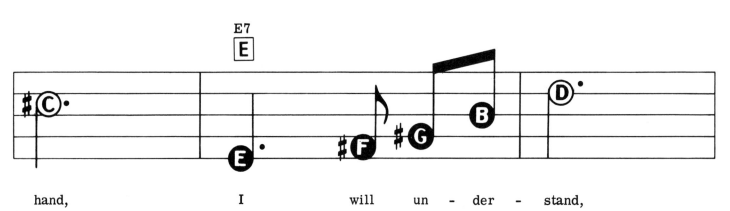

hand, I will un - der - stand,

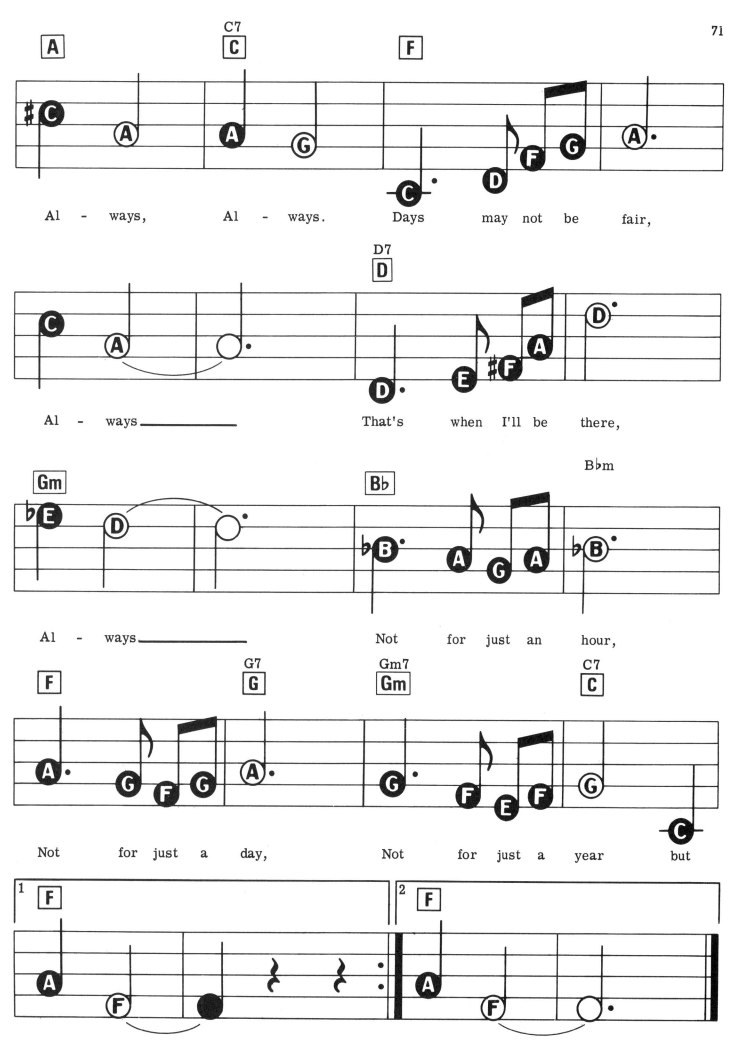

1926
Bye Bye Blackbird
from PETE KELLY'S BLUES

Lyric by Mort Dixon
Music by Ray Henderson

Registration 2
Rhythm: Fox Trot or Swing

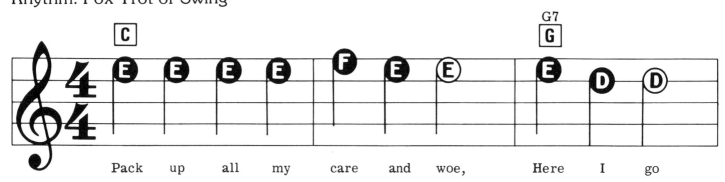

Pack up all my care and woe, Here I go

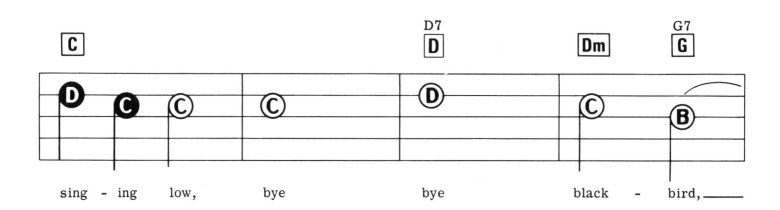

sing - ing low, bye bye black - bird, _____

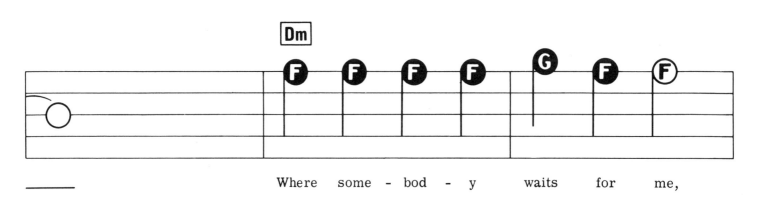

_____ Where some - bod - y waits for me,

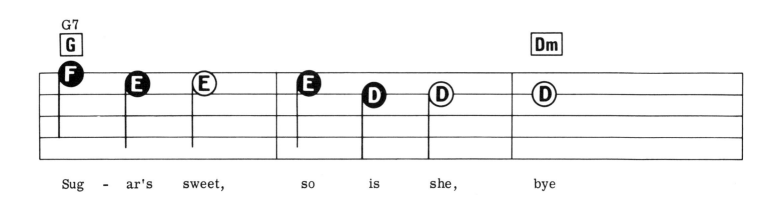

Sug - ar's sweet, so is she, bye

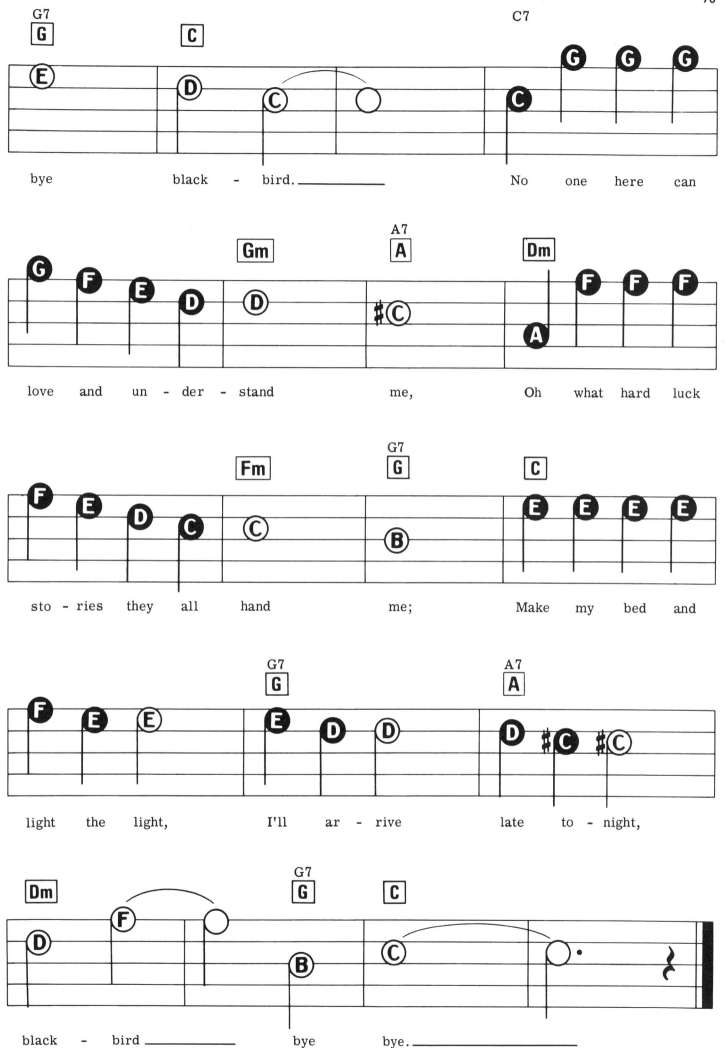

74

1927
My Blue Heaven

Registration 9
Rhythm: Swing

Lyric by George Whiting
Music by Walter Donaldson

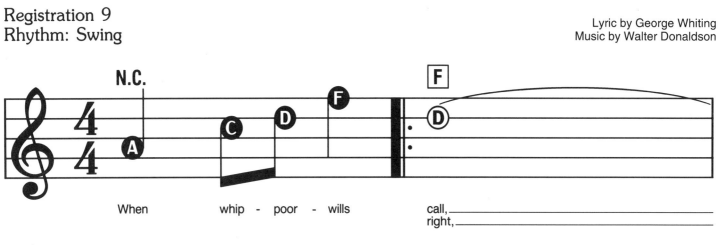

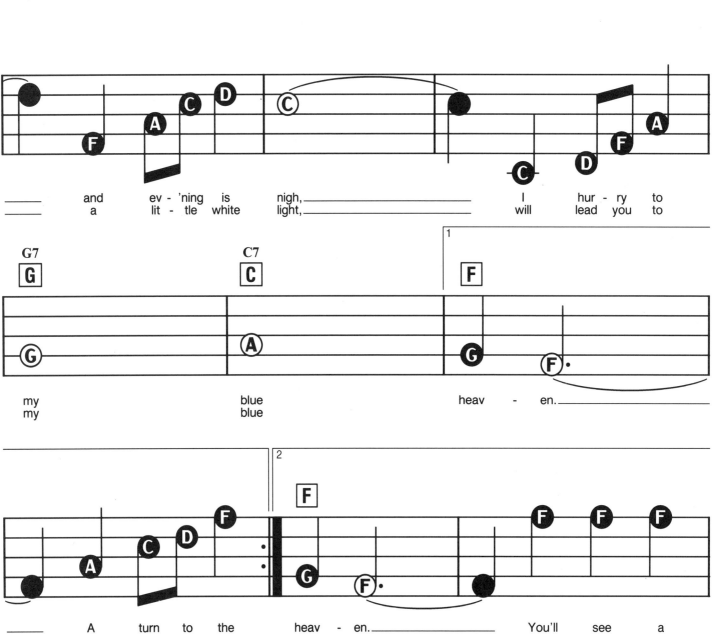

75

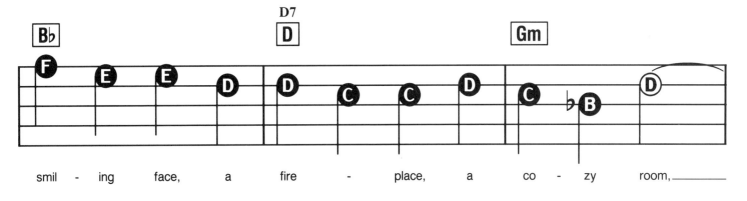

smil - ing face, a fire - place, a co - zy room,

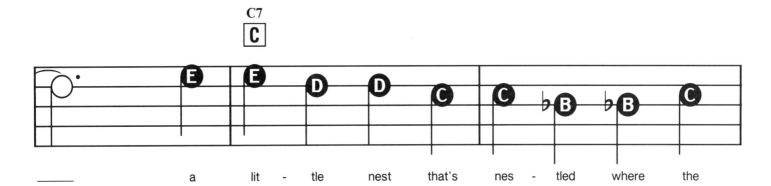

_____ a lit - tle nest that's nes - tled where the

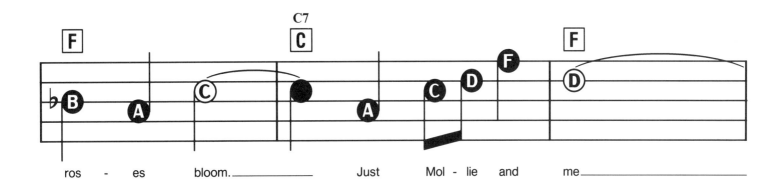

ros - es bloom. _____ Just Mol - lie and me _____

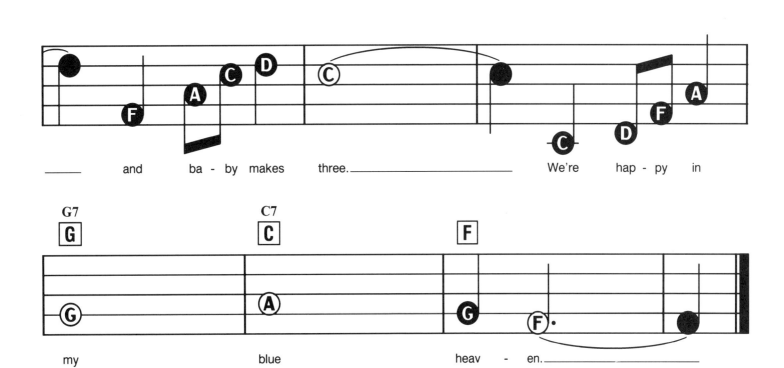

_____ and ba - by makes three. _____ We're hap - py in

my blue heav - en. _____

1928
Can't Help Lovin' Dat Man
from SHOW BOAT

Registration 5
Rhythm: Ballad or Swing

Lyrics by Oscar Hammerstein II
Music by Jerome Kern

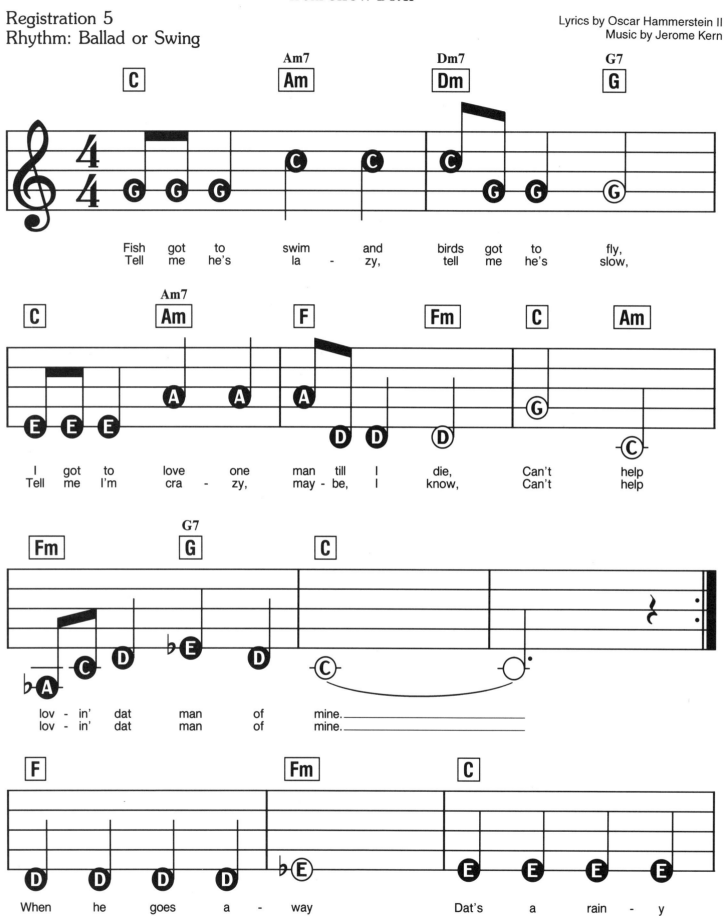

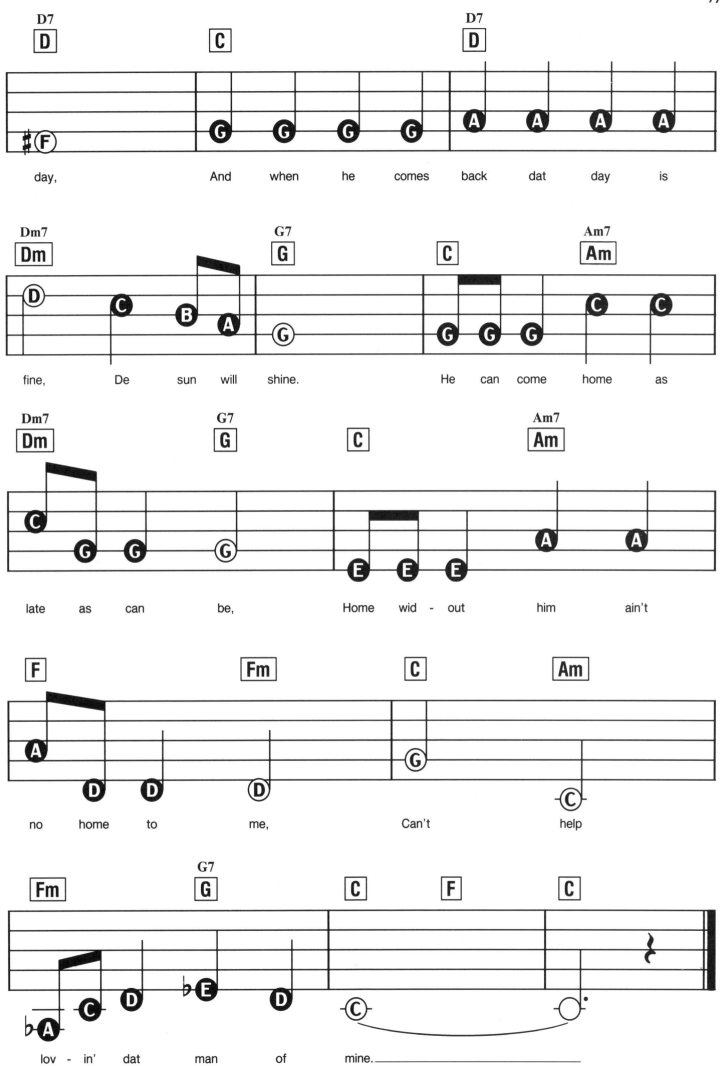

1929
Ain't Misbehavin'
from AIN'T MISBEHAVIN'

Registration 7
Rhythm: Fox Trot or Swing

Words by Andy Razaf
Music by Thomas "Fats" Waller and Harry Brooks

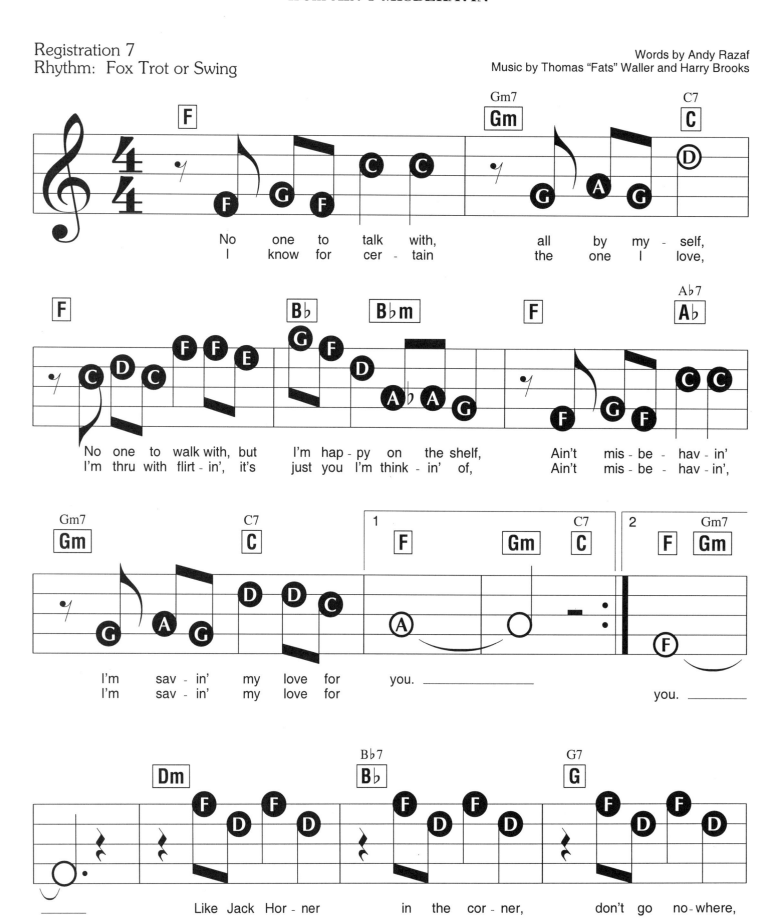

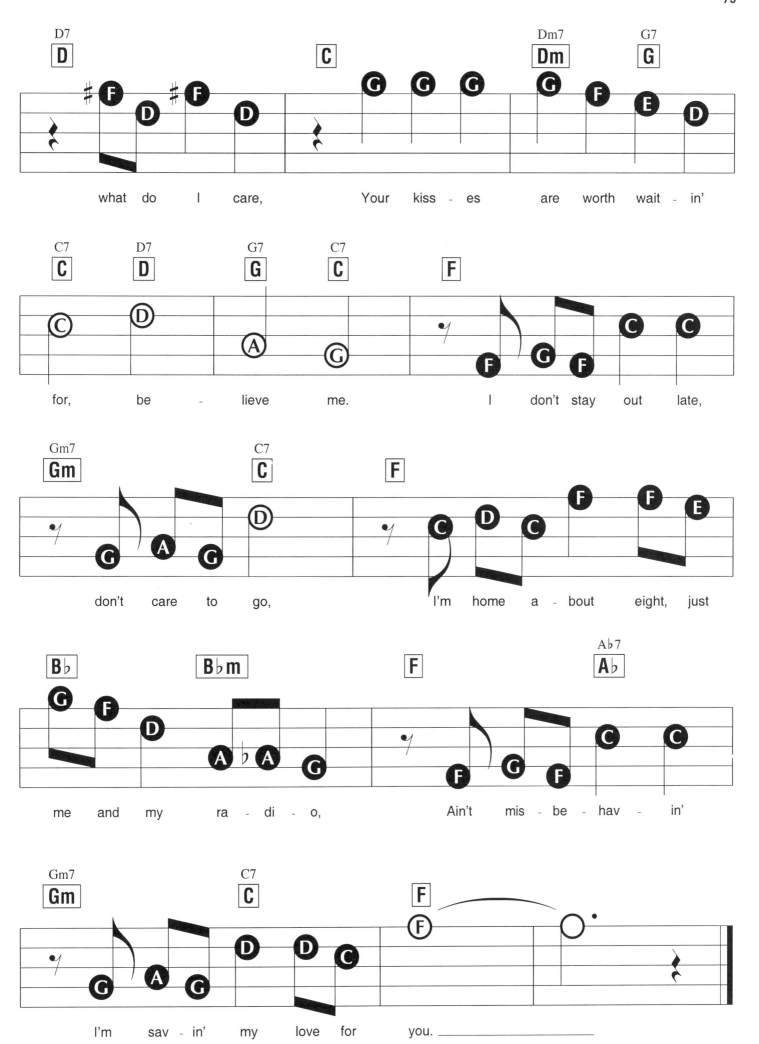

1930
Body and Soul

Registration 1
Rhythm: Fox Trot or Swing

Words by Edward Heyman, Robert Sour and Frank Eyton
Music by John Green

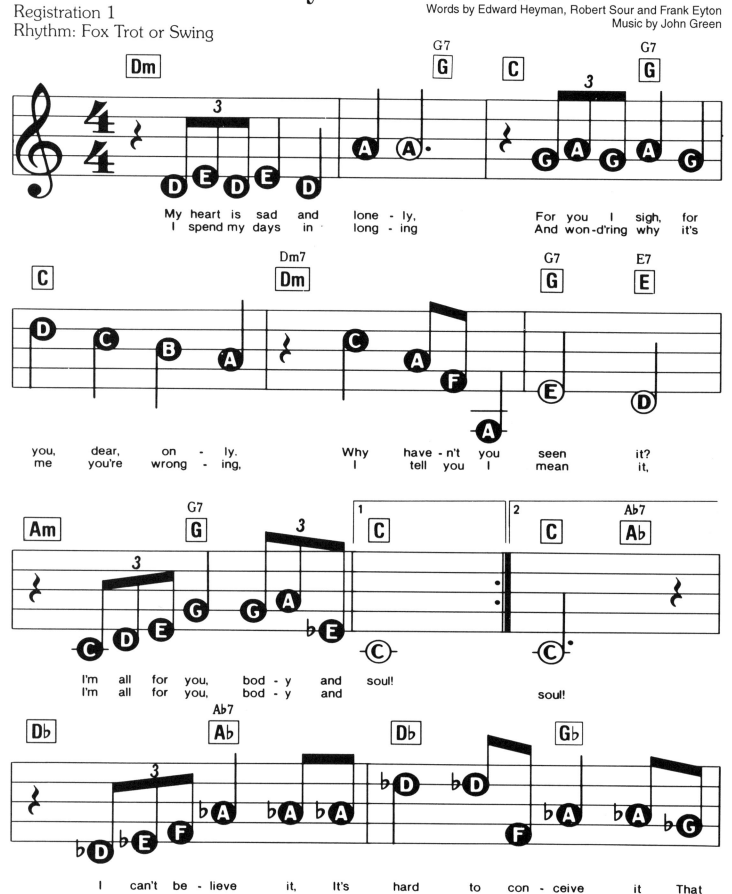

81

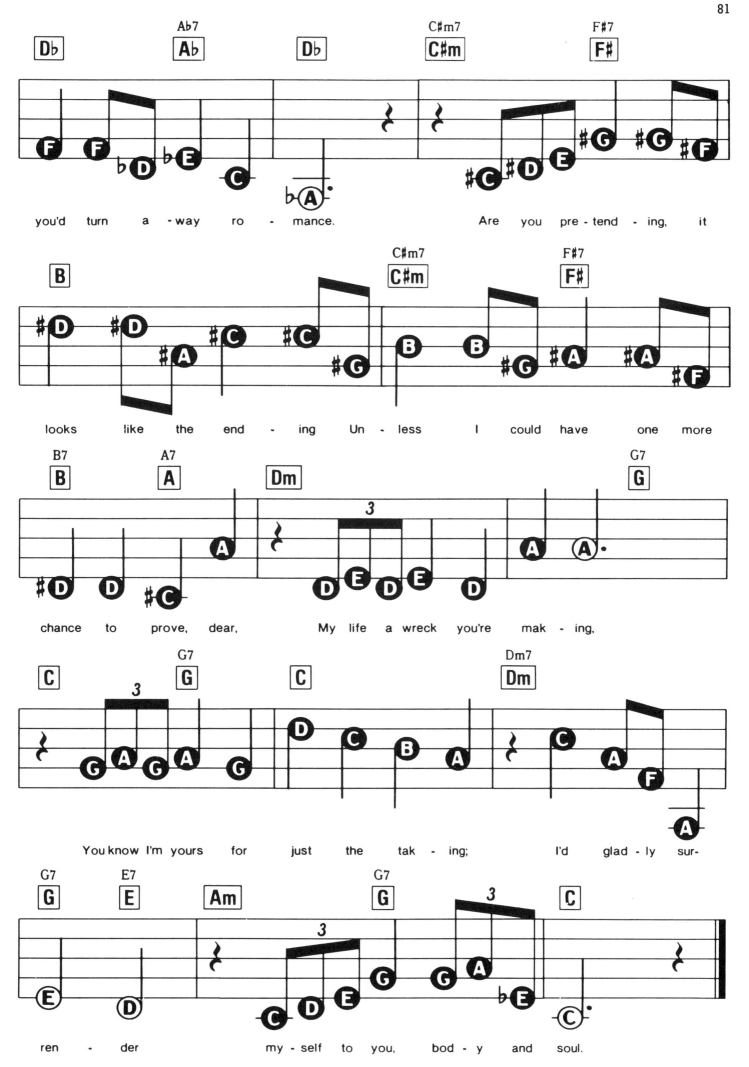

1931
Star Dust

Registration 5
Rhythm: Swing or Jazz

Words by Mitchell Parish
Music by Hoagy Carmichael

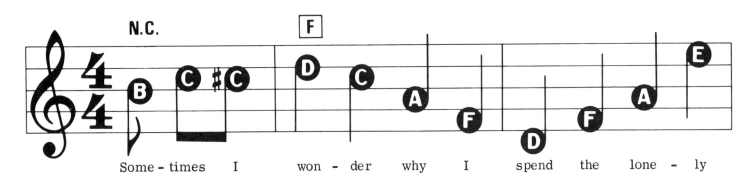

Some - times I   won - der why I   spend the   lone - ly

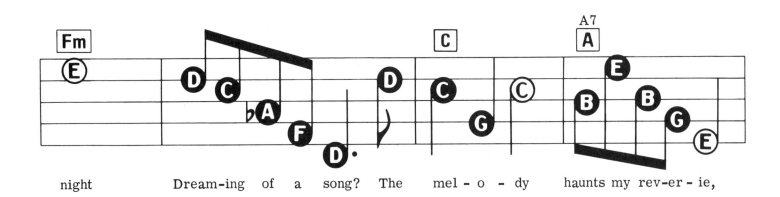

night   Dream-ing of a   song? The   mel - o - dy   haunts my rev-er - ie,

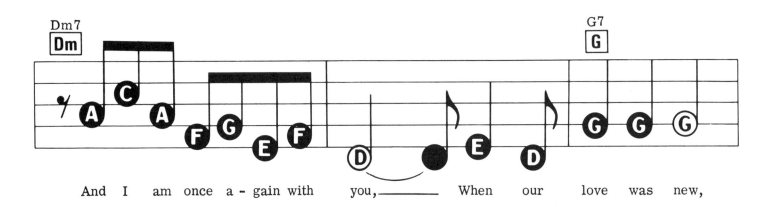

And I   am once a - gain with   you,_____ When   our love was new,

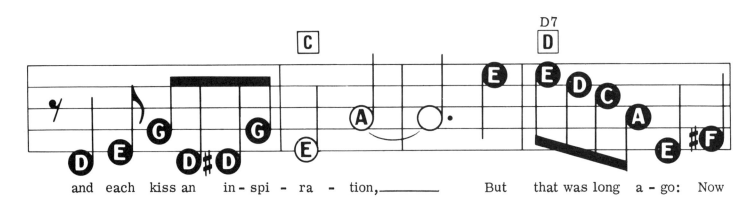

and each kiss an   in - spi - ra - tion,_____ But   that was long a - go: Now

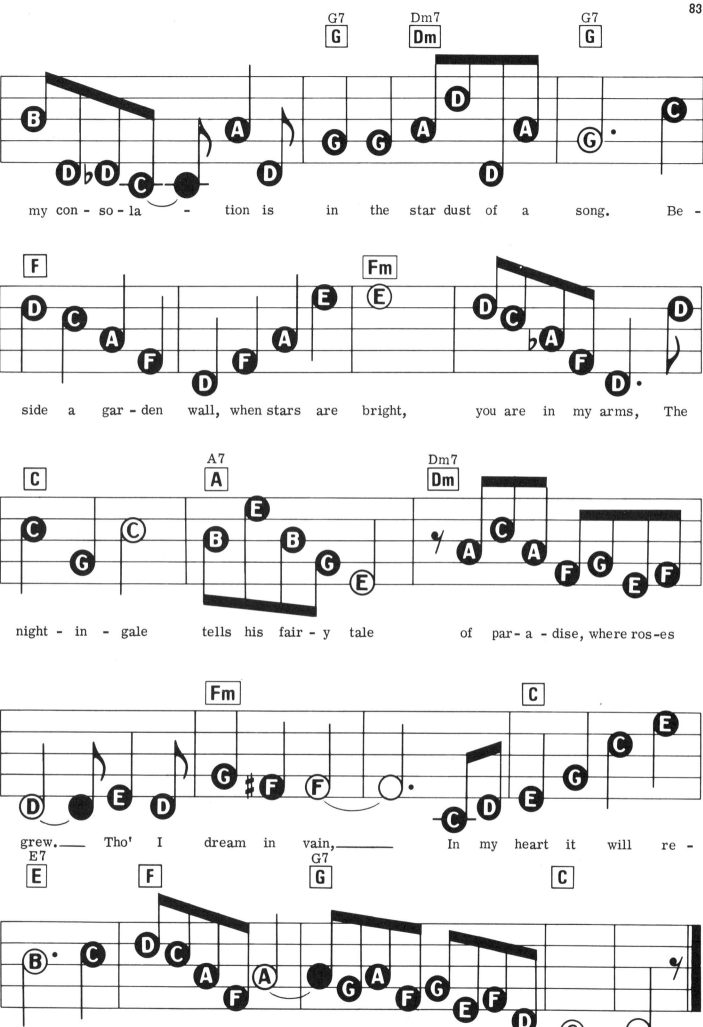

1932
April in Paris

Registration 2
Rhythm: Fox Trot or Swing

Words by E.Y. Harburg
Music by Vernon Duke

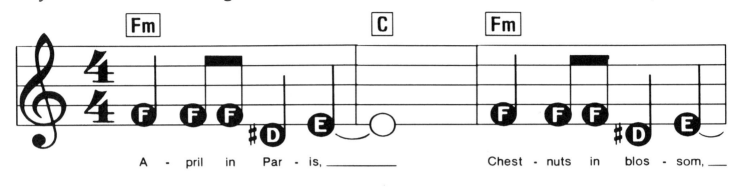

A - pril in Par - is, _____ Chest - nuts in blos - som, _____

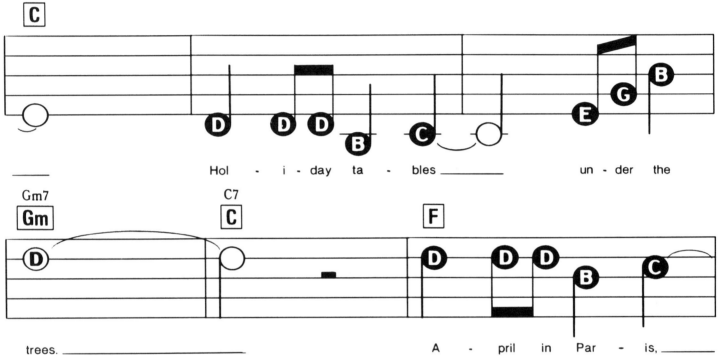

_____ Hol - i - day ta - bles _____ un - der the

trees. _____ A - pril in Par - is, _____

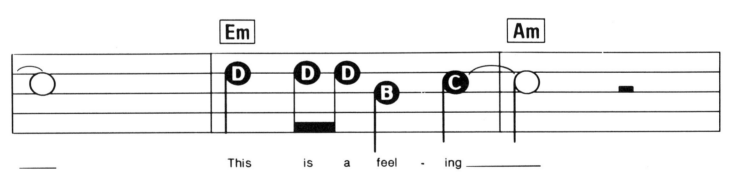

_____ This is a feel - ing _____

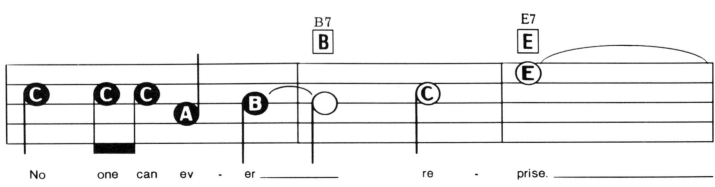

No one can ev - er _____ re - prise. _____

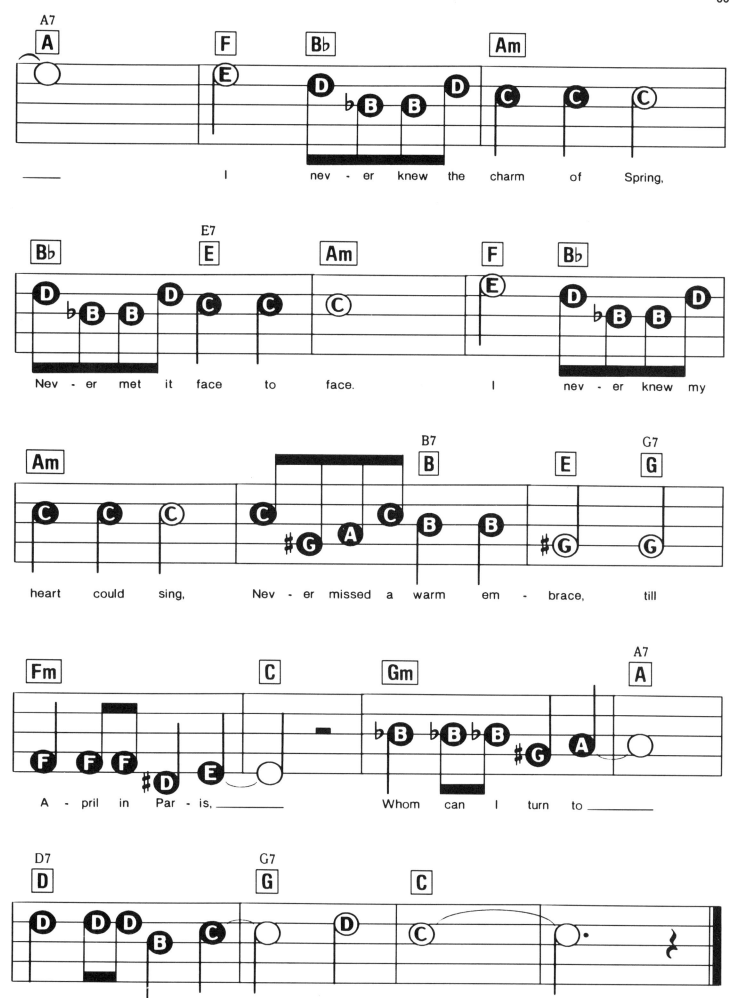

1933
Stormy Weather
(Keeps Rainin' All the Time)
from COTTON CLUB PARADE OF 1933

Lyric by Ted Koehler
Music by Harold Arlen

Registration 2
Rhythm: Ballad or Rhythm 'n' Blues

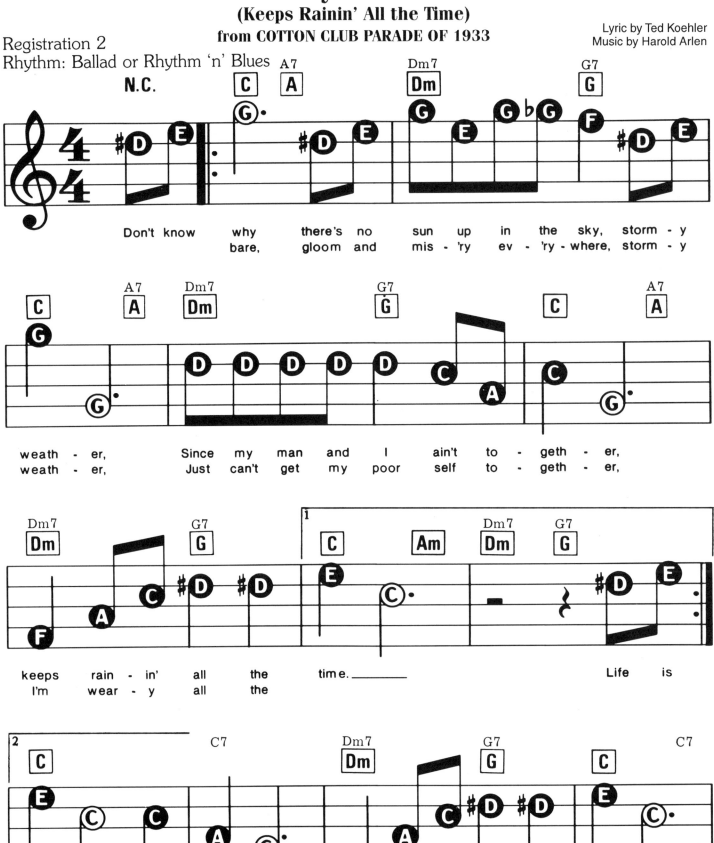

Don't know why there's no sun up in the sky, storm-y
bare, gloom and mis-'ry ev-'ry-where, storm-y

weath-er, Since my man and I ain't to-geth-er,
weath-er, Just can't get my poor self to-geth-er,

keeps rain-in' all the time._____ Life is
I'm wear-y all the

time,_____ the time,_____ So wear-y all the time._____

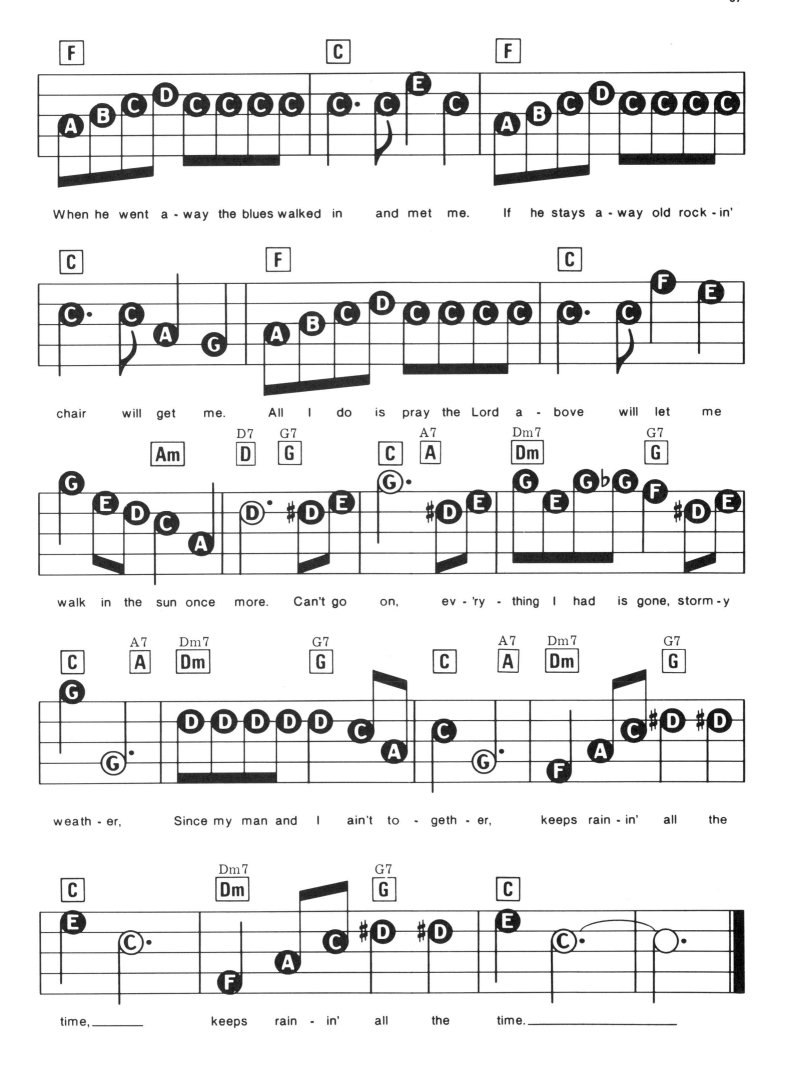

1934
Moonglow

Registration 2
Rhythm: Fox Trot

Words and Music by Will Hudson,
Eddie DeLange and Irving Mills

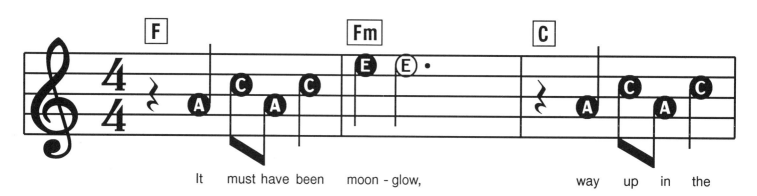

It must have been moon - glow, way up in the

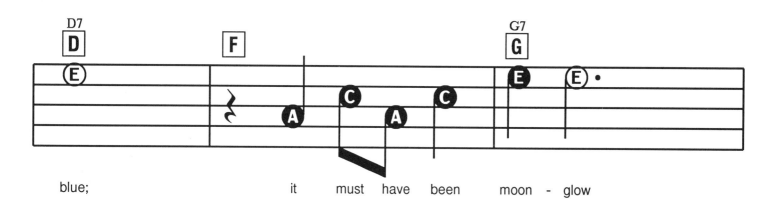

blue; it must have been moon - glow

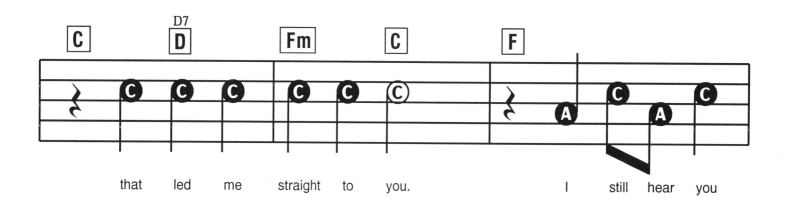

that led me straight to you. I still hear you

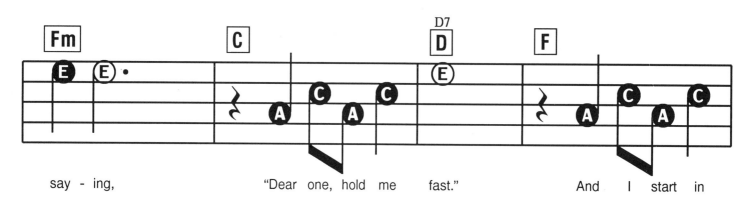

say - ing, "Dear one, hold me fast." And I start in

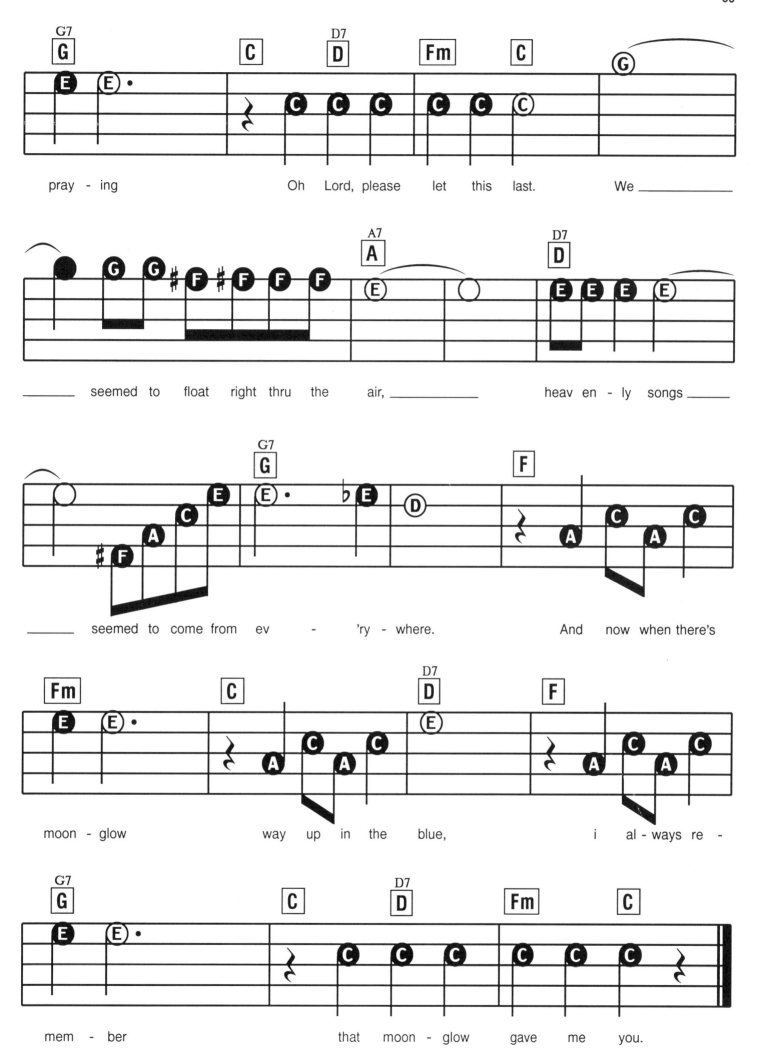

1935
Cheek to Cheek
from the RKO Radio Motion Picture TOP HAT

Registration 1
Rhythm: Fox Trot or Swing

Words and Music by
Irving Berlin

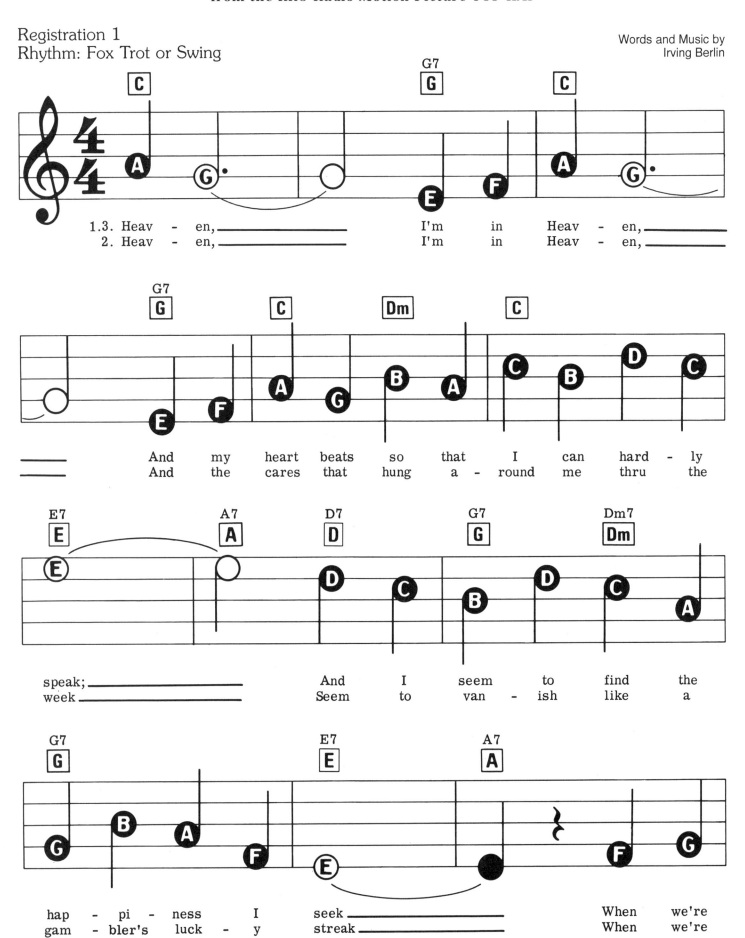

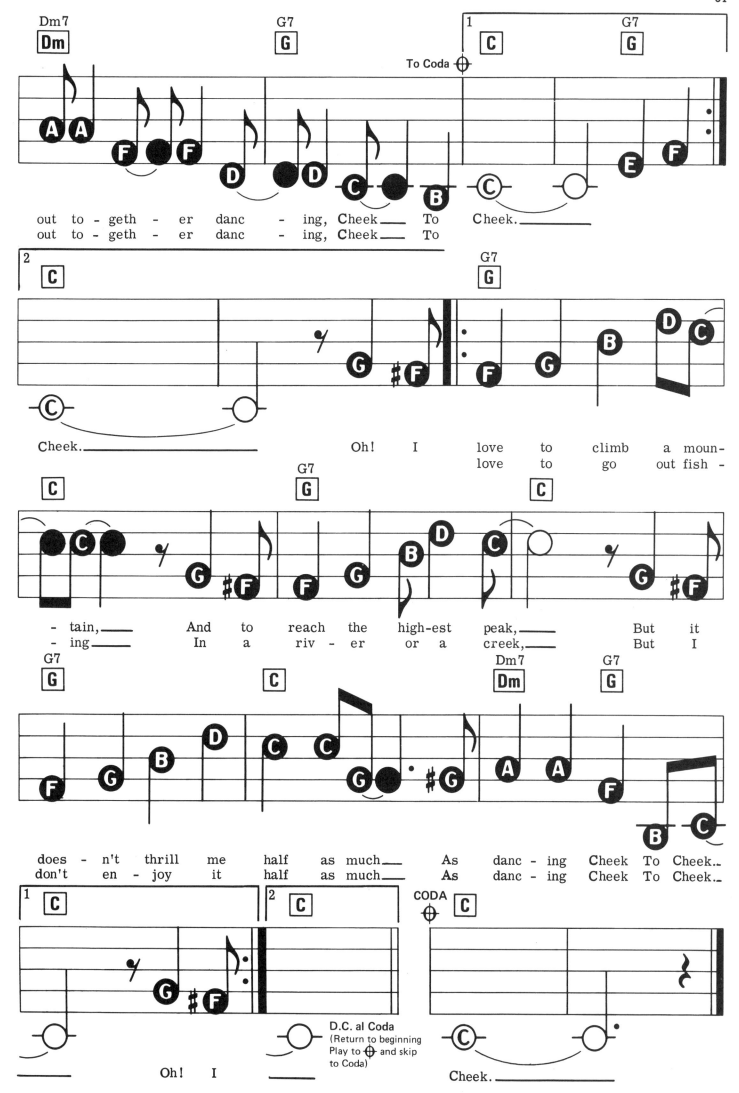

1936
Pennies from Heaven
from PENNIES FROM HEAVEN

Registration 2
Rhythm: Fox Trot or Swing

Words by John Burke
Music by Arthur Johnston

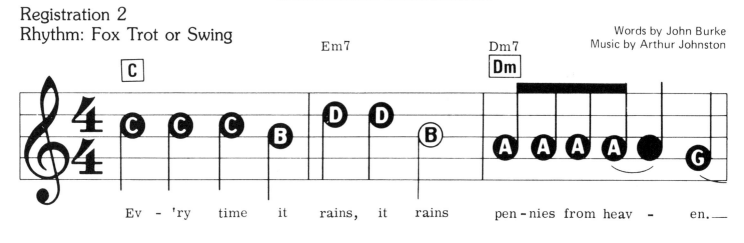

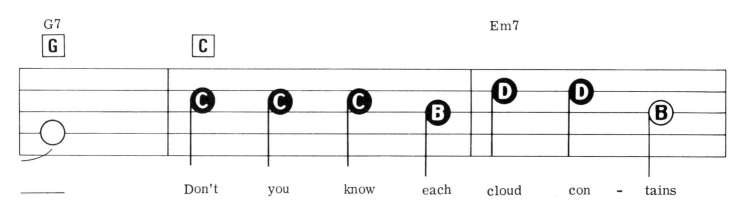

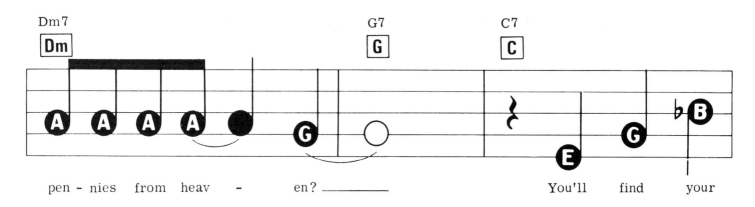

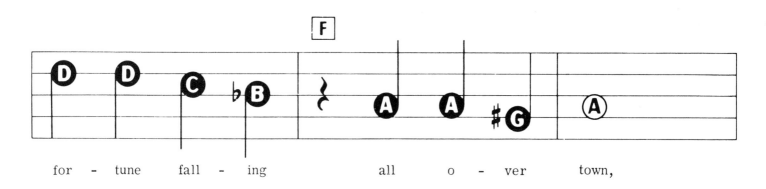

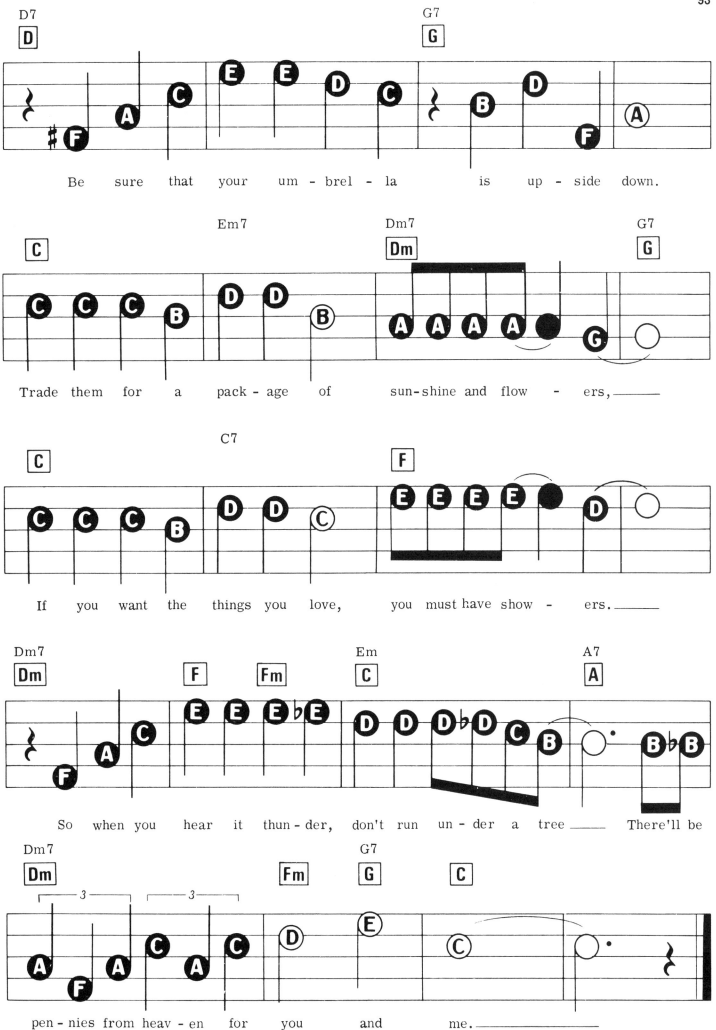

1937
Stompin' at the Savoy

Registration 2
Rhythm: Swing

Words and Music by Benny Goodman, Edgar Sampson,
Chick Webb and Andy Razaf

Sa - voy, the home of sweet ro - mance; Sa -

voy, it wins you at a glance; Sa - voy, gives hap - py feet a

chance to dance. Your form just like a cling - in'

vine, Your lips so warm and sweet as wine, Your

cheek so soft and close to mine, di - vine!

95

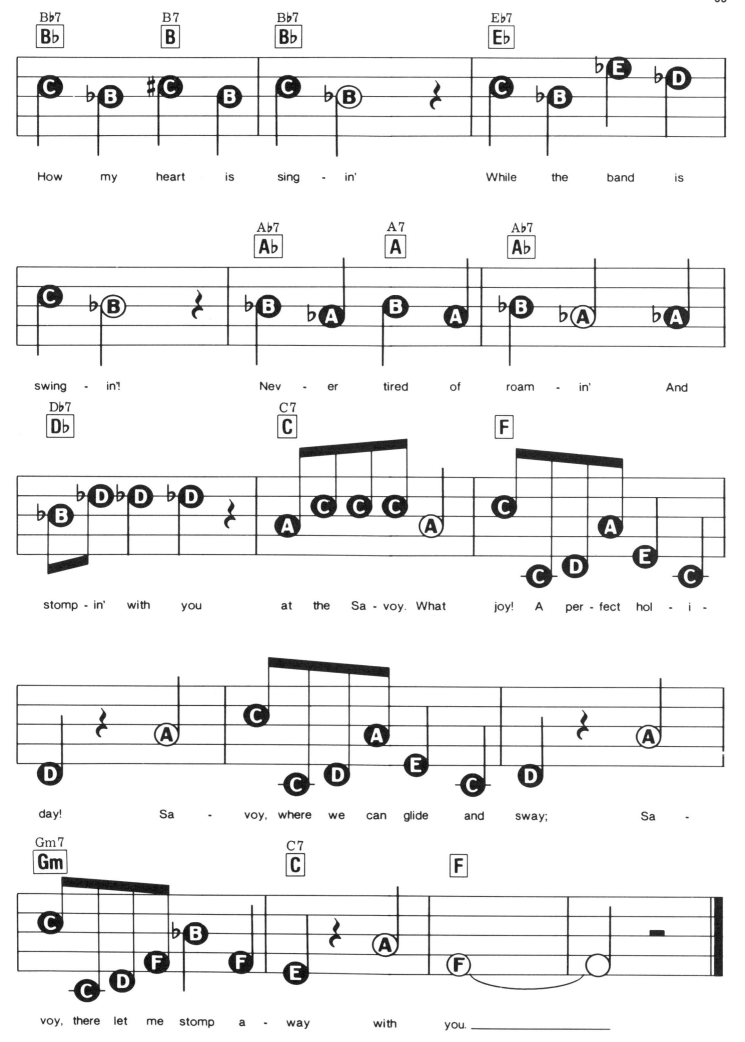

1938
Heart and Soul
from the Paramount Short Subject A SONG IS BORN

Registration 8
Rhythm: Swing

Words by Frank Loesser
Music by Hoagy Carmichael

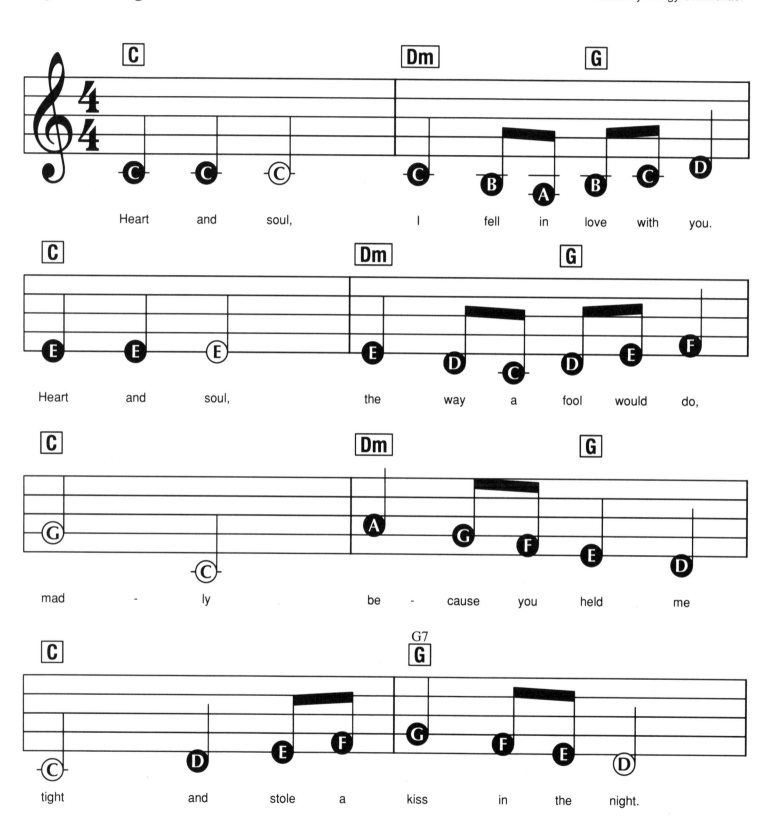

97

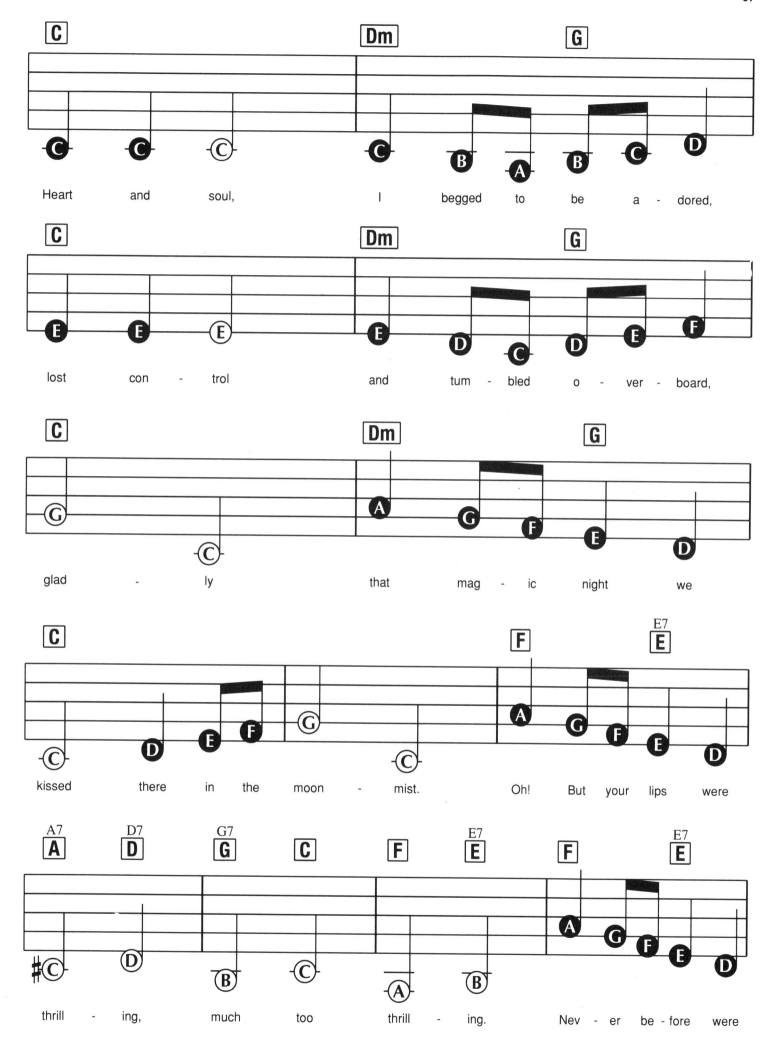

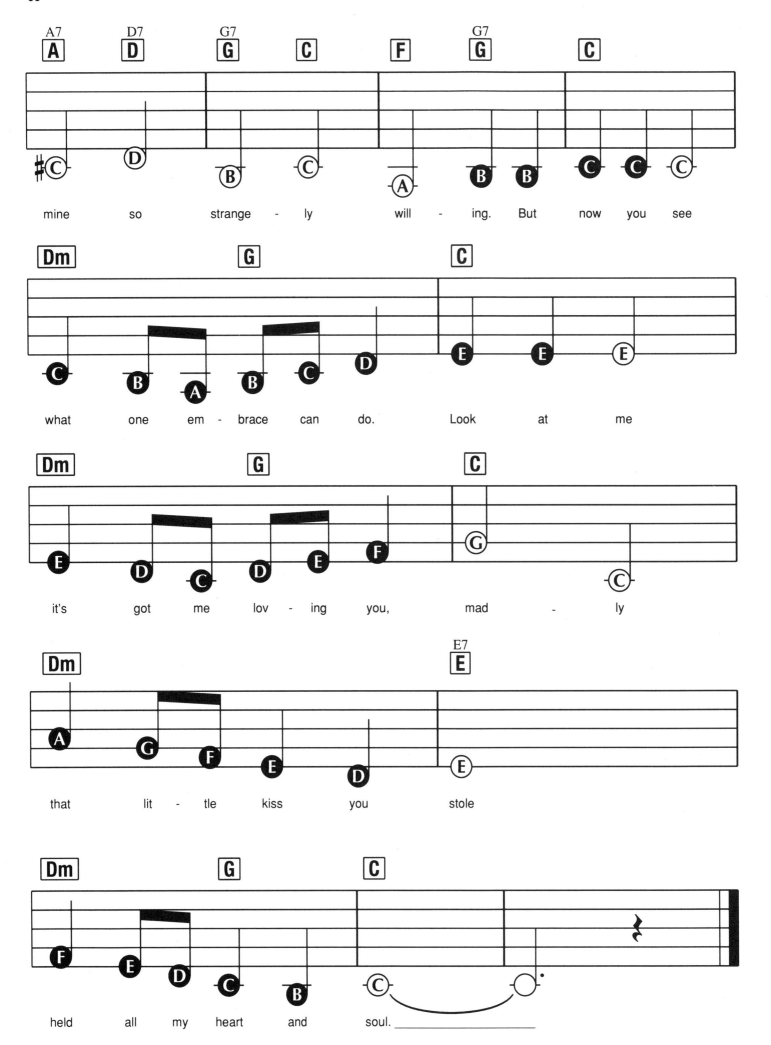

1939
All the Things You Are
from VERY WARM FOR MAY

Registration 2
Rhythm: Ballad or Swing

Lyrics by Oscar Hammerstein II
Music by Jerome Kern

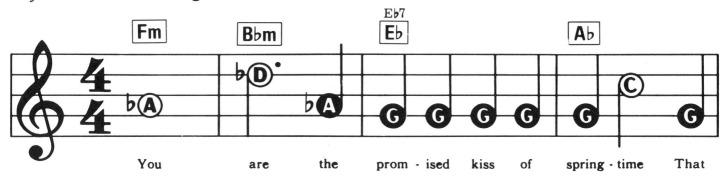

You are the prom - ised kiss of spring - time That

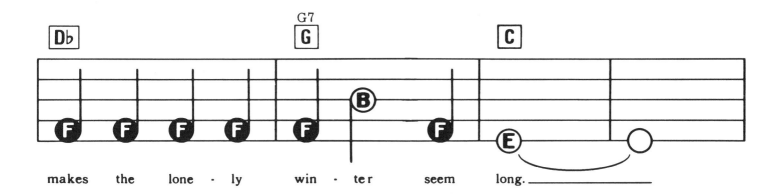

makes the lone - ly win - te r seem long._____

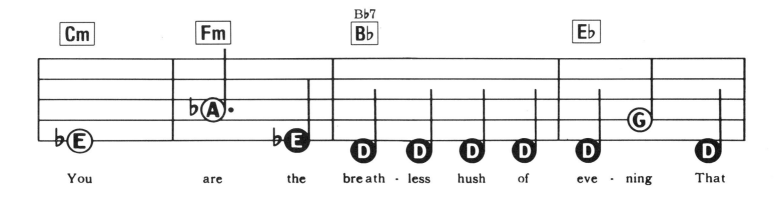

You are the breath - less hush of eve - ning That

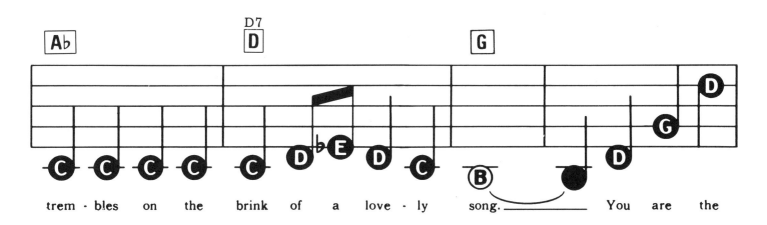

trem - bles on the brink of a love - ly song._____ You are the

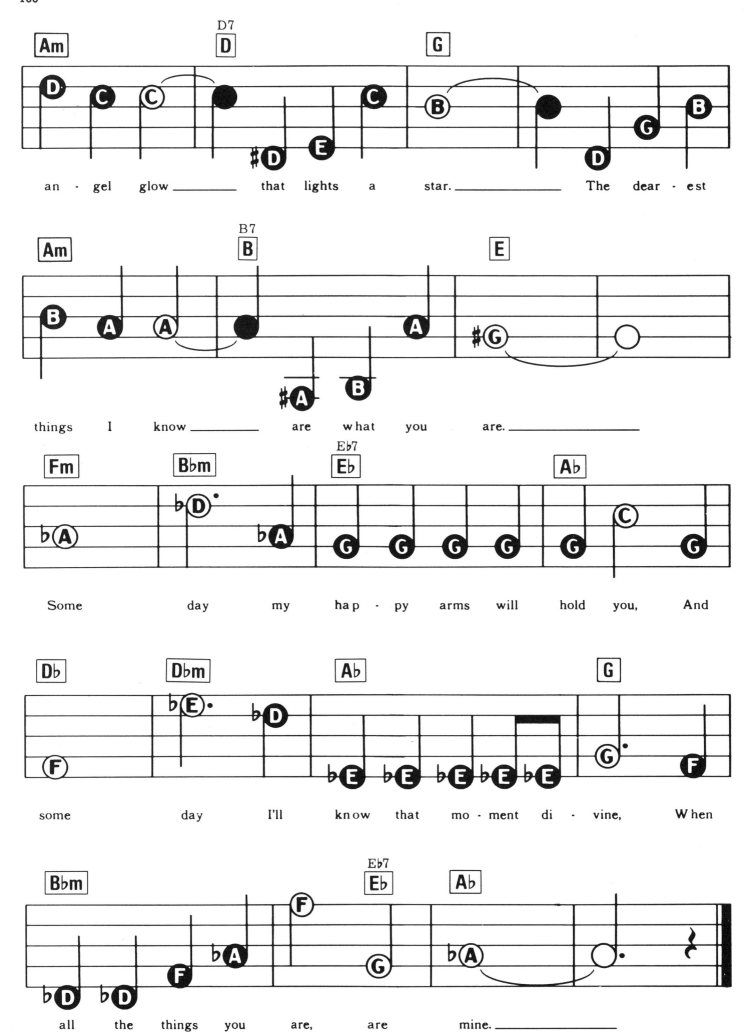

1940
In the Mood

Registration 8
Rhythm: Swing

By Joe Garland

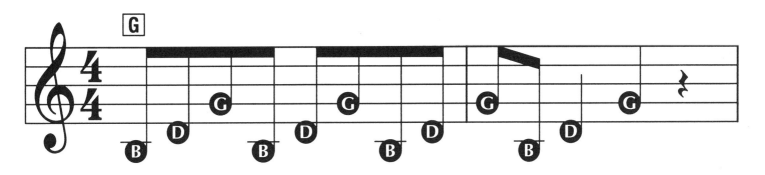

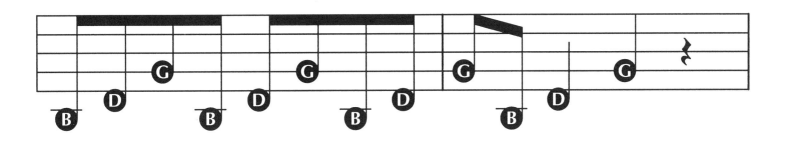

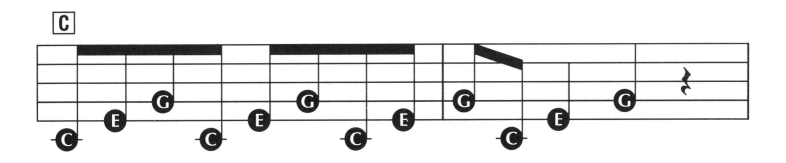

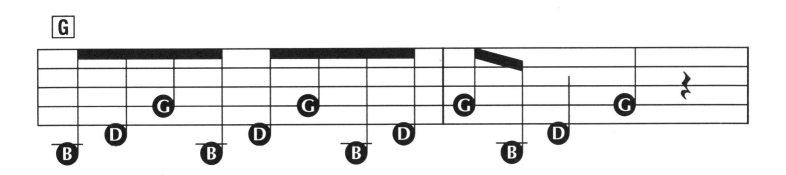

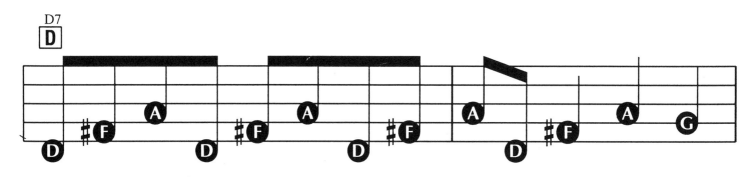

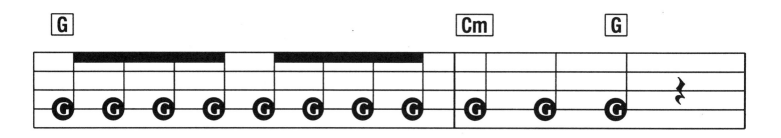

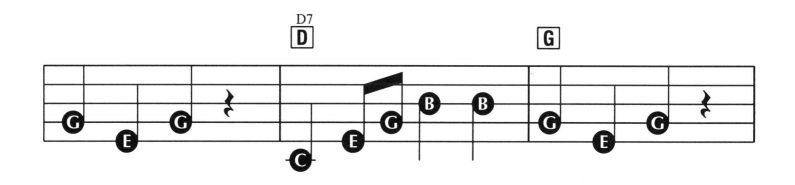

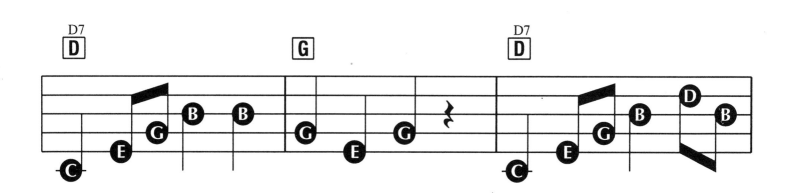

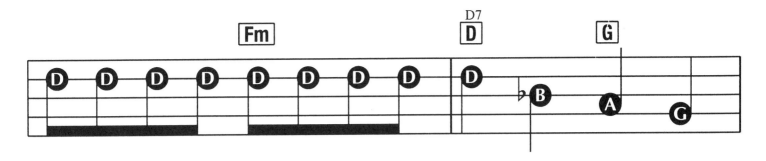

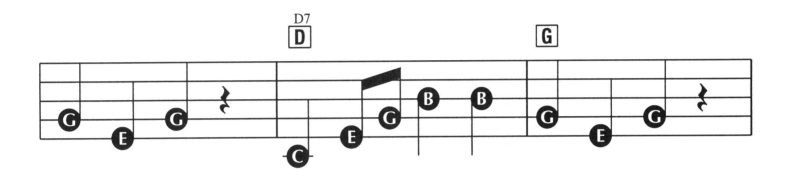

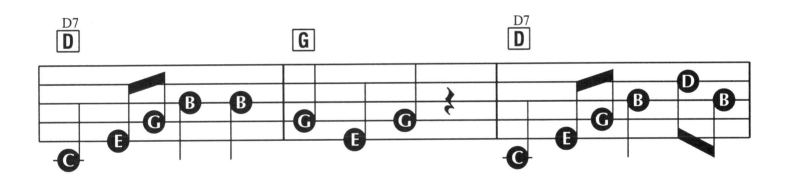

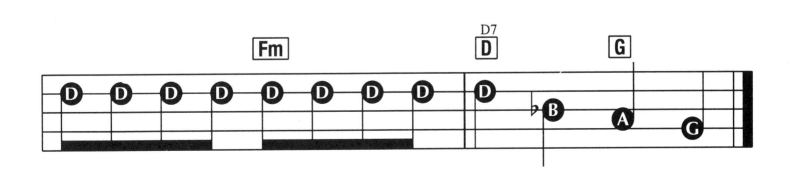

1941
Bewitched
from PAL JOEY

Registration 10
Rhythm: Ballad or Fox Trot

Words by Lorenz Hart
Music by Richard Rodgers

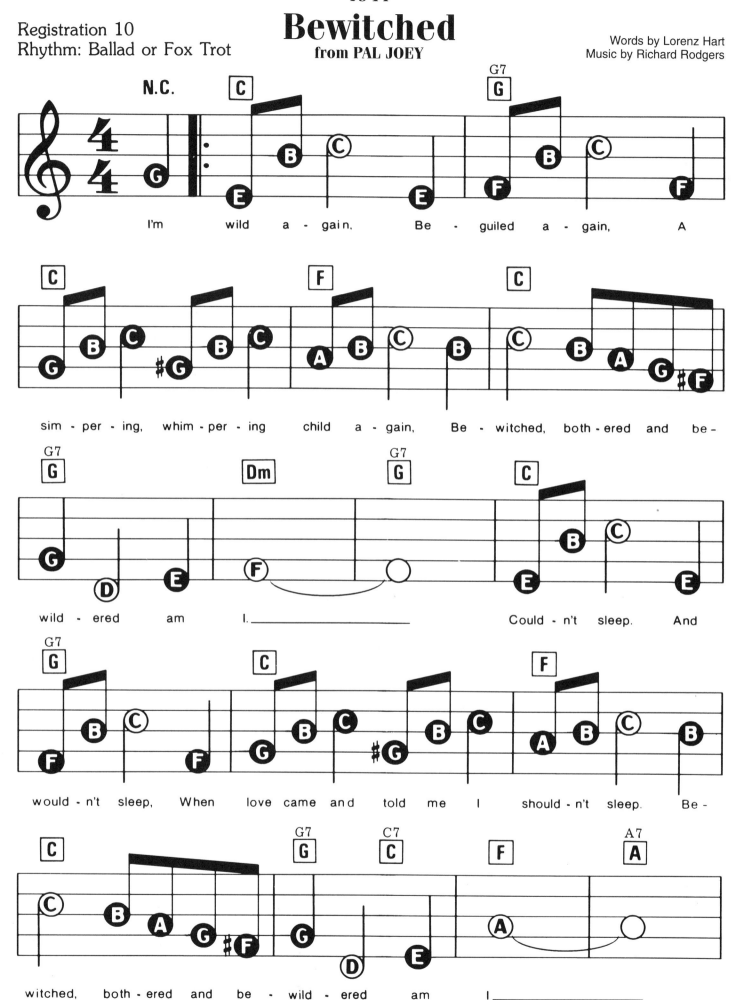

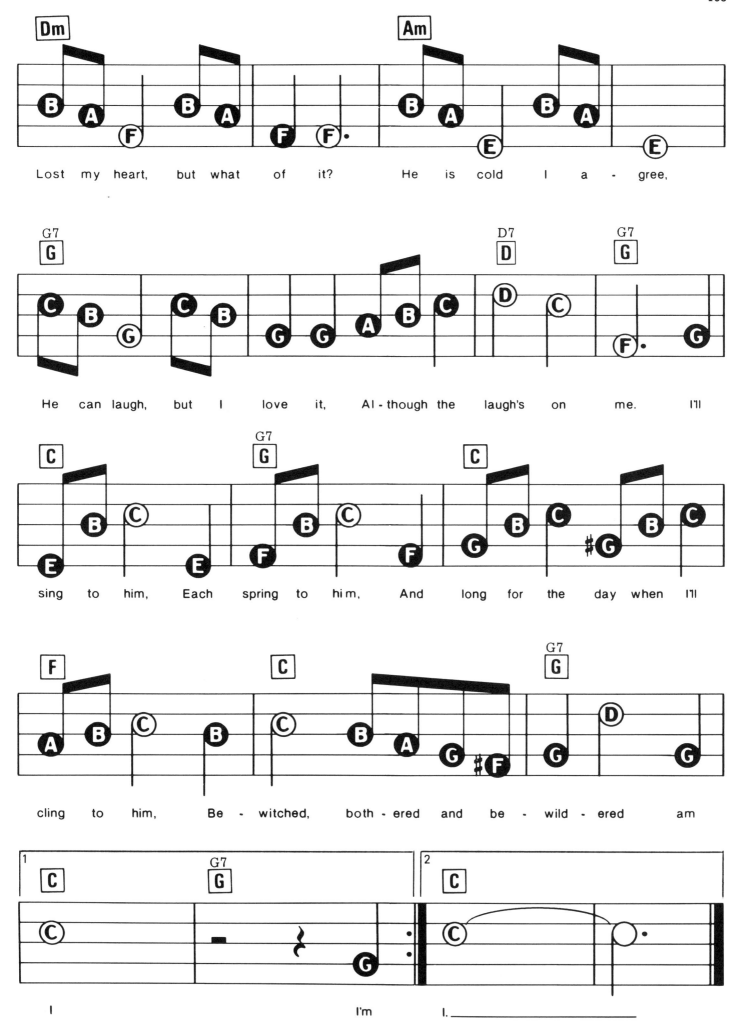

1942
A String of Pearls

Registration 4
Rhythm: Swing

Words by Eddie De Lange
Music by Jerry Gray

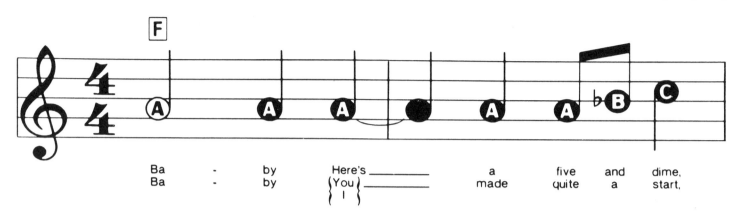

Ba - by Here's _____ a made five and dime,
Ba - by (You) _____ a made quite a start,
{ I }

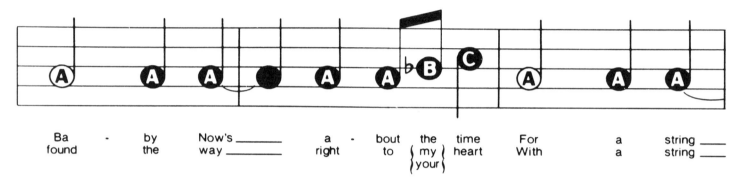

Ba - by Now's _____ a - bout the time For a string _____
found the way _____ right to {my} heart With a string _____
{your}

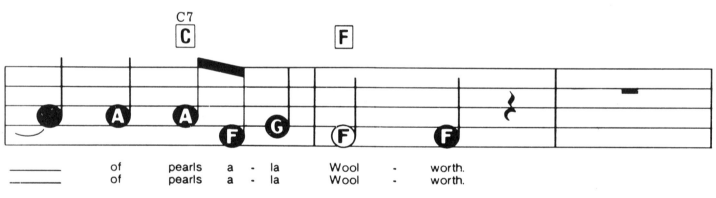

_____ of pearls a - la Wool - worth.
_____ of pearls a - la Wool - worth.

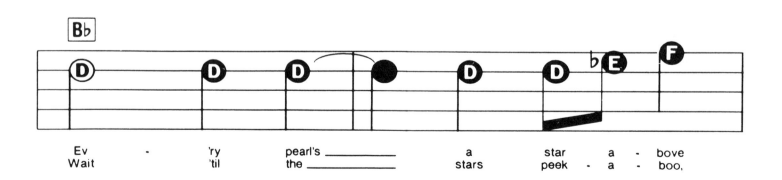

Ev - 'ry pearl's _____ a star a - bove
Wait 'til the _____ a stars peek - a - boo,

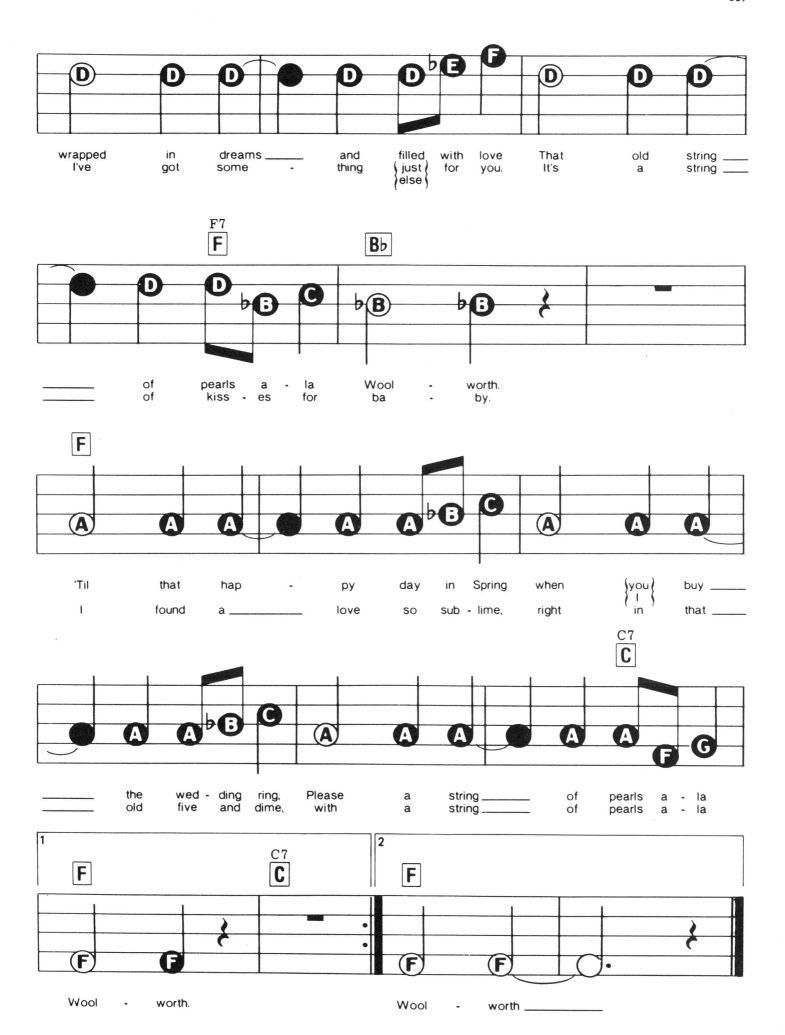

1943

I've Heard That Song Before

from the Motion Picture YOUTH ON PARADE

Registration 2
Rhythm: Fox Trot or Swing

Lyric by Sammy Cahn
Music by Jule Styne

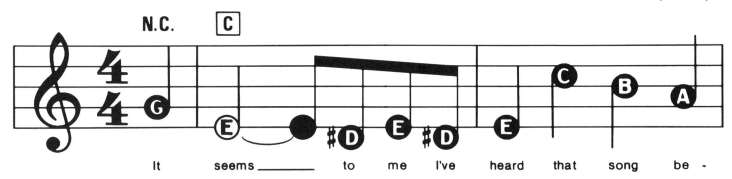

It seems _____ to me I've heard that song be-

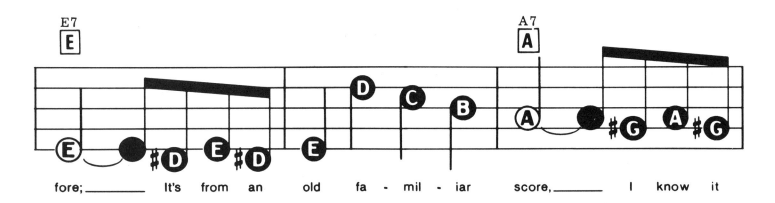

fore; _____ It's from an old fa-mil-iar score, _____ I know it

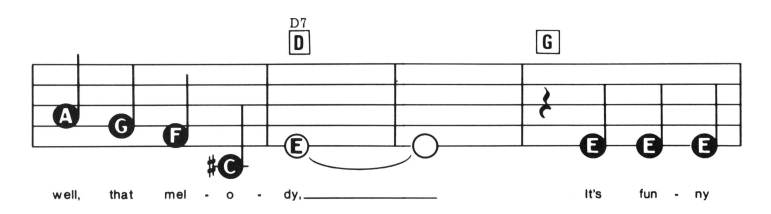

well, that mel-o-dy, _____ It's fun-ny

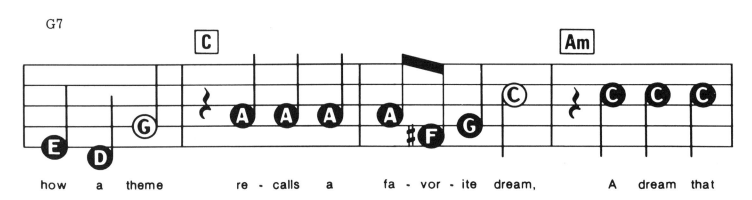

how a theme re-calls a fa-vor-ite dream, A dream that

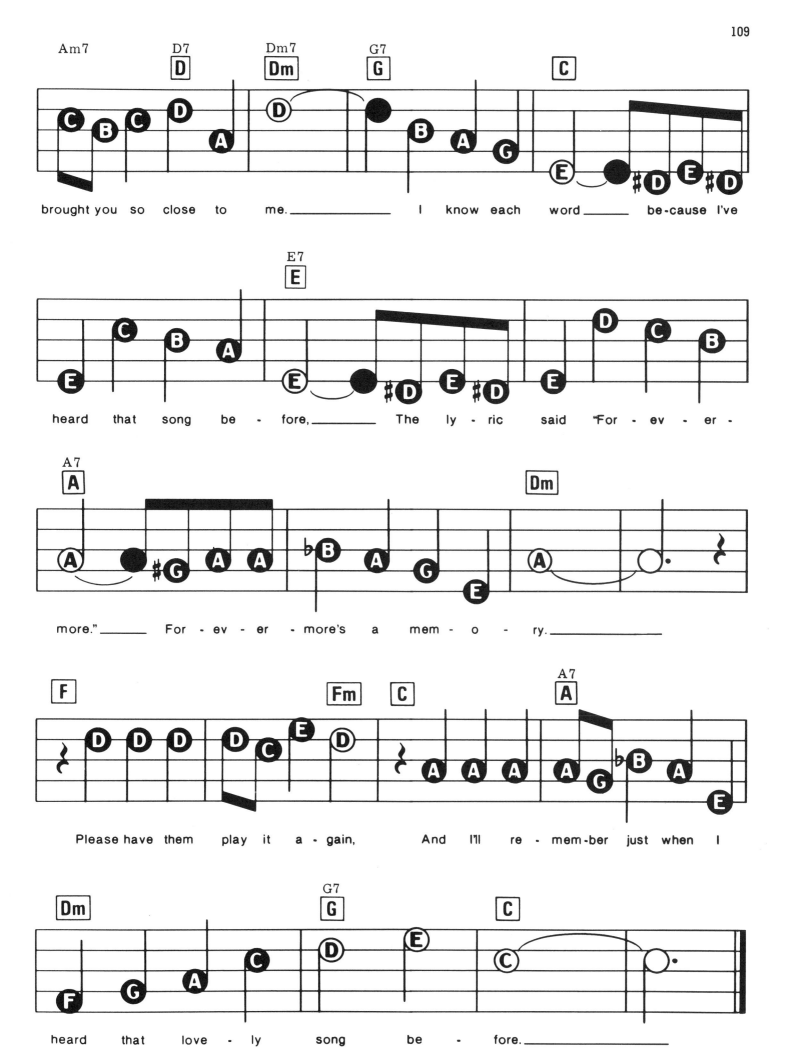

1944
I'll Be Seeing You
from RIGHT THIS WAY

Lyric by Irving Kahal
Music by Sammy Fain

Registration 5
Rhythm: Swing

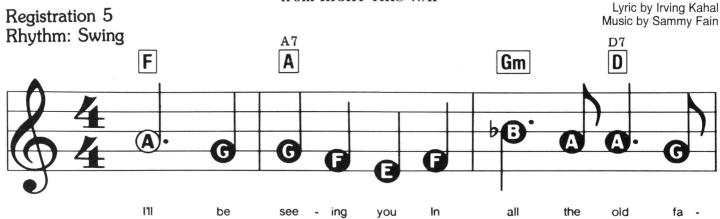

I'll be see - ing you In all the old fa -

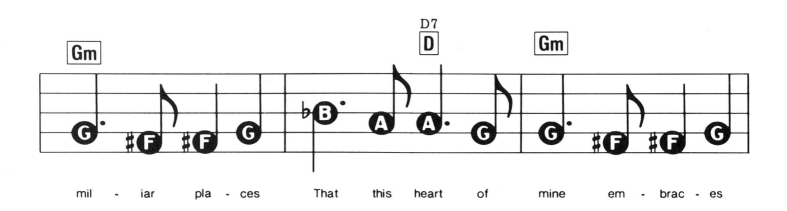

mil - iar pla - ces That this heart of mine em - brac - es

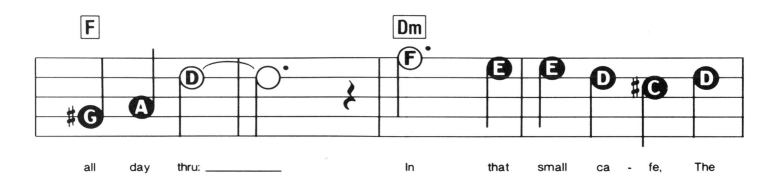

all day thru: _____ In that small ca - fe, The

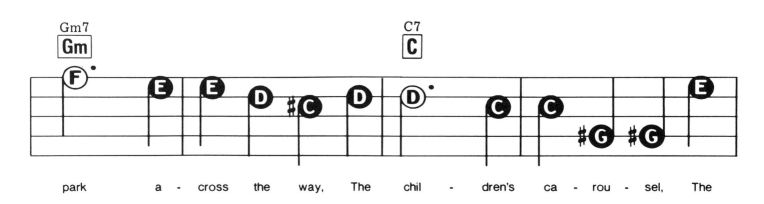

park a - cross the way, The chil - dren's ca - rou - sel, The

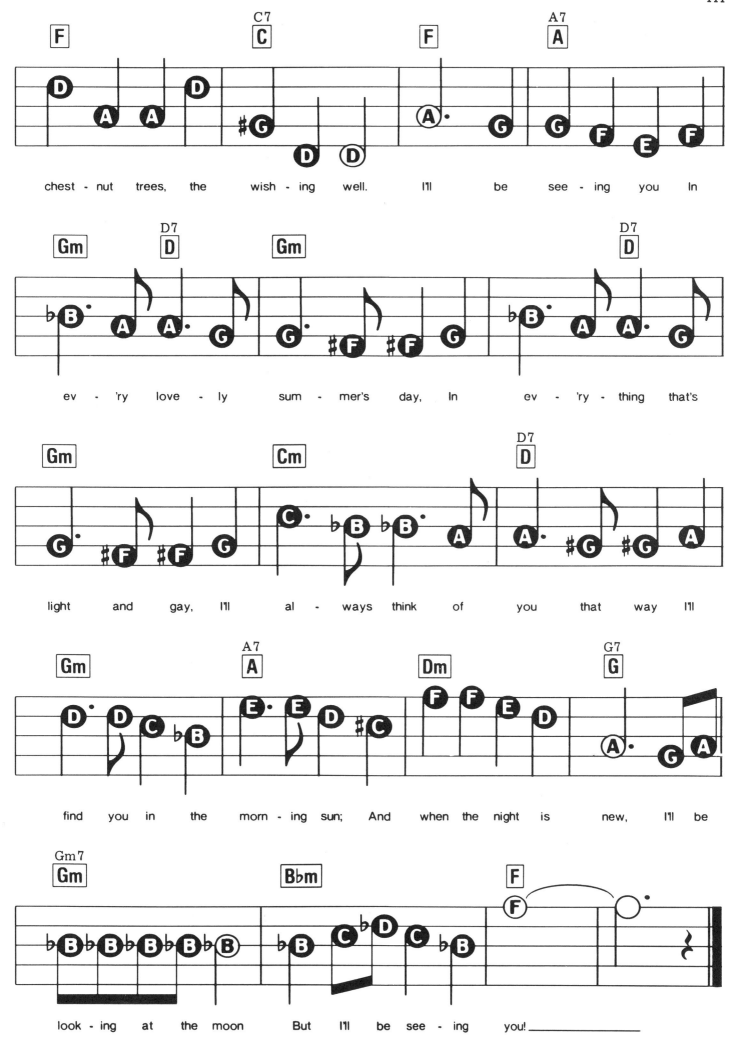

1945
Sentimental Journey

Registration 2
Rhythm: Fox Trot or Swing

Words and Music by Bud Green,
Les Brown and Ben Homer

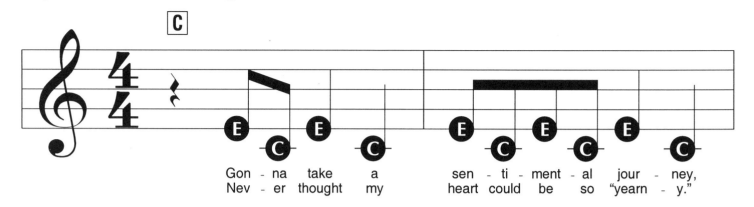

Gon - na take a sen - ti - ment - al jour - ney,
Nev - er thought my heart could be so "yearn - y."

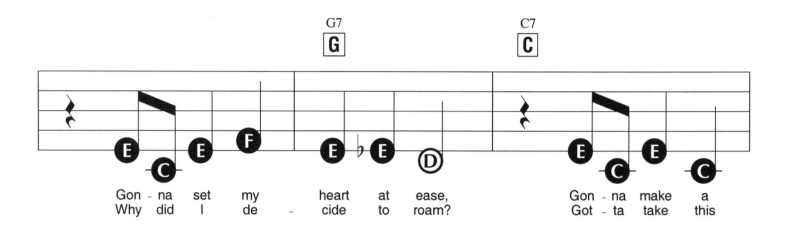

Gon - na set my heart at ease, Gon - na make a
Why did I de - cide to roam? Got - ta take this

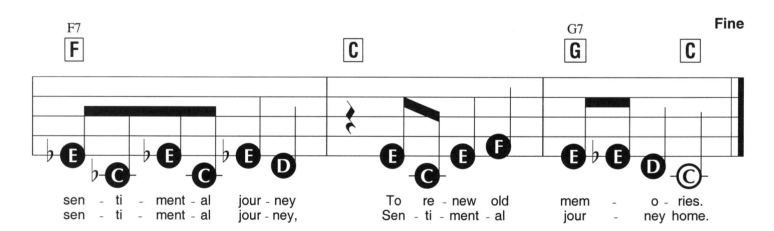

sen - ti - ment - al jour - ney To re - new old mem - o - ries.
sen - ti - ment - al jour - ney, Sen - ti - ment - al jour - ney home.

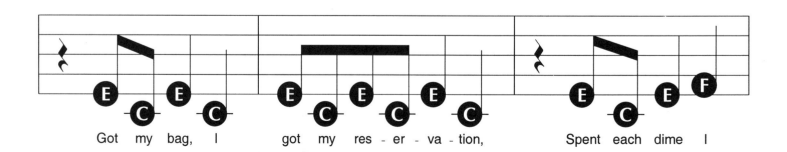

Got my bag, I got my res - er - va - tion, Spent each dime I

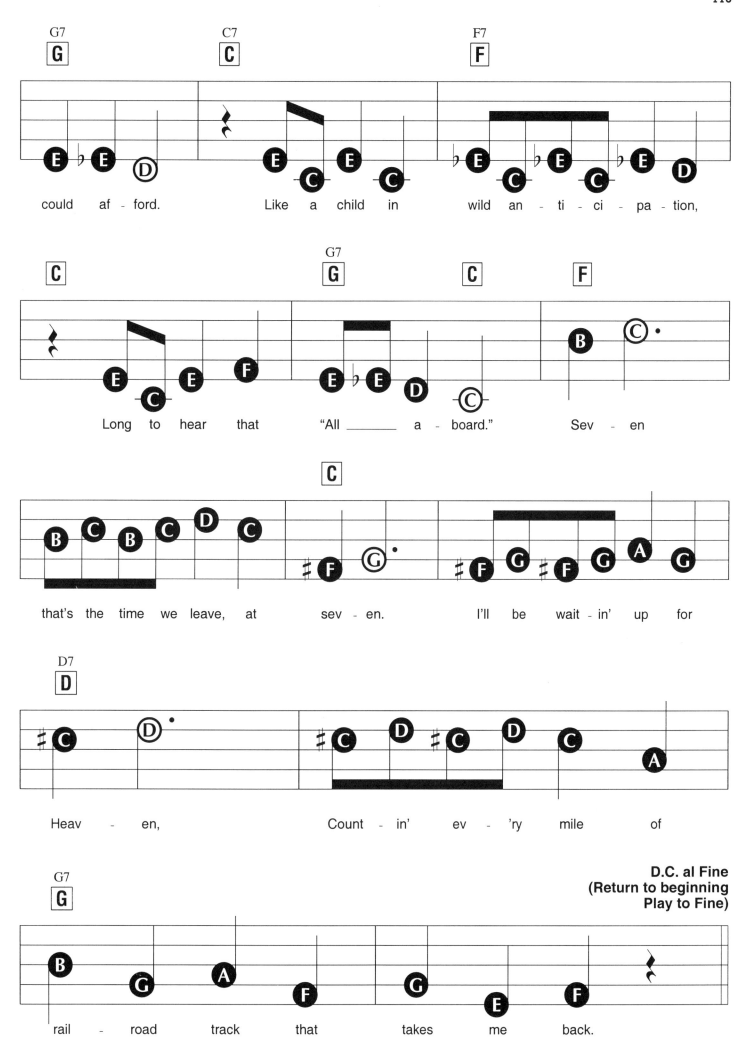

D.C. al Fine
(Return to beginning
Play to Fine)

1946

Come Rain or Come Shine
from ST. LOUIS WOMAN

Words by Johnny Mercer
Music by Harold Arlen

Registration 7
Rhythm: Ballad or Swing

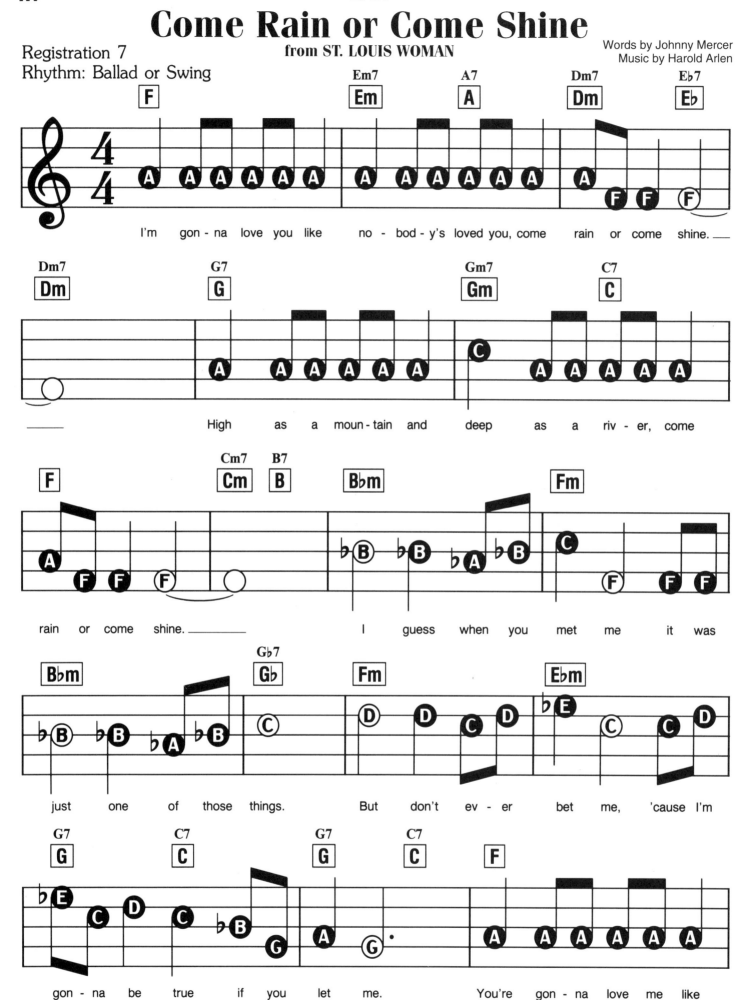

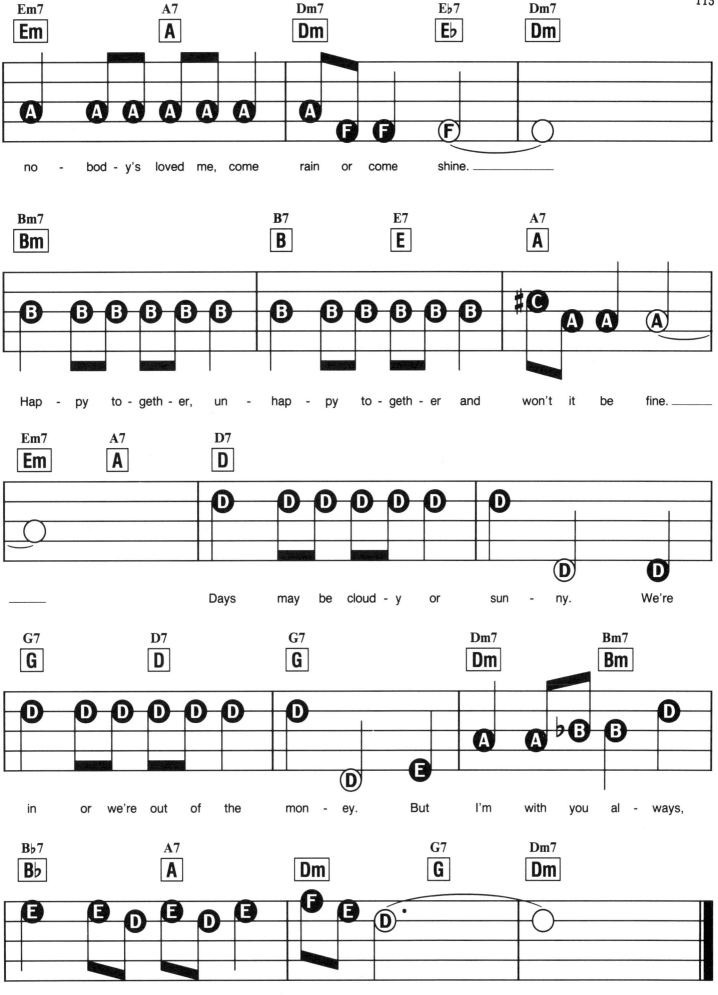

1947
Old Devil Moon
from FINIAN'S RAINBOW

Registration 3
Rhythm: Ballad or Fox Trot

Words by E. Y. Harburg
Music by Burton Lane

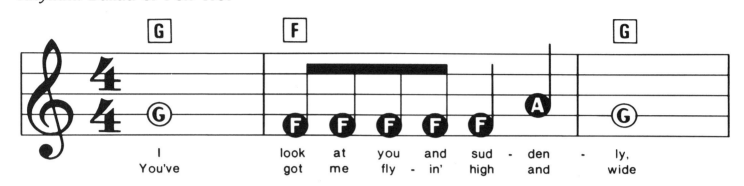

I look at you and sud - den - ly,
You've got me fly - in' high and wide

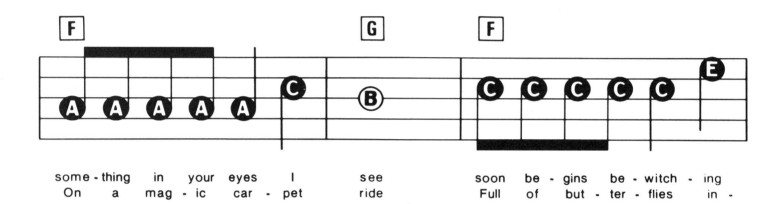

some - thing in your eyes I see soon be - gins be - witch - ing
On a mag - ic car - pet ride Full of but - ter - flies in -

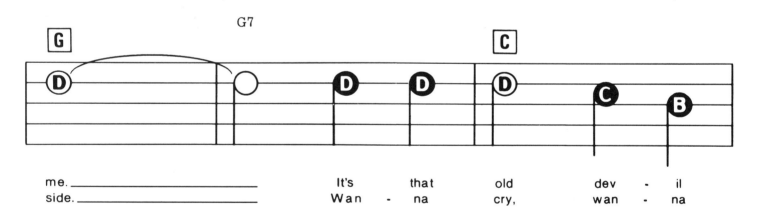

me. _____ It's that old dev - il
side. _____ Wan - na cry, wan - na

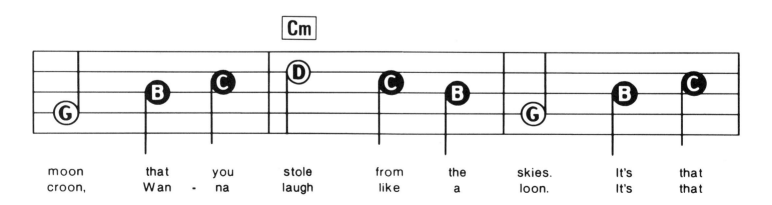

moon, that you stole from the skies. It's that
croon, Wan - na laugh like a loon. It's that

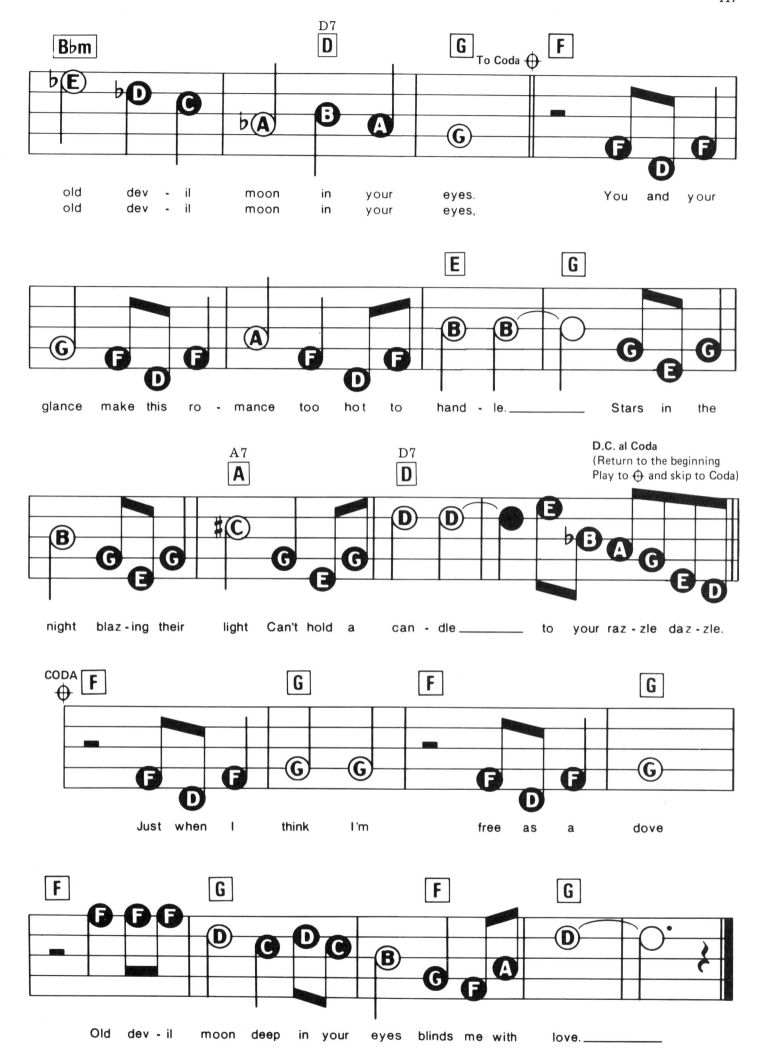

1948
Nature Boy

Registration 3
Rhythm: Waltz

Words and Music by
Eden Ahbez

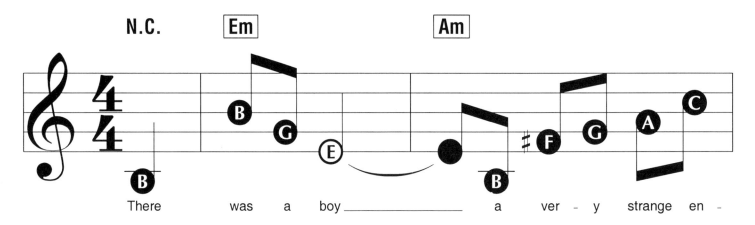

There was a boy _____ a ver - y strange en -

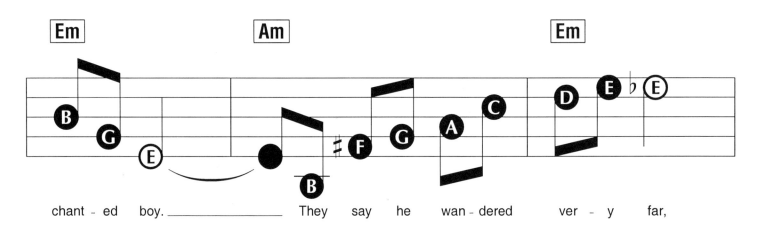

chant - ed boy. _____ They say he wan - dered ver - y far,

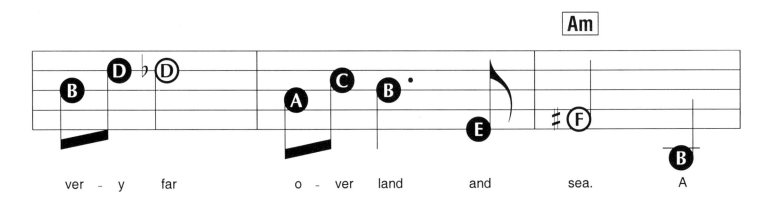

ver - y far o - ver land and sea. A

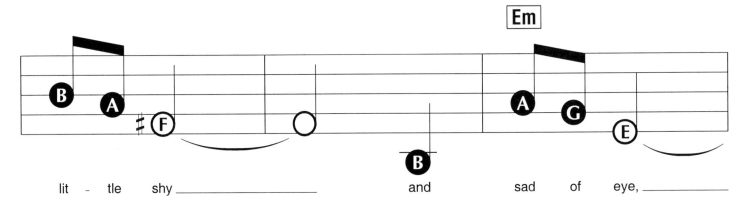

lit - tle shy _____ and sad of eye, _____

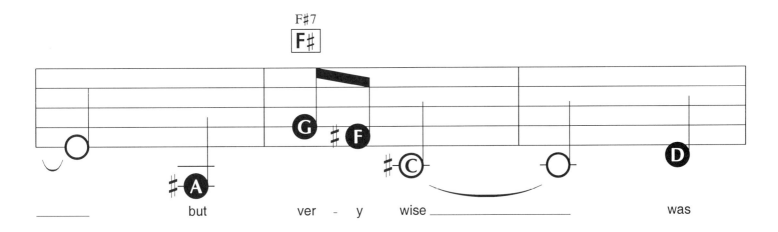

but ver - y wise _____ was

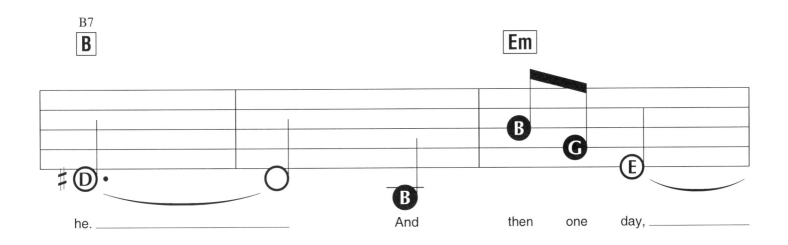

he. _____ And then one day, _____

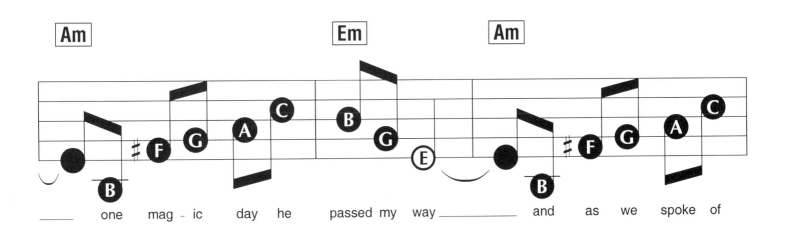

_____ one mag - ic day he passed my way _____ and as we spoke of

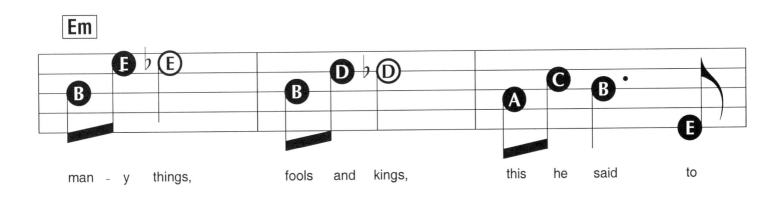

man - y things, fools and kings, this he said to

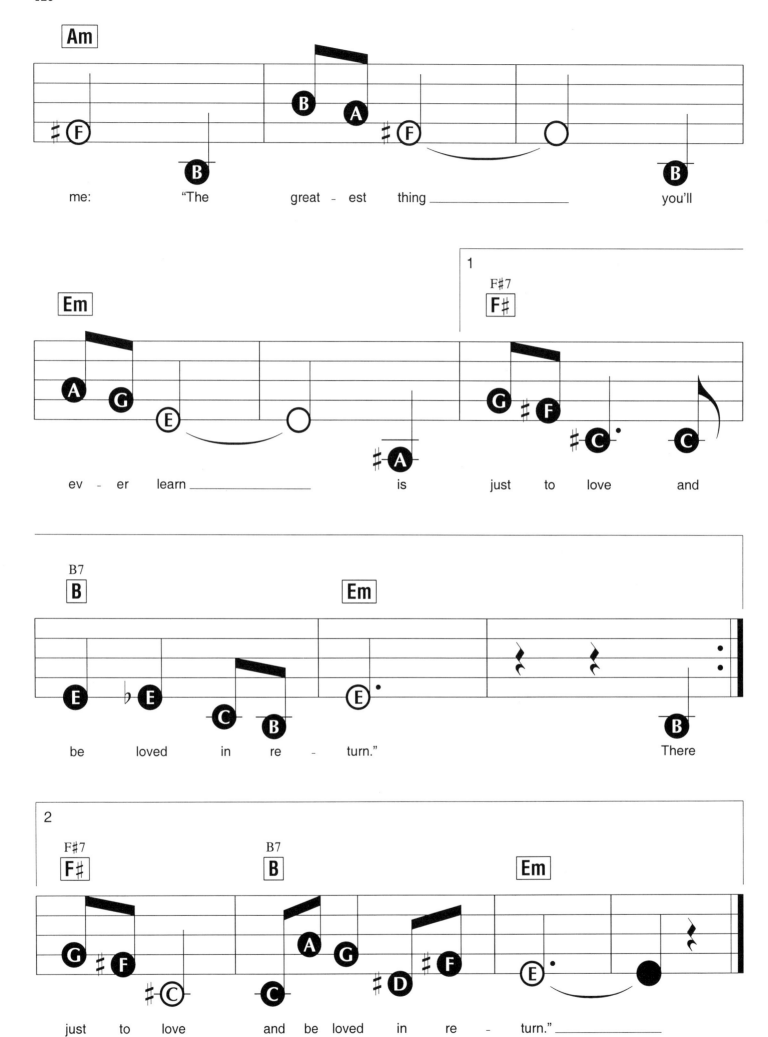

1949
Some Enchanted Evening
from SOUTH PACIFIC

Registration 1
Rhythm: Fox Trot

Lyrics by Oscar Hammerstein II
Music by Richard Rodgers

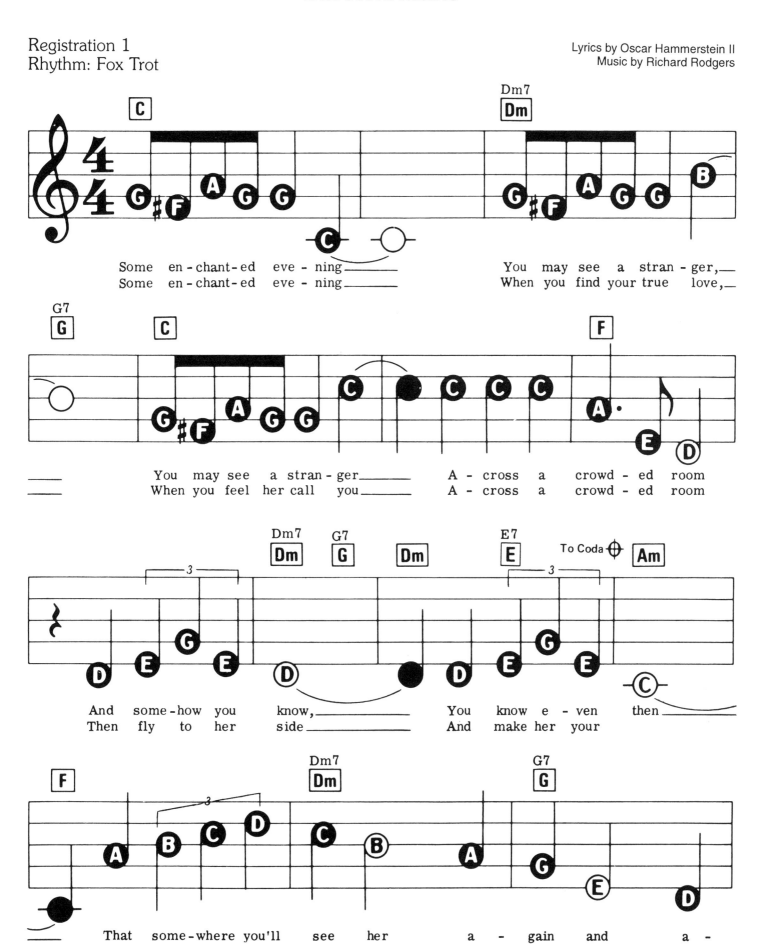

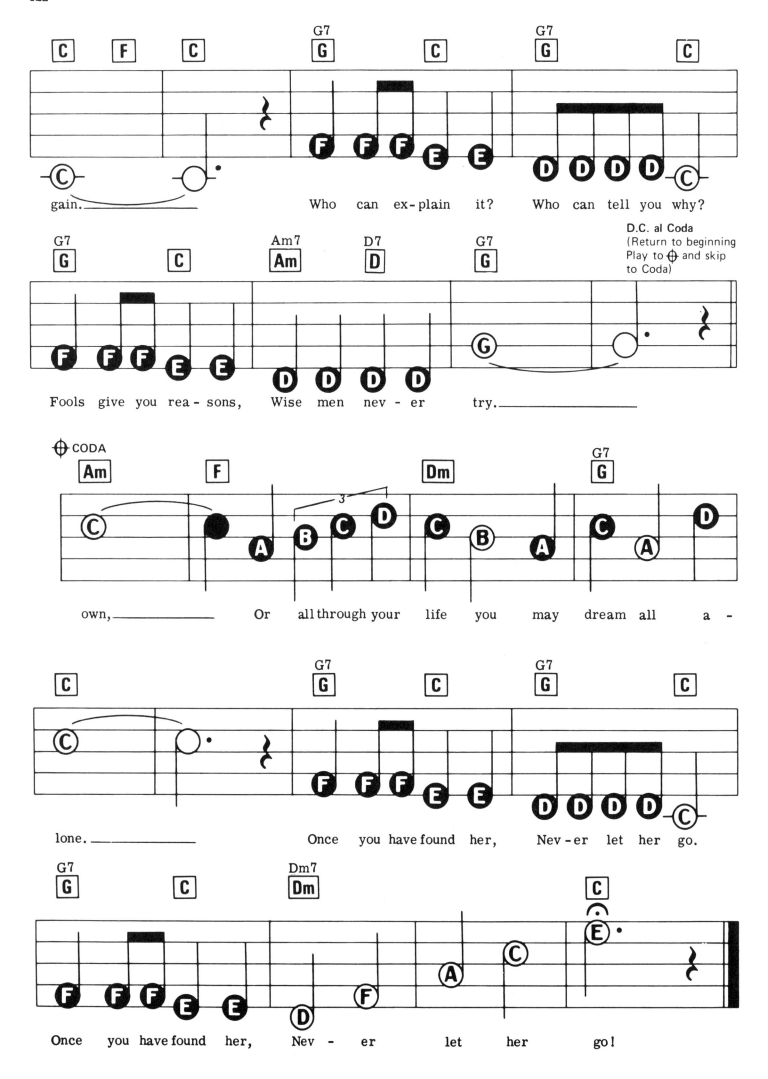

1950
Tennessee Waltz

Registration 4
Rhythm: Waltz

Words and Music by Redd Stewart
and Pee Wee King

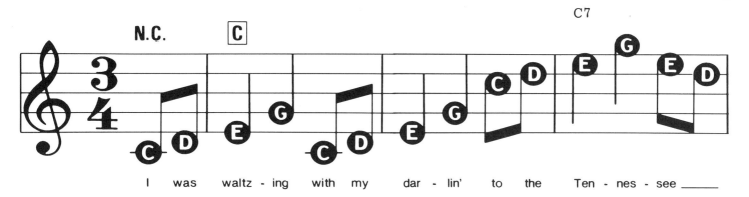

I was waltz - ing with my dar - lin' to the Ten - nes - see _____

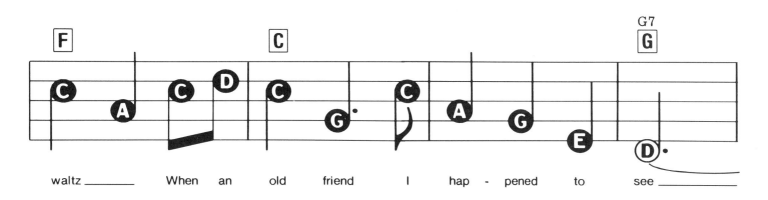

waltz _____ When an old friend I hap - pened to see _____

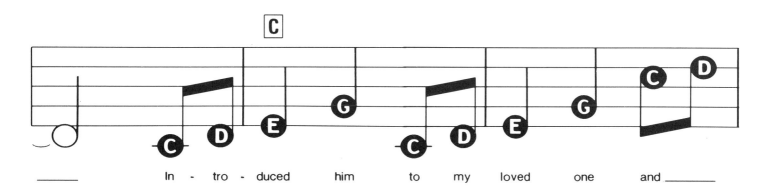

_____ In - tro - duced him to my loved one and _____

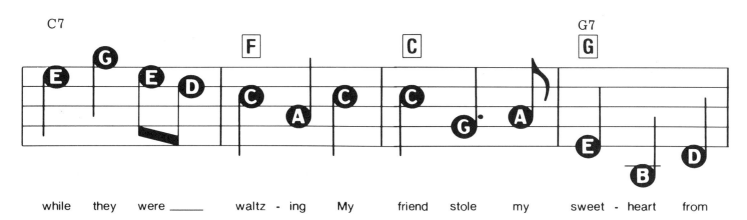

while they were _____ waltz - ing My friend stole my sweet - heart from

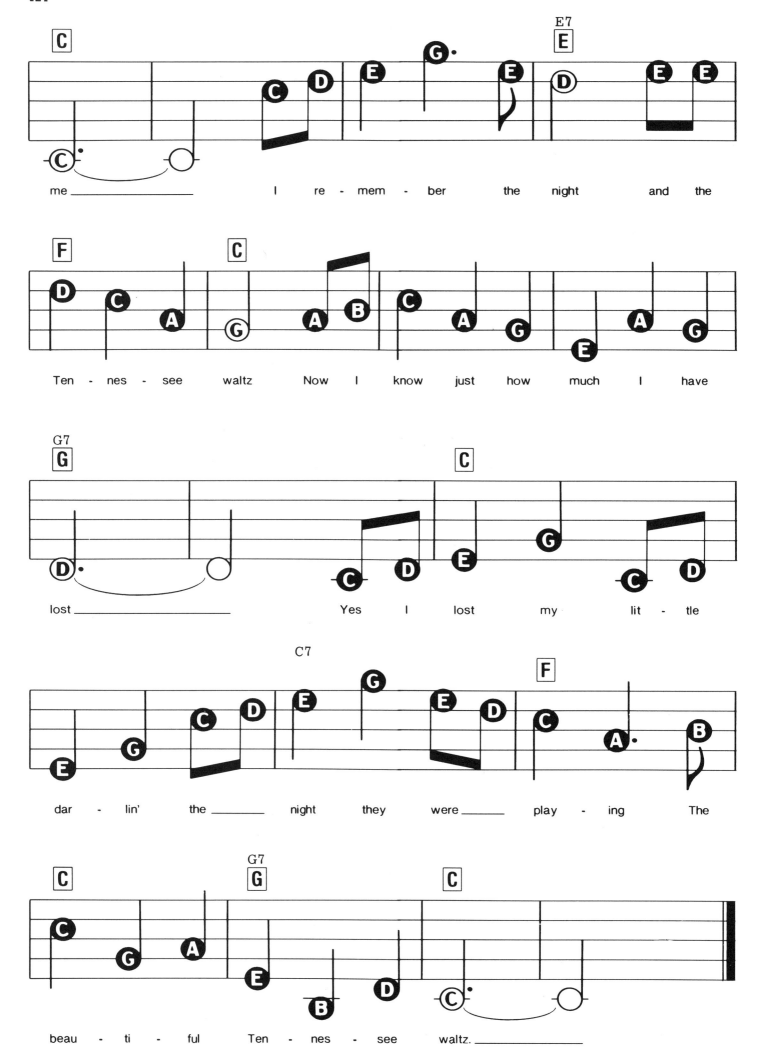

1951
How High the Moon
from TWO FOR THE SHOW

Registration 3
Rhythm: Swing or Fox Trot

Words by Nancy Hamilton
Music by Morgan Lewis

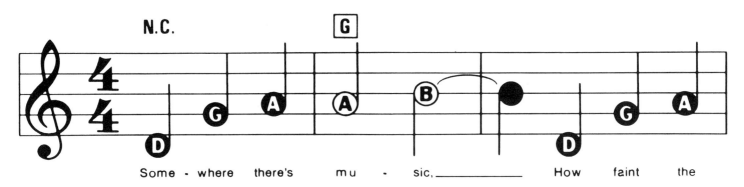

Some - where there's mu - sic, _____ How faint the

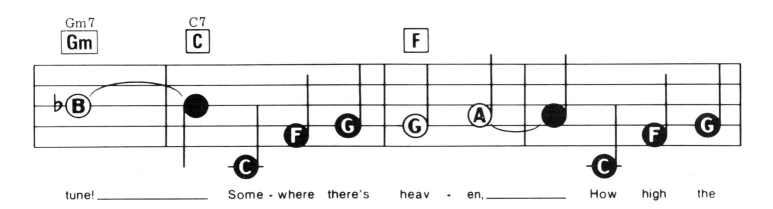

tune! _____ Some - where there's heav - en, _____ How high the

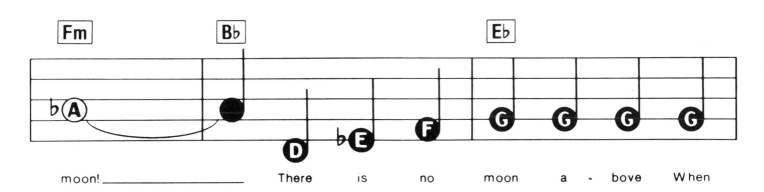

moon! _____ There is no moon a - bove When

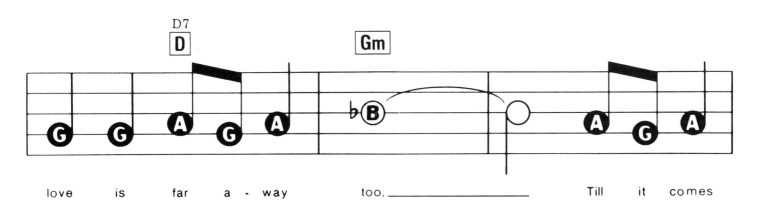

love is far a - way too, _____ Till it comes

126

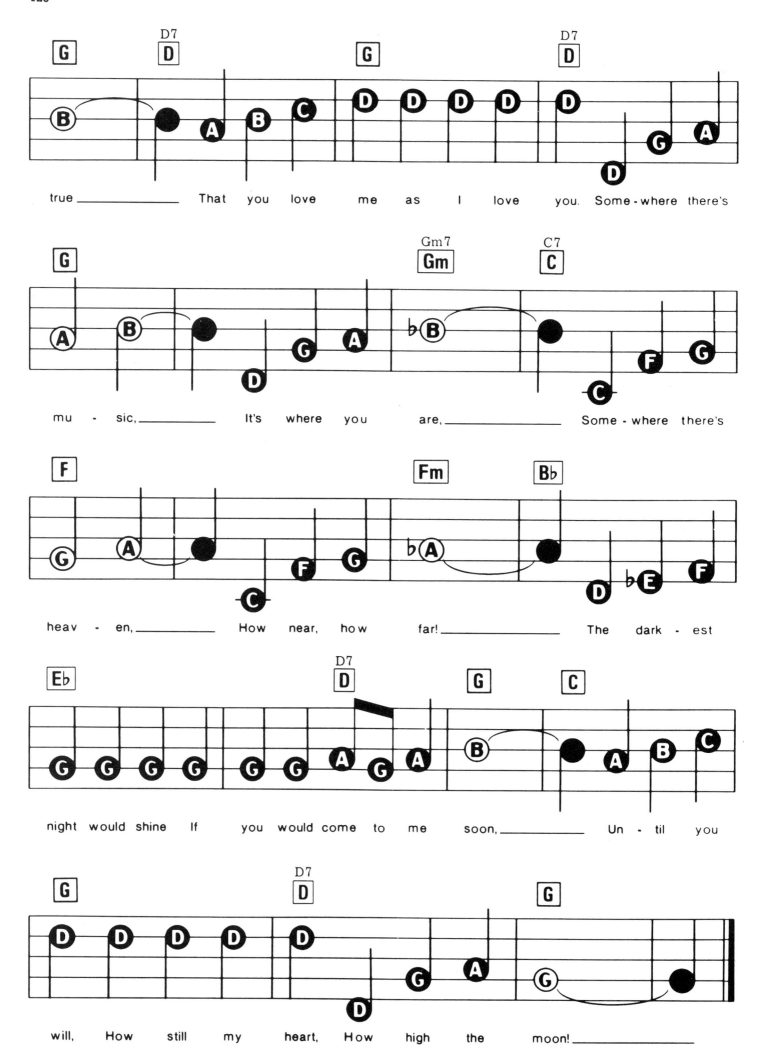

1952
When I Fall in Love

Registration 10
Rhythm: Fox Trot or Ballad

Words by Edward Heyman
Music by Victor Young

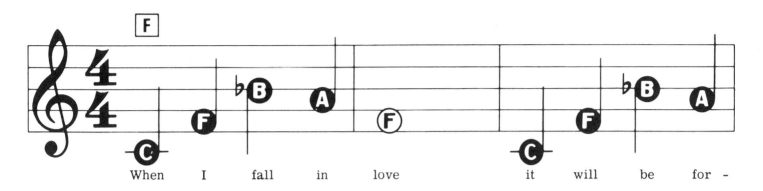

When I fall in love it will be for -

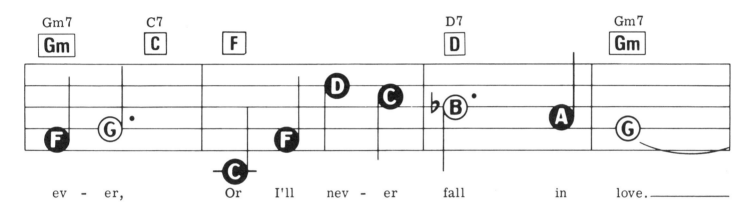

ev - er, Or I'll nev - er fall in love._____

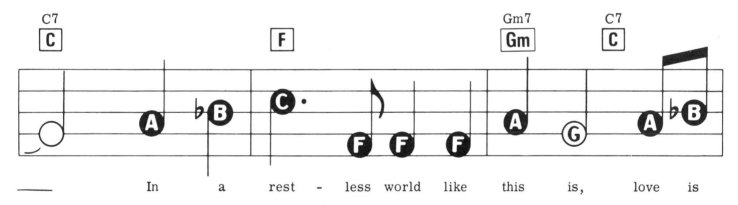

_____ In a rest - less world like this is, love is

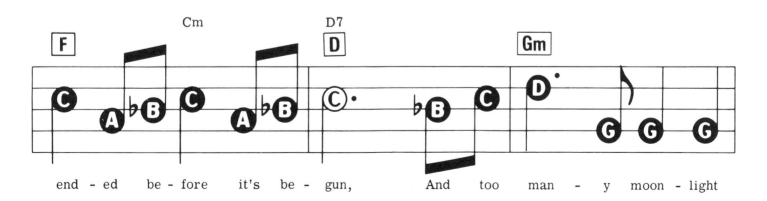

end - ed be - fore it's be - gun, And too man - y moon - light

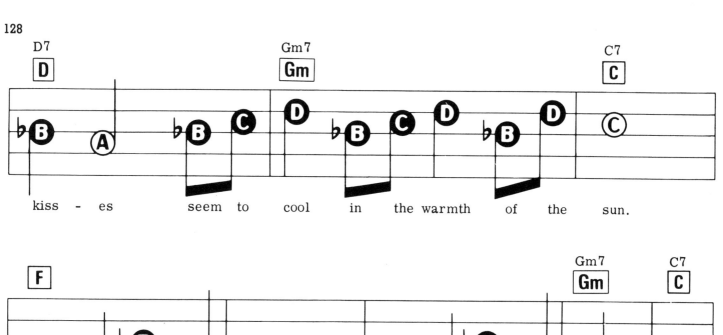

kiss - es   seem to cool   in the warmth of the sun.

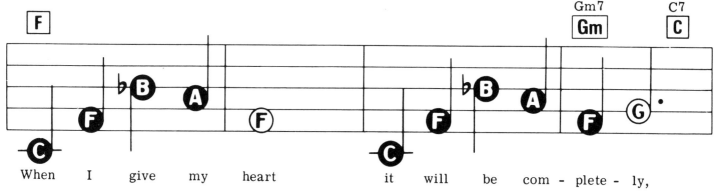

When   I   give   my   heart   it   will   be   com - plete - ly,

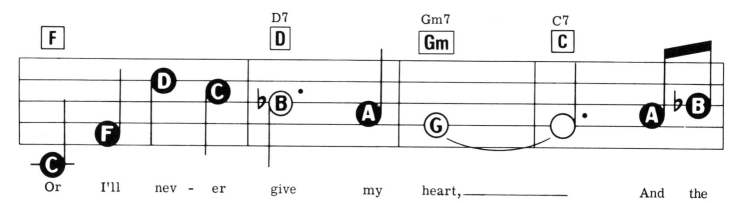

Or   I'll   nev - er   give   my   heart,_____   And   the

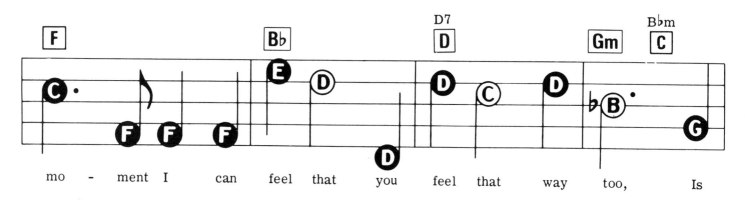

mo - ment I   can   feel that   you   feel that   way   too,   Is

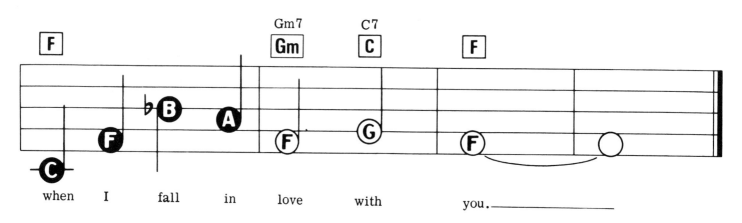

when   I   fall   in   love   with   you._____

1953
That's Amoré
(That's Love)
from the Paramount Picture THE CADDY

Registration 3
Rhythm: Waltz

Words by Jack Brooks
Music by Harry Warren

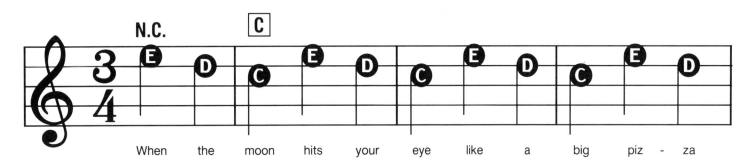

When the moon hits your eye like a big piz - za

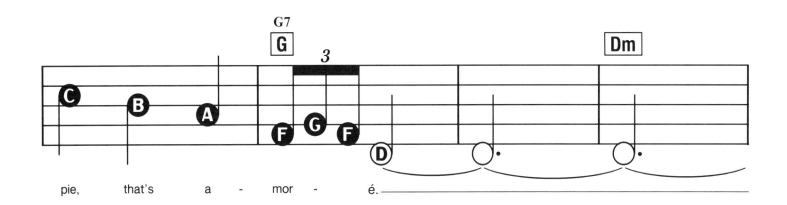

pie, that's a - mor - é. _____

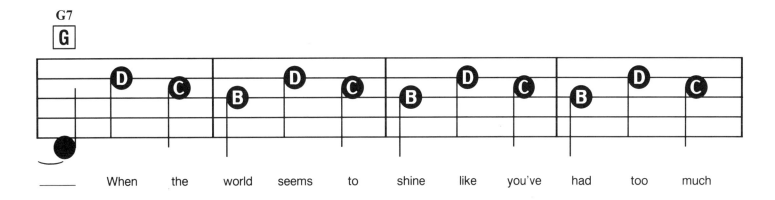

_____ When the world seems to shine like you've had too much

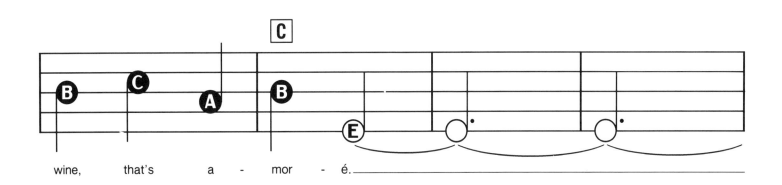

wine, that's a - mor - é. _____

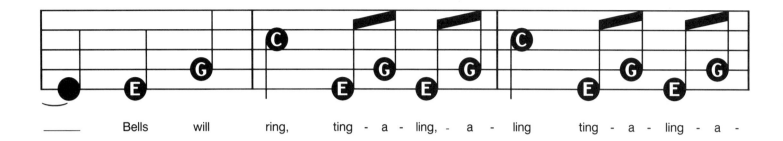

Bells will ring, ting - a - ling, - a - ling ting - a - ling - a -

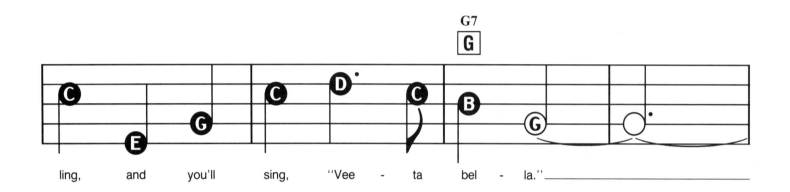

G7

ling, and you'll sing, "Vee - ta bel - la."

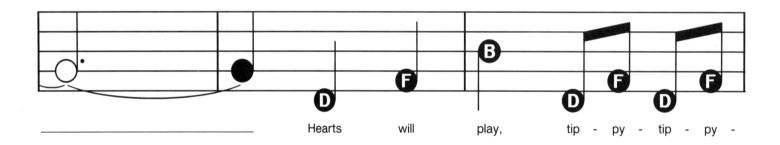

Hearts will play, tip - py - tip - py -

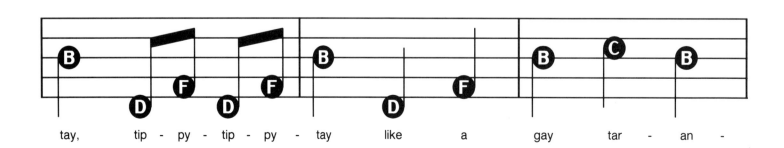

tay, tip - py - tip - py - tay like a gay tar - an -

131

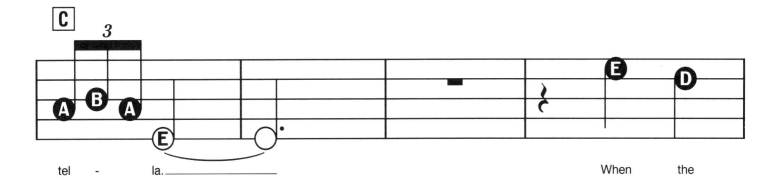

tel - la.   When the

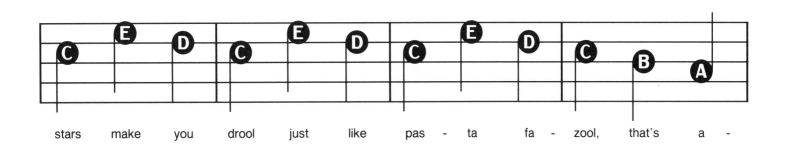

stars make you drool just like pas - ta fa - zool, that's a -

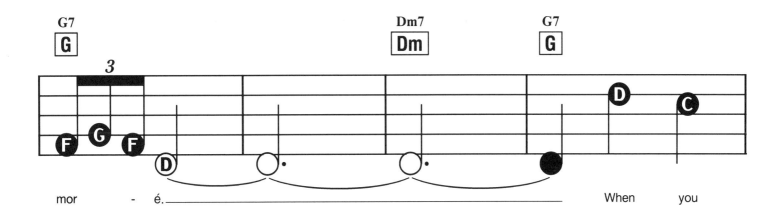

mor - é.   When you

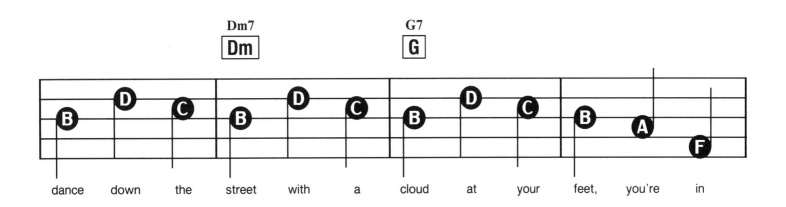

dance down the street with a cloud at your feet, you're in

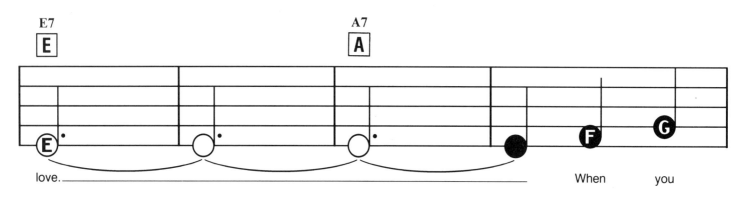

E7

love. When you

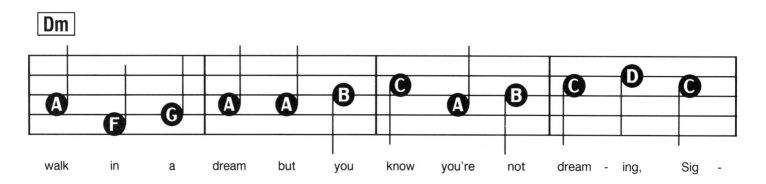

Dm

walk in a dream but you know you're not dream - ing, Sig -

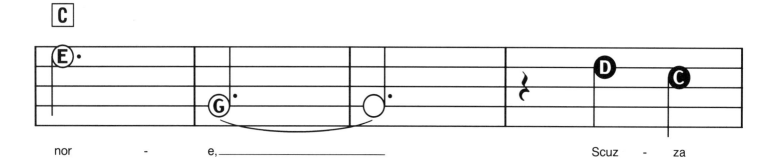

C

nor - e, Scuz - za

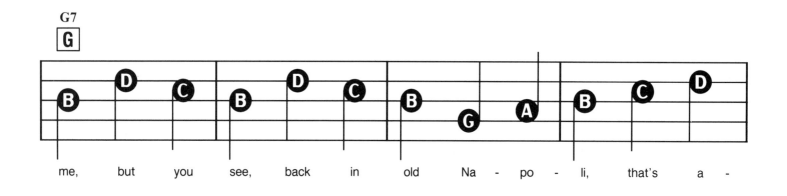

G7

me, but you see, back in old Na - po - li, that's a -

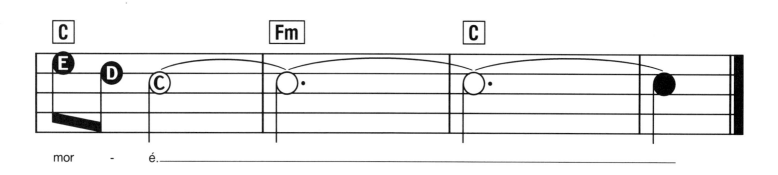

C   **Fm**   **C**

mor - é.

1954
Three Coins in the Fountain

Registration 2
Rhythm: Swing

Words by Sammy Cahn
Music by Jule Styne

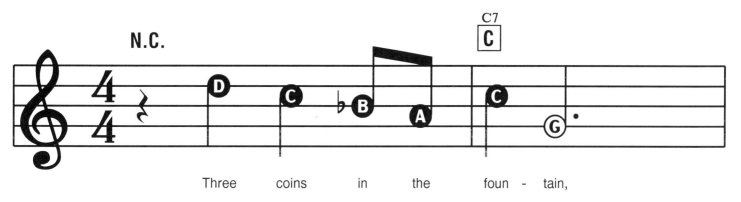

Three coins in the foun - tain,

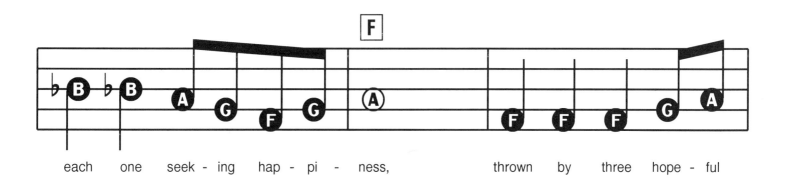

each one seek - ing hap - pi - ness, thrown by three hope - ful

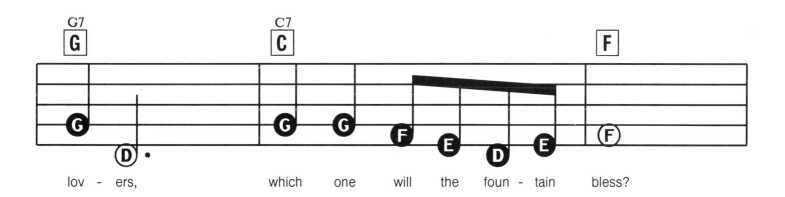

lov - ers, which one will the foun - tain bless?

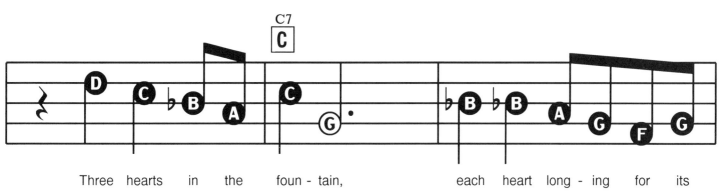

Three hearts in the foun - tain, each heart long - ing for its

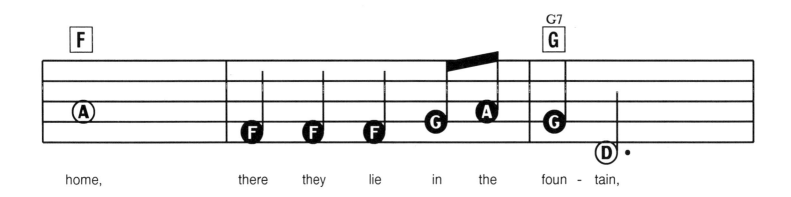

home, there they lie in the foun - tain,

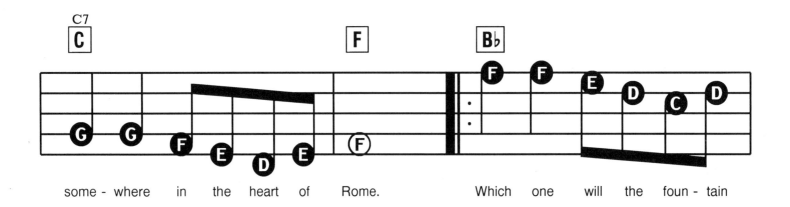

some - where in the heart of Rome. Which one will the foun - tain

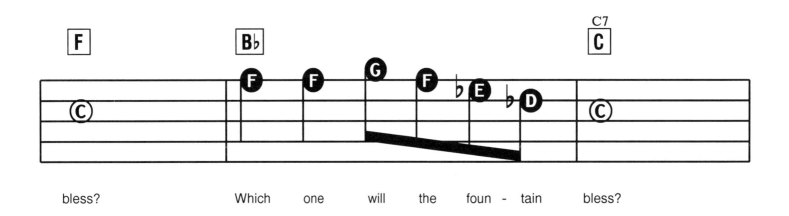

bless? Which one will the foun - tain bless?

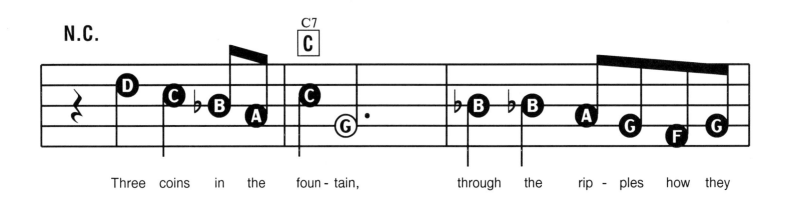

Three coins in the foun - tain, through the rip - ples how they

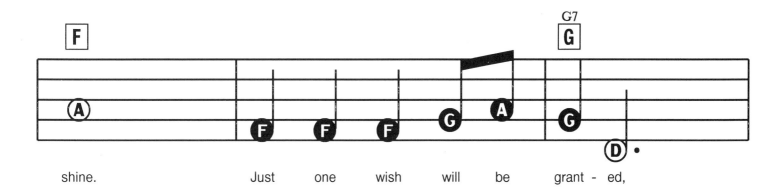

shine.   Just   one   wish   will   be   grant - ed,

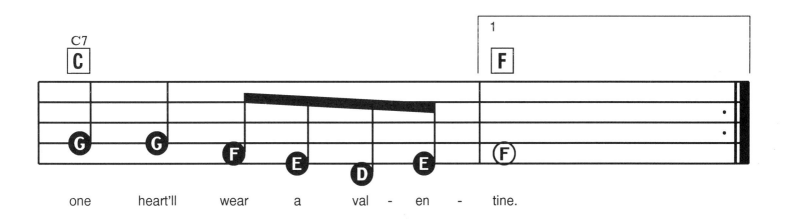

one   heart'll   wear   a   val - en - tine.

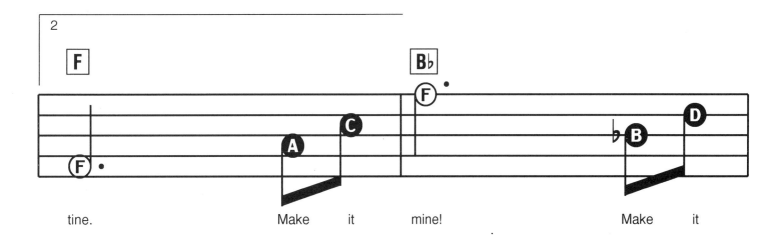

tine.   Make   it   mine!   Make   it

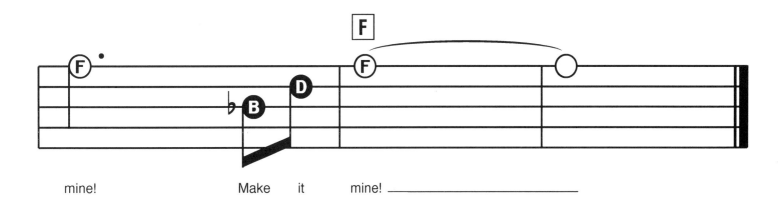

mine!   Make   it   mine! _____

1955
Rock Around the Clock

Registration 8
Rhythm: Rock

Words and Music by Max C. Freedman
and Jimmy DeKnight

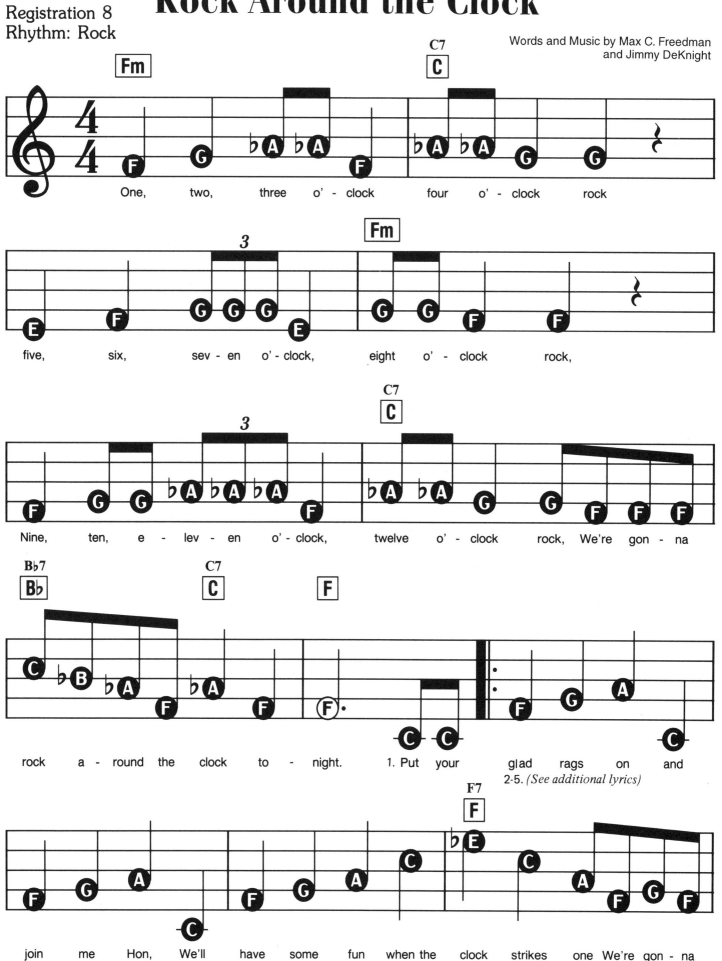

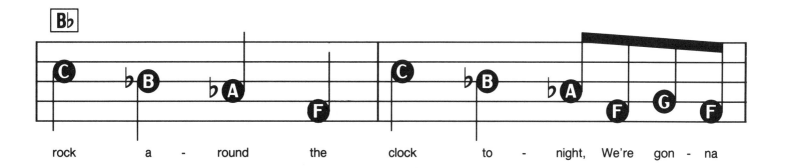

rock a - round the clock to - night, We're gon - na

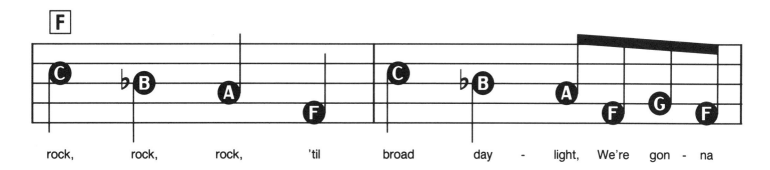

rock, rock, rock, 'til broad day - light, We're gon - na

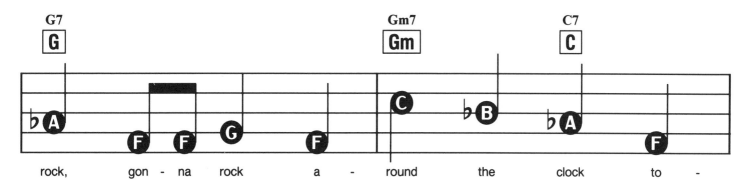

rock, gon - na rock a - round the clock to -

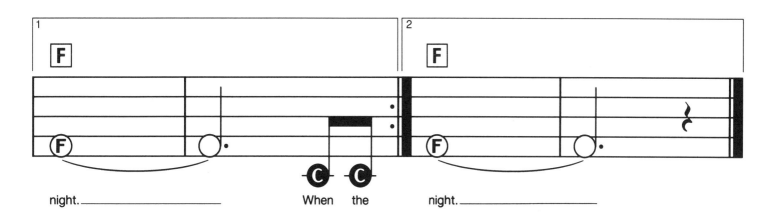

1.
night._____ When the

2.
night._____

Additional Lyrics

2. When the clock strikes two, and three and four,
   If the band slows down we'll yell for more,
   We're gonna rock around the clock tonight,
   We're gonna rock, rock, rock, etc. . . .

3. When the chimes ring five and six and seven,
   We'll be rockin' up in seventh heav'n,
   We're gonna rock around the clock tonight,
   We're gonna rock, rock, rock, etc. . . .

4. When it's eight, nine, ten, eleven, too,
   I'll be goin' strong and so will you,
   We're gonna rock around the clock tonight,
   We're gonna rock, rock, rock, etc. . . .

5. When the clock strikes twelve, we'll cool off, then,
   Start a rockin' 'round the clock again,
   We're gonna rock around the clock tonight,
   We're gonna rock, rock, rock, etc. . . .

1956

Don't Be Cruel
(To a Heart That's True)

Registration 4
Rhythm: Rock

Words and Music by Otis Blackwell
and Elvis Presley

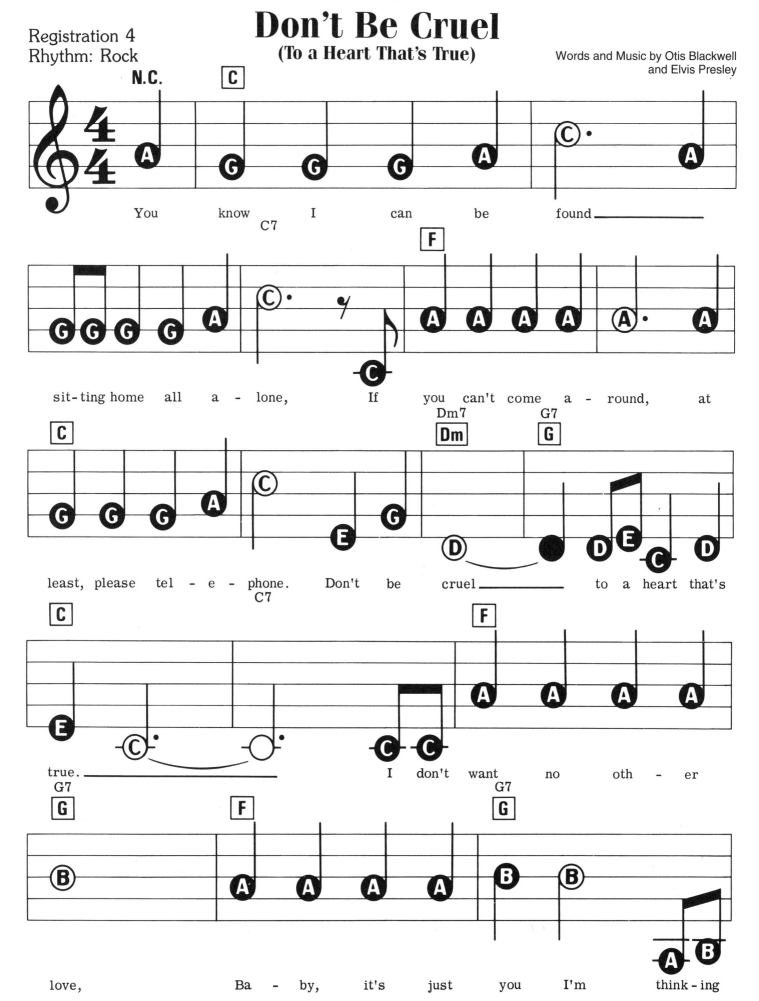

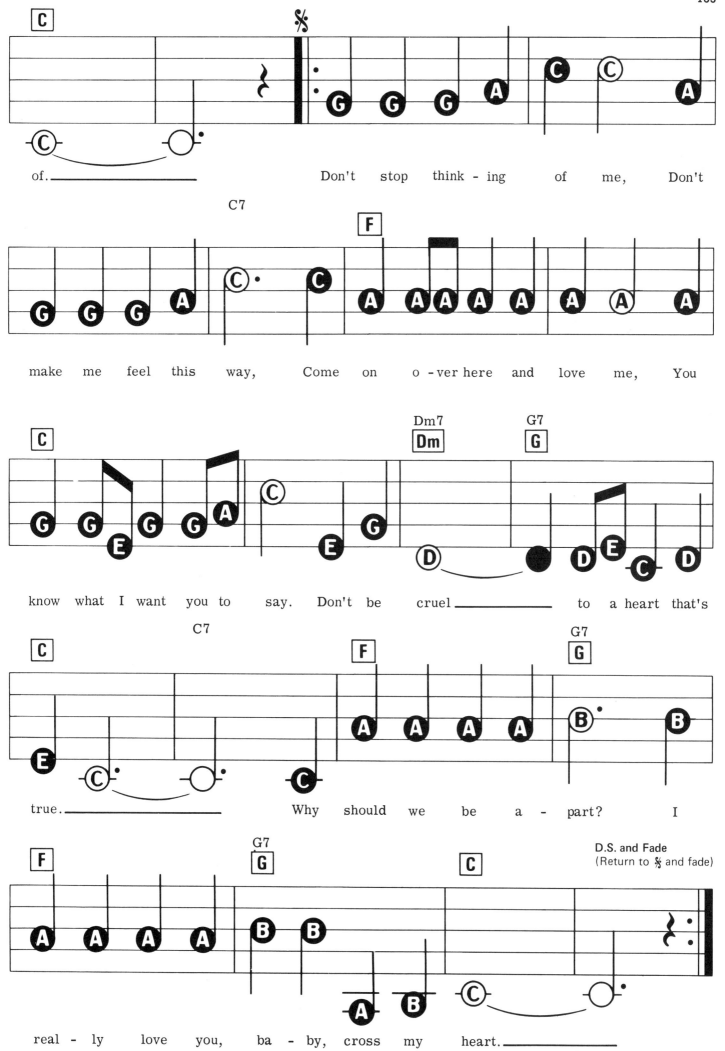

1957
That'll Be the Day

Registration 8
Rhythm: Swing or Shuffle

Words and Music by Jerry Allison,
Norman Petty and Buddy Holly

N.C. F

Well,___ that - 'll be the day, when you say, good-bye, Yes,___

C C7

that - 'll be the day, when you make me cry, Ah, you

F C

say you're gon - na leave, you know it's a lie, 'cause that - 'll be the day___

G7 C7
G C F

___ when I die. Well, When Cu - pid shot his dart,

C F

He shot it at your heart, So if we ev - er part and

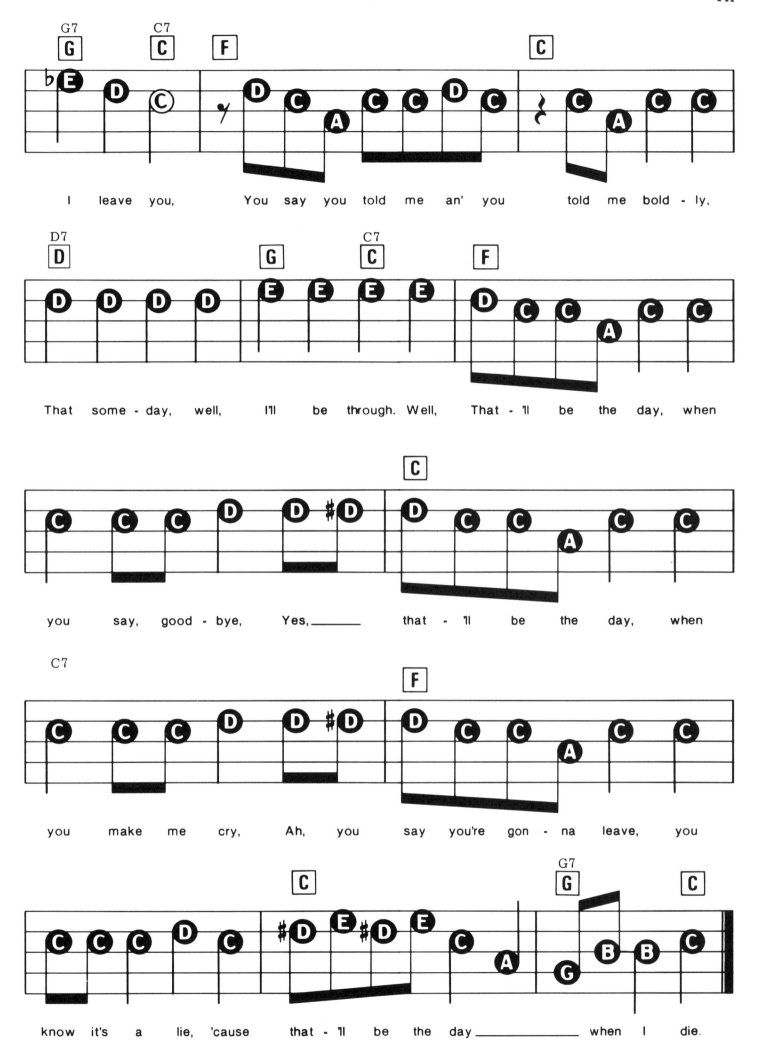

1958

Witchcraft

Registration 9
Rhythm: Swing

Lyric by Carolyn Leigh
Music by Cy Coleman

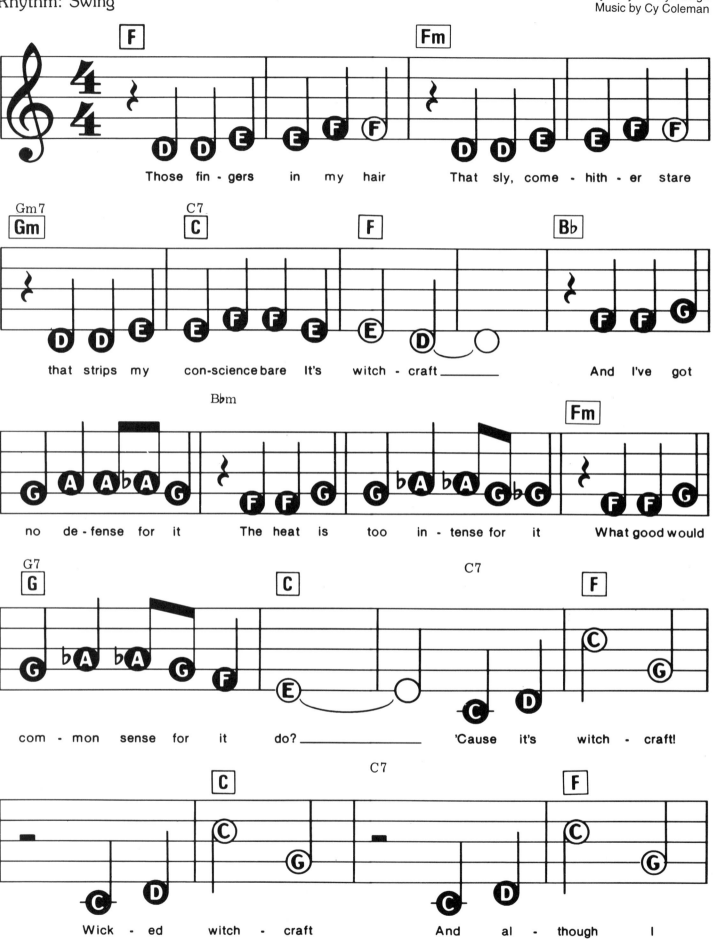

143

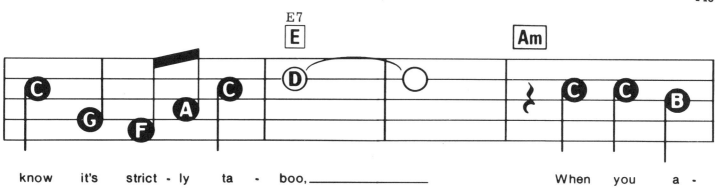

know it's strict-ly ta - boo,_____ When you a -

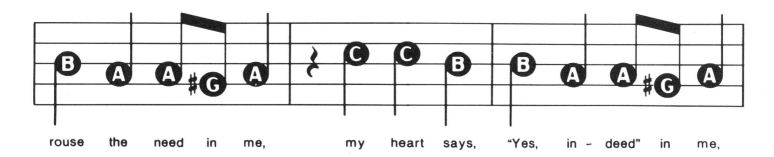

rouse the need in me, my heart says, "Yes, in - deed" in me,

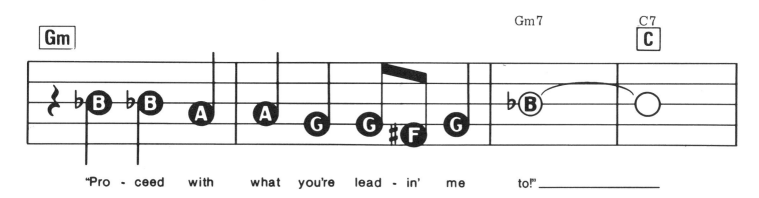

"Pro - ceed with what you're lead - in' me to!"_____

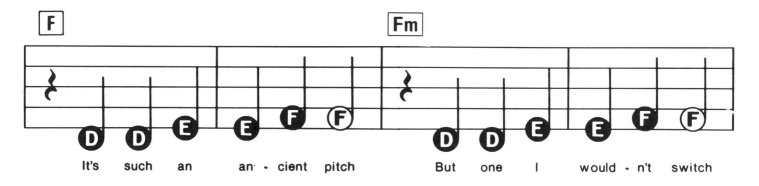

It's such an an - cient pitch But one I would - n't switch

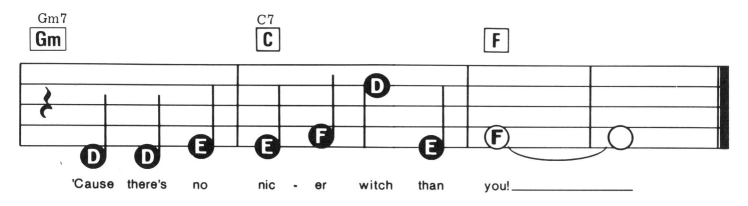

'Cause there's no nic - er witch than you!_____

1959
The Sound of Music
from THE SOUND OF MUSIC

Registration 5
Rhythm: Fox Trot

Lyrics by Oscar Hammerstein II
Music by Richard Rodgers

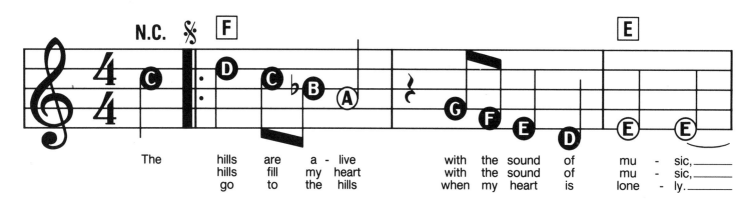

The hills are a - live with the sound of mu - sic,____
hills fill my heart with the sound of mu - sic,____
go to the hills when my heart is lone - ly.____

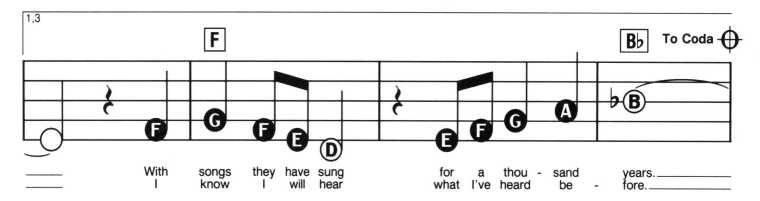

____ With songs they have sung for a thou - sand years._____
I know I will hear what I've heard be - fore._____

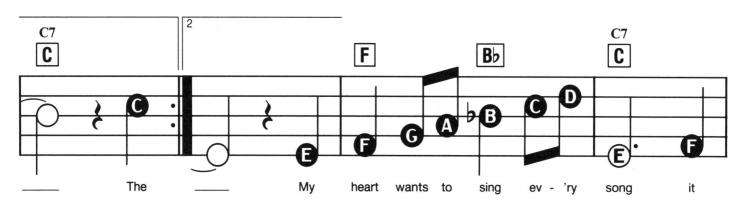

____ The ____ My heart wants to sing ev - 'ry song it

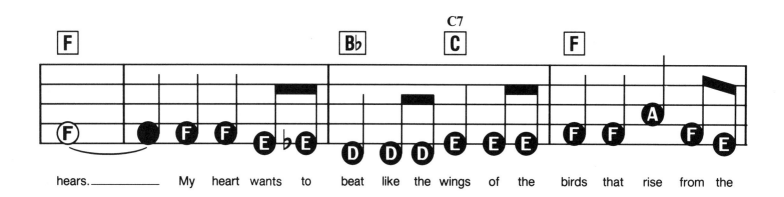

hears._____ My heart wants to beat like the wings of the birds that rise from the

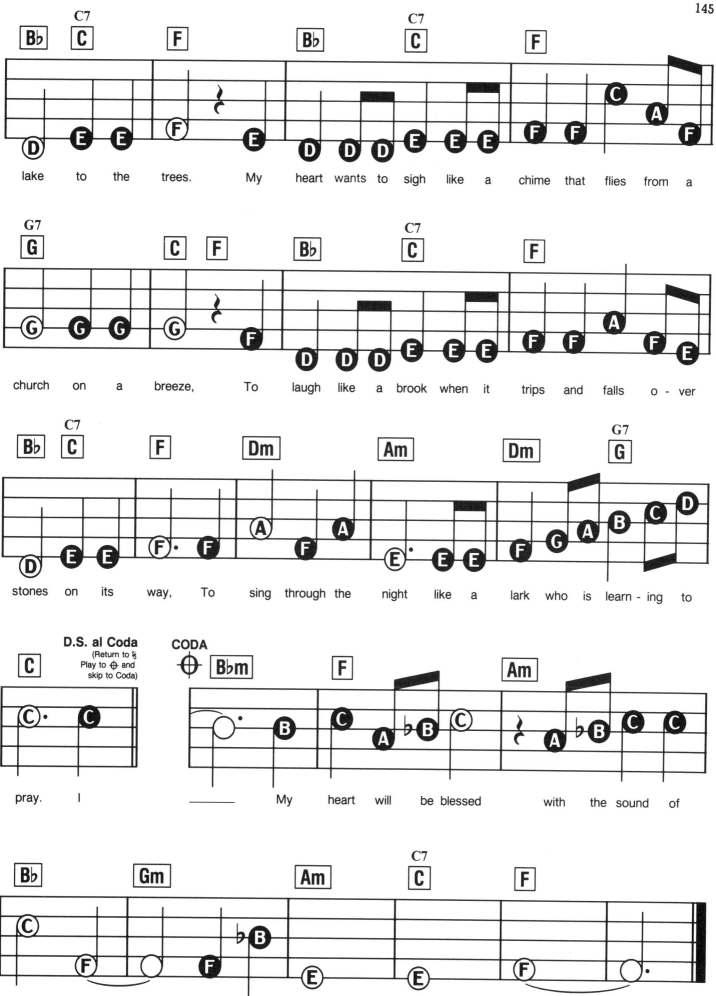

1960
Georgia on My Mind

Registration 4
Rhythm: Swing

Words by Stuart Gorrell
Music by Hoagy Carmichael

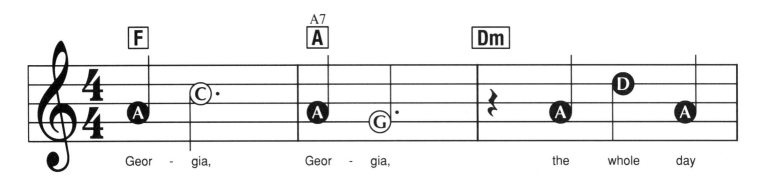

Geor - gia, Geor - gia, the whole day

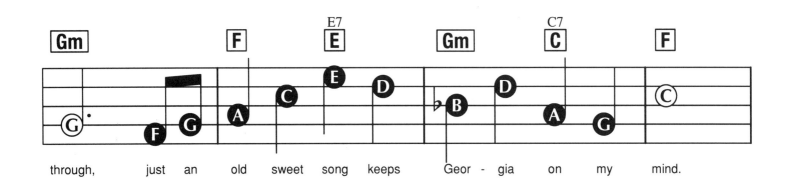

through, just an old sweet song keeps Geor - gia on my mind.

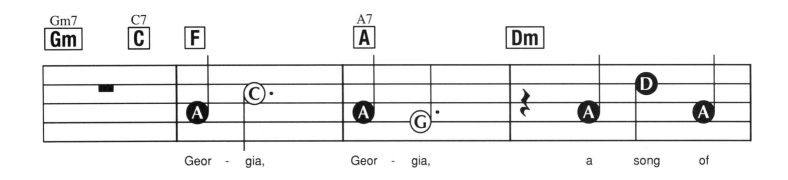

Geor - gia, Geor - gia, a song of

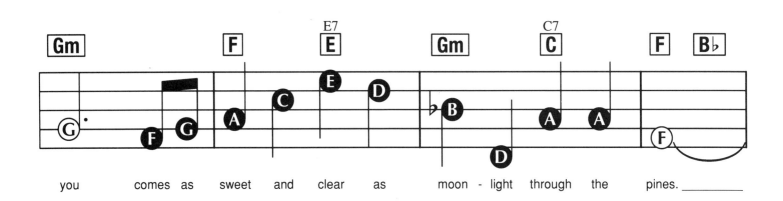

you comes as sweet and clear as moon - light through the pines. _____

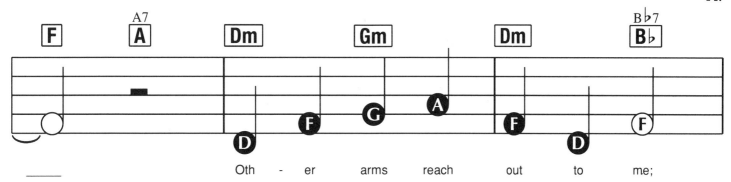

_____ Oth - er arms reach out to me;

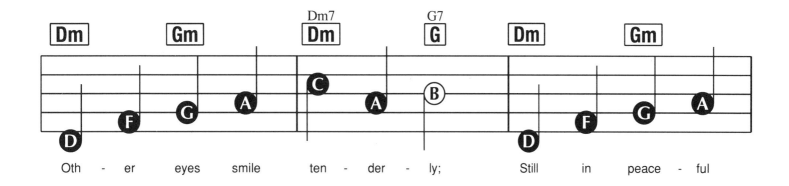

Oth - er eyes smile ten - der - ly; Still in peace - ful

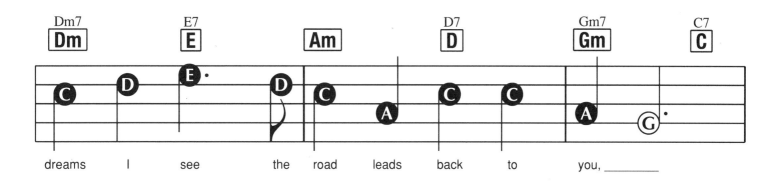

dreams I see the road leads back to you, _____

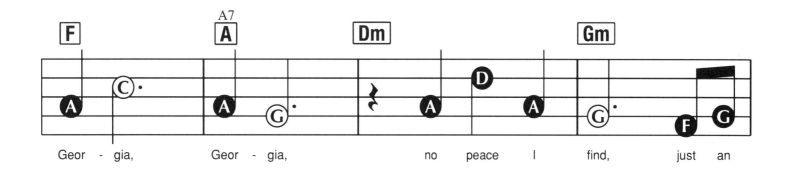

Geor - gia, Geor - gia, no peace I find, just an

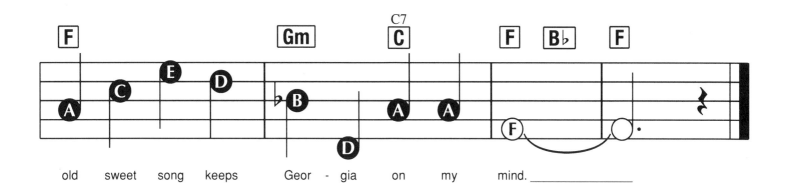

old sweet song keeps Geor - gia on my mind. _____

1961
Moon River
from the Paramount Picture BREAKFAST AT TIFFANY'S

Registration 7
Rhythm: Waltz

Words by Johnny Mercer
Music by Henry Mancini

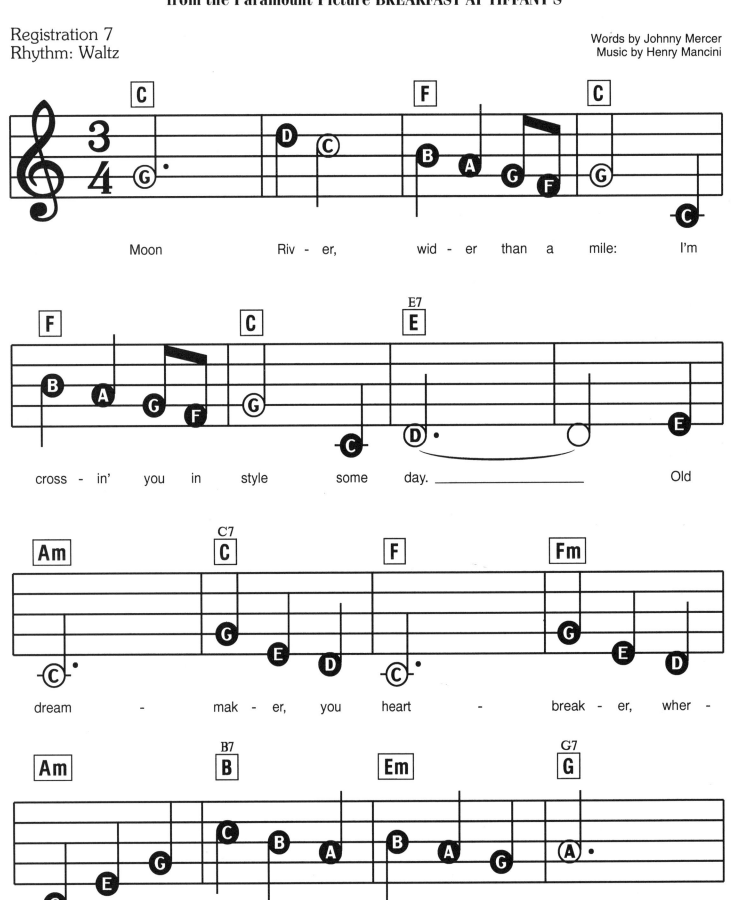

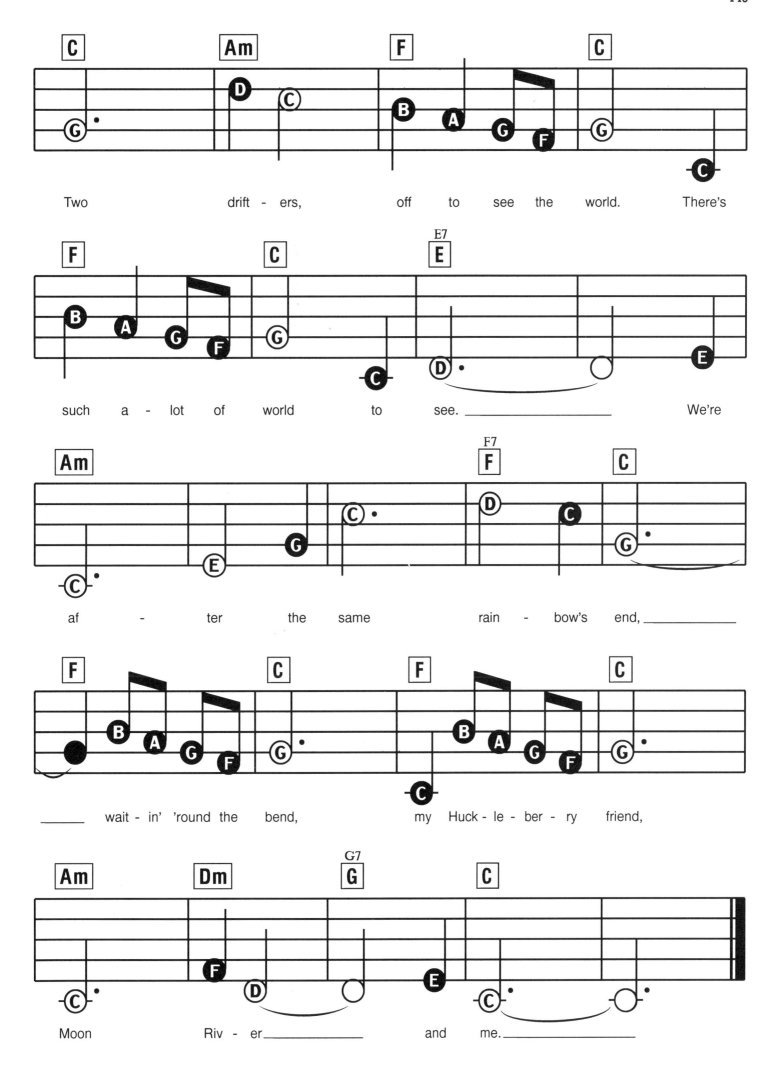

1962
The Twist

Registration 5
Rhythm: Rock

Words and Music by
Hank Ballard

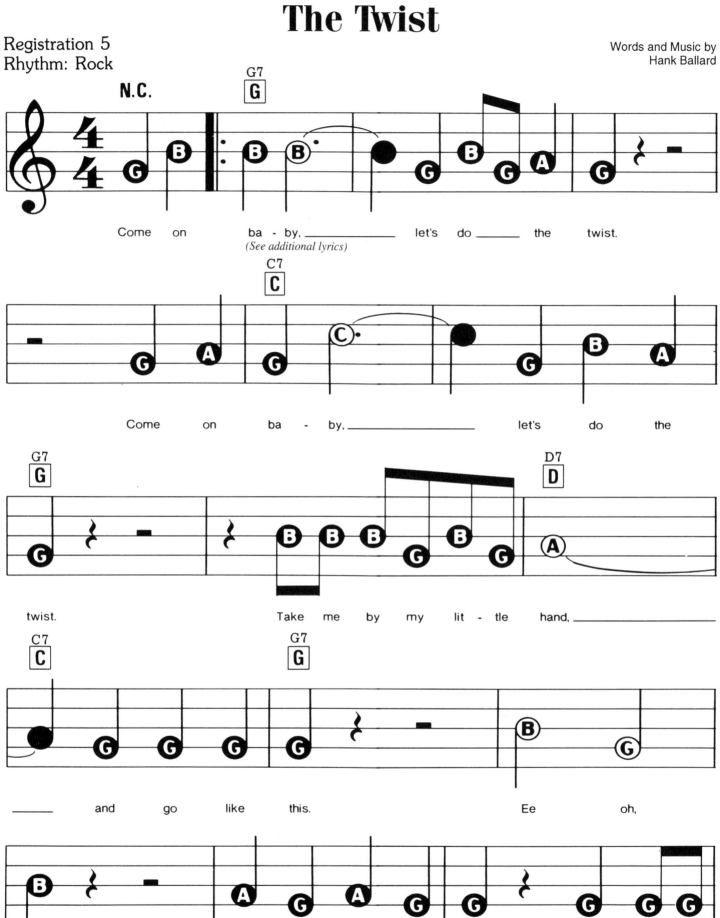

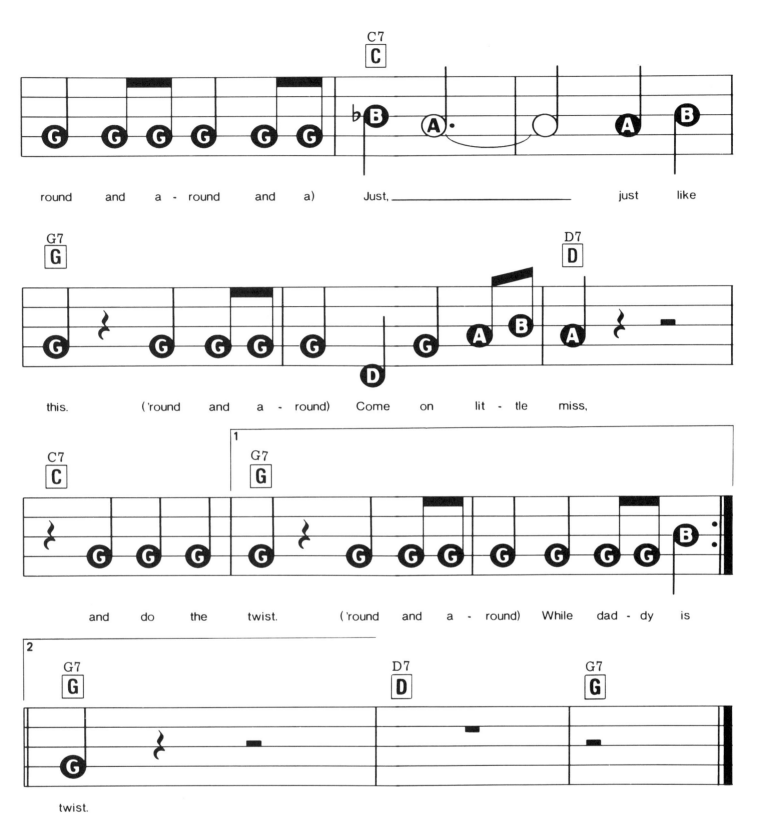

Additional Lyrics

Verse 2
While daddy is sleeping and mama ain't around,
While daddy is sleeping and mama ain't around,
We're gonna twisty, twisty, twisty until we tear the house down.

You should see my little sis,
You should see my little sis,
She knows how to rock and she knows how to twist.

1963

More
(Ti Guardero' Nel Cuore)
from the film MONDO CANE

Registration 2
Rhythm: Bossa Nova or Latin

Music by Nino Oliviero and Riz Ortolani
Italian Lyrics by Marcello Ciorciolini
English Lyrics by Norman Newell

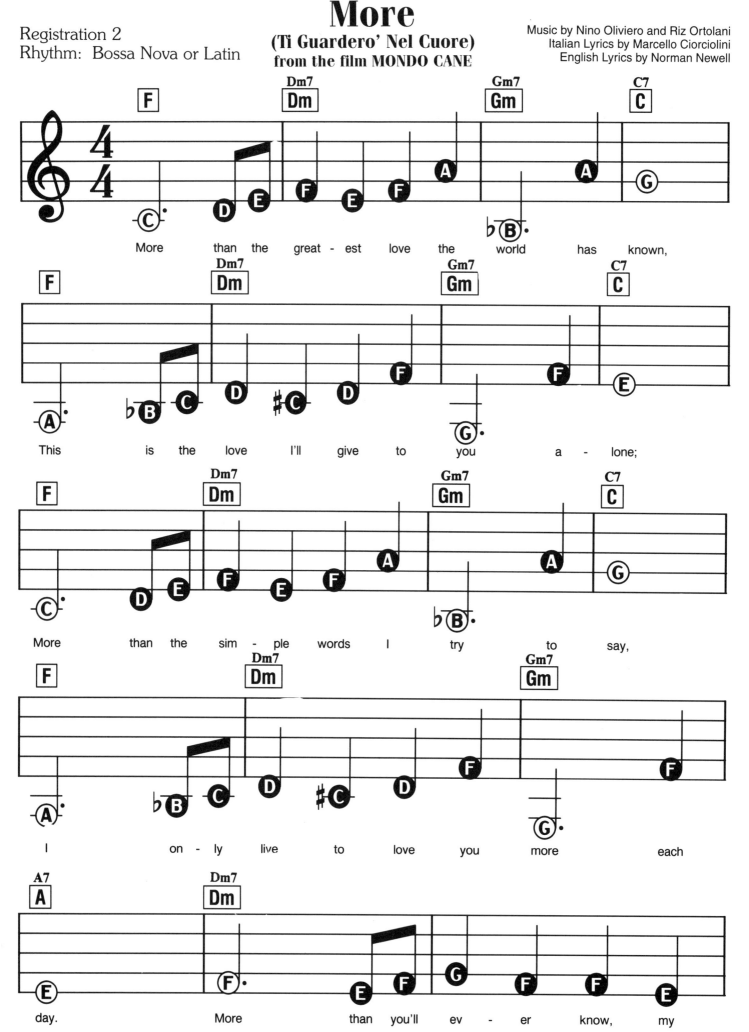

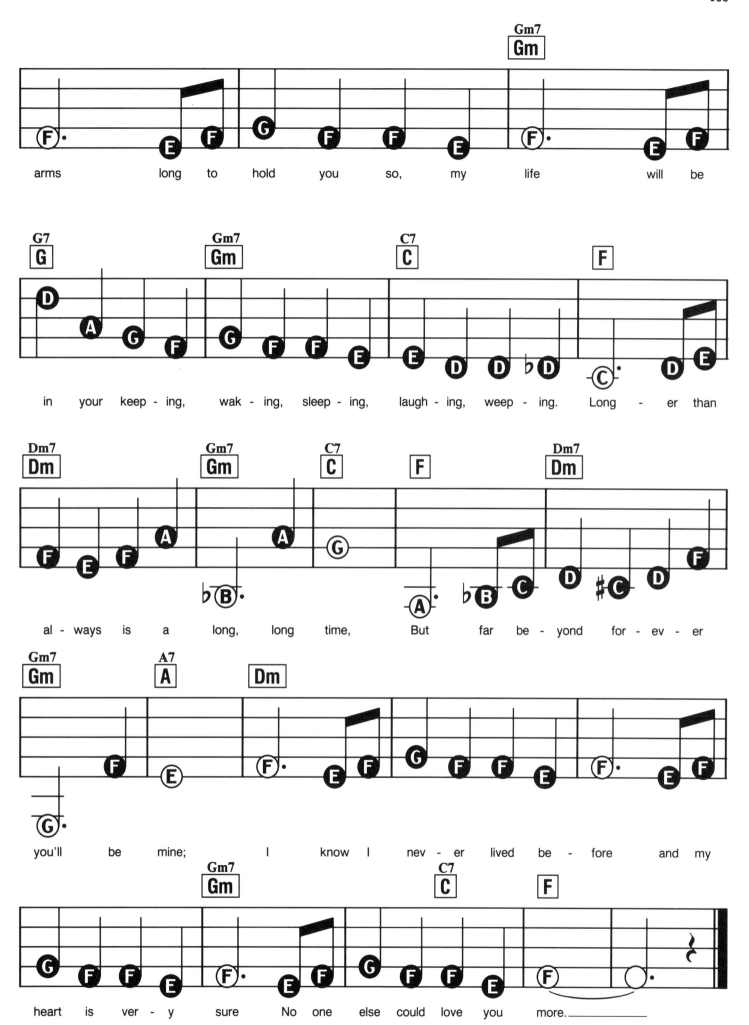

1964
I Want to Hold Your Hand

Registration 3
Rhythm: Rock

Words and Music by John Lennon
and Paul McCartney

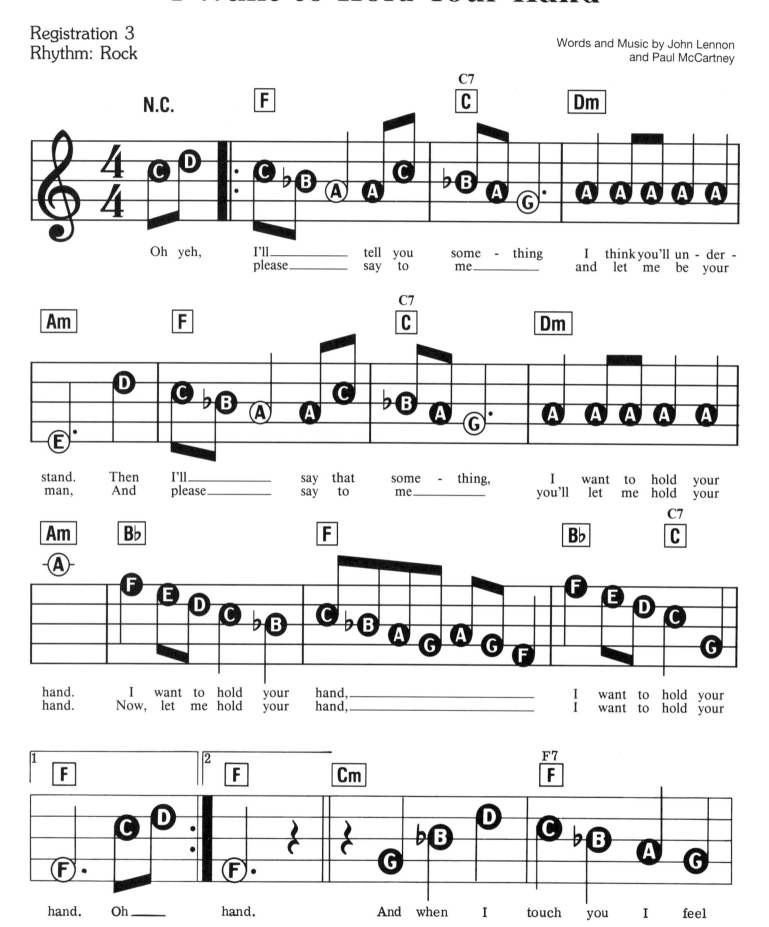

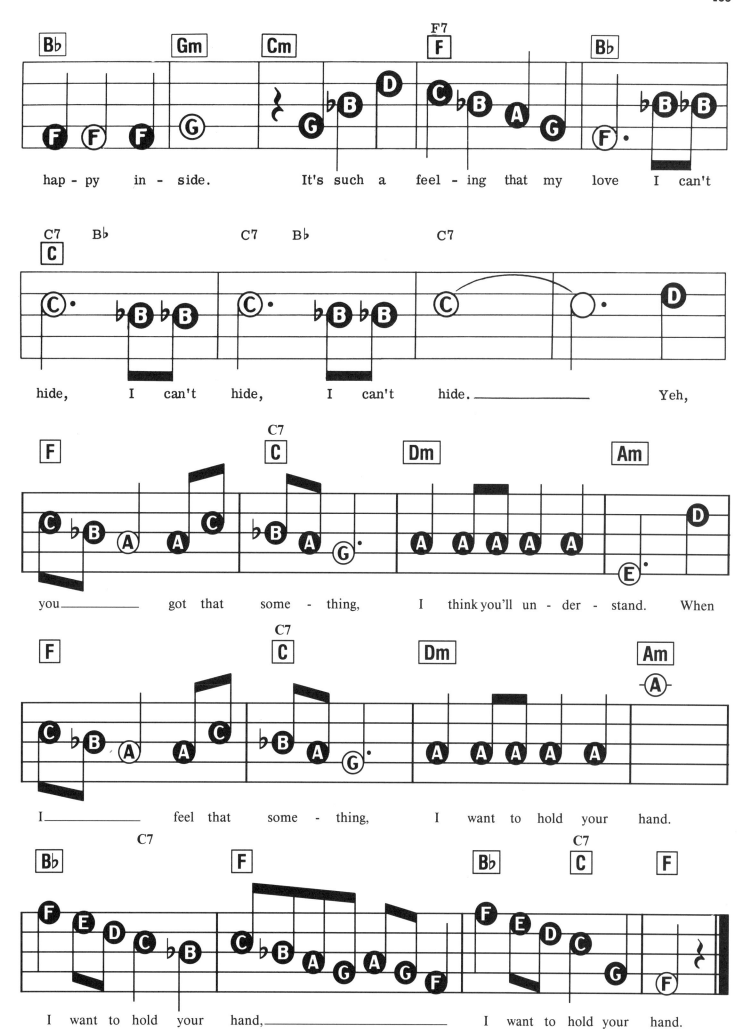

1965
Downtown

Registration 5
Rhythm: Rock

Words and Music by
Tony Hatch

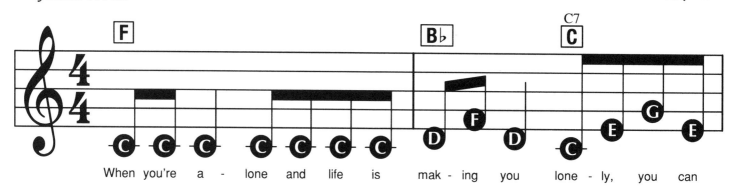

When you're a - lone and life is mak - ing you lone - ly, you can

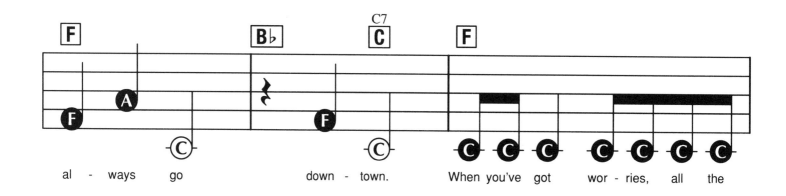

al - ways go down - town. When you've got wor - ries, all the

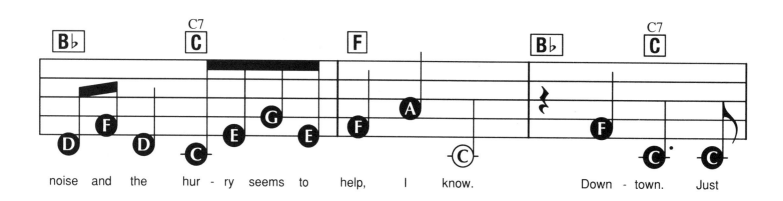

noise and the hur - ry seems to help, I know. Down - town. Just

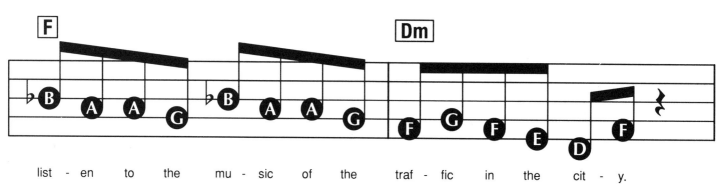

list - en to the mu - sic of the traf - fic in the cit - y.

MCA Music Publishing

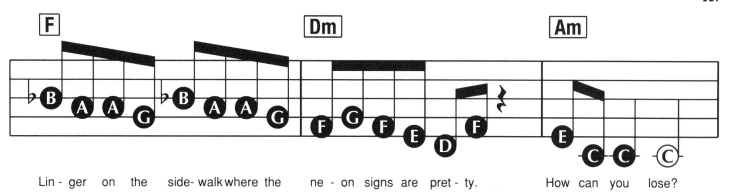

Lin - ger on the side- walk where the ne - on signs are pret - ty. How can you lose?

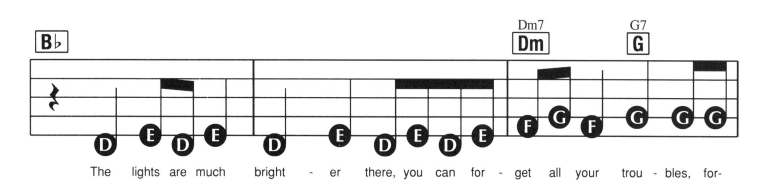

The lights are much bright - er there, you can for - get all your trou - bles, for-

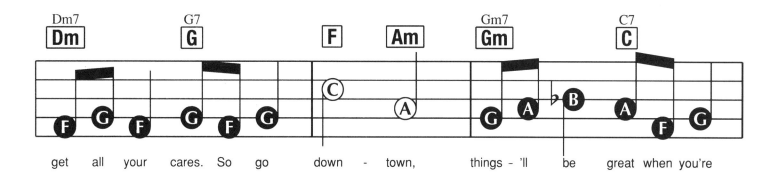

get all your cares. So go down - town, things - 'll be great when you're

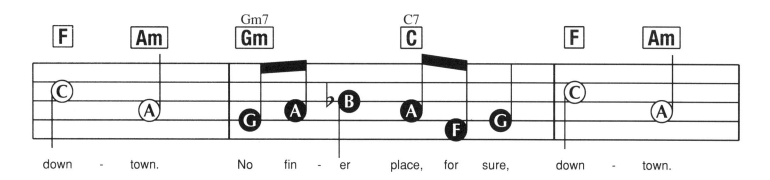

down - town. No fin - er place, for sure, down - town.

Repeat and Fade

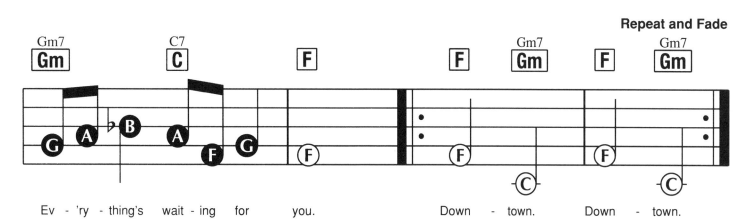

Ev - 'ry - thing's wait - ing for you. Down - town. Down - town.

1966
California Dreamin'

Registration 5
Rhythm: Rock

Words and Music by John Phillips
and Michelle Phillips

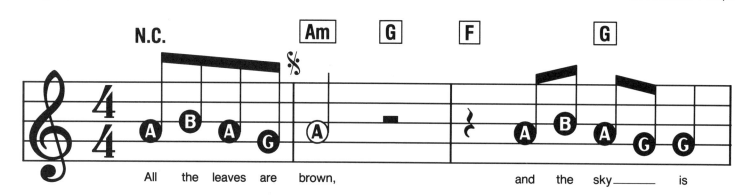

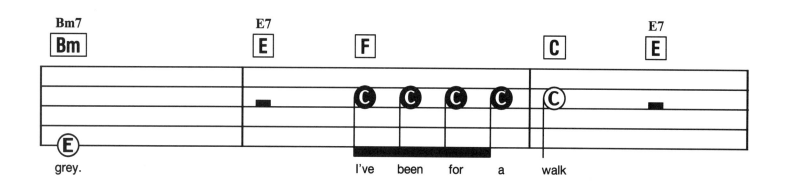

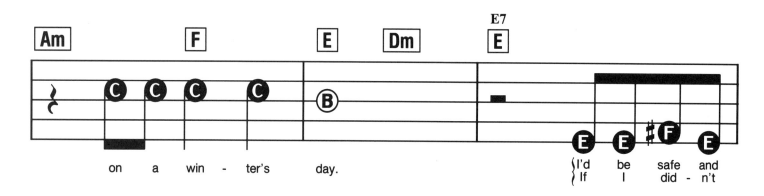

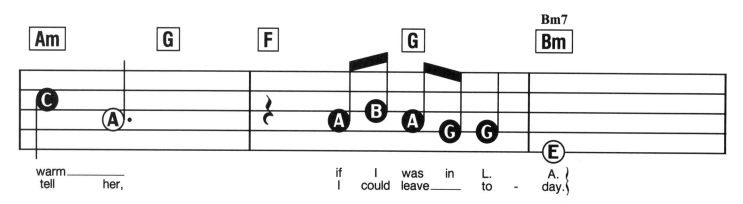

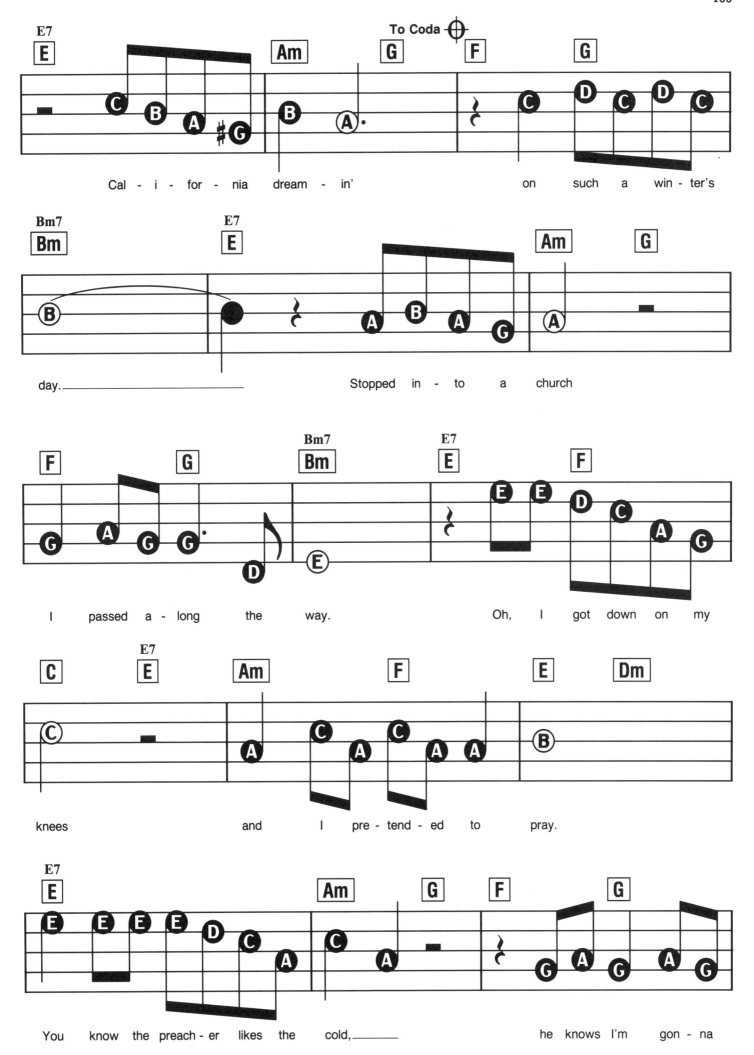

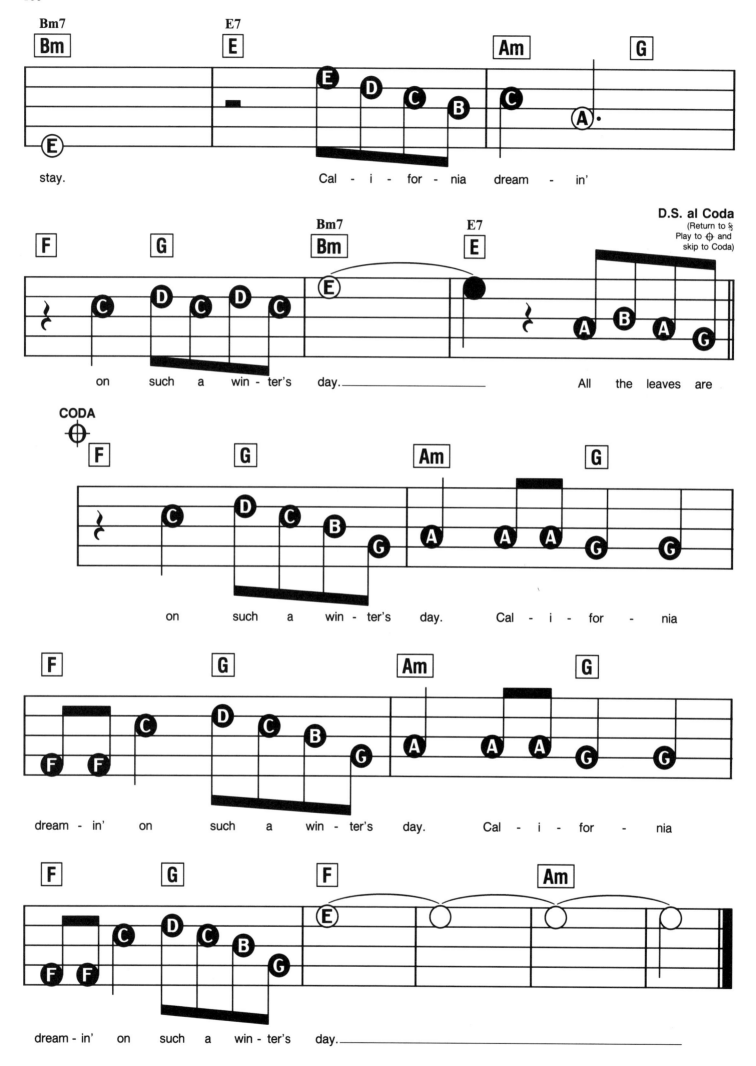

1967
All You Need Is Love

Registration 5
Rhythm: Shuffle or Swing

Words and Music by John Lennon
and Paul McCartney

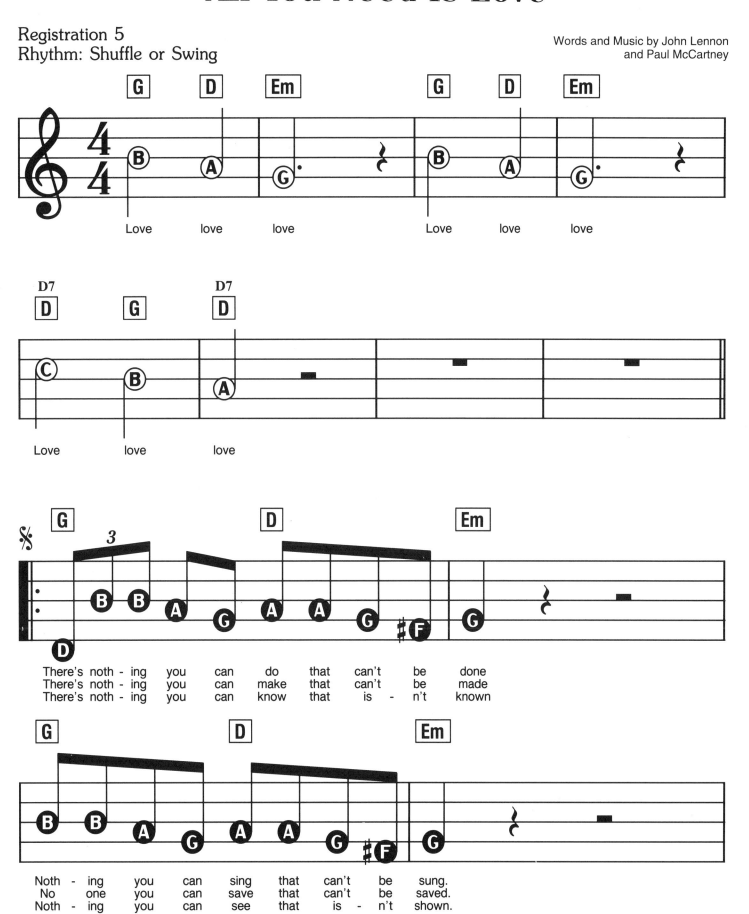

162

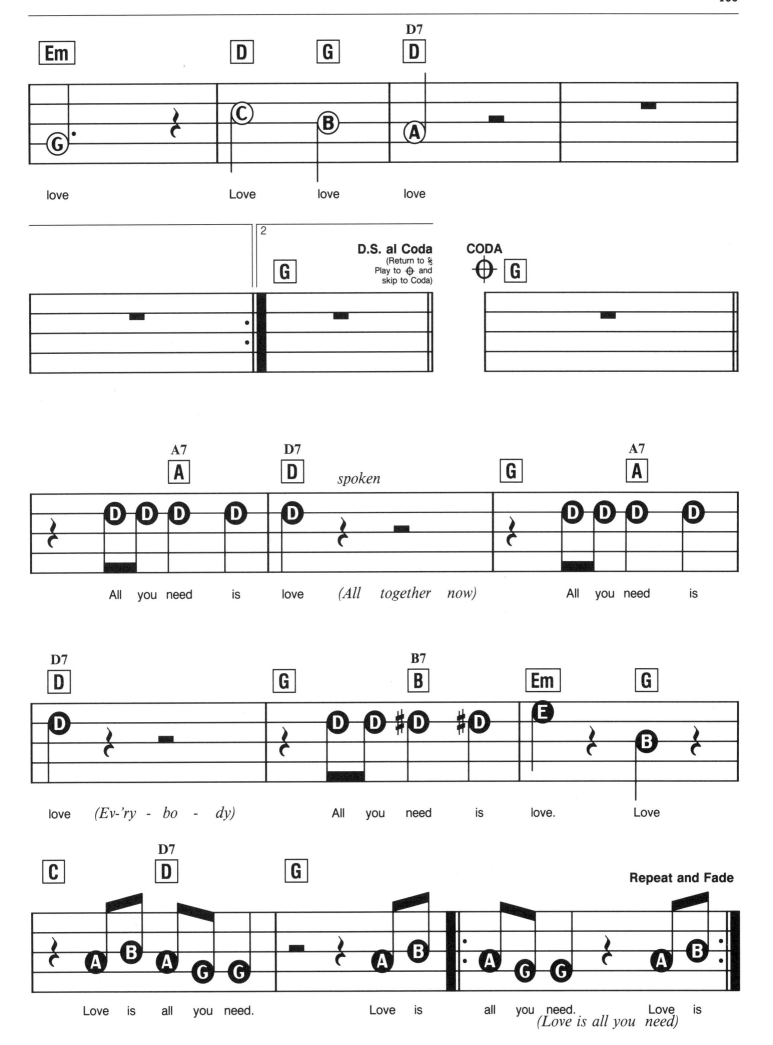

1968

I Heard It Through the Grapevine

Registration 7
Rhythm: Rock or 8-Beat

Words and Music by Norman Whitfield
and Barrett Strong

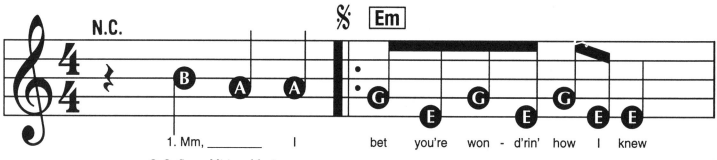

2, 3. *See additional lyrics*

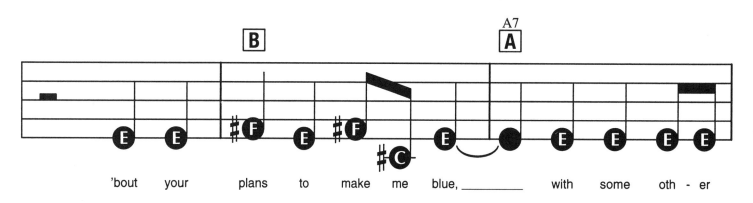

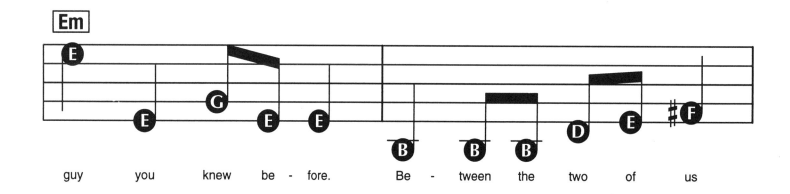

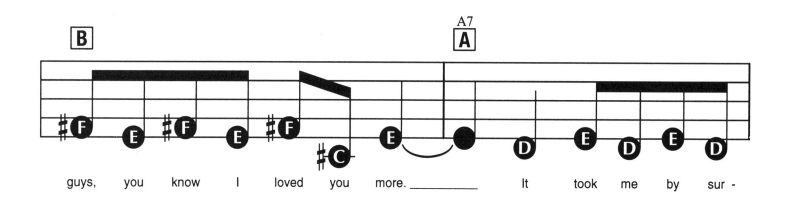

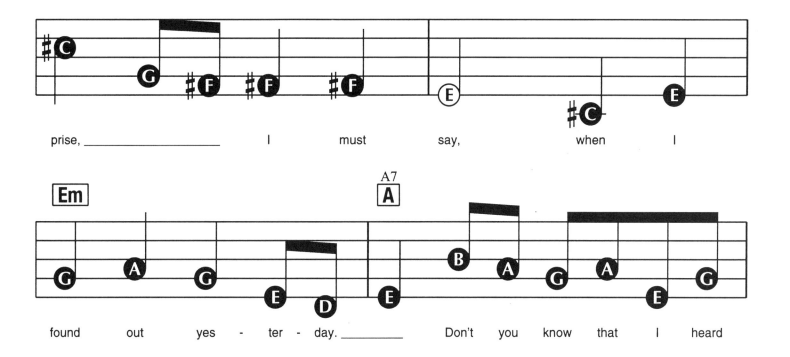

prise, _____ I must say, when I

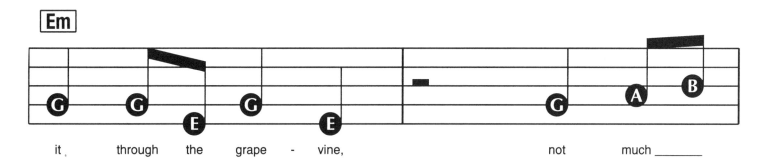

found out yes - ter - day. _____ Don't you know that I heard

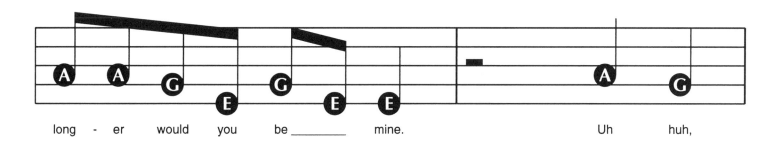

it through the grape - vine, not much _____

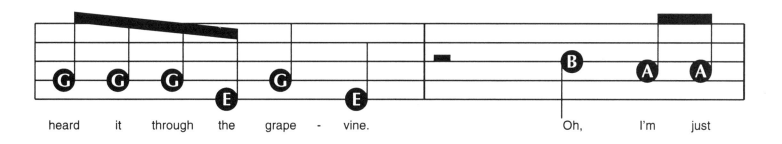

long - er would you be _____ mine. Uh huh,

heard it through the grape - vine. Oh, I'm just

CODA

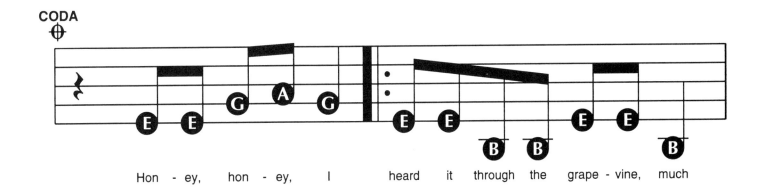

Hon - ey, hon - ey, I heard it through the grape - vine, much

Repeat and Fade

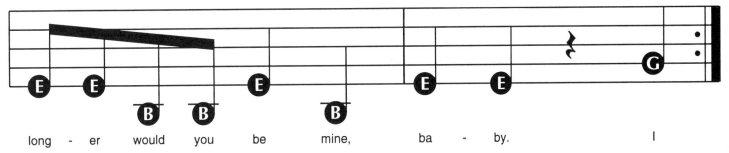

long - er would you be mine, ba - by. I

Additional Lyrics

2. I know a man ain't supposed to cry,
   but these tears I can't hold inside.
   Losin' you would end my life, you see,
   'cause you mean that much to me.
   You could have told me yourself
   that you loved someone else.
   Instead, I heard it through the grapevine,
   not much longer would you be mine.
   Oh, I heard it through the grapevine,
   and I'm just about to lose my mind.

3. People say believe half of what you see,
   oh, and none of what you hear.
   But I can't help but be confused.
   If it's true please tell me, dear.
   Do you plan to let me go
   for the other guy you loved before?

1969

Leaving on a Jet Plane

Registration 2
Rhythm: Fox Trot or Swing

Words and Music by
John Denver

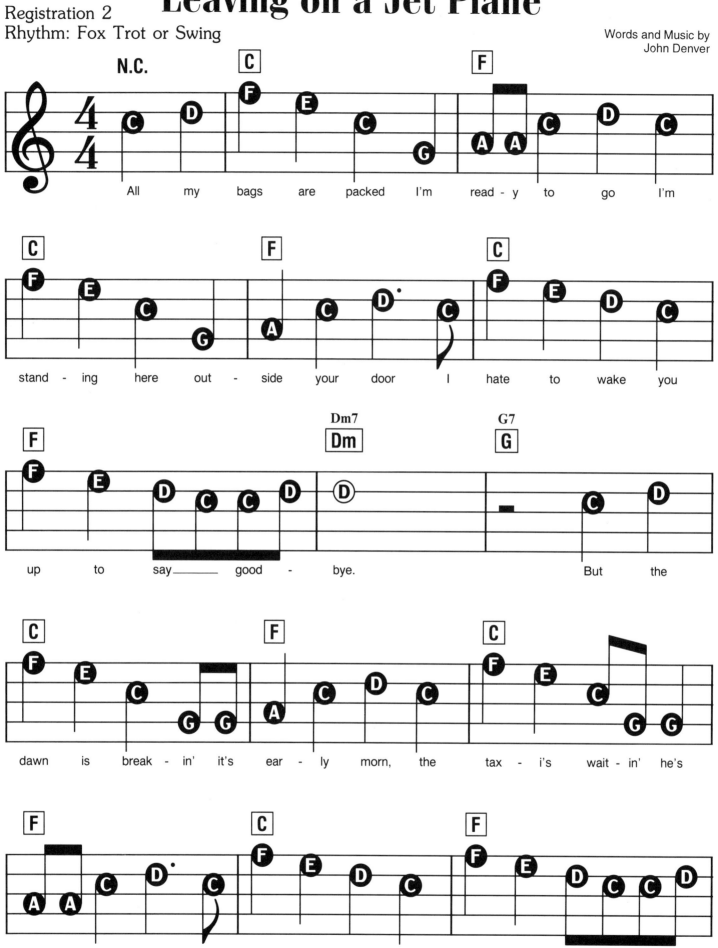

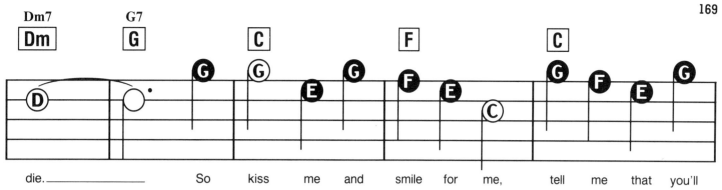

die._____ So kiss me and smile for me, tell me that you'll

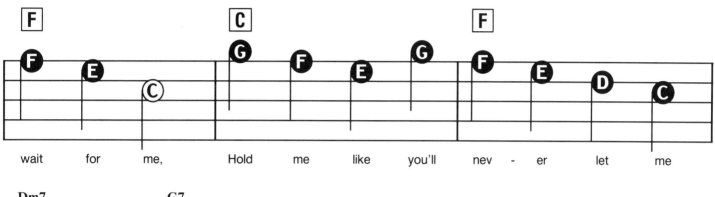

wait for me, Hold me like you'll nev - er let me

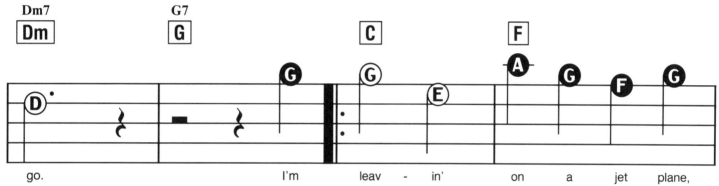

go. I'm leav - in' on a jet plane,

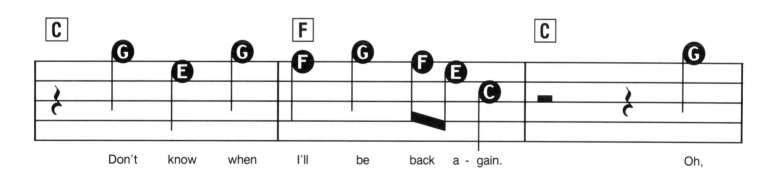

Don't know when I'll be back a - gain. Oh,

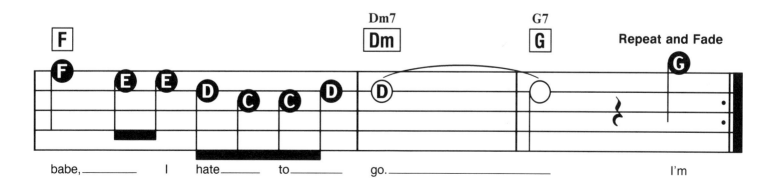

babe,_____ I hate_____ to_____ go._____ I'm

1970
(They Long to Be)
Close to You

Registration 2
Rhythm: Slow Rock

Lyric by Hal David
Music by Burt Bacharach

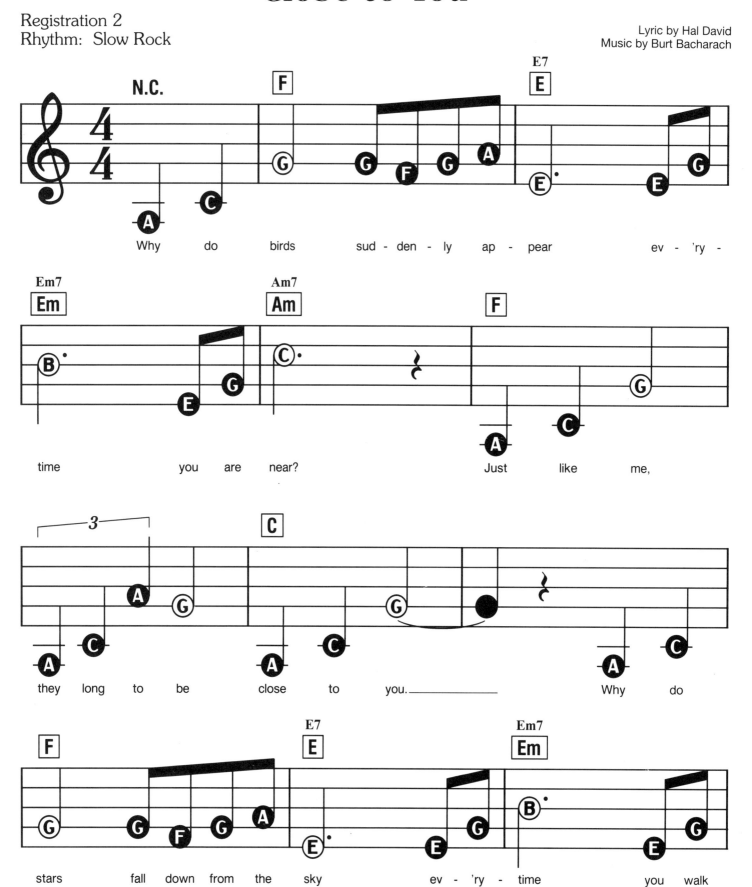

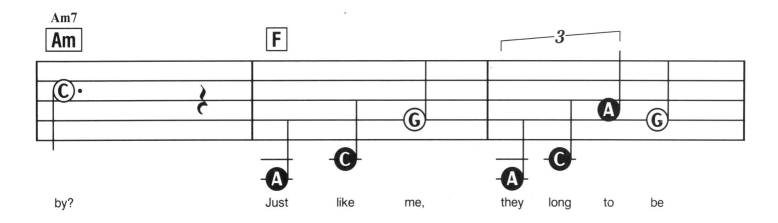

by?   Just   like   me,   they   long   to   be

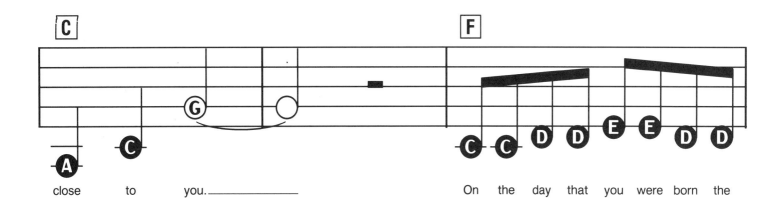

close   to   you._____   On   the   day   that   you   were   born   the

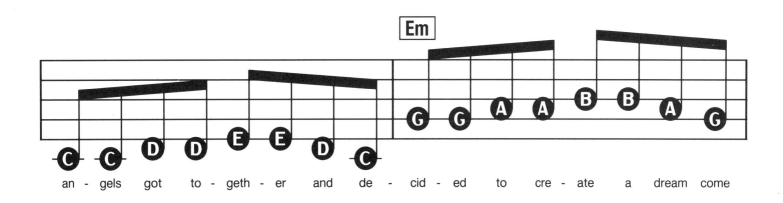

an - gels   got   to - geth - er   and   de - cid - ed   to   cre - ate   a   dream   come

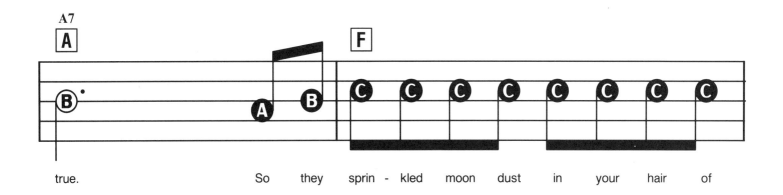

true.   So   they   sprin - kled   moon   dust   in   your   hair   of

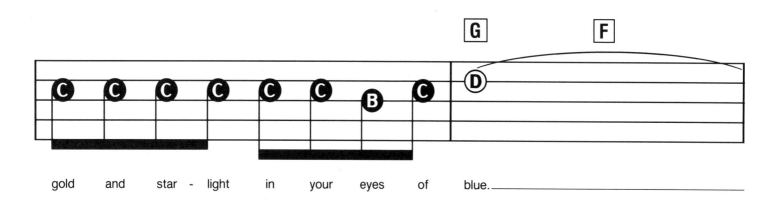

gold and star - light in your eyes of blue.

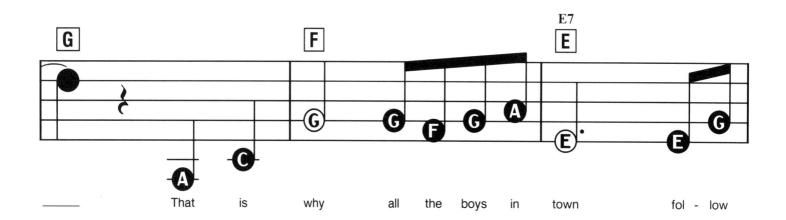

That is why all the boys in town fol - low

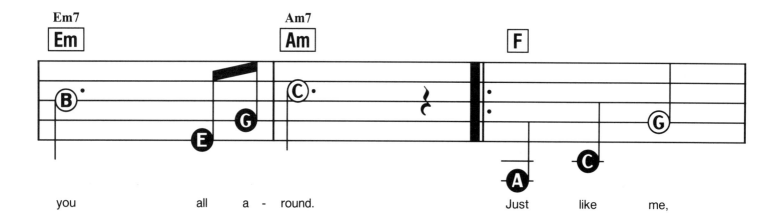

you all a - round. Just like me,

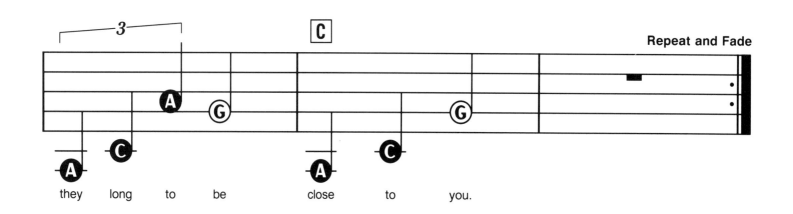

they long to be close to you.

1971
You've Got a Friend

Registration 3
Rhythm: Slow Rock or Ballad

Words and Music by
Carole King

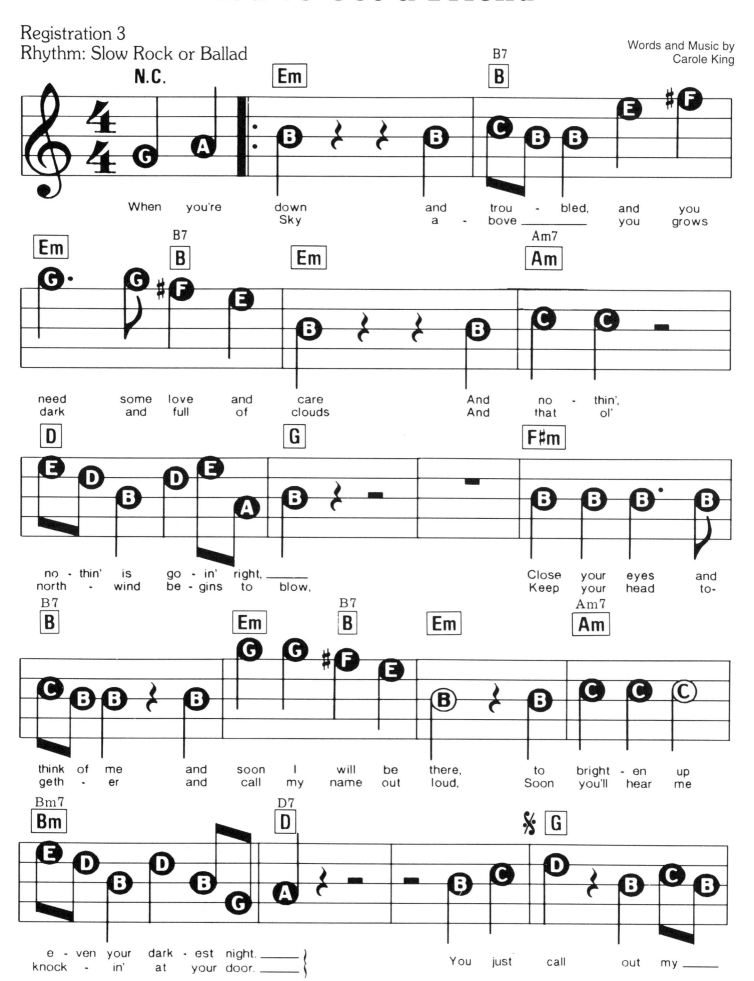

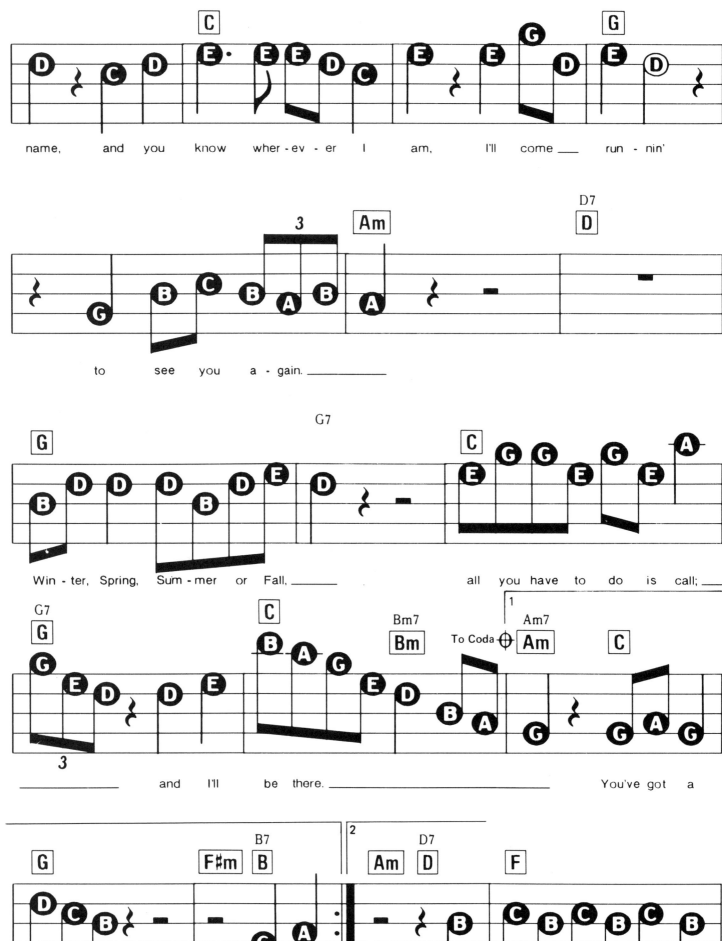

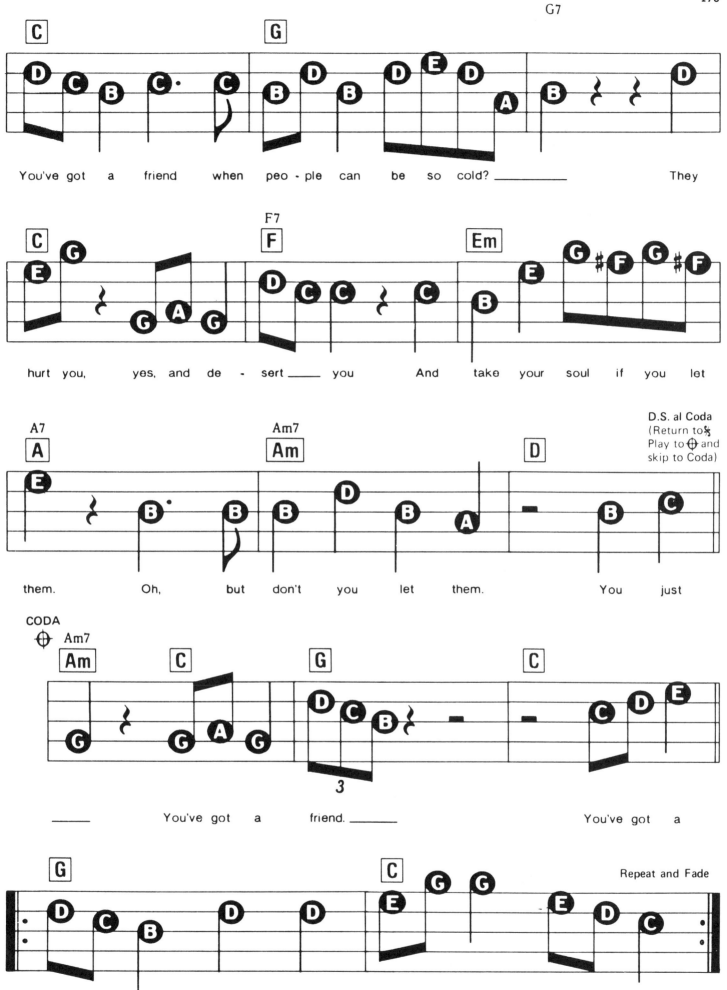

1972
American Pie

Registration 2
Rhythm: Rock

Words and Music by
Don McLean

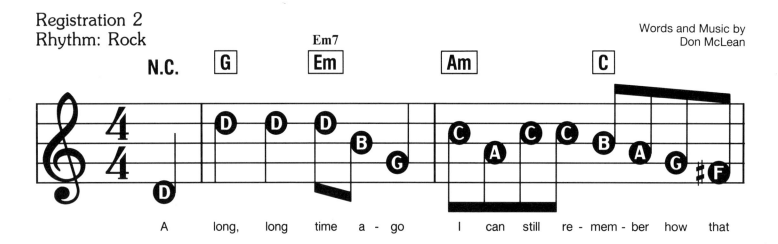

A long, long time a-go I can still re-mem-ber how that

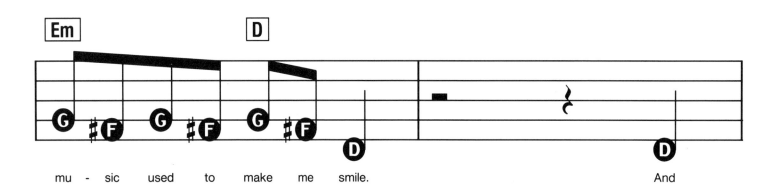

mu - sic used to make me smile. And

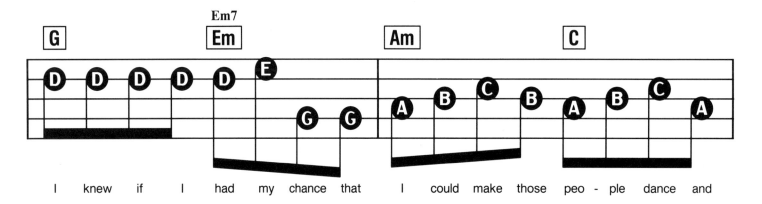

I knew if I had my chance that I could make those peo-ple dance and

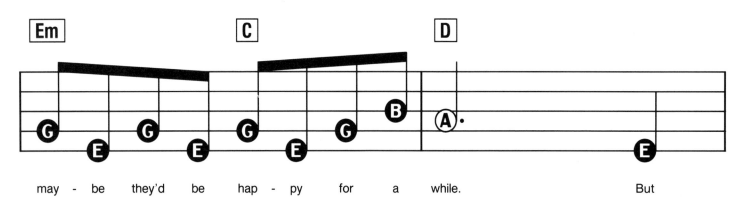

may - be they'd be hap - py for a while. But

MCA Music Publishing

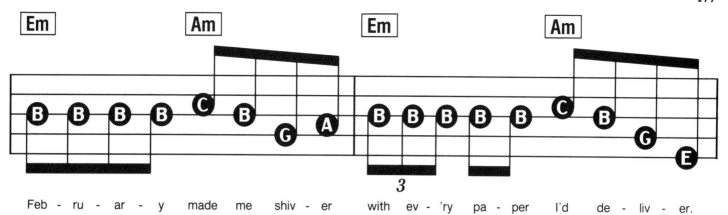

Feb - ru - ar - y made me shiv - er with ev - 'ry pa - per I'd de - liv - er.

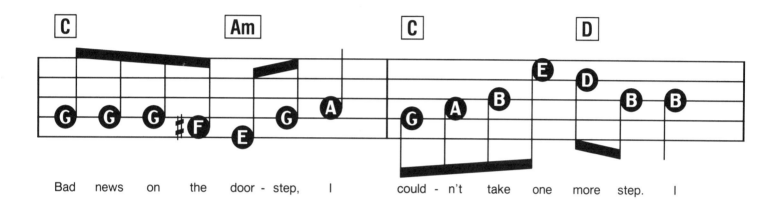

Bad news on the door - step, I could - n't take one more step. I

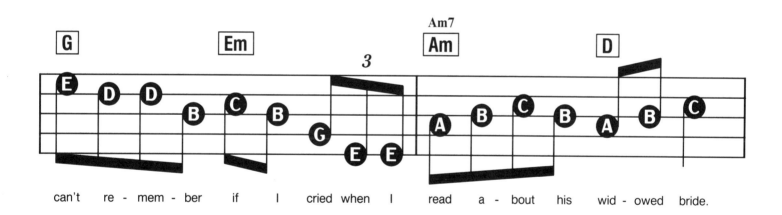

can't re - mem - ber if I cried when I read a - bout his wid - owed bride.

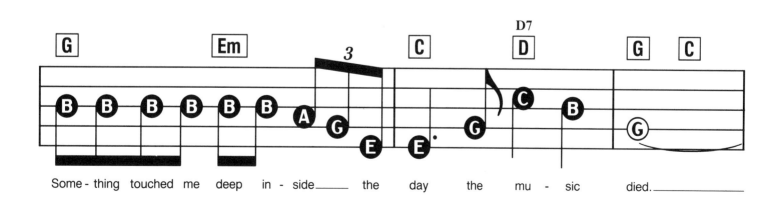

Some - thing touched me deep in - side____ the day the mu - sic died._____

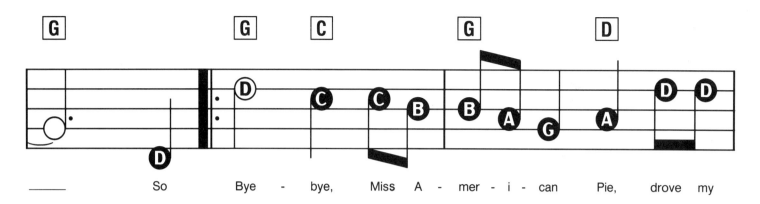

So Bye - bye, Miss A - mer - i - can Pie, drove my

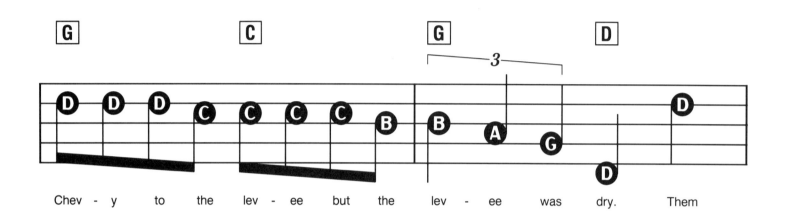

Chev - y to the lev - ee but the lev - ee was dry. Them

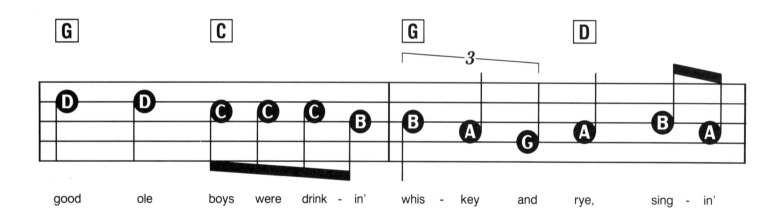

good ole boys were drink - in' whis - key and rye, sing - in'

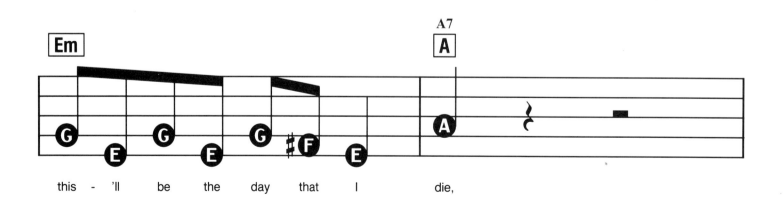

this - 'll be the day that I die,

179

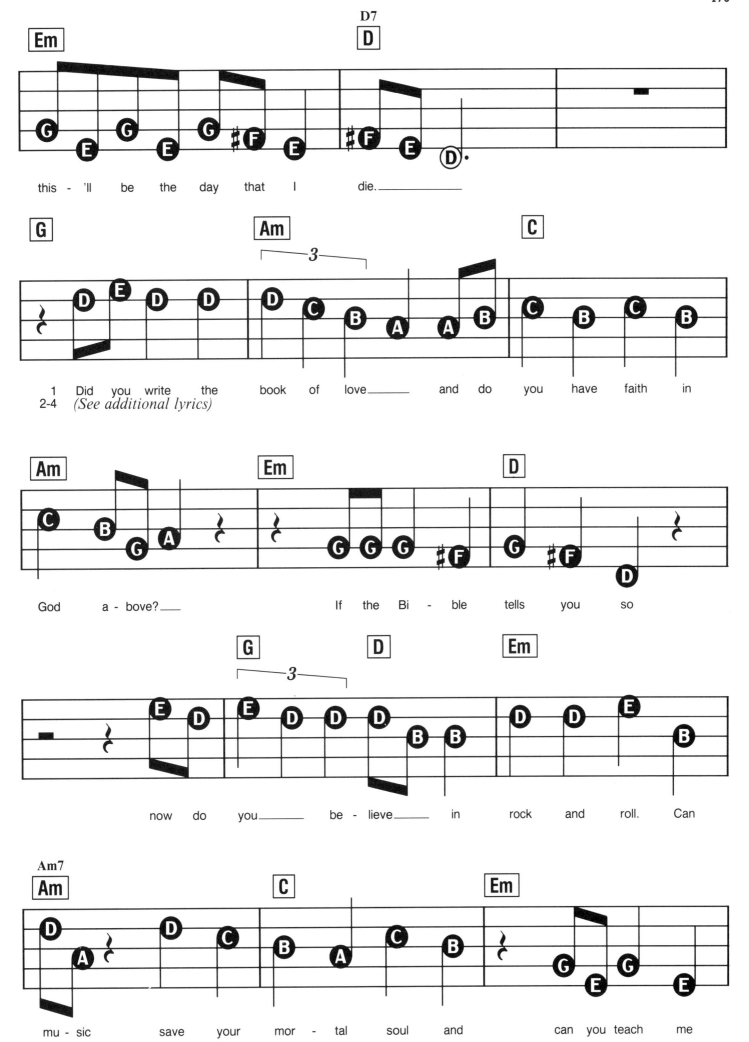

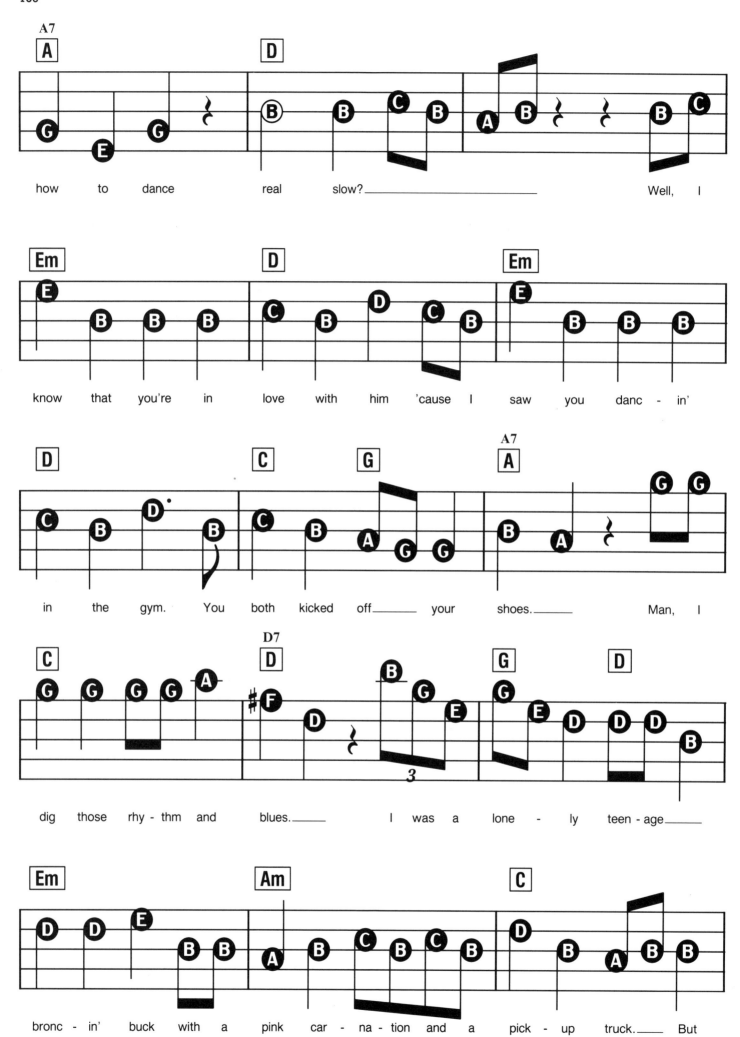

181

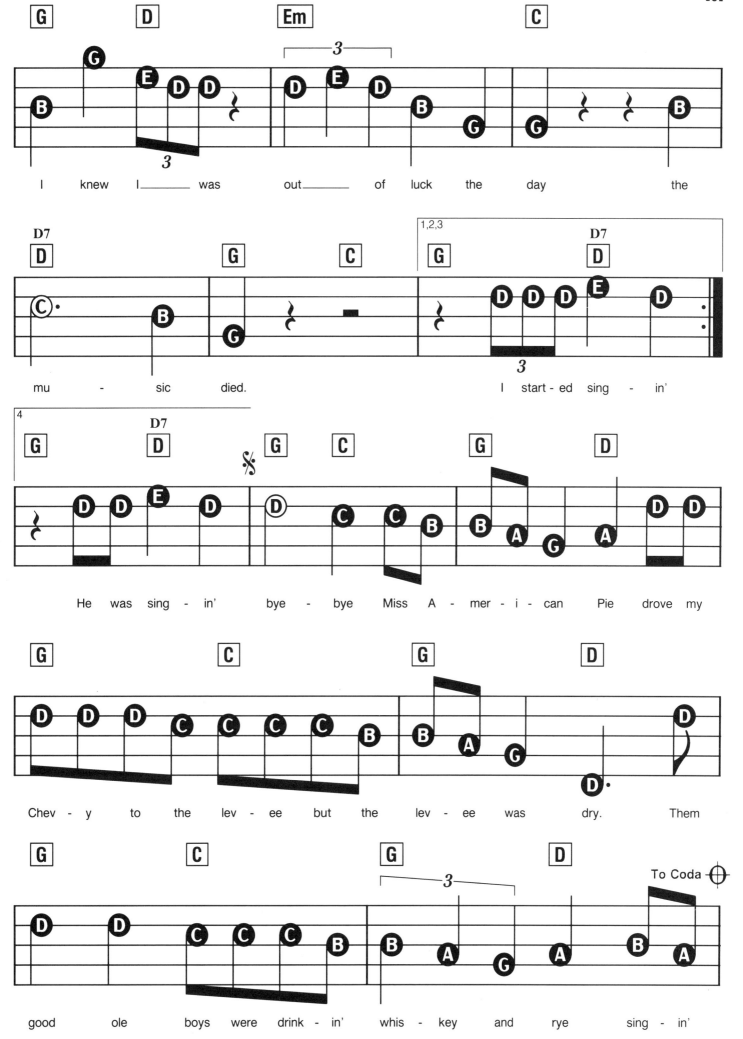

182

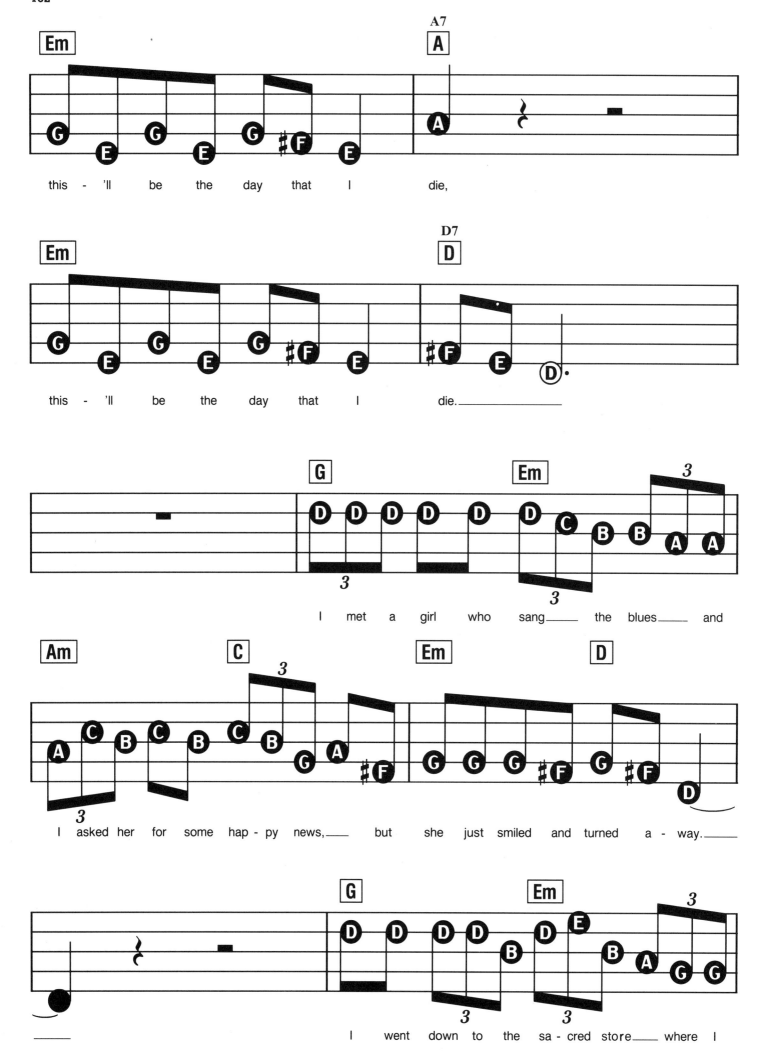

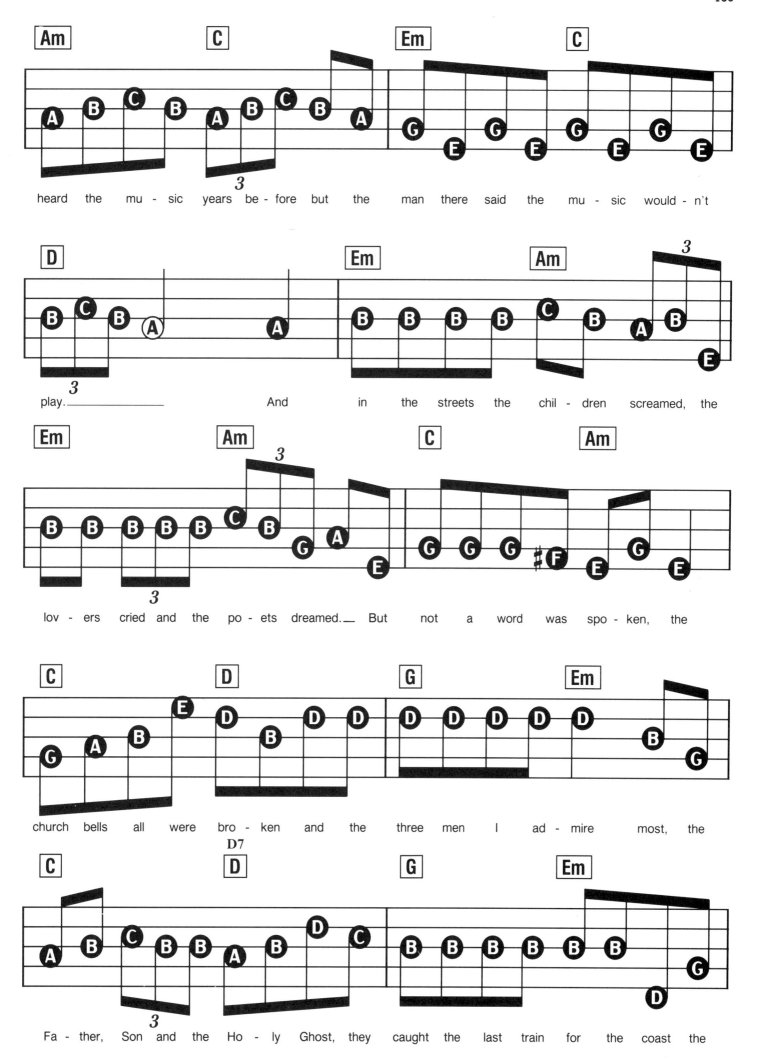

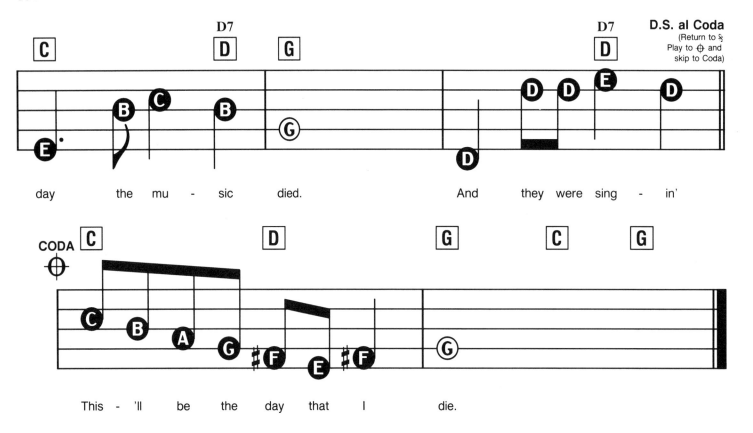

D.S. al Coda
(Return to 𝄋
Play to ⊕ and
skip to Coda)

day   the   mu - sic   died.   And   they   were   sing - in'

CODA

This - 'll   be   the   day   that   I   die.

Additional Lyrics

2. Now for ten years we've been on our own, and moss grows fat on a rollin' stone
   But that's not how it used to be when the jester sang for the king and queen
   In a coat he borrowed from James Dean and a voice that came from you and me
   Oh and while the king was looking down, the jester stole his thorny crown
   The courtroom was adjourned, no verdict was returned
   And while Lenin read a book on Marx the quartet practiced in the park
   And we sang dirges in the dark
   The day the music died
   We were singin'. . . bye-bye. . .,*etc.*

3. Helter-skelter in the summer swelter the birds flew off with a fallout shelter
   Eight miles high and fallin' fast, it landed foul on the grass
   The players tried for a forward pass, with the jester on the sidelines in a cast
   Now the half-time air was sweet perfume while the sergeants played a marching tune
   We all got up to dance but we never got the chance
   'Cause the players tried to take the field, the marching band refused to yield
   Do you recall what was revealed
   The day the music died
   We started singin'. . . bye-bye. . .,*etc.*

4. And there we were all in one place, a generation lost in space
   With no time left to start again
   So come on, Jack be nimble, Jack be quick, Jack Flash sat on a candlestick
   'Cause fire is the devil's only friend
   And as I watched him on the stage my hands were clenched in fists of rage
   No angel born in hell could break that Satan's spell
   And as the flames climbed high into the night to light the sacrificial rite
   I saw Satan laughing with delight the day the music died.
   He was singin'. . . bye-bye. . .,*etc.*

1973
You Are the Sunshine of My Life

Registration 7
Rhythm: 8 Beat or Bossa Nova

Words and Music by
Stevie Wonder

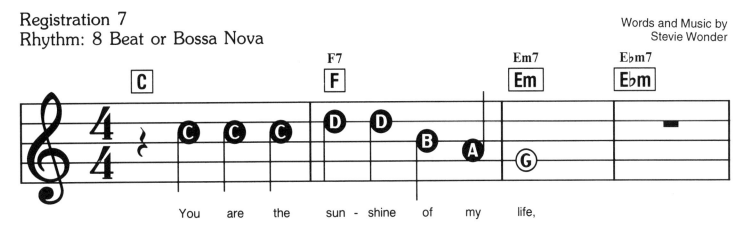

You are the sun - shine of my life,

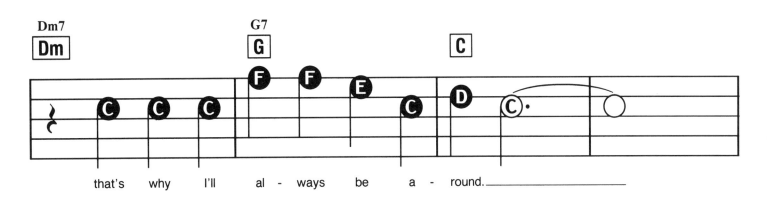

that's why I'll al - ways be a - round.

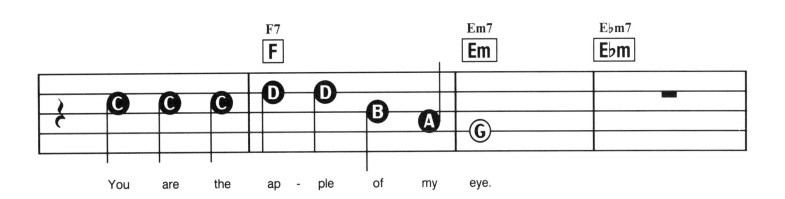

You are the ap - ple of my eye.

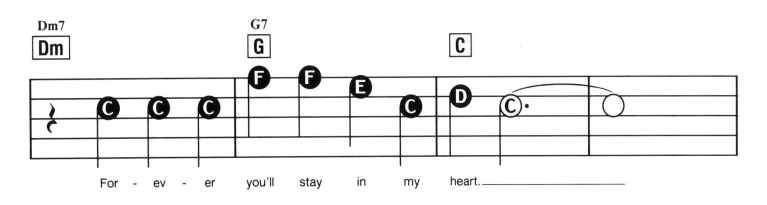

For - ev - er you'll stay in my heart.

186

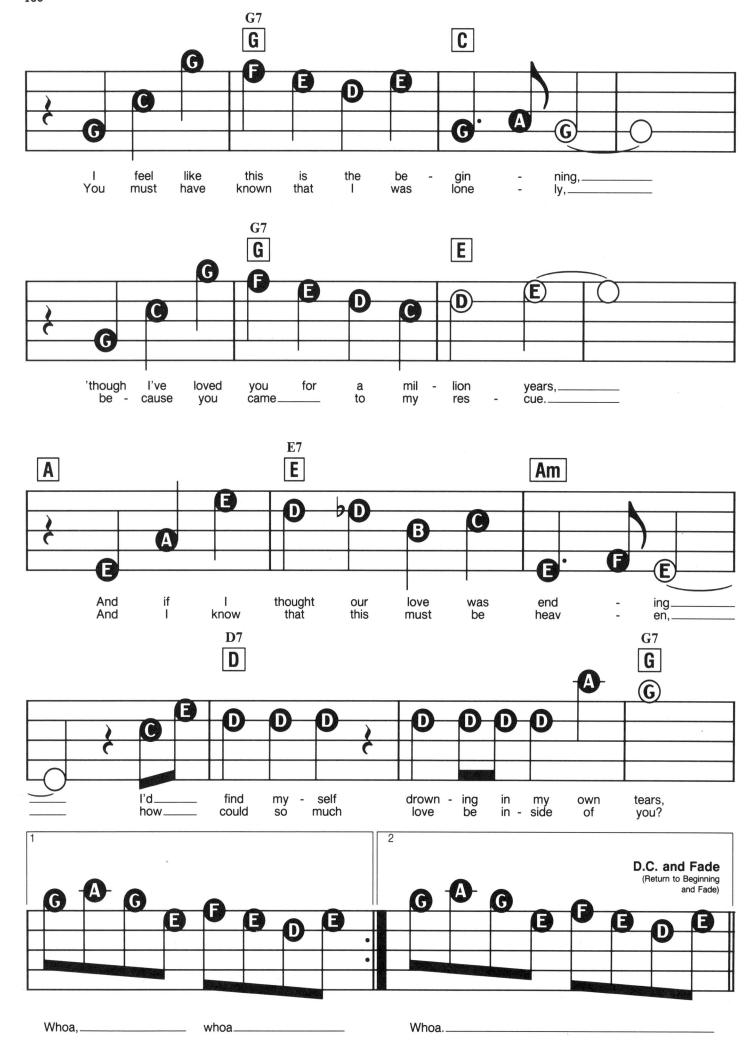

1974
The Way We Were
from the Motion Picture THE WAY WE WERE

Words by Alan and Marilyn Bergman
Music by Marvin Hamlisch

Registration 8
Rhythm: Slow Rock or Ballad

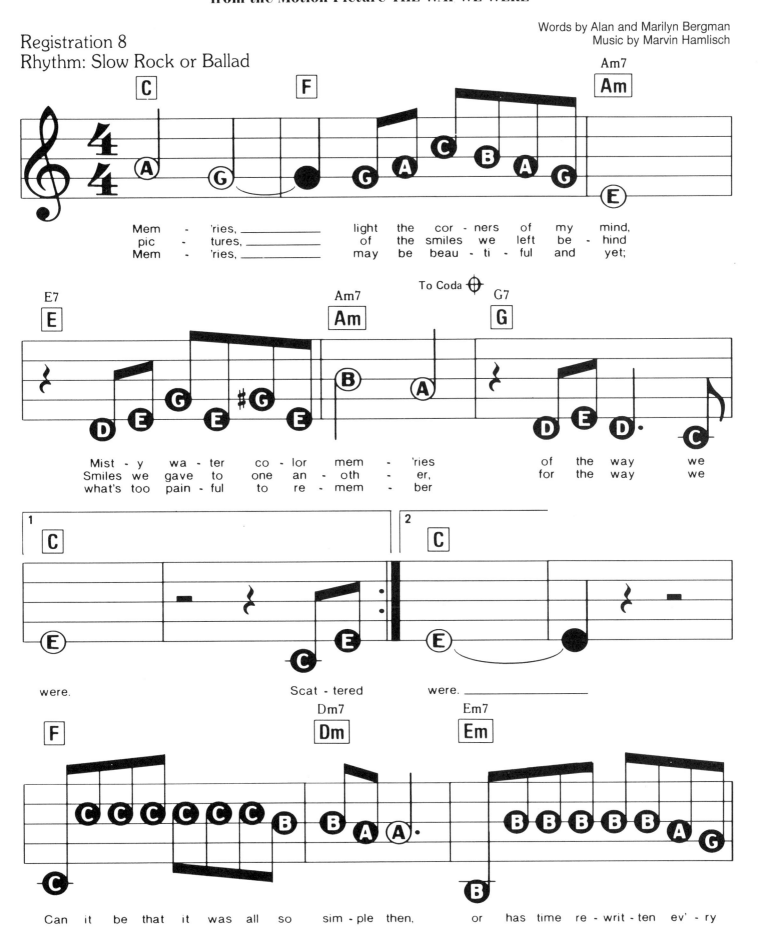

188

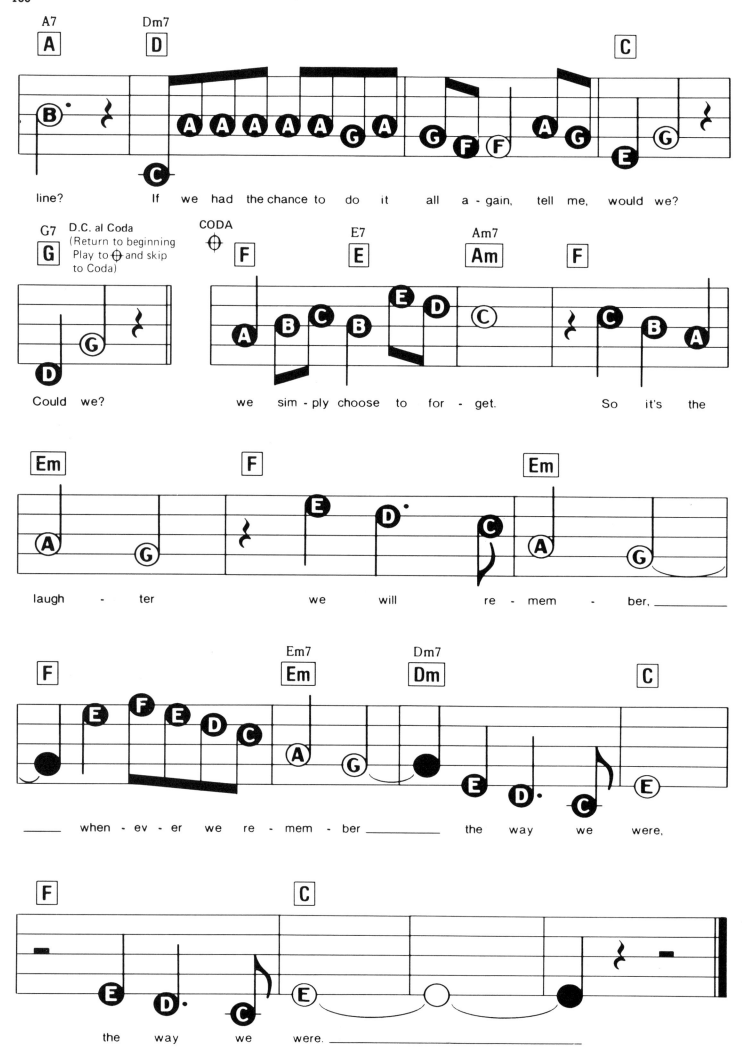

1975
Jive Talkin'
from SATURDAY NIGHT FEVER

Registration 4
Rhythm: Rock or Disco

Words and Music by Barry Gibb,
Maurice Gibb and Robin Gibb

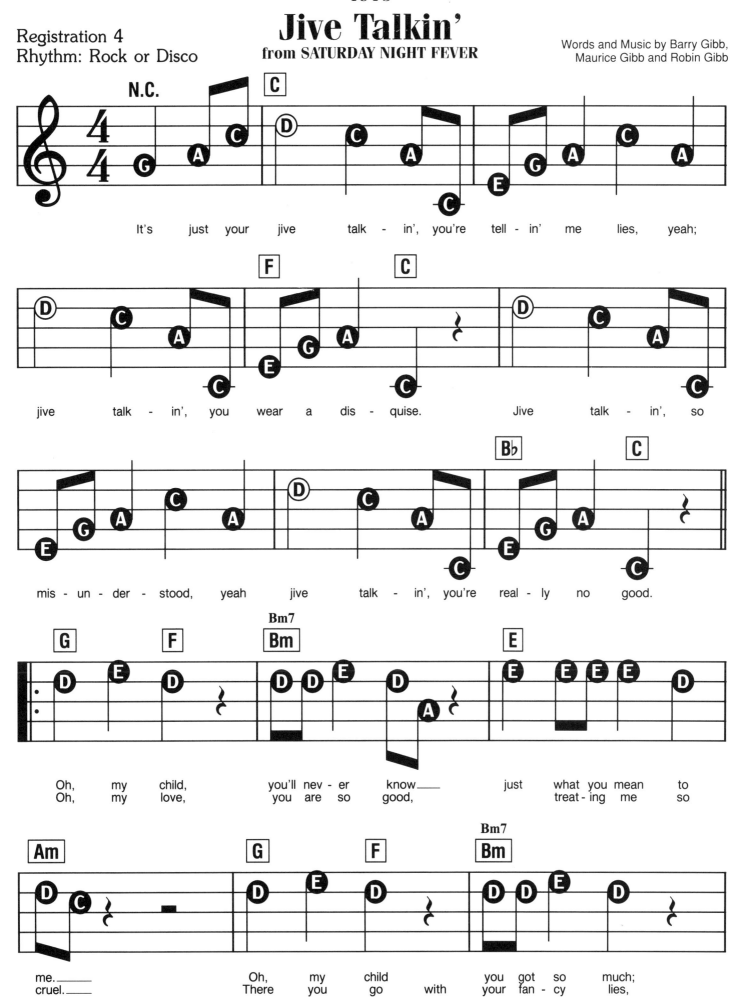

1976
I Write the Songs

Registration 7
Rhythm: Rock or 8 Beat

Words and Music by
Bruce Johnston

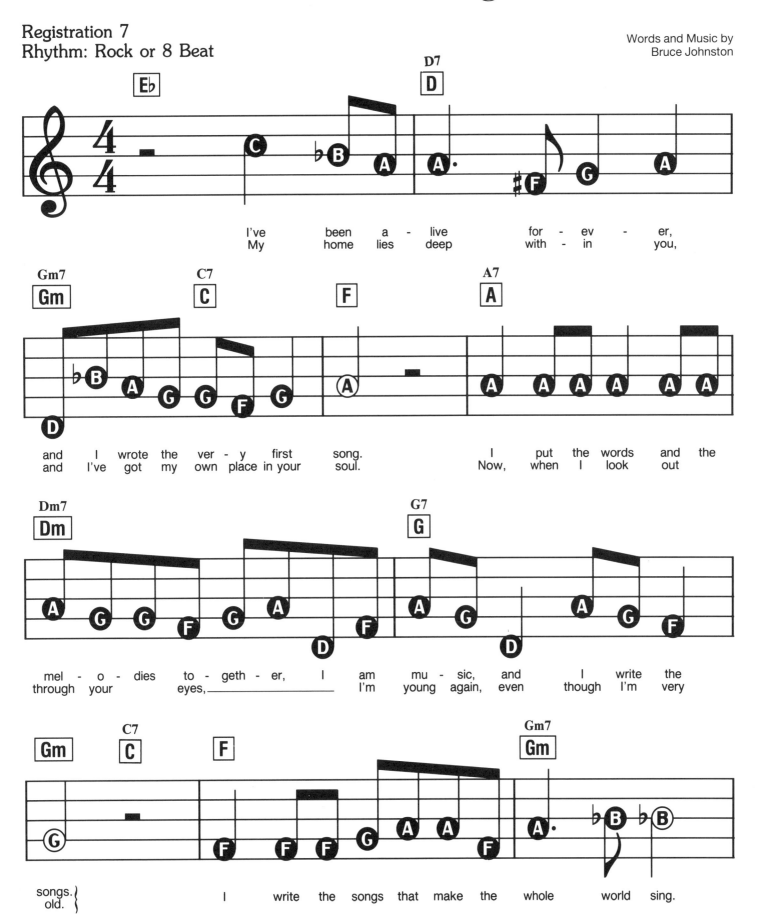

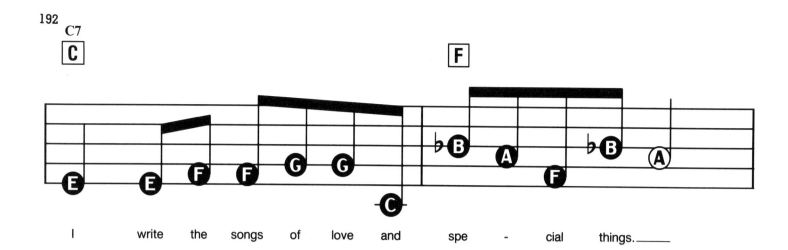

I write the songs of love and spe - cial things.____

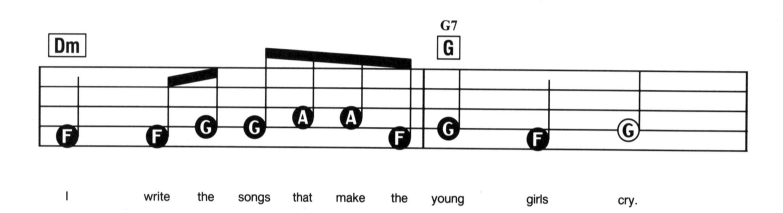

I write the songs that make the young girls cry.

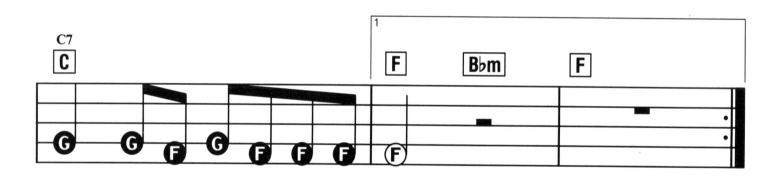

I write the songs, I write the songs.

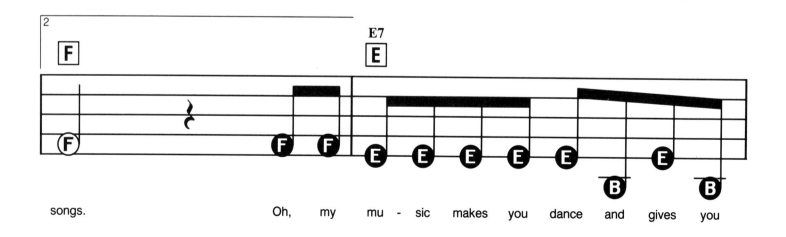

songs. Oh, my mu - sic makes you dance and gives you

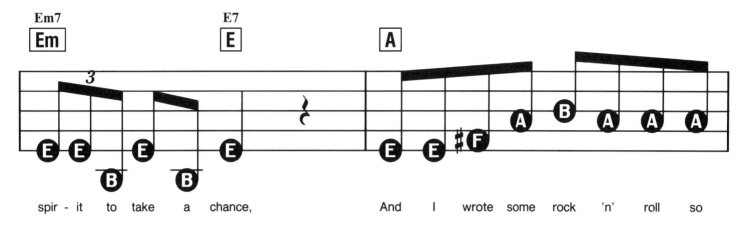

spir - it   to   take   a   chance,   And   I   wrote   some   rock   'n'   roll   so

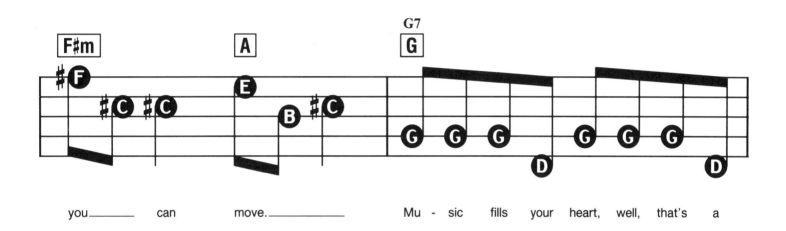

you_____   can   move._____   Mu - sic   fills   your   heart,   well,   that's   a

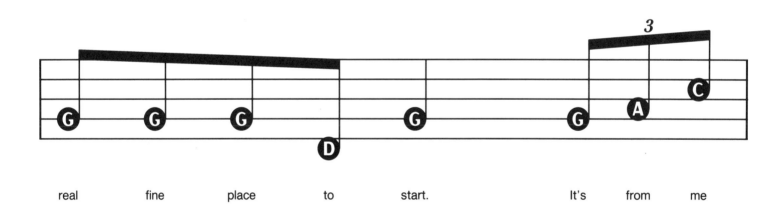

real   fine   place   to   start.   It's   from   me

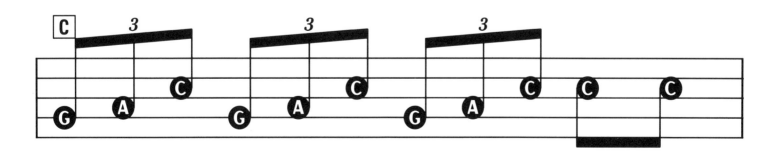

it's   for   you,   it's   from   you,   it's   for   me,   it's   a

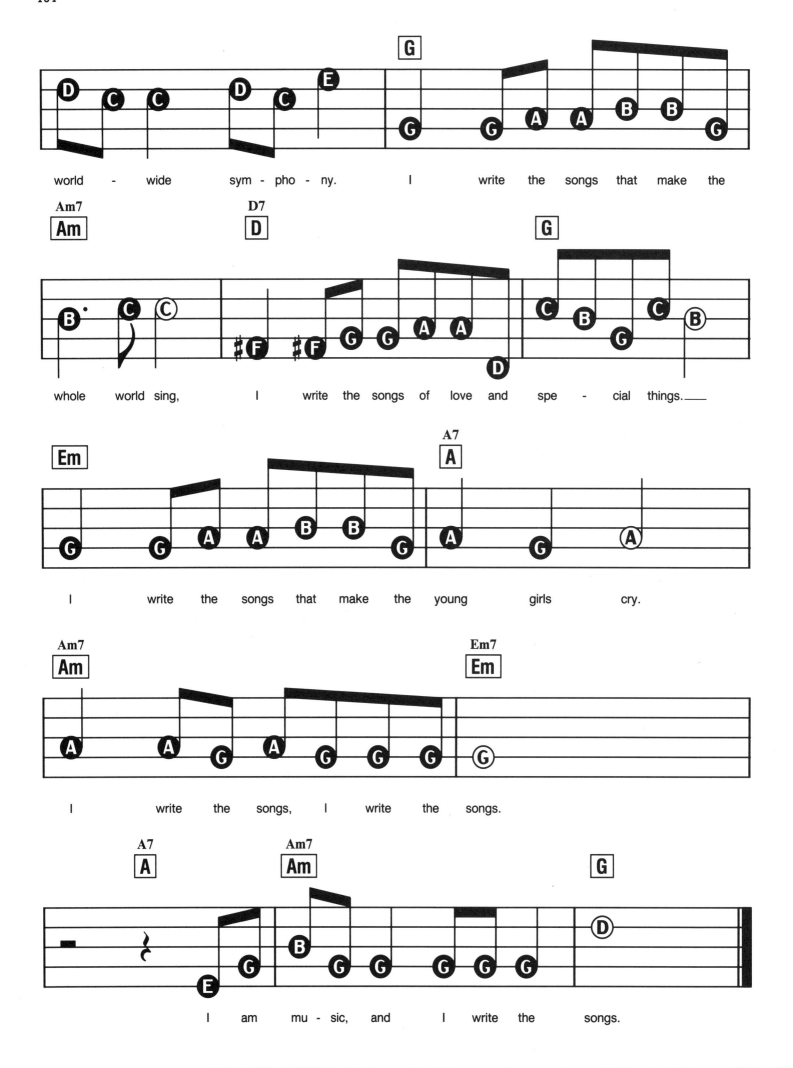

1977

You Light Up My Life

Registration 7
Rhythm: Waltz

Words and Music by
Joseph Brooks

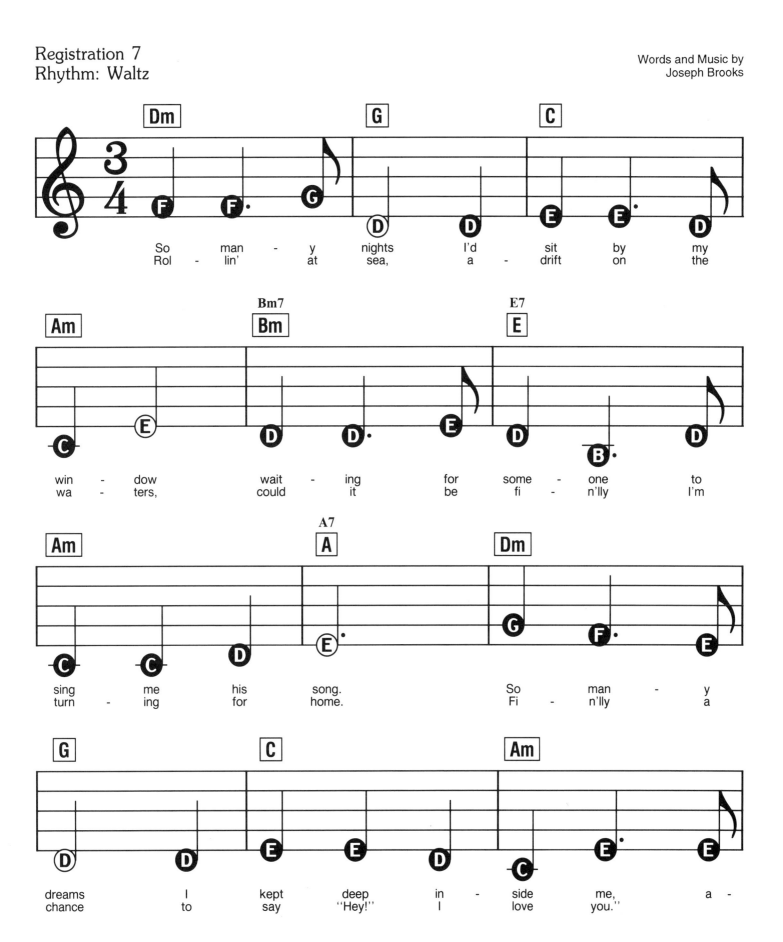

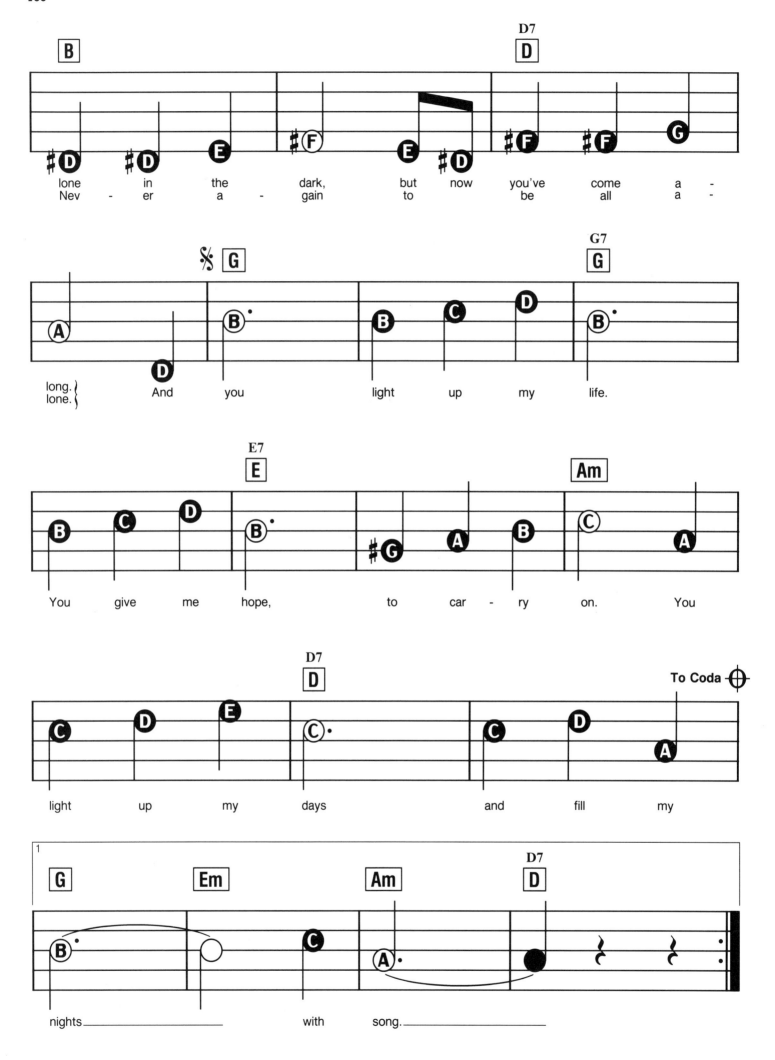

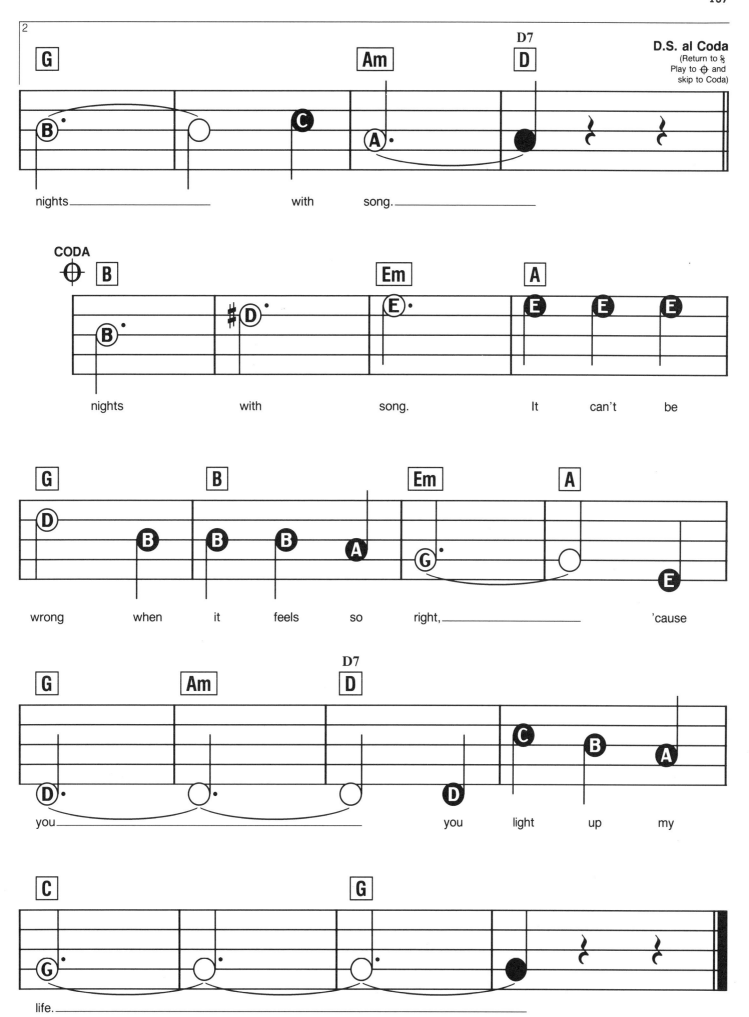

1978
Just the Way You Are

Registration 4
Rhythm: Rock or Jazz Rock

Words and Music by
Billy Joel

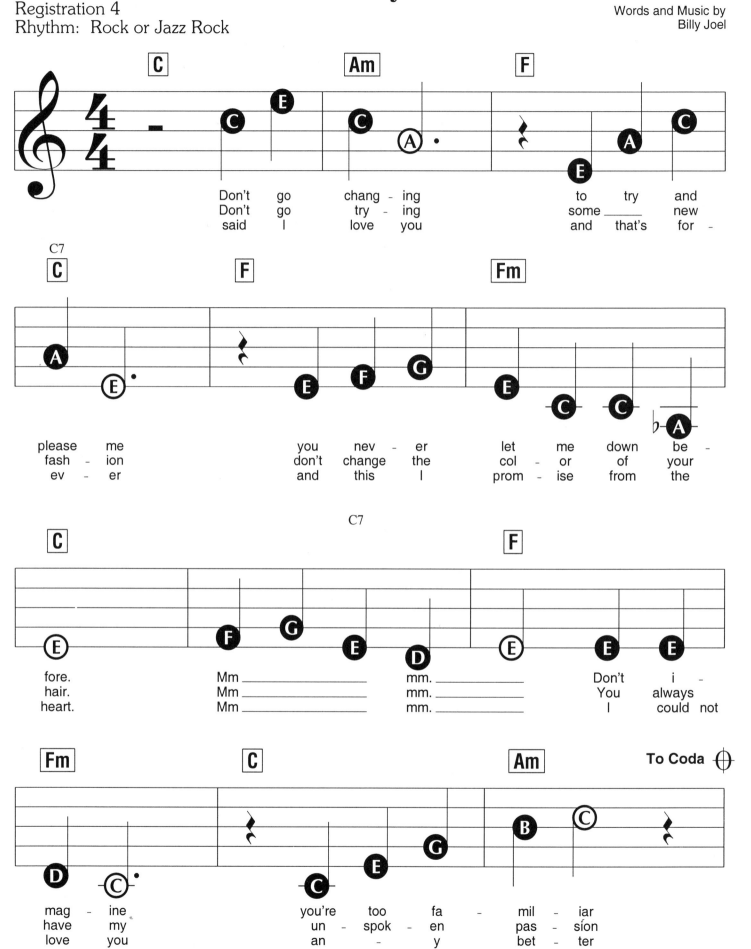

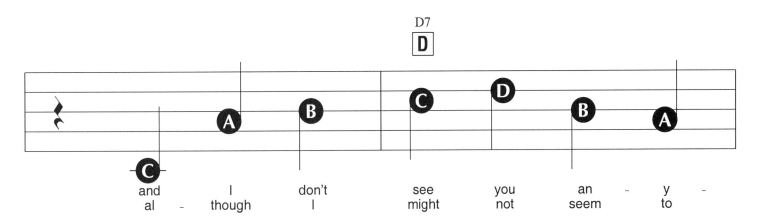

and   I   don't   see   you   an   -   y   -
al - though   I   might   not   seem   to

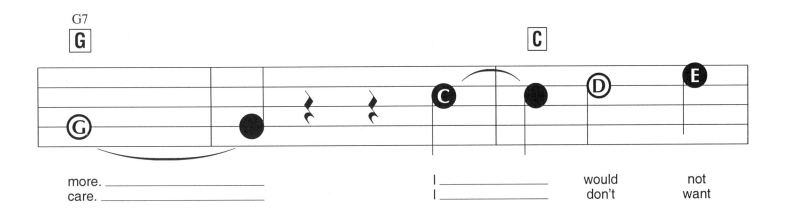

more. _____   I _____ would   not
care. _____   I _____ don't   want

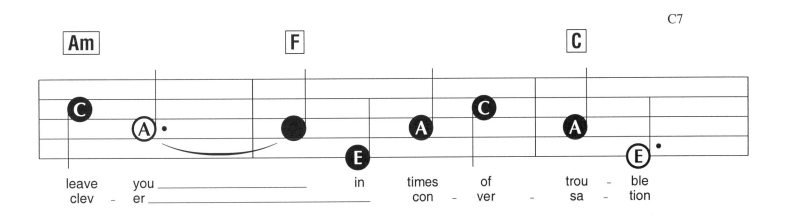

leave   you _____ in   times   of   trou - ble
clev - er _____ con - ver - sa - tion

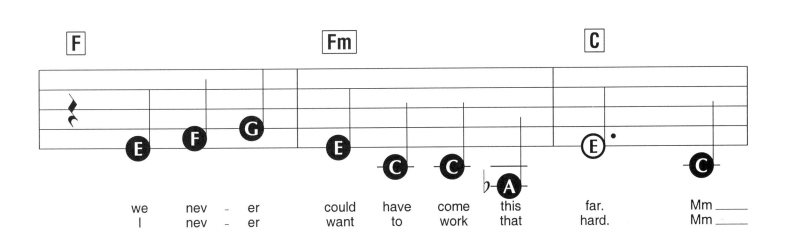

we   nev - er   could   have   come   this   far.   Mm _____
I   nev - er   want   to   work   that   hard.   Mm _____

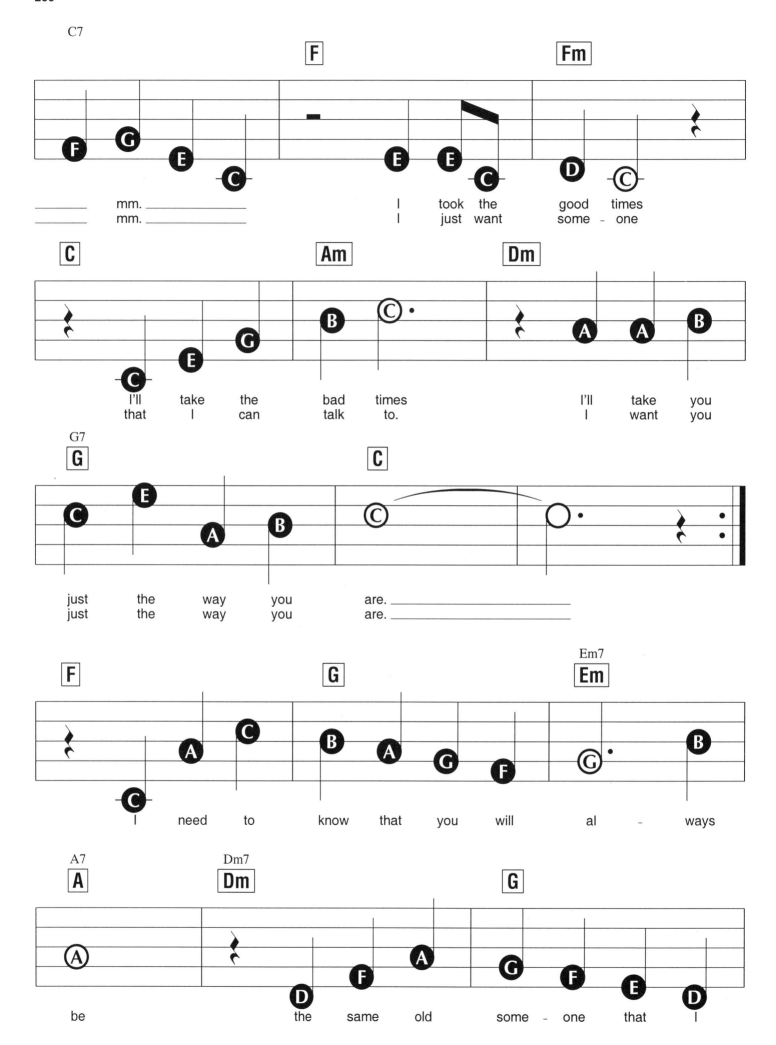

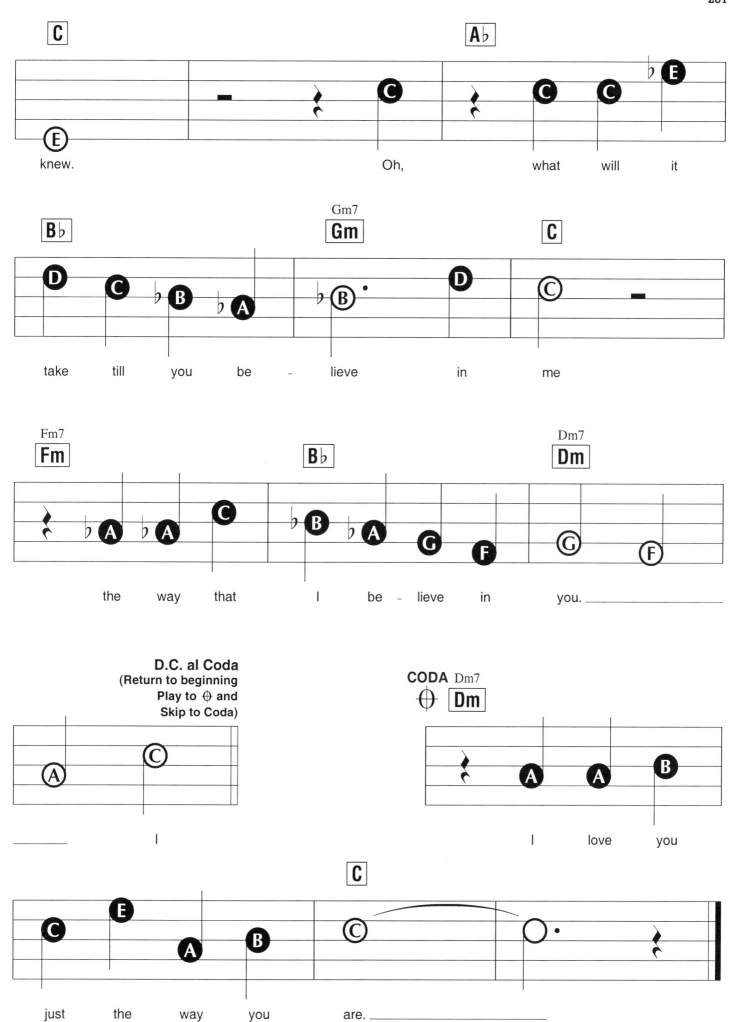

1979
I Will Survive

Registration 5
Rhythm: Rock or Disco

Words and Music by Dino Fekaris
and Freddie Perren

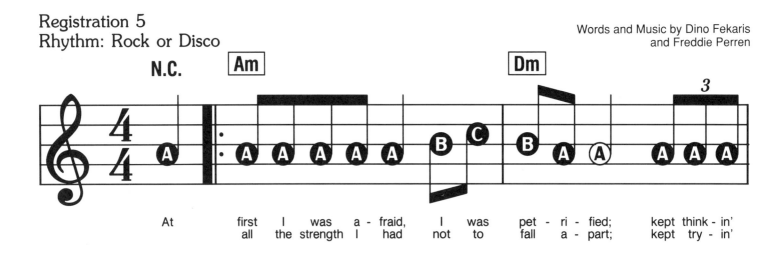

At first I was a-fraid, I was pet-ri-fied; kept think-in'
all the strength I had not to fall a-part; kept try-in'

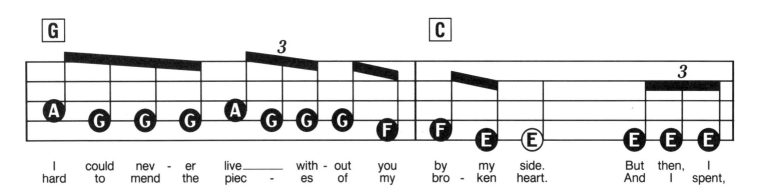

I could nev-er live_____ with-out you by my side. But then, I
hard to mend the piec-es of my bro-ken heart. And I spent,

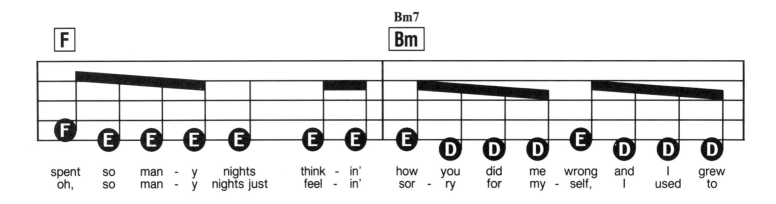

spent so man-y nights think-in' how you did me wrong and I grew
oh, so man-y nights just feel-in' sor-ry for my-self, I used to

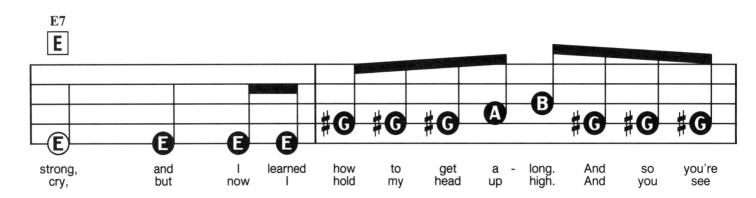

strong, and I learned how to get a-long. And so you're
cry, but now I hold my head up high. And you see

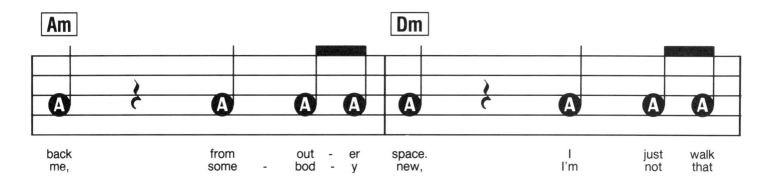
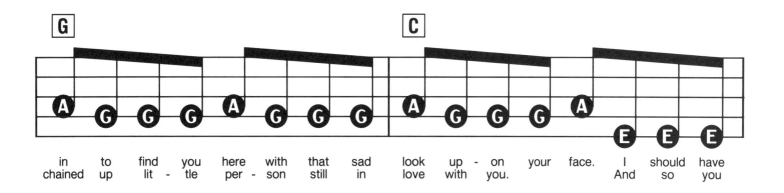
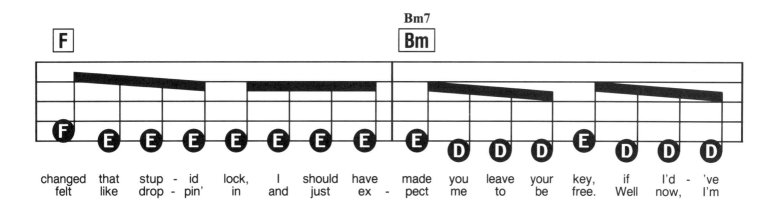
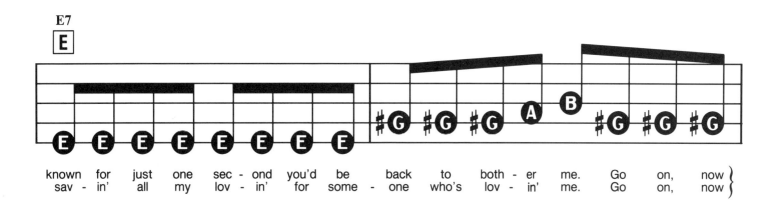

204

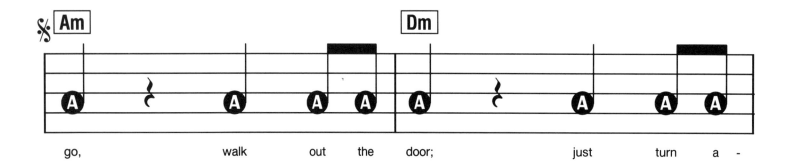

go, walk out the door; just turn a -

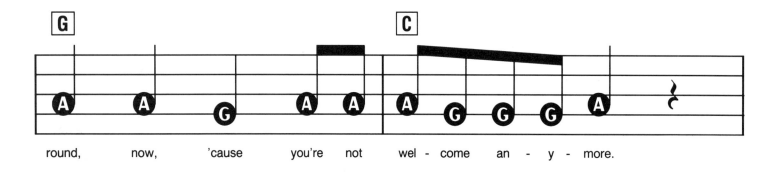

round, now, 'cause you're not wel - come an - y - more.

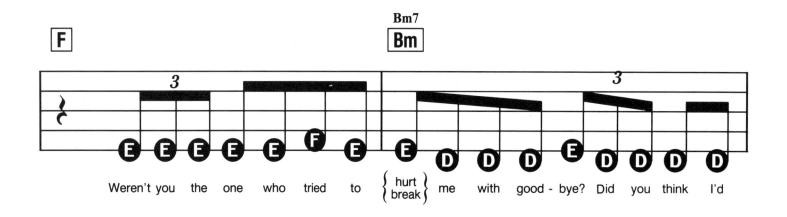

Weren't you the one who tried to {hurt break} me with good - bye? Did you think I'd

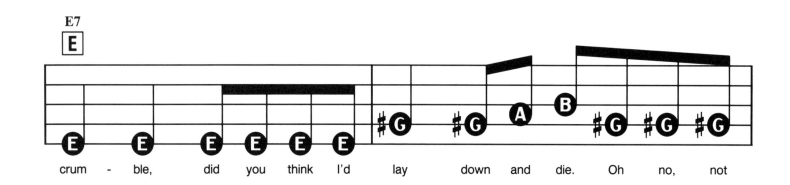

crum - ble, did you think I'd lay down and die. Oh no, not

205

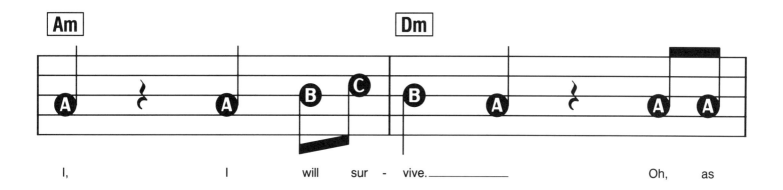

I, I will sur - vive._____ Oh, as

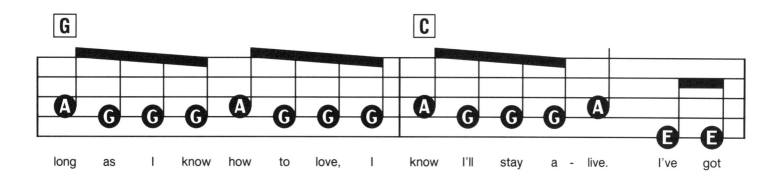

long as I know how to love, I know I'll stay a - live. I've got

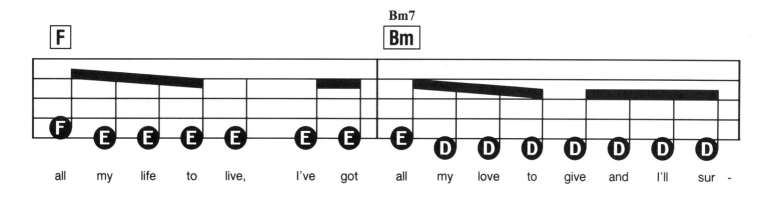

all my life to live, I've got all my love to give and I'll sur -

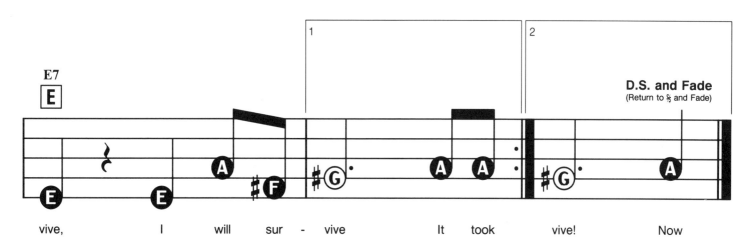

vive, I will sur - vive It took vive! Now

1980
Another One Bites the Dust

Registration 8
Rhythm: Rock

Words and Music by
John Deacon

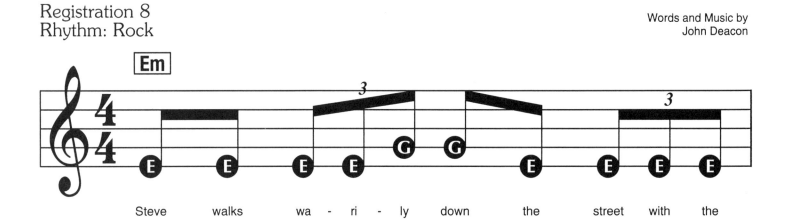

Steve walks wa - ri - ly down the street with the

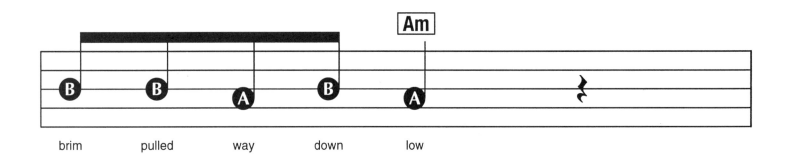

brim pulled way down low

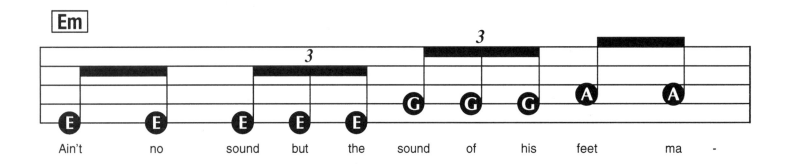

Ain't no sound but the sound of his feet ma -

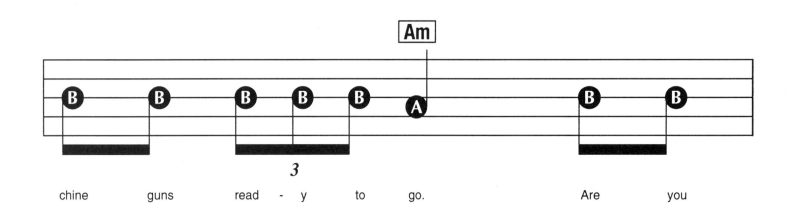

chine guns read - y to go. Are you

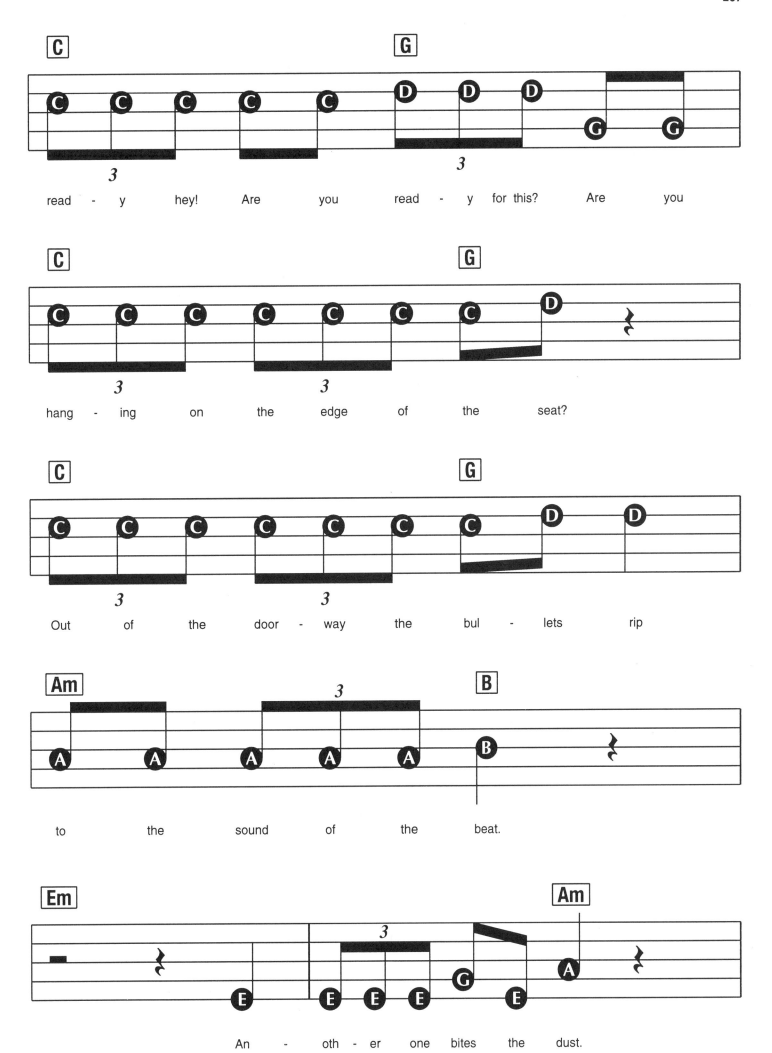

208

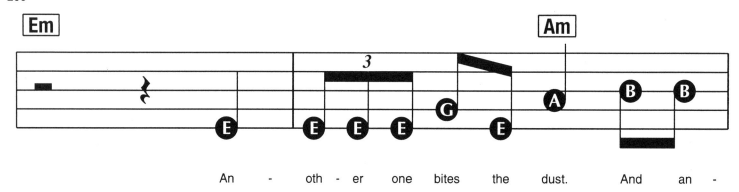

An - oth - er one bites the dust. And an -

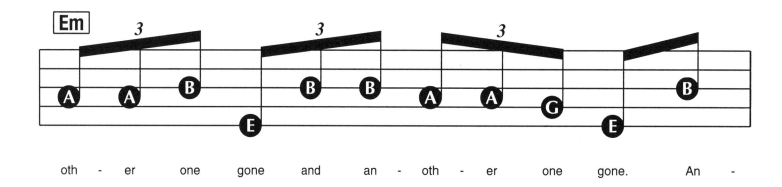

oth - er one gone and an - oth - er one gone. An -

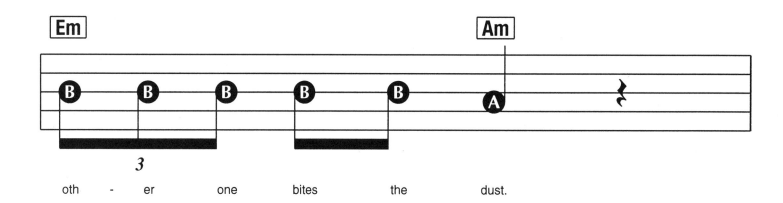

oth - er one bites the dust.

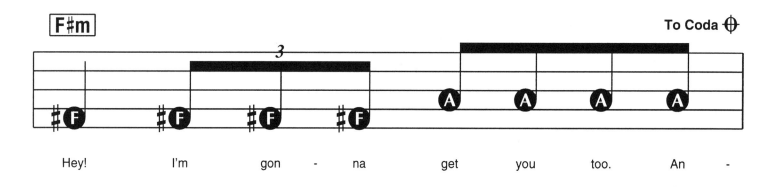

Hey! I'm gon - na get you too. An -

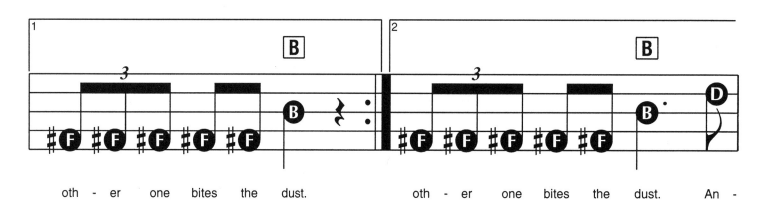

oth - er one bites the dust. oth - er one bites the dust. An -

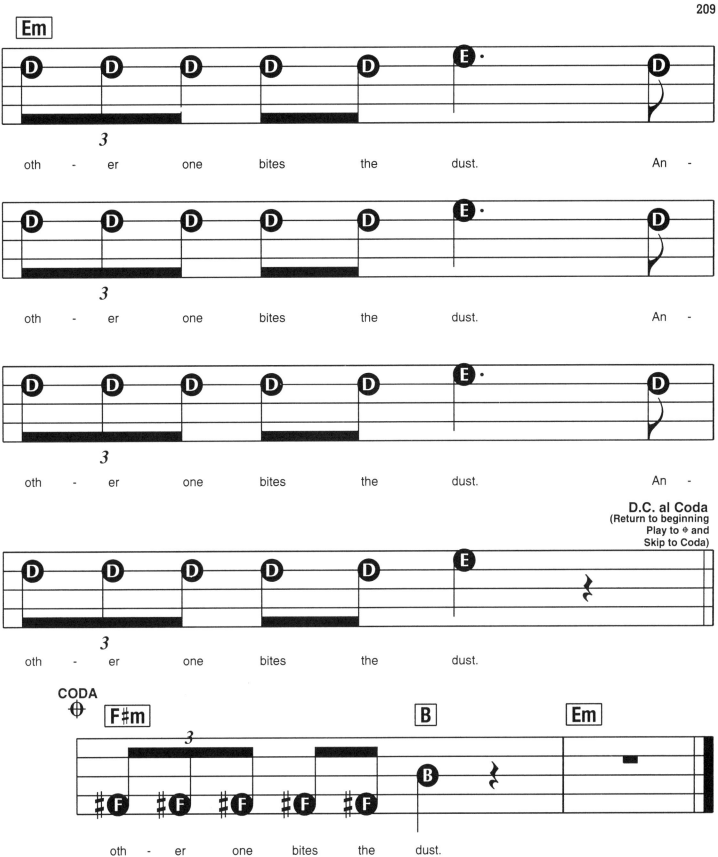

Additional Lyrics

2. How do you think I'm going to get along
   Without you when you're gone?
   You took me for everything that I had
   And kicked me out on my own

   Are you happy are you satisfied?
   How long can you stand the heat?
   Out of the doorway the bullets rip
   To the sound of the beat

3. There are plenty of ways you can hurt a man
   And bring him to the ground
   You can beat him
   You can cheat him
   You can treat him bad and leave him
   When he's down
   But I'm ready yes I'm ready for you
   I'm standing on my own two feet
   Out of the doorway the bullets rip
   Repeating to the sound of the beat
   Another one bites the dust

1981
Endless Love
from ENDLESS LOVE

Registration 1
Rhythm: Rock or 8 Beat

Words and Music by
Lionel Richie

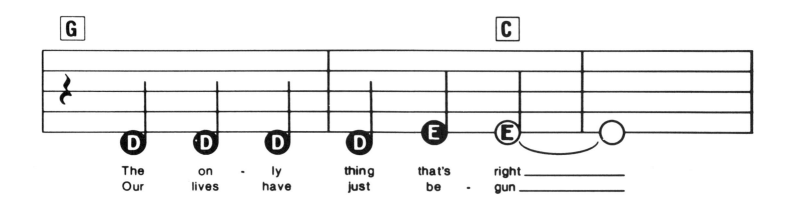

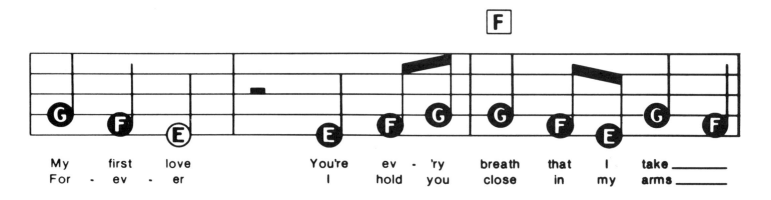

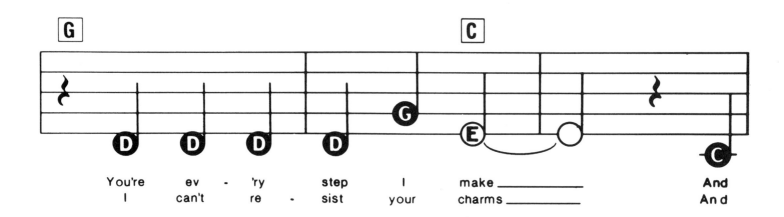

211

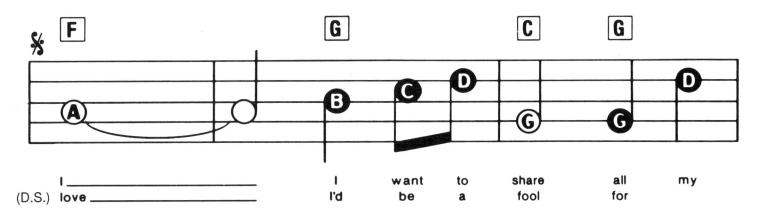

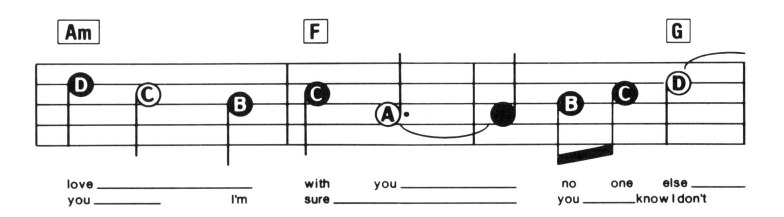

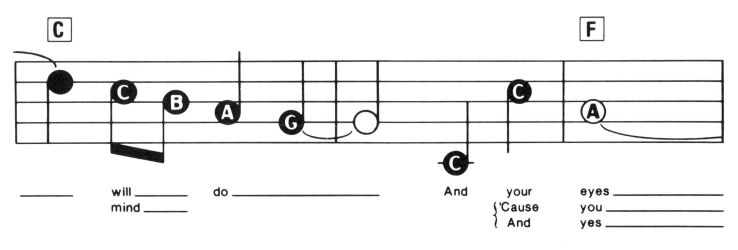

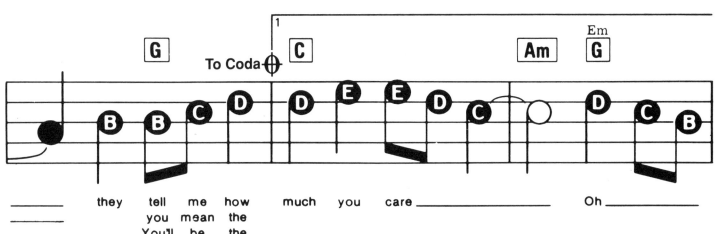

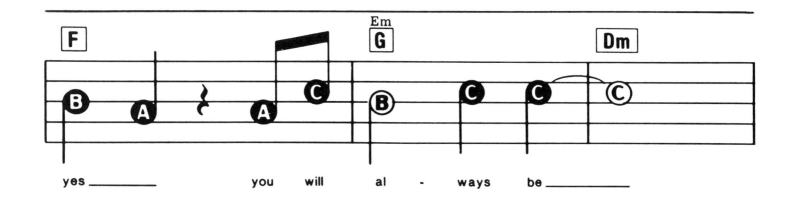

yes _____ you will al - ways be _____

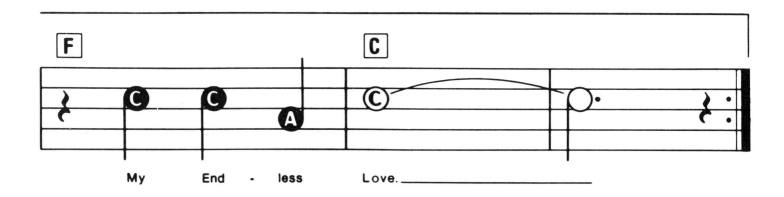

My End - less Love. _____

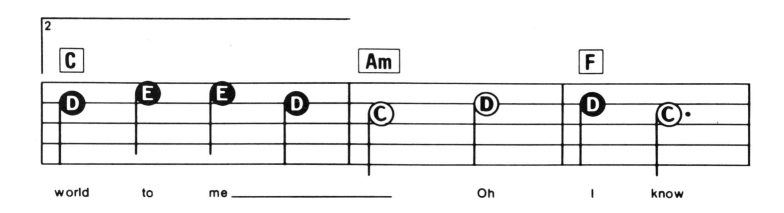

world to me _____ Oh I know

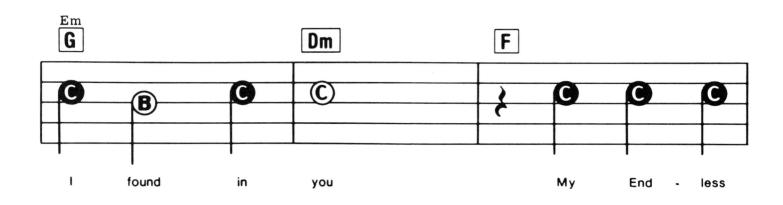

I found in you My End - less

D.S. al Coda
(Return to %
Play to ⊕ and
Skip to Coda)

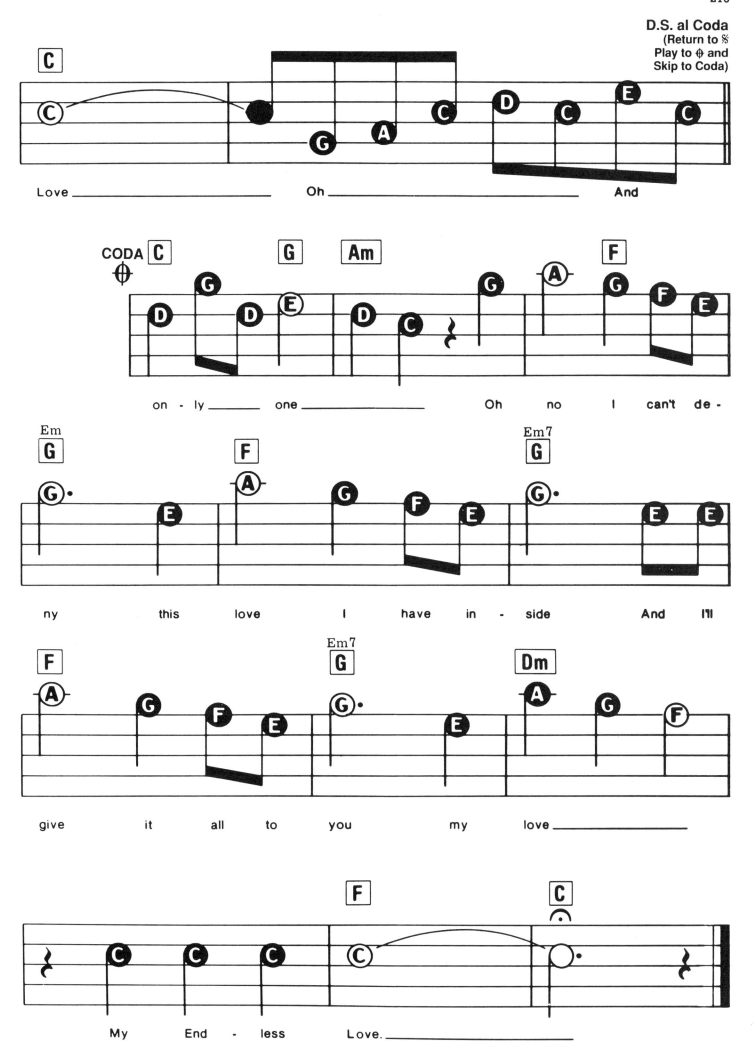

1982
Up Where We Belong
from the Paramount Picture AN OFFICER AND A GENTLEMAN

Registration 10
Rhythm: Rock

Words by Will Jennings
Music by Buffy Sainte-Marie and Jack Nitzsche

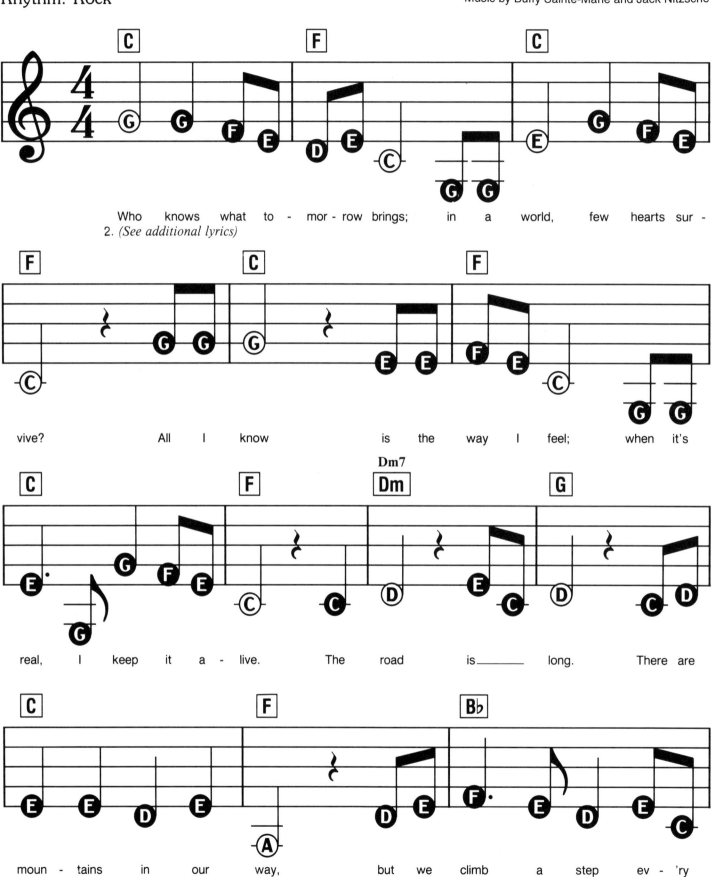

Who knows what to - mor - row brings; in a world, few hearts sur -
2. *(See additional lyrics)*

vive? All I know is the way I feel; when it's

real, I keep it a - live. The road is_____ long. There are

moun - tains in our way, but we climb a step ev - 'ry

215

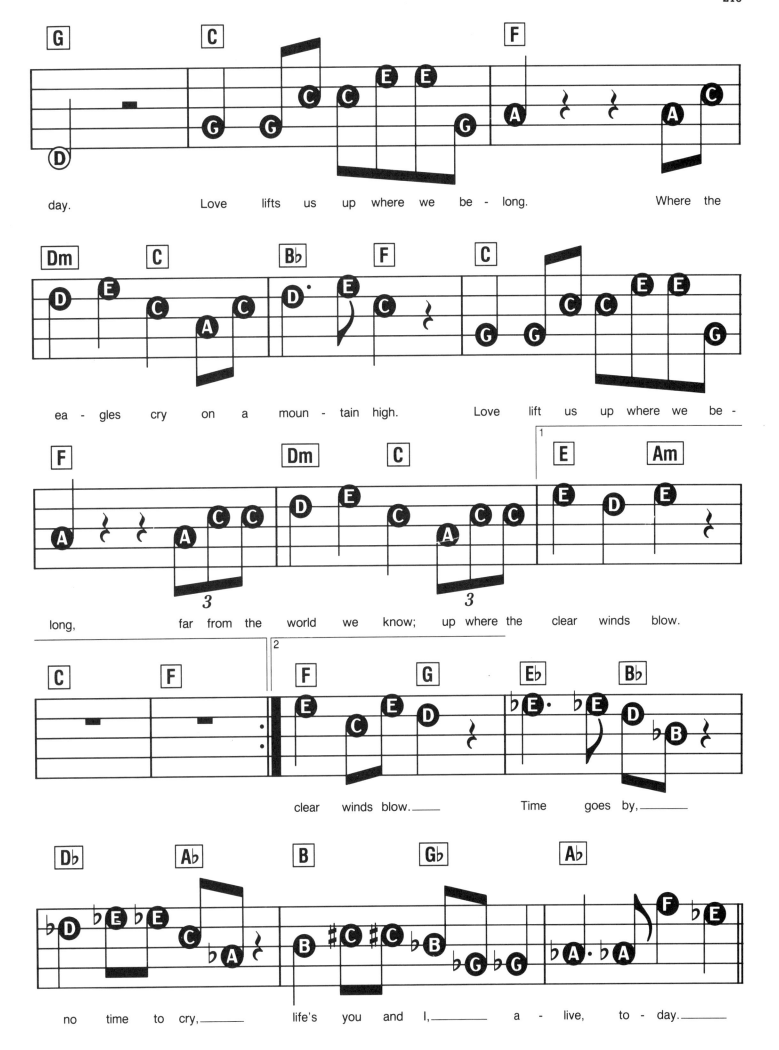

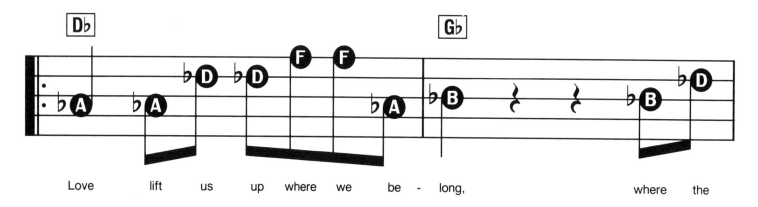

Love lift us up where we be - long, where the

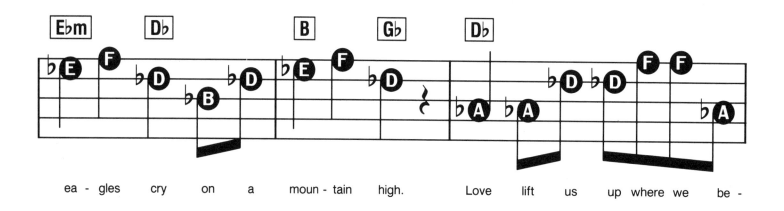

ea - gles cry on a moun - tain high. Love lift us up where we be -

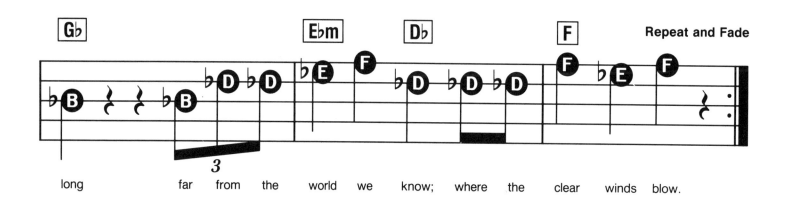

long far from the world we know; where the clear winds blow.

Additional Lyrics

2. Some hang on to "used to be,"
Live their lives looking behind.
All we have is here and now;
All our life, out there to find.
The road is long.
There are mountains in our way,
But we climb them a step every day.

1983
Every Breath You Take

Registration 1
Rhythm: Rock or 8 Beat

Written and Composed by
Sting

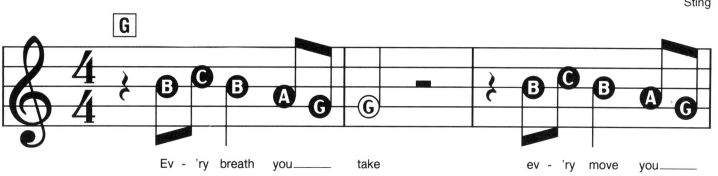

Ev - 'ry breath you_____ take   ev - 'ry move you_____

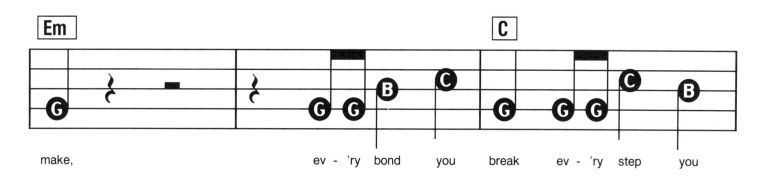

make,   ev - 'ry bond you break   ev - 'ry step you

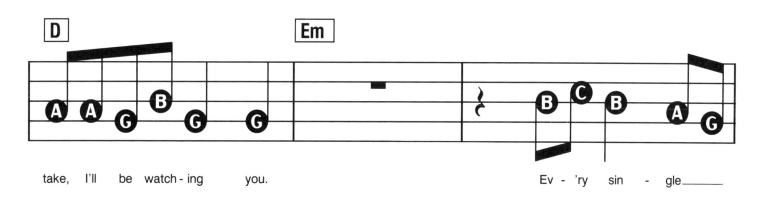

take, I'll be watch - ing   you.   Ev - 'ry sin - gle_____

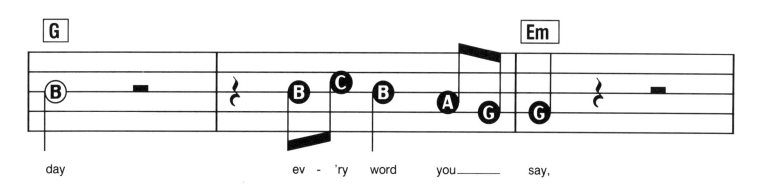

day   ev - 'ry word you_____ say,

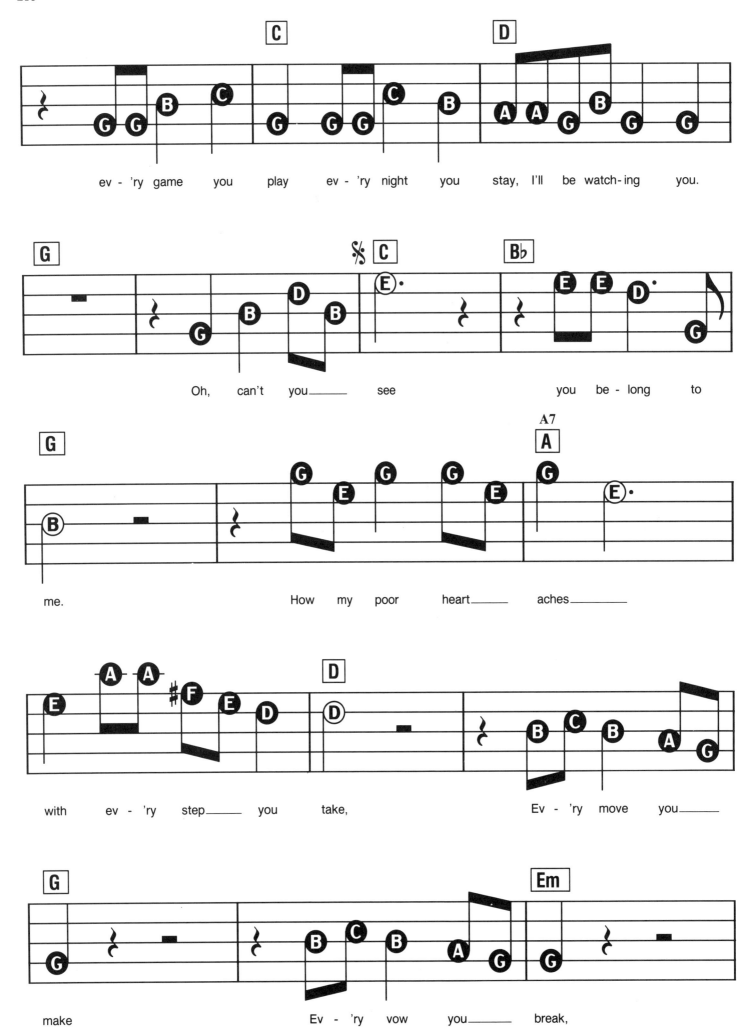

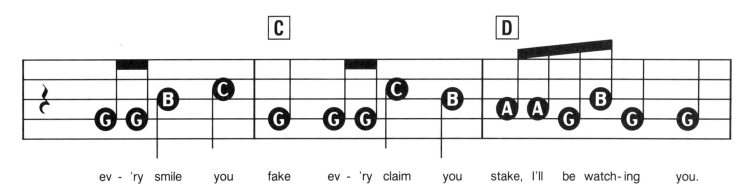

ev - 'ry smile you fake ev - 'ry claim you stake, I'll be watch- ing you.

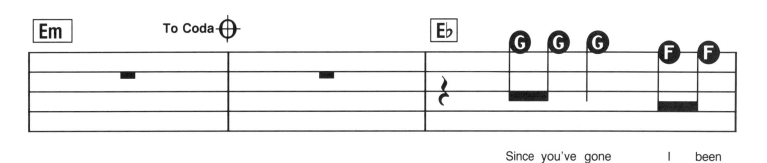

Since you've gone I been

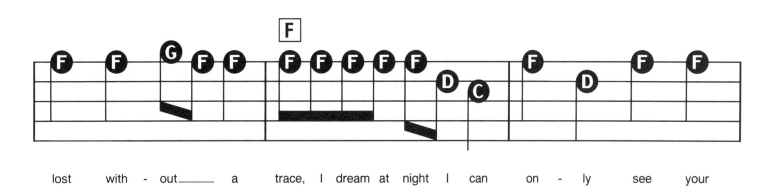

lost with - out_____ a trace, I dream at night I can on - ly see your

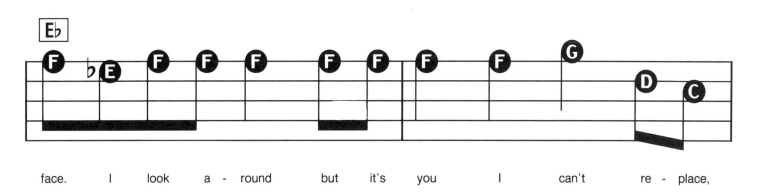

face. I look a - round but it's you I can't re - place,

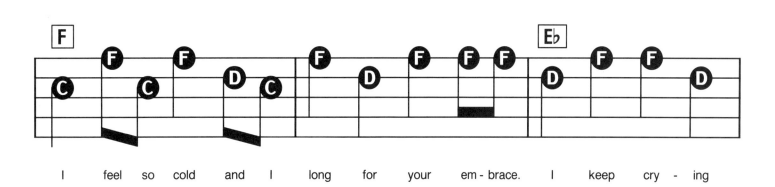

I feel so cold and I long for your em - brace. I keep cry - ing

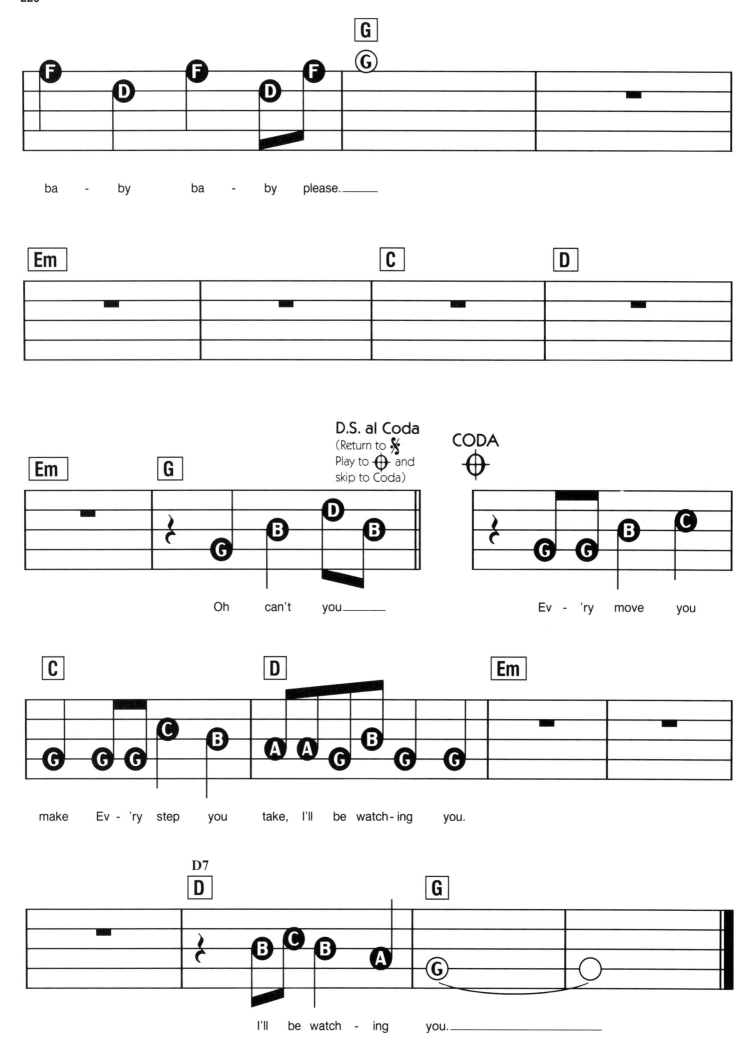

1984
Footloose
Theme from the Paramount Motion Picture FOOTLOOSE

Registration 4
Rhythm: Rock or 8 Beat

Words by Dean Pitchford and Kenny Loggins
Music by Kenny Loggins

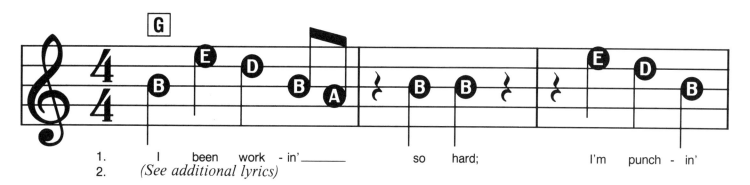

1. I been work - in' _____ so hard; I'm punch - in'
2. *(See additional lyrics)*

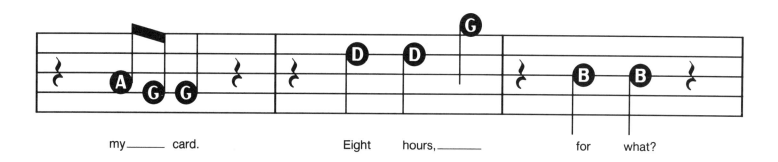

my _____ card. Eight hours, _____ for what?

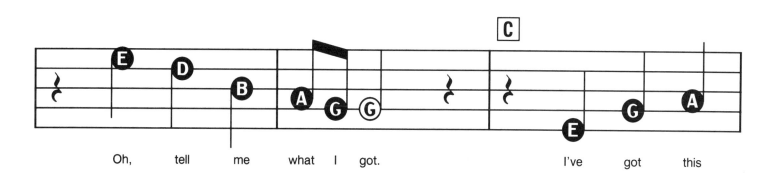

Oh, tell me what I got. I've got this

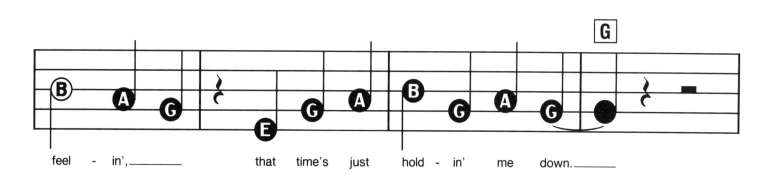

feel - in', _____ that time's just hold - in' me down. _____

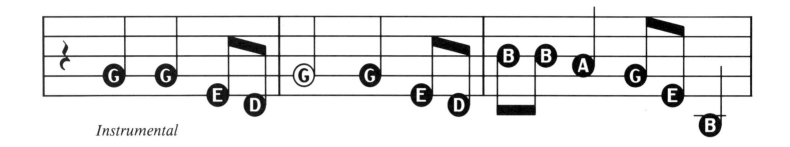

Instrumental

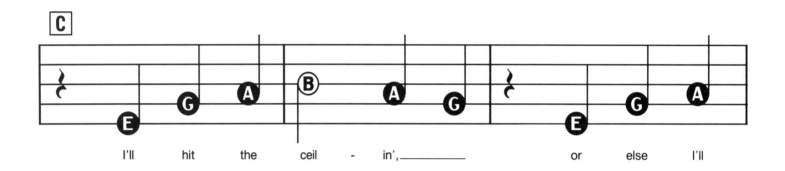

I'll   hit   the   ceil - in',_____   or   else   I'll

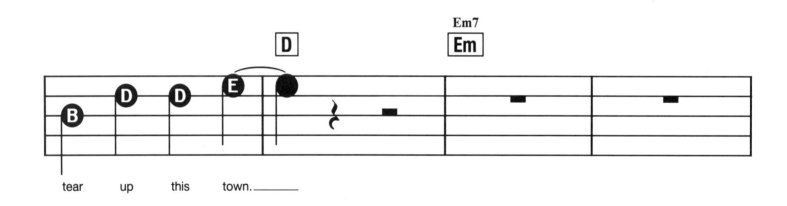

tear   up   this   town._____

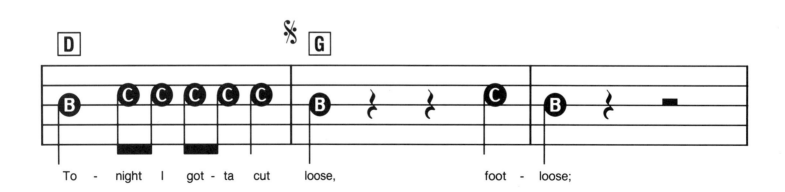

To - night I got - ta cut   loose,   foot - loose;

223

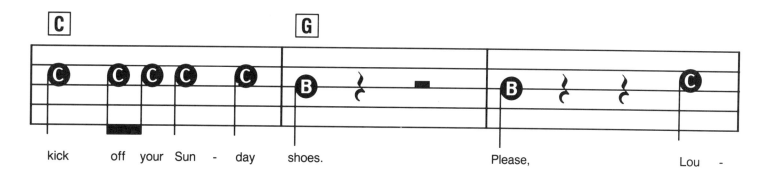

kick off your Sun - day shoes. Please, Lou -

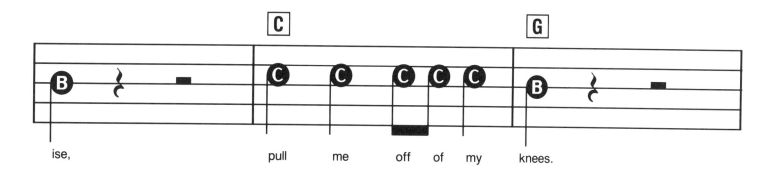

ise, pull me off of my knees.

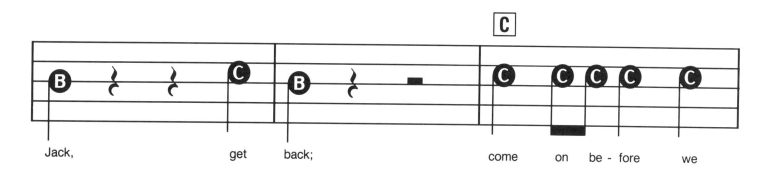

Jack, get back; come on be - fore we

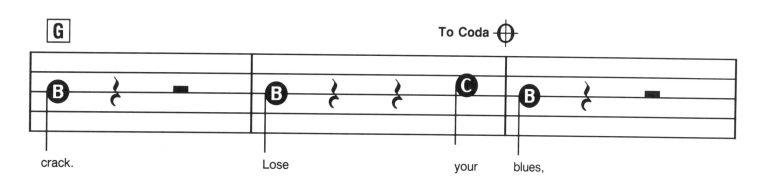

crack. Lose your blues,

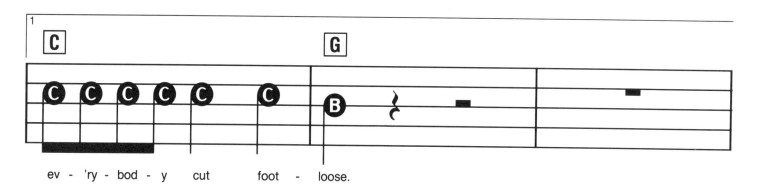

ev - 'ry - bod - y cut foot - loose.

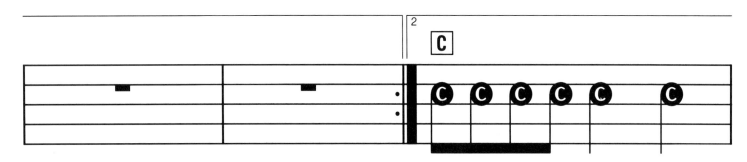

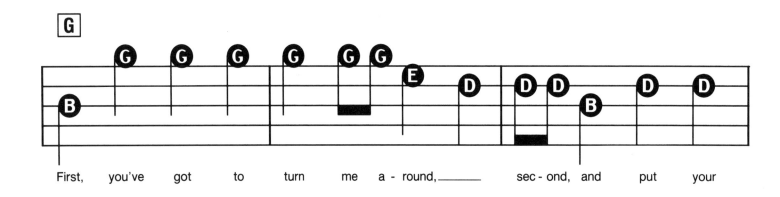

First, you've got to turn me a - round,_____ sec - ond, and put your

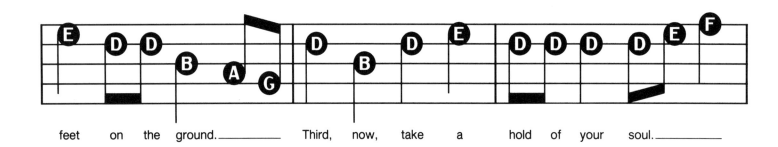

feet on the ground._____ Third, now, take a hold of your soul._____

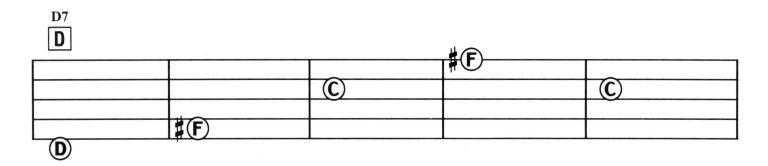

D.S. al Coda
(Return to %
Play to ⊕ and
skip to Coda)

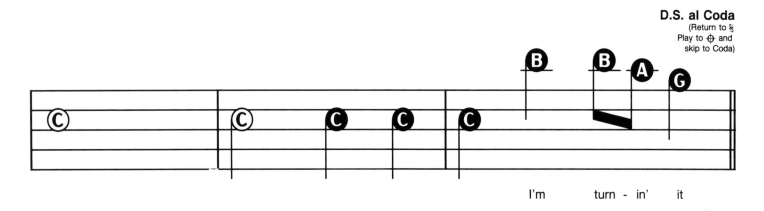

I'm turn - in' it

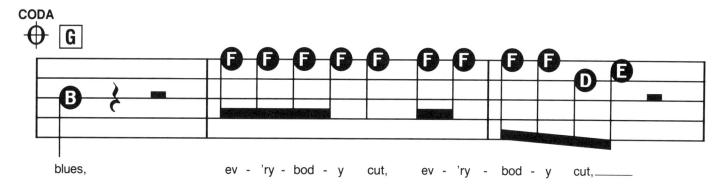

blues,   ev - 'ry - bod - y cut,   ev - 'ry - bod - y cut,_____

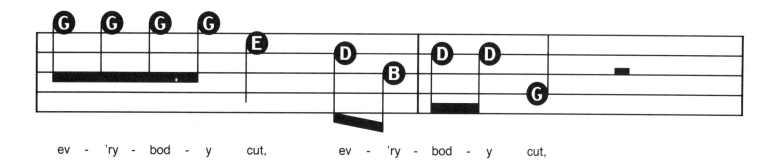

ev - 'ry - bod - y cut,   ev - 'ry - bod - y cut,

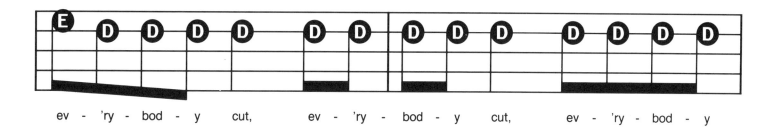

ev - 'ry - bod - y cut,   ev - 'ry - bod - y cut,   ev - 'ry - bod - y

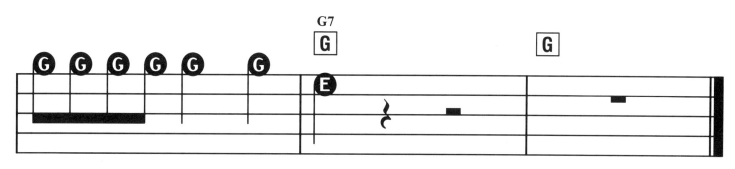

ev - 'ry - bod - y cut   foot - loose.

Additional Lyrics

Verse 2:
You're playin' so cool
Obeying every rule
Dig way down in your heart
You're burnin', yearnin' for some...
Somebody to tell you
That life ain't a-passin' you by.
I'm tryin' to tell you
It will if you don't even try;
You can fly if you'd only cut

Chorus:
Loose, footloose,
Kick off your Sunday shoes.
Ooh-ee, Marie,
Shake it, shake it for me.
Whoa, Milo,
Come on, come on let's go.
Lose your blues,
Everybody cut footloose.

1985

Careless Whisper

Registration 1
Rhythm: Rock or Jazz Rock

Words and Music by George Michael
and Andrew Ridgeley

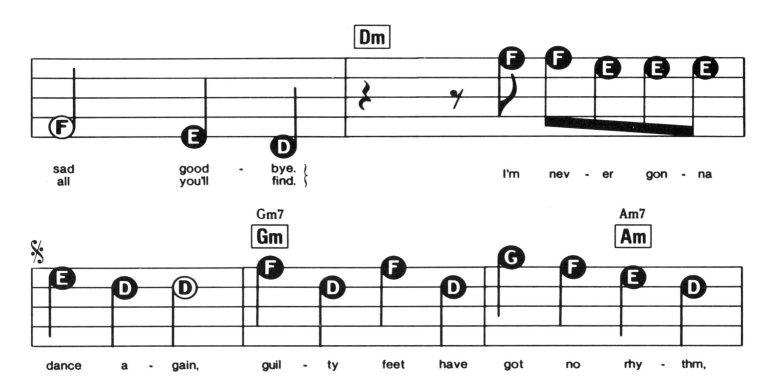

sad good - bye.
all you'll find.
I'm nev - er gon - na

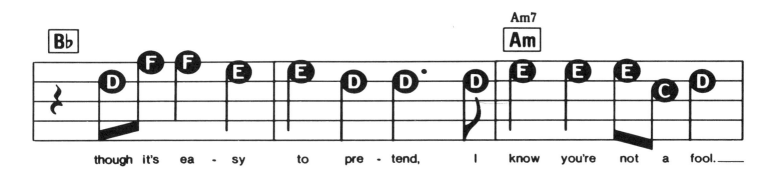

dance a - gain, guil - ty feet have got no rhy - thm,

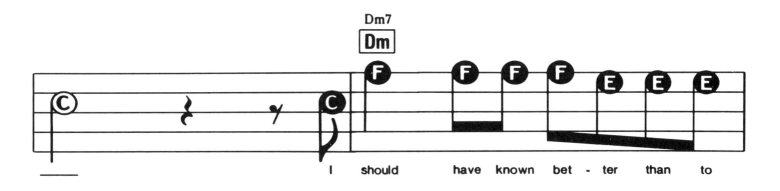

though it's ea - sy to pre - tend, I know you're not a fool.___

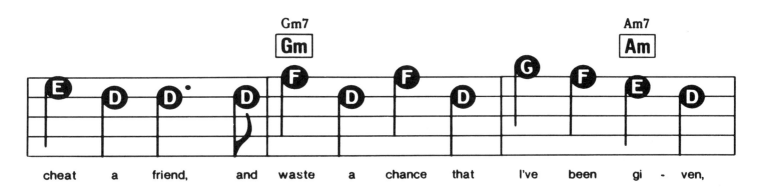

I should have known bet - ter than to

cheat a friend, and waste a chance that I've been gi - ven,

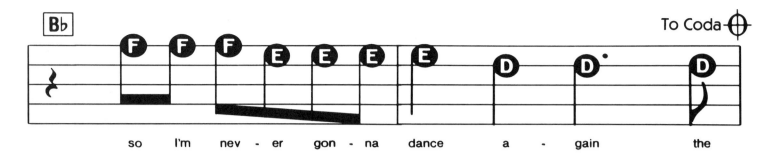

so I'm nev - er gon - na dance a - gain the

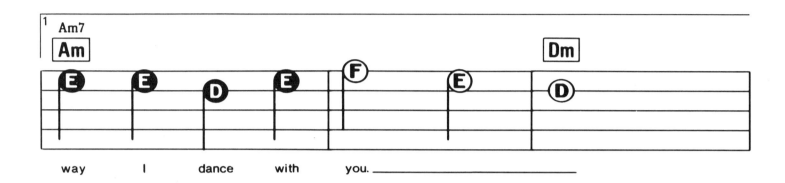

way I dance with you. _____

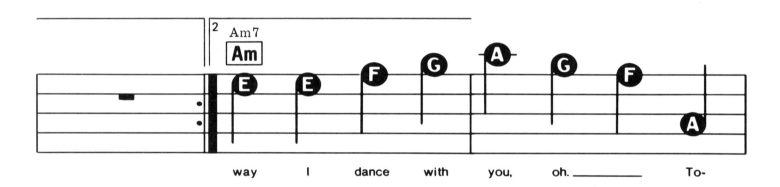

way I dance with you, oh. _____ To-

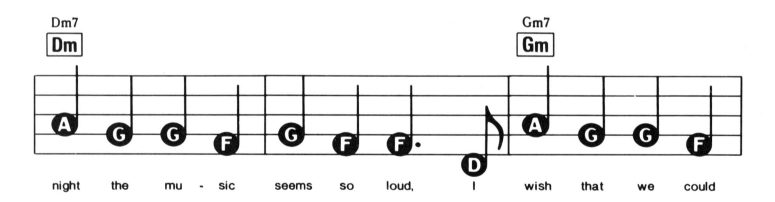

night the mu - sic seems so loud, I wish that we could

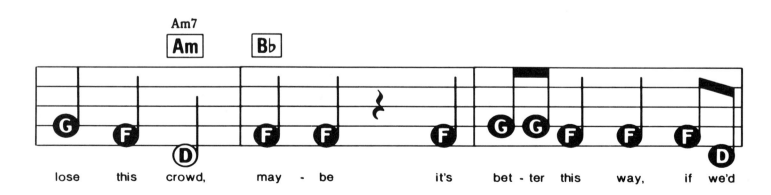

lose this crowd, may - be it's bet - ter this way, if we'd

229

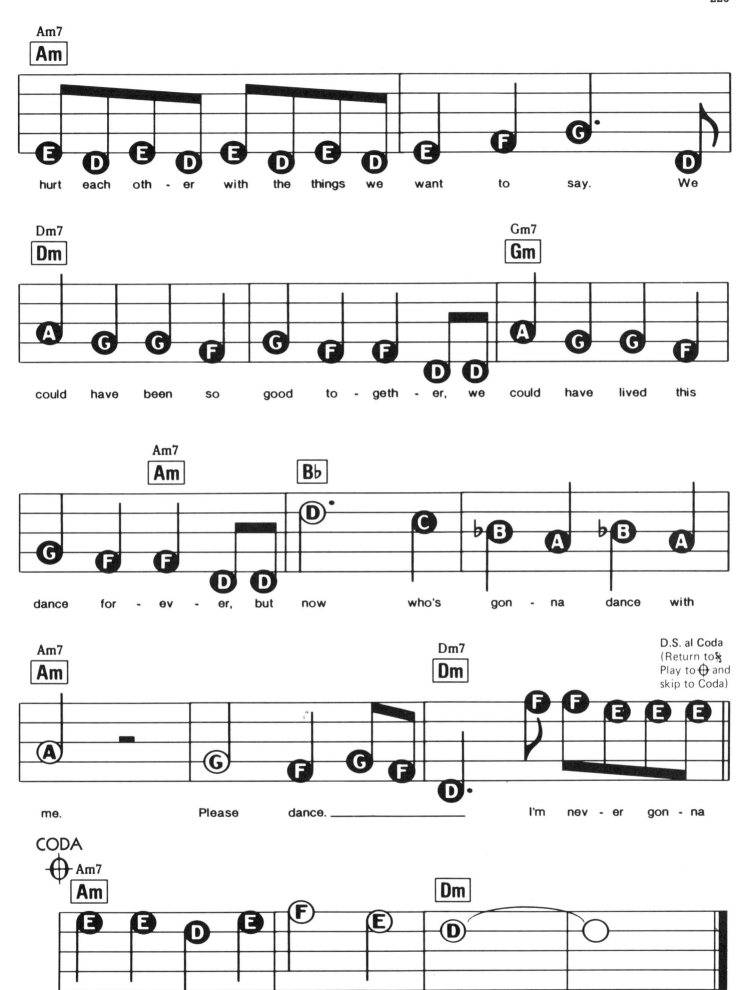

1986
Somewhere Out There
from AN AMERICAN TAIL

Registration 4
Rhythm: Ballad

Words and Music by James Horner,
Barry Mann and Cynthia Weil

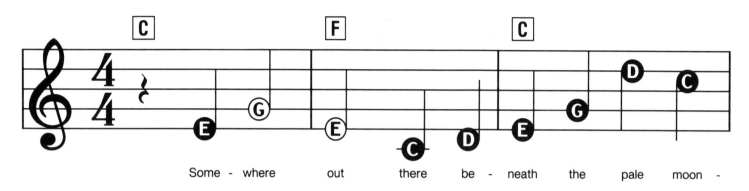

Some - where   out   there   be - neath   the   pale   moon -

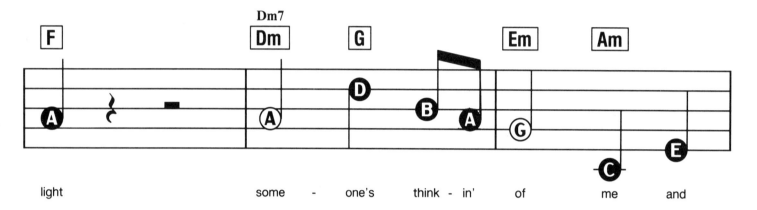

light   some - one's   think - in'   of   me   and

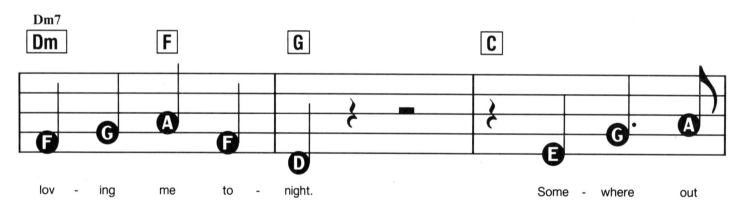

lov - ing   me   to - night.   Some - where   out

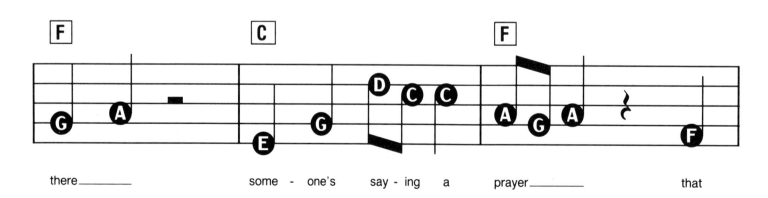

there_____   some - one's   say - ing   a   prayer_____   that

MCA Music Publishing

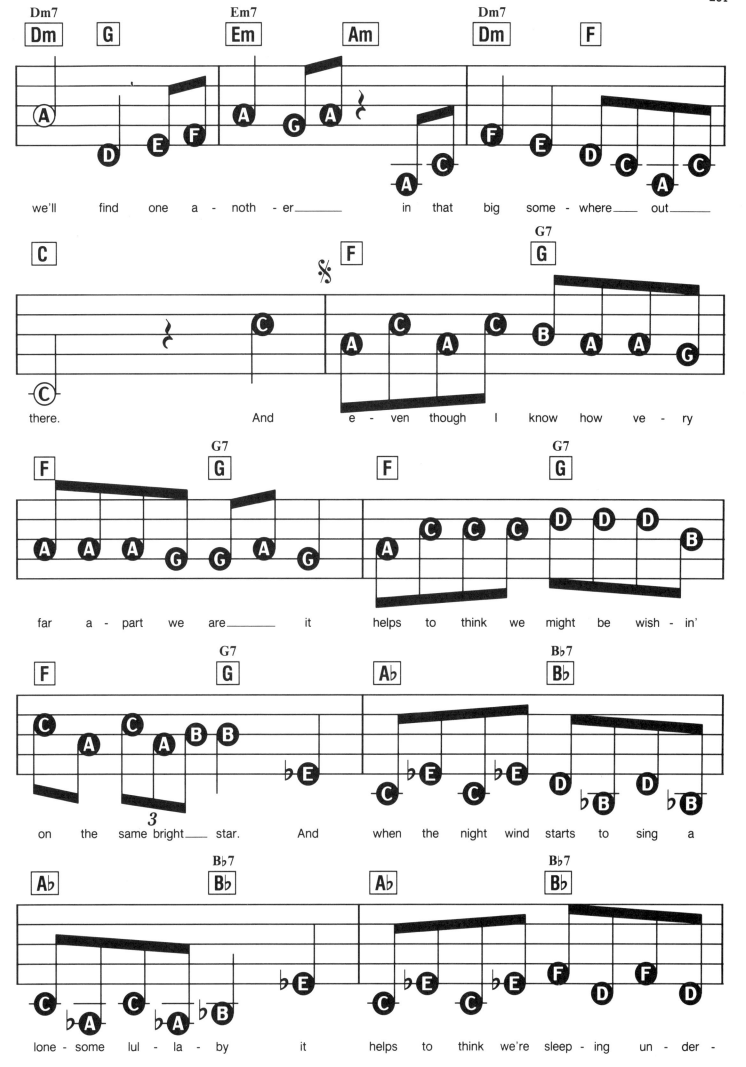

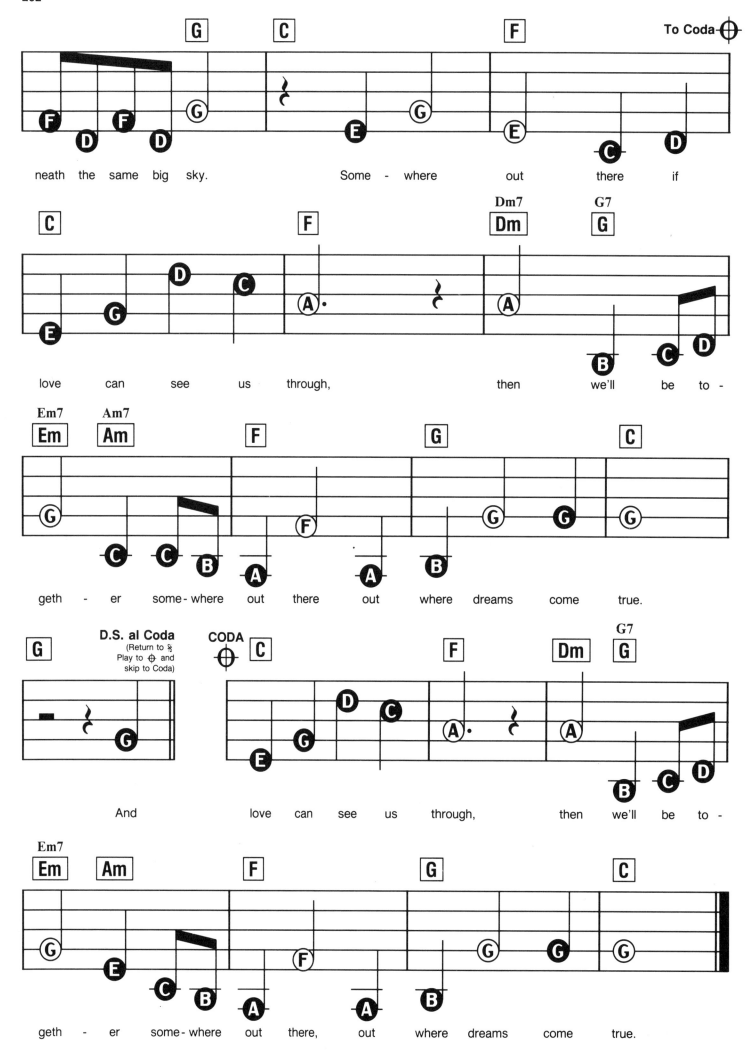

1987
(I've Had)
The Time of My Life
from DIRTY DANCING

Registration 1
Rhythm: Rock or 16 Beat

Words and Music by Franke Previte,
John DeNicola and Donald Markowitz

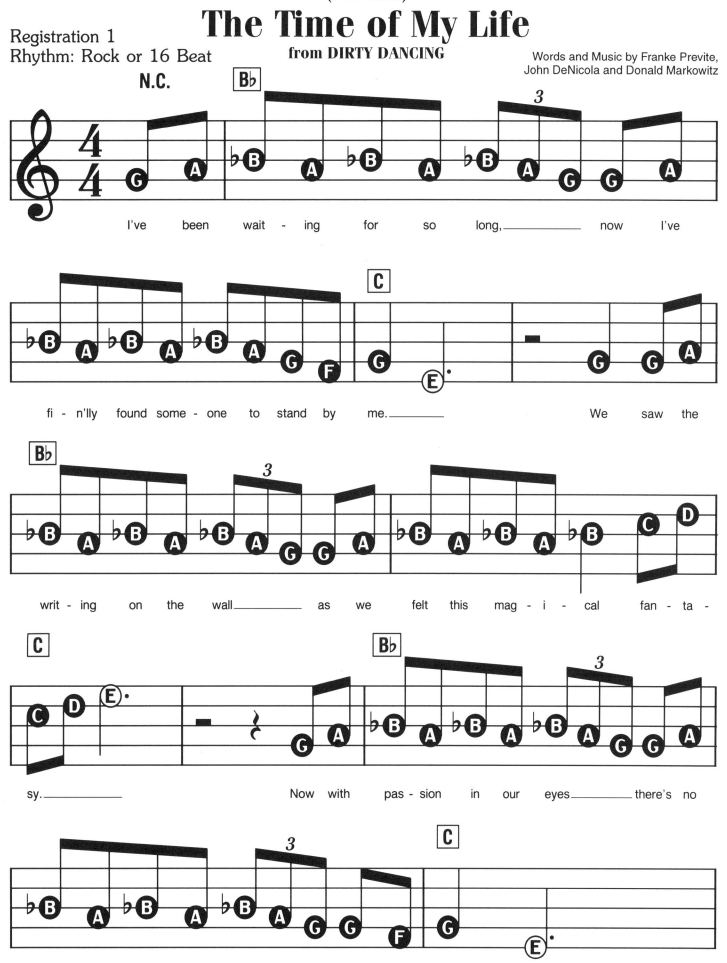

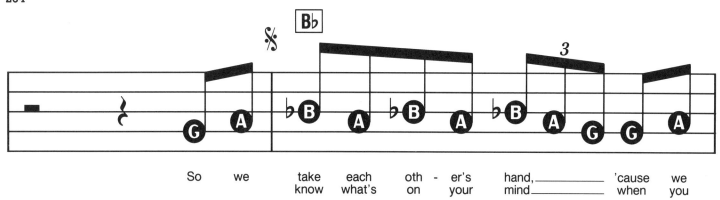

So we take each oth - er's hand,_____ 'cause we
know what's on your mind_____ when you

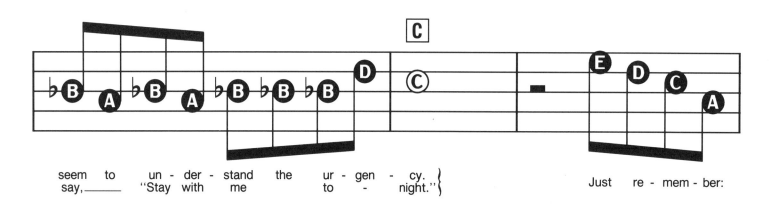

seem to un - der - stand the ur - gen - cy.
say,_____ "Stay with me to - night."

Just re - mem - ber:

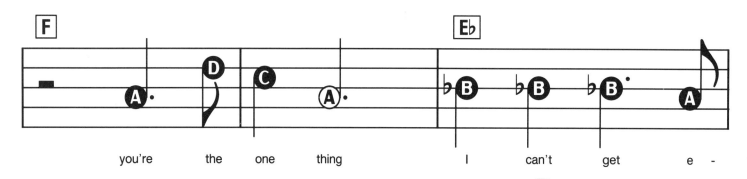

you're the one thing I can't get e -

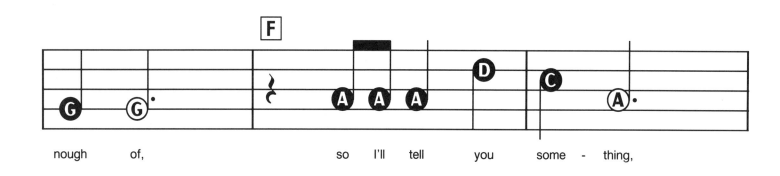

nough of, so I'll tell you some - thing,

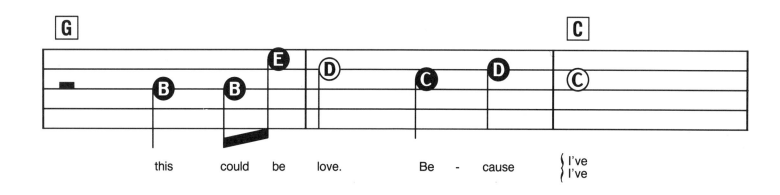

this could be love. Be - cause I've
I've

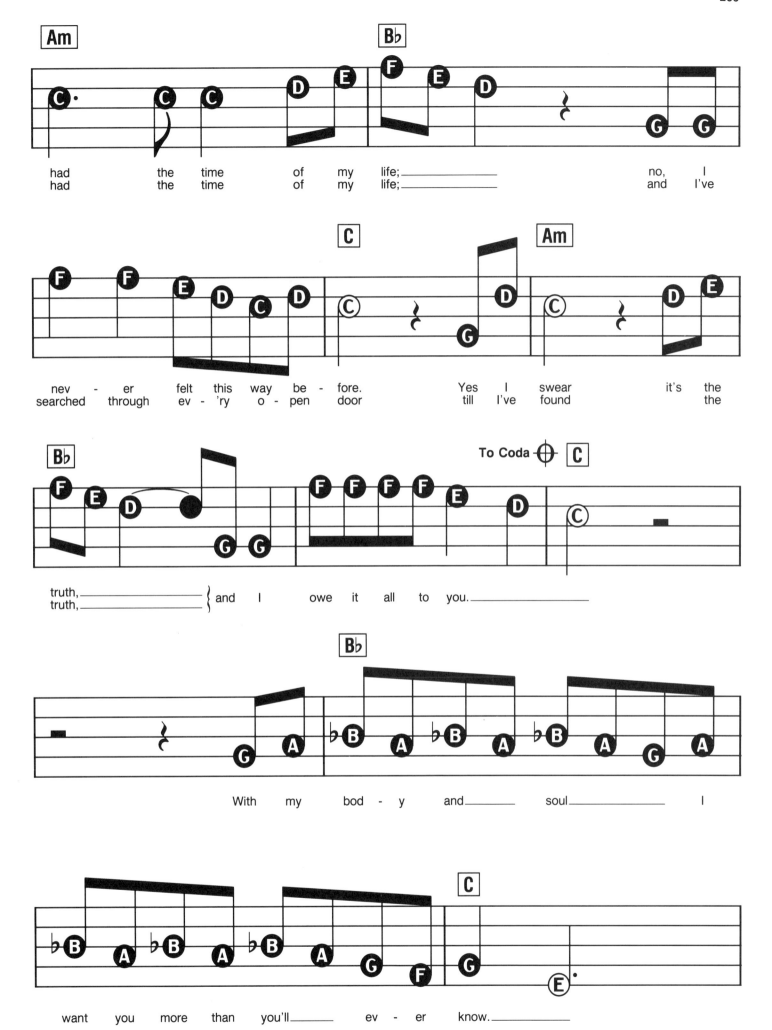

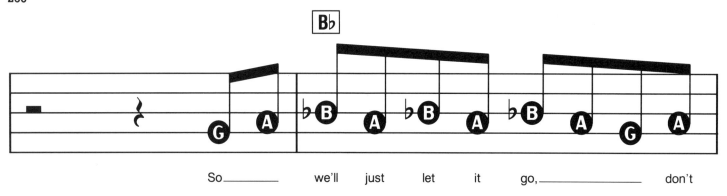

So_____ we'll just let it go,_____ don't

D.S. al Coda
(Return to 𝄋
Play to ⊕ and
skip to Coda)

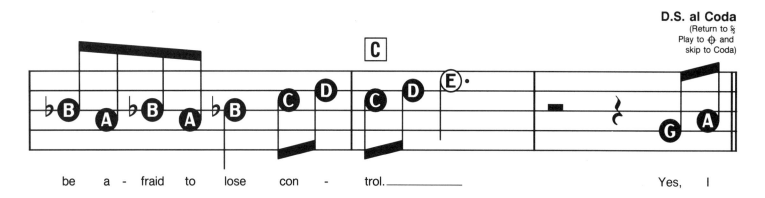

be a - fraid to lose con - trol._____ Yes, I

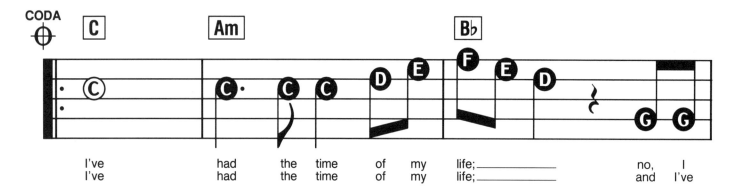

I've had the time of my life;_____ no, I
I've had the time of my life;_____ and I've

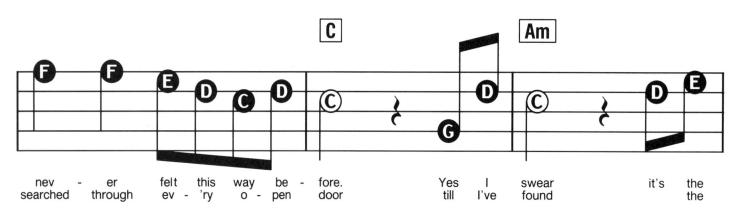

nev - er felt this way be - fore. Yes I swear it's the
searched through ev - 'ry o - pen door till I've found the

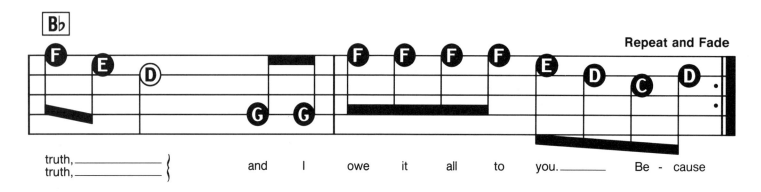

truth,_____ }
truth,_____ } and I owe it all to you._____ Be - cause

1988
All I Ask of You
from THE PHANTOM OF THE OPERA

Registration 9
Rhythm: 8 Beat or Pops

Music by Andrew Lloyd Webber
Lyrics by Charles Hart
Additional Lyrics by Richard Stilgoe

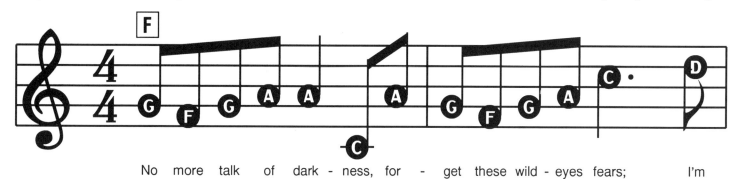

No more talk of dark - ness, for - get these wild - eyes fears; I'm

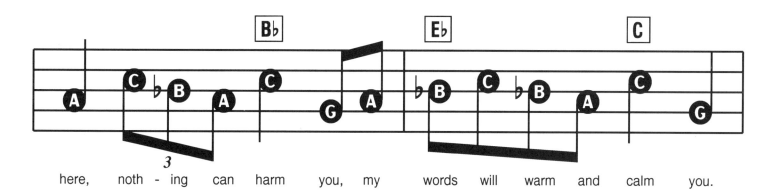

here, noth - ing can harm you, my words will warm and calm you.

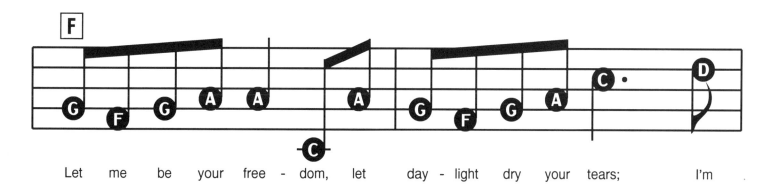

Let me be your free - dom, let day - light dry your tears; I'm

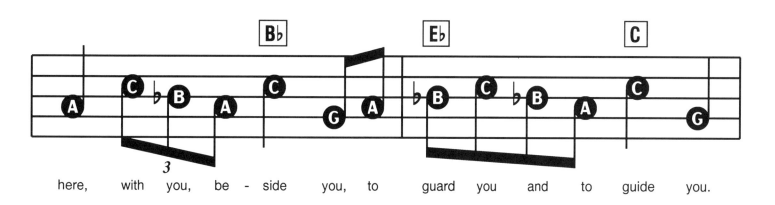

here, with you, be - side you, to guard you and to guide you.

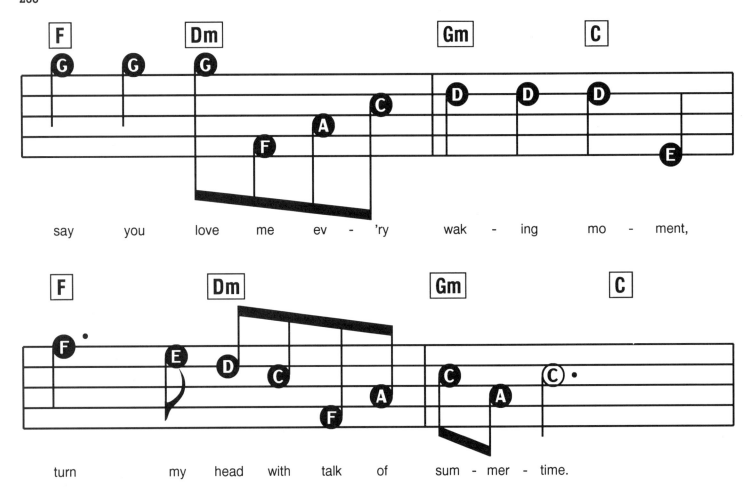

say   you   love   me   ev - 'ry   wak - ing   mo - ment,

turn   my   head   with   talk   of   sum - mer - time.

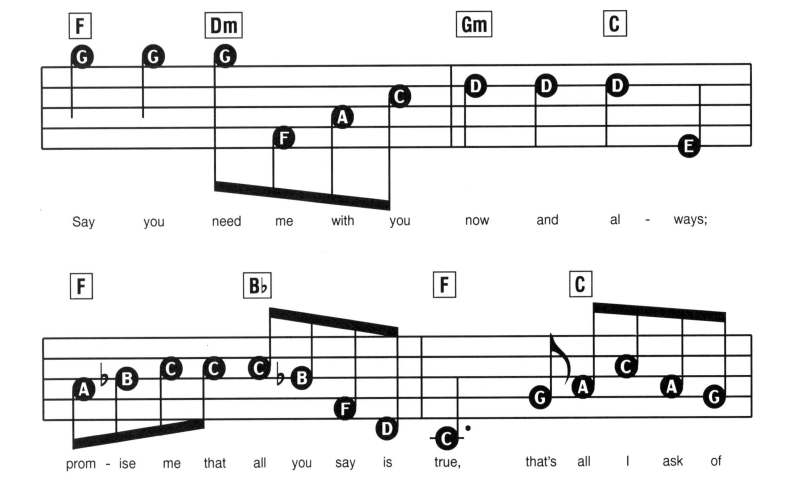

Say   you   need   me   with   you   now   and   al - ways;

prom - ise   me   that   all   you   say   is   true,   that's   all   I   ask   of

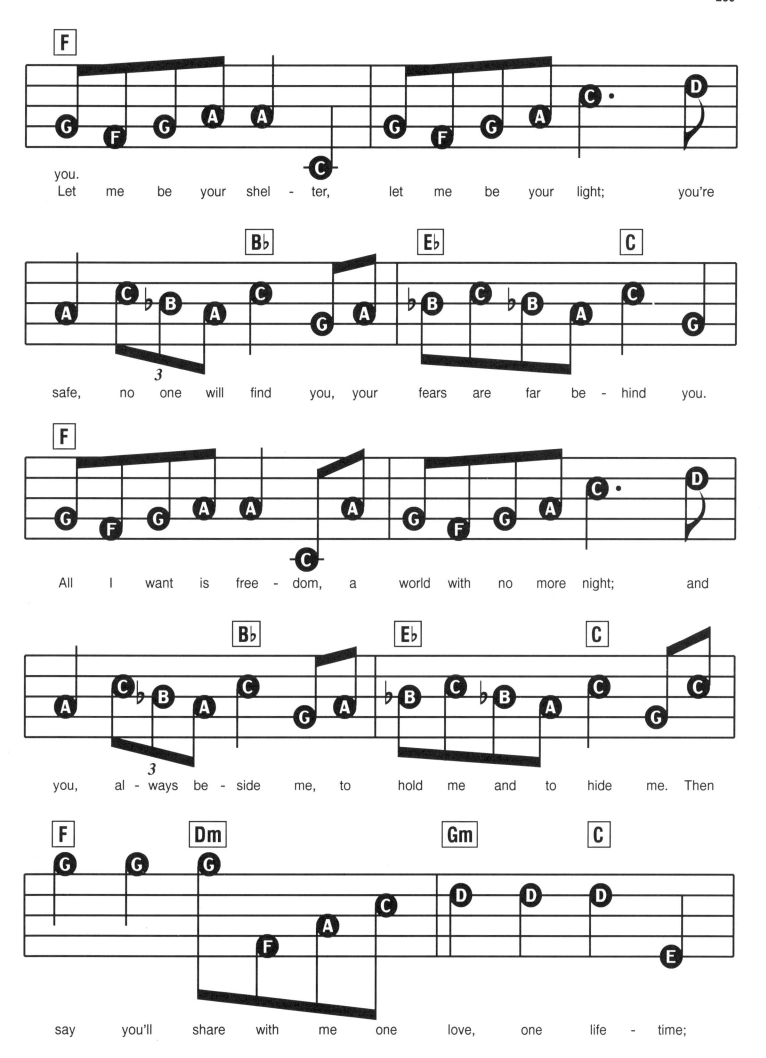

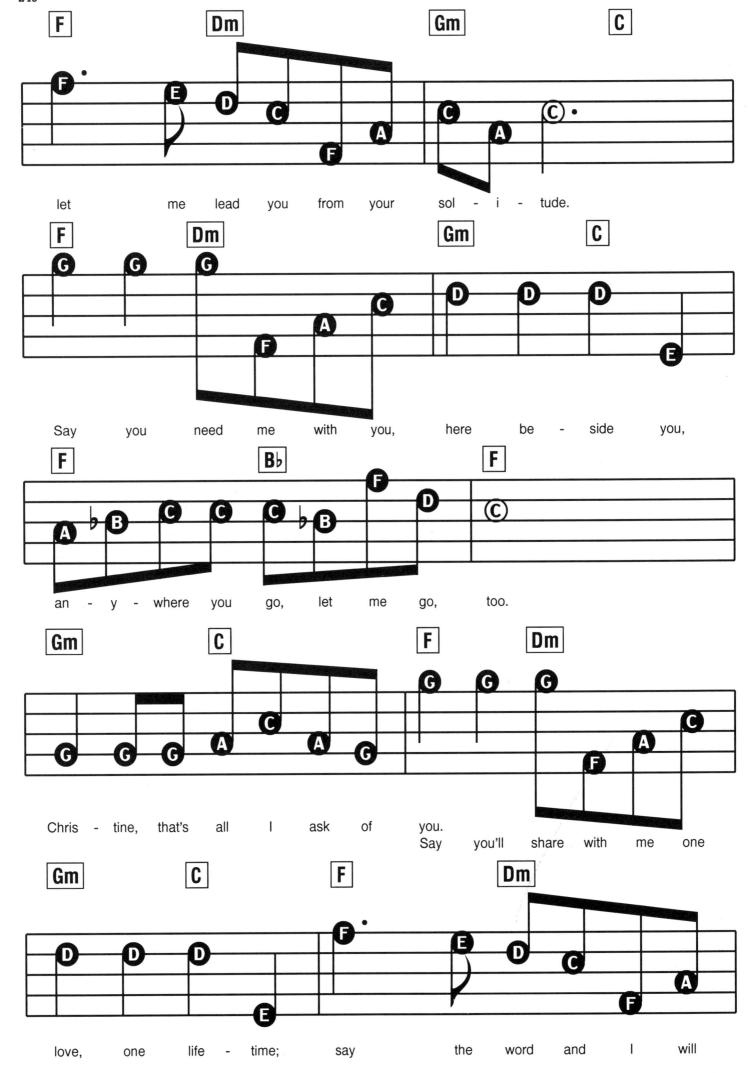

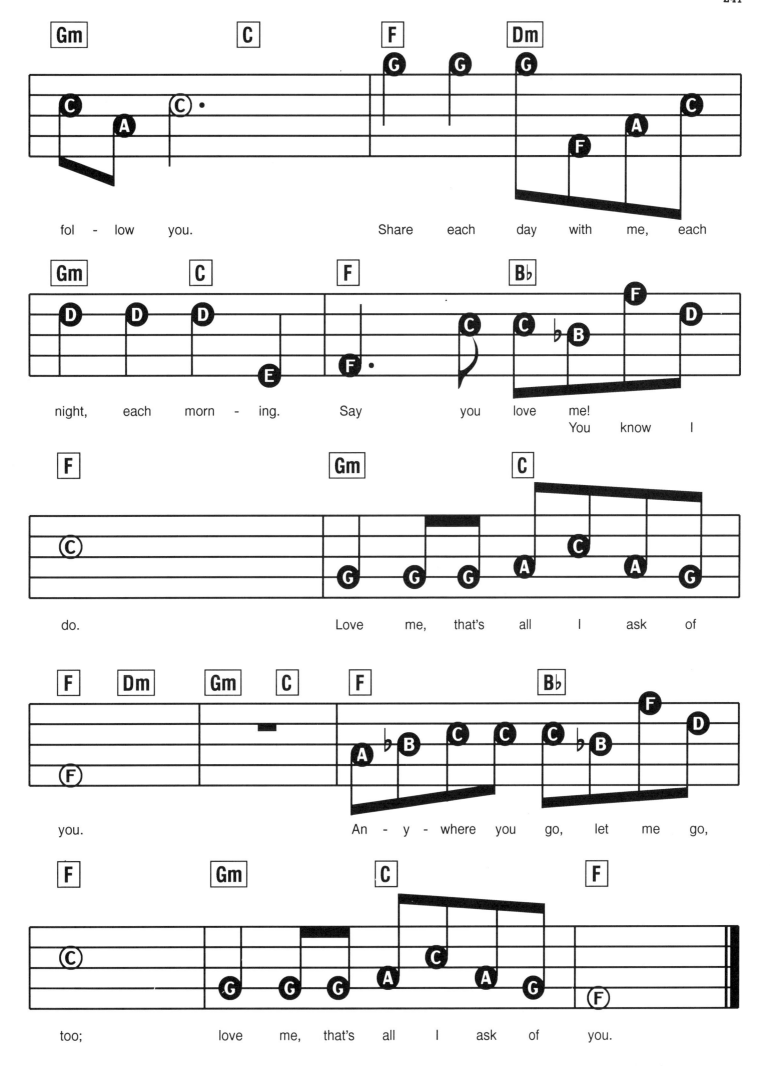

1989
Don't Know Much

Registration 7
Rhythm: Pops or 8 Beat

Words and Music by Barry Mann,
Cynthia Weil and Tom Snow

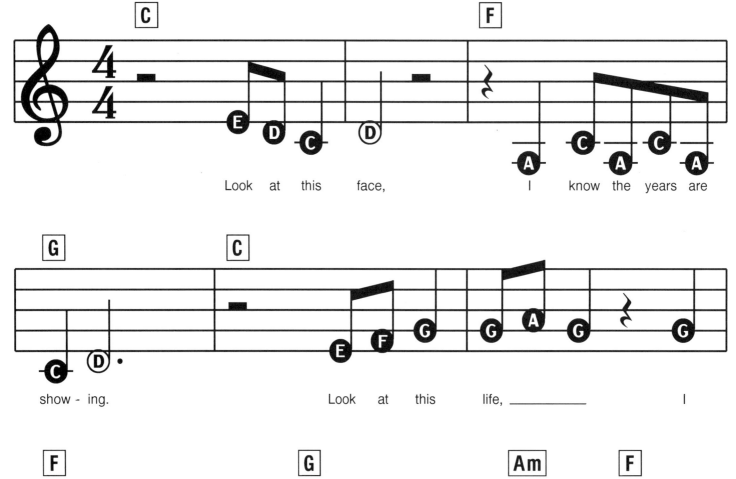

Look at this face, I know the years are

show - ing. Look at this life, _____ I

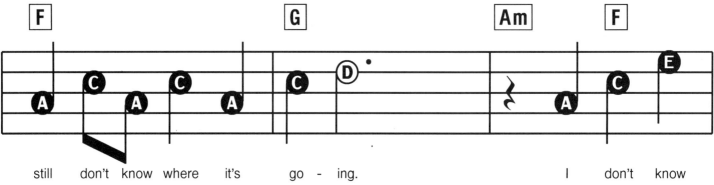

still don't know where it's go - ing. I don't know

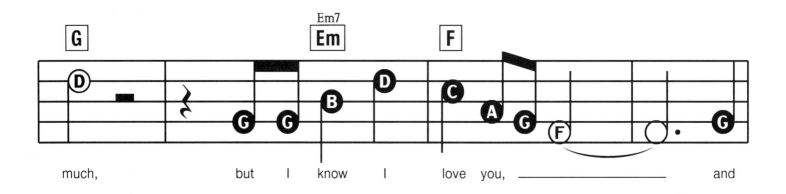

much, but I know I love you, _____ and

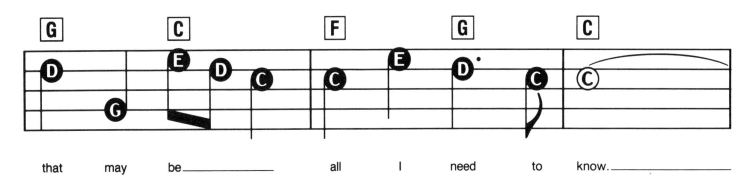

that may be_____ all I need to know._____

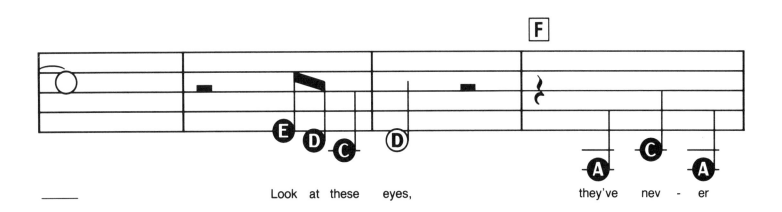

_____ Look at these eyes, they've nev - er

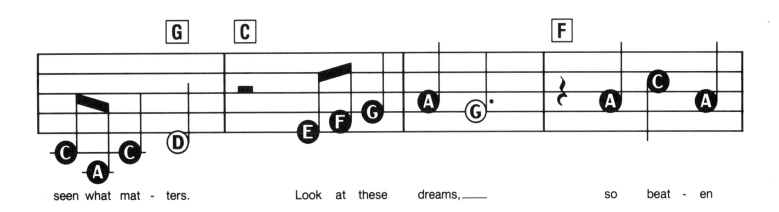

seen what mat - ters. Look at these dreams,_____ so beat - en

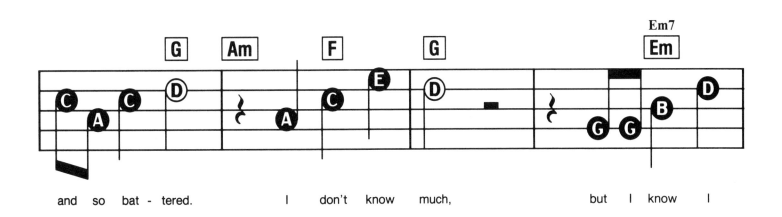

and so bat - tered. I don't know much, but I know I

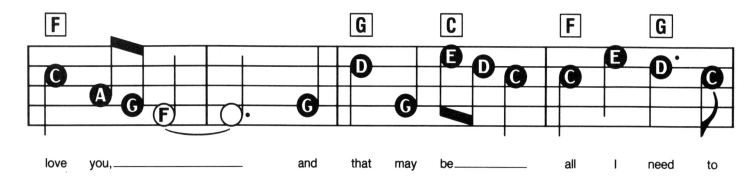

love you,_____ and that may be_____ all I need to

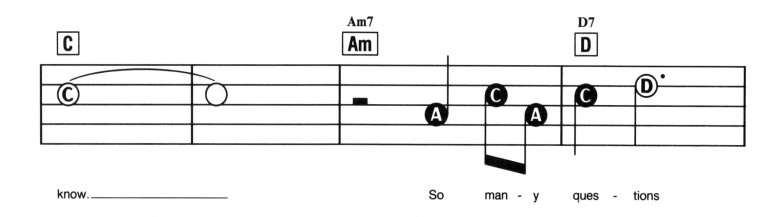

know._____ So man - y ques - tions

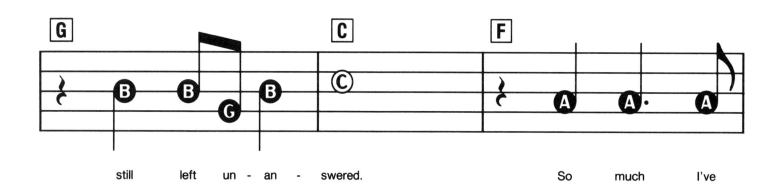

still left un - an - swered. So much I've

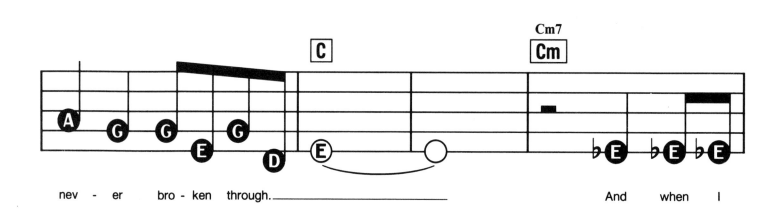

nev - er bro - ken through._____ And when I

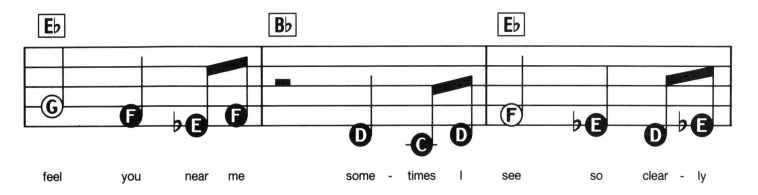

feel   you   near me   some - times I   see   so   clear - ly

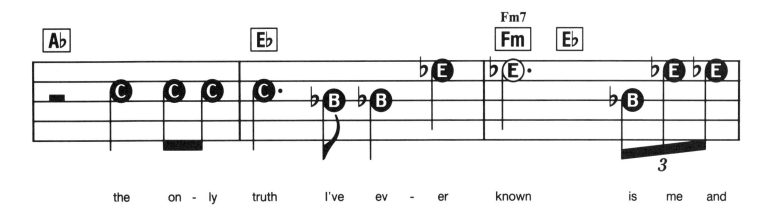

the   on - ly   truth   I've   ev - er   known   is   me   and

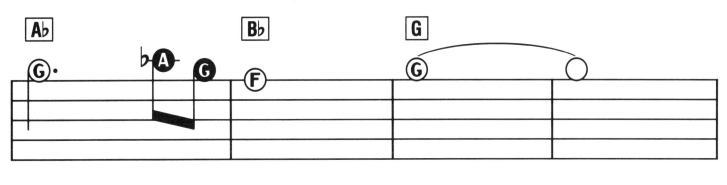

you.

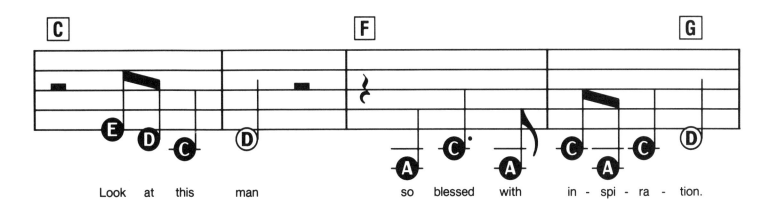

Look   at   this   man   so   blessed   with   in - spi - ra - tion.

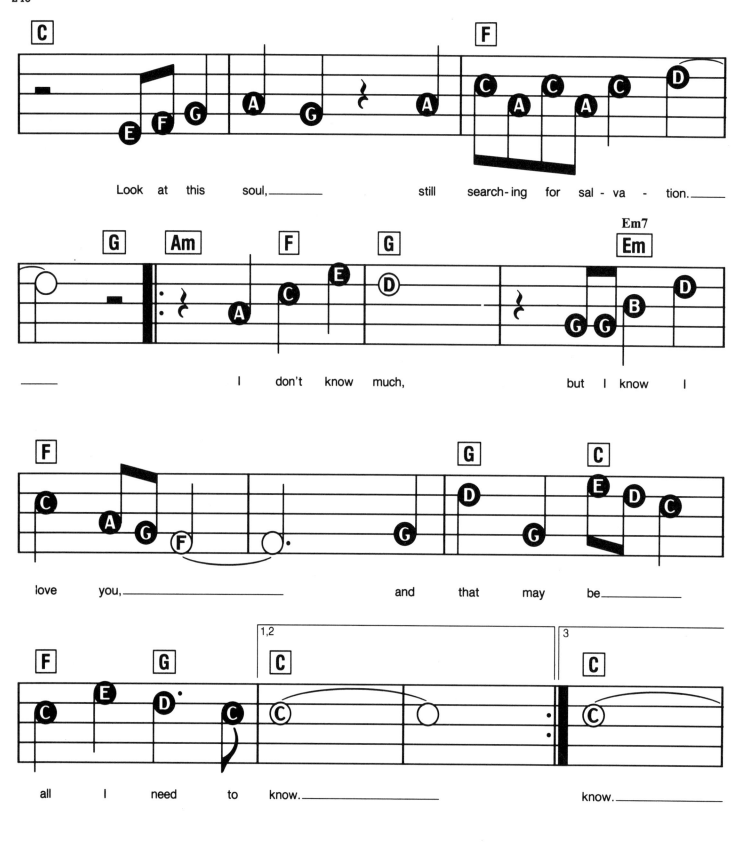

Look at this soul,_____ still search-ing for sal - va - tion._____

_____ I don't know much, but I know I

love you,_____ and that may be_____

all I need to know._____ know._____

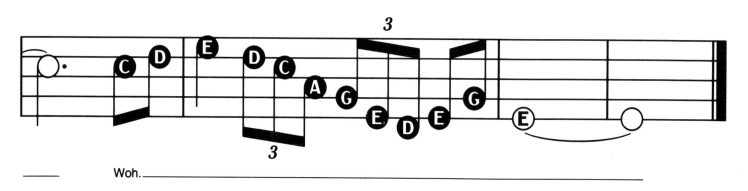

_____ Woh._____

1990

From a Distance

Registration 7
Rhythm: 8 Beat or Pops

Words and Music by
Julie Gold

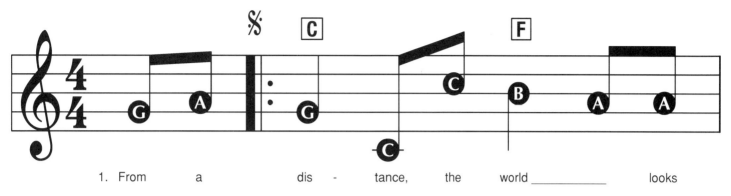

1. From a dis - tance, the world _____ looks

(See Additional Lyrics)

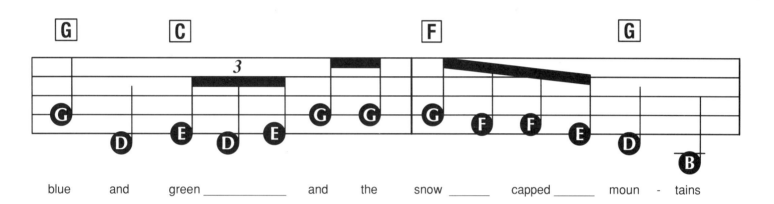

blue and green _____ and the snow _____ capped _____ moun - tains

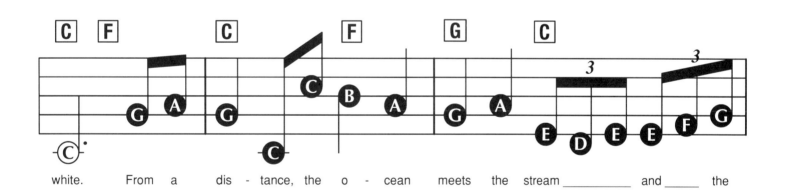

white. From a dis - tance, the o - cean meets the stream _____ and _____ the

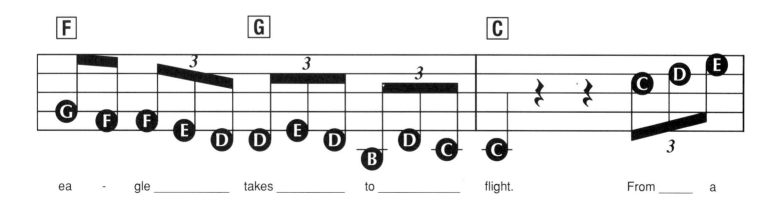

ea - gle _____ takes _____ to _____ flight. From _____ a

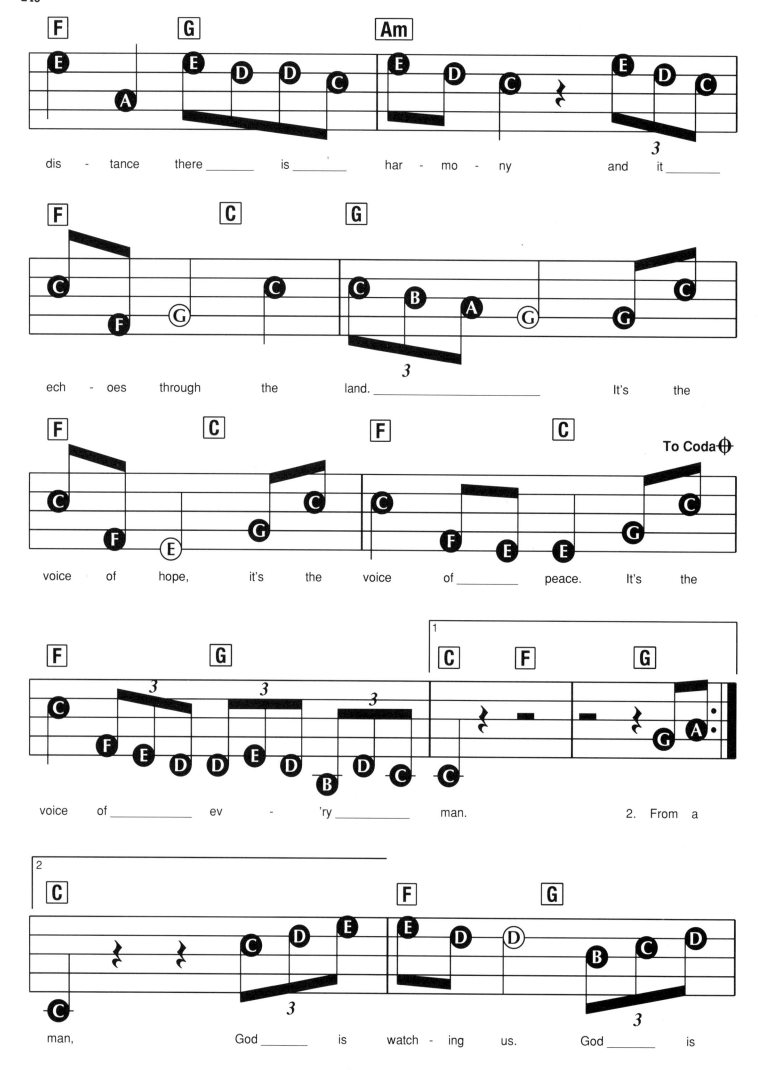

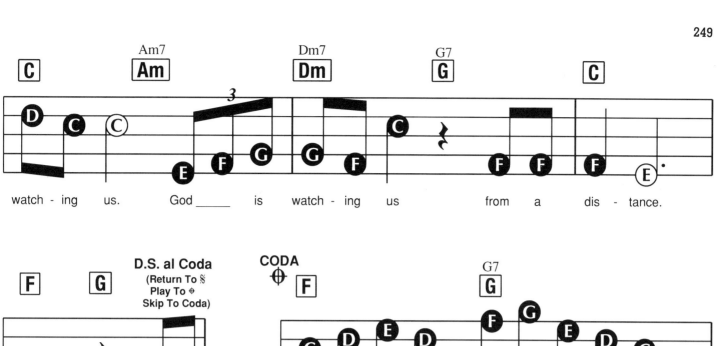

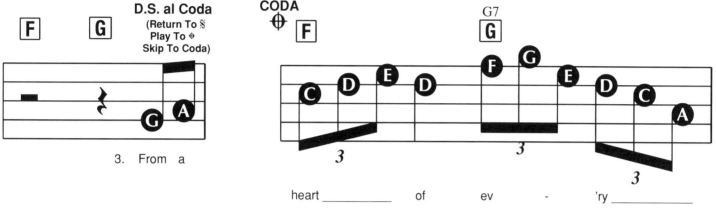

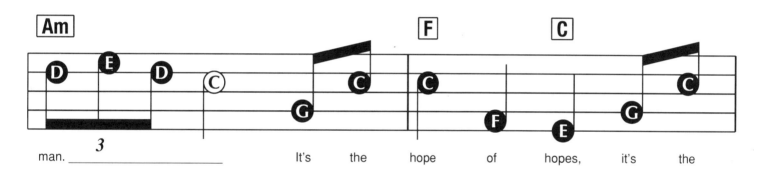

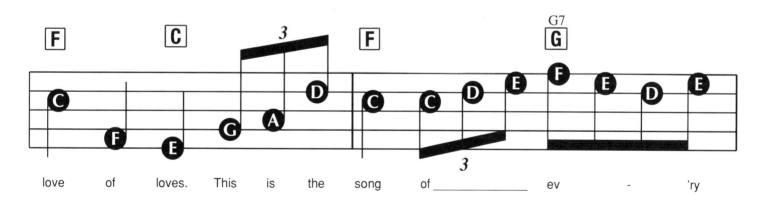

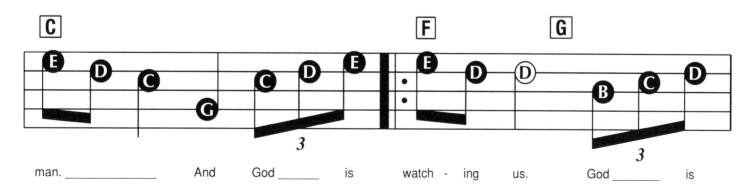

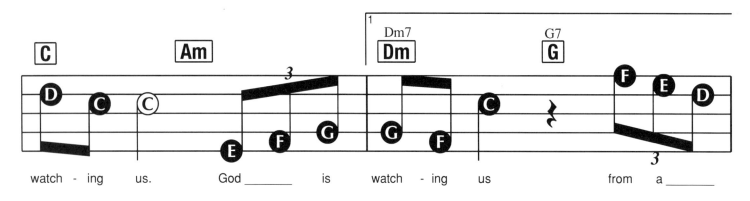

watch - ing us. God _____ is watch - ing us from a _____

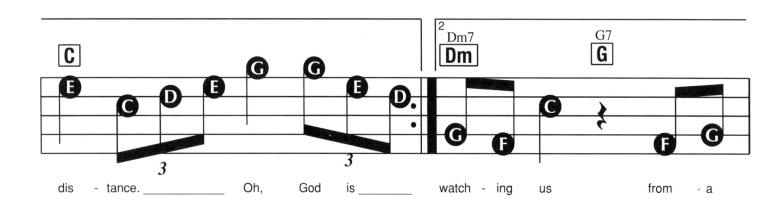

dis - tance. _____ Oh, God is _____ watch - ing us from a

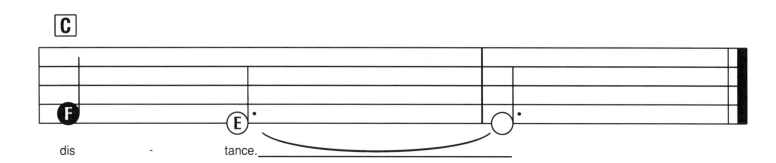

dis - tance. _____

Additional Lyrics

2. From a distance, we all have enough,
   And no one is in need.
   There are no guns, no bombs, no diseases,
   No hungry mouths to feed.
   From a distance, we are instruments
   Marching in a common band;
   Playing songs of hope, playing songs of peace,
   They're the songs of every man.

3. From a distance, you look like my friend
   Even though we are at war.
   From a distance I just cannot comprehend
   What all this fighting is for.
   From a distance there is harmony
   And it echos through the land.
   It's the hope of hopes, it's the love of loves.
   It's the heart of every man.

1991
Beauty and the Beast
from Walt Disney's BEAUTY AND THE BEAST

Registration 1
Rhythm: Pops or 8 Beat

Lyrics by Howard Ashman
Music by Alan Menken

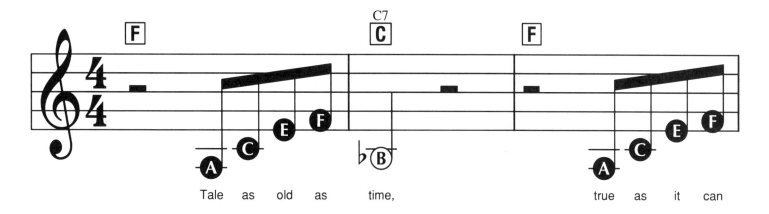

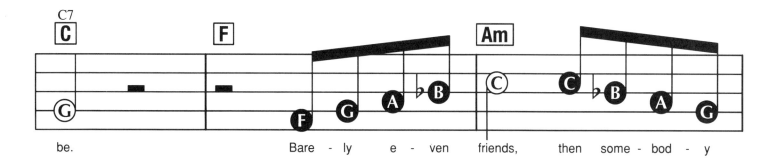

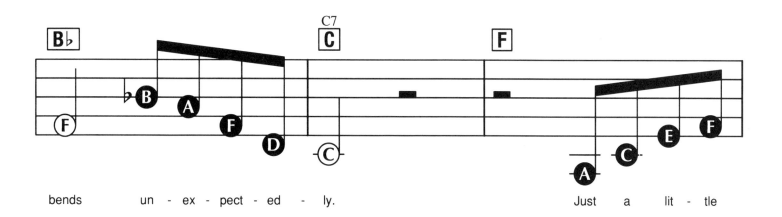

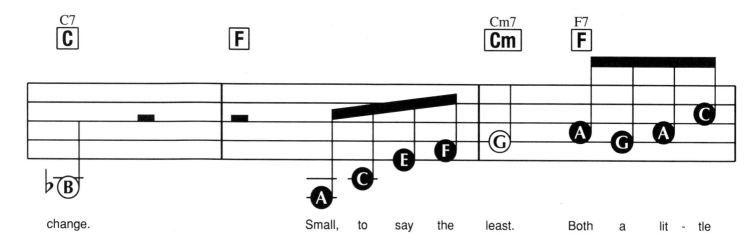

change.   Small, to say the least. Both a lit - tle

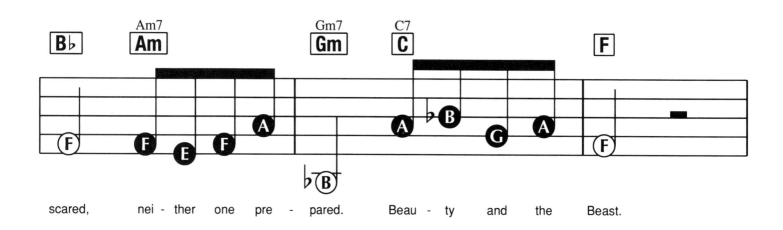

scared, nei - ther one pre - pared. Beau - ty and the Beast.

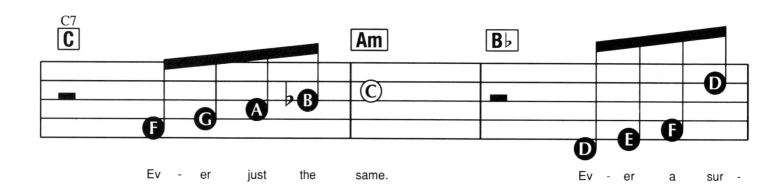

Ev - er just the same.   Ev - er a sur -

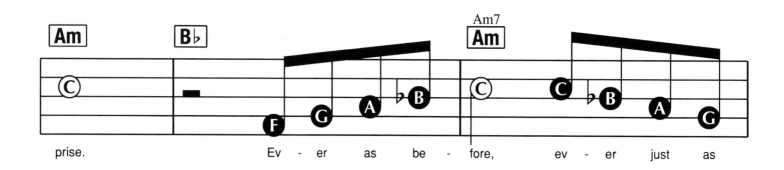

prise.   Ev - er as be - fore, ev - er just as

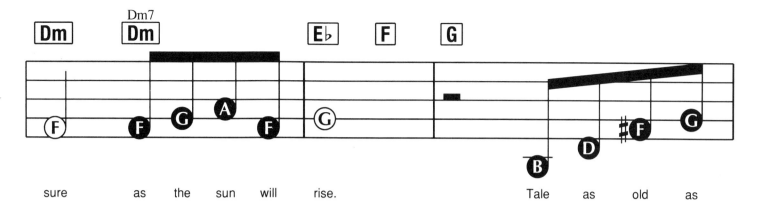

sure   as   the   sun   will   rise.   Tale   as   old   as

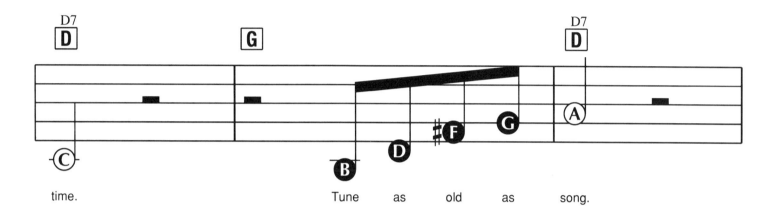

time.   Tune   as   old   as   song.

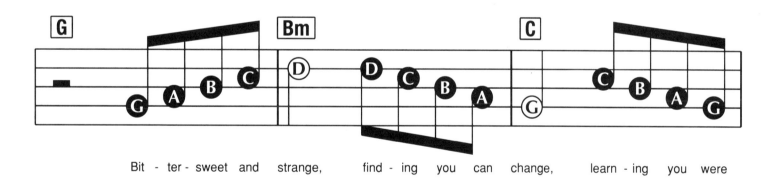

Bit - ter - sweet and   strange,   find - ing   you   can   change,   learn - ing   you   were

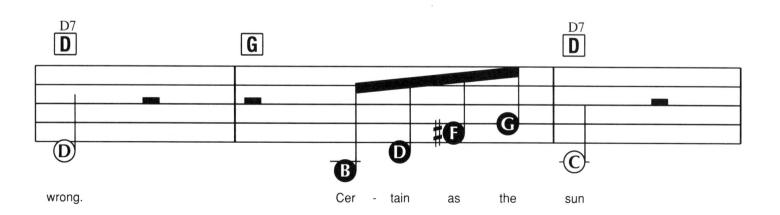

wrong.   Cer - tain   as   the   sun

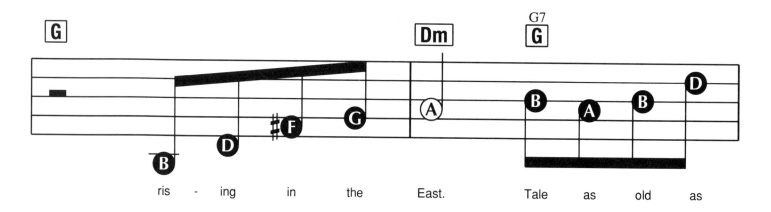

ris - ing in the East. Tale as old as

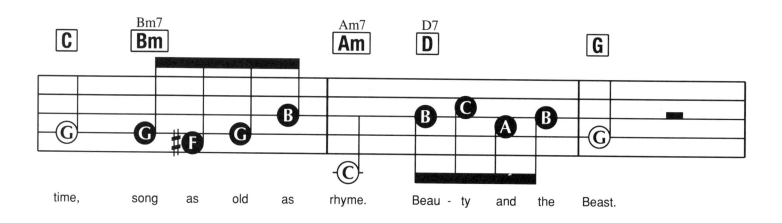

time, song as old as rhyme. Beau - ty and the Beast.

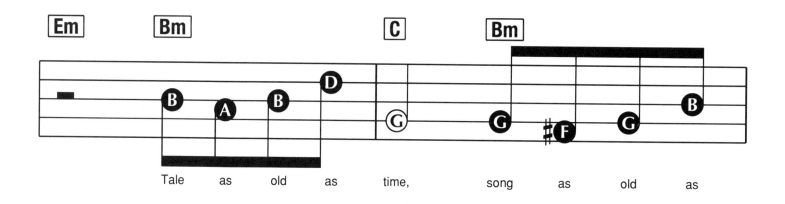

Tale as old as time, song as old as

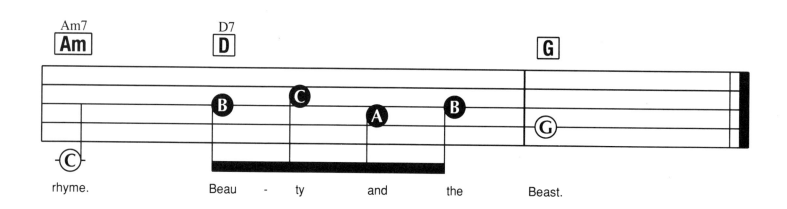

rhyme. Beau - ty and the Beast.

1992
Tears in Heaven

Registration 8
Rhythm: 8 Beat

Words and Music by Eric Clapton
and Will Jennings

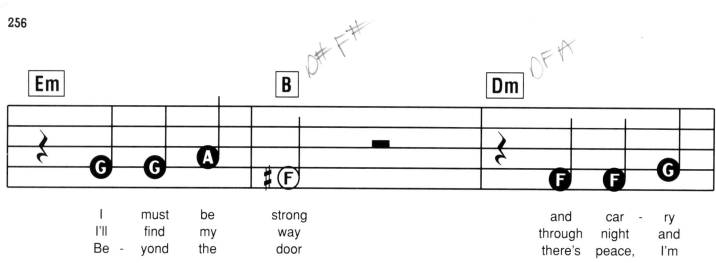

I must be strong
I'll find my way
Be - yond the door

and car - ry
through night and
there's peace, I'm

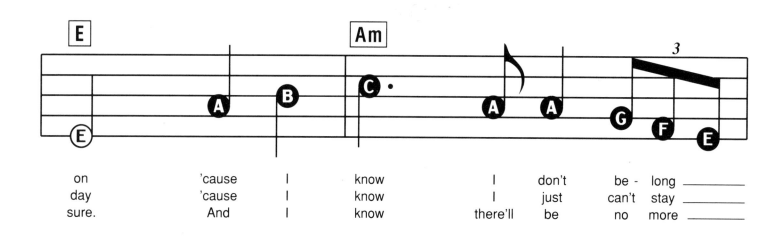

on 'cause I know I don't be - long
day 'cause I know I just can't stay
sure. And I know there'll be no more

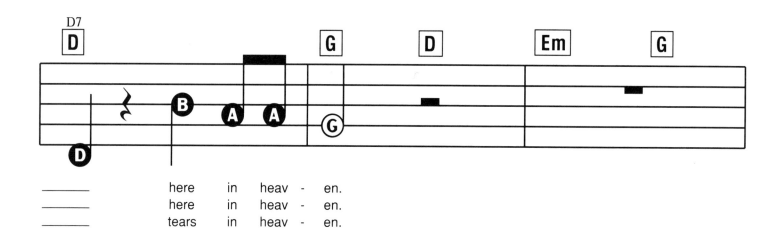

here in heav - en.
here in heav - en.
tears in heav - en.

To Next Strain

257

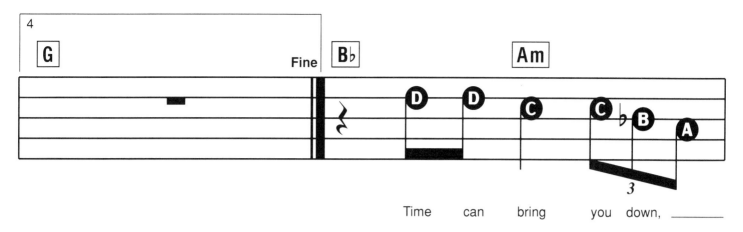

Time can bring you down, _____

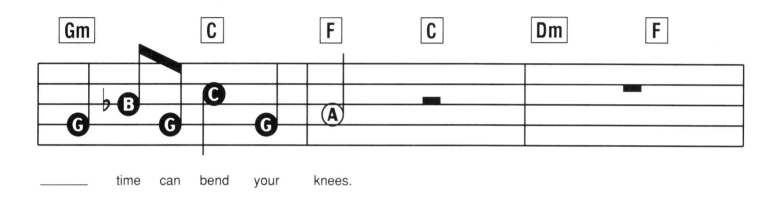

_____ time can bend your knees.

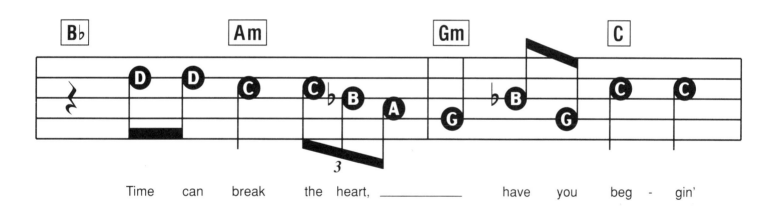

Time can break the heart, _____ have you beg - gin'

D.C. al Fine
(Return to beginning and
Play to Fade)

D7

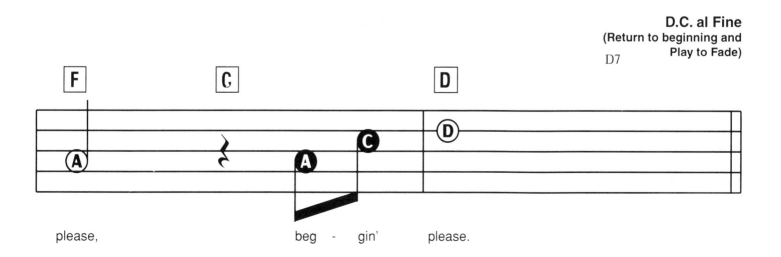

please,   beg - gin'   please.

1993
A Whole New World
from Walt Disney's ALADDIN

Registration 1
Rhythm: 8 Beat or Pops

Music by Alan Menken
Lyrics by Tim Rice

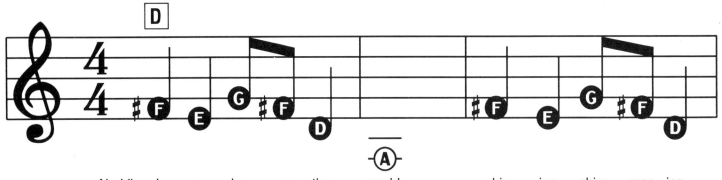

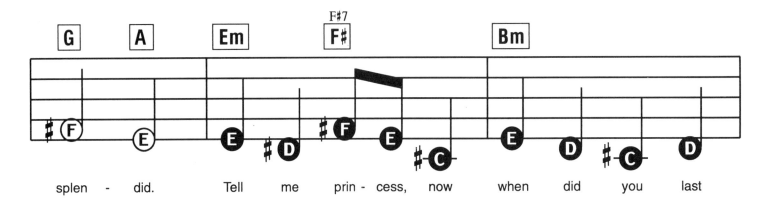

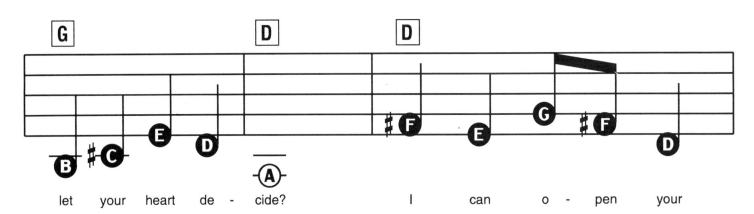

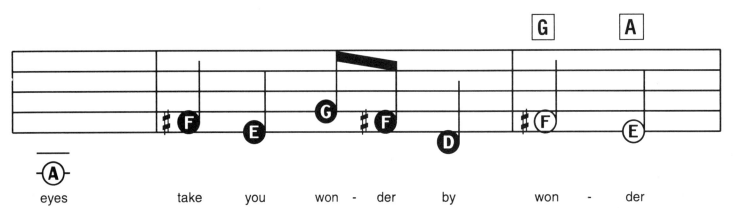

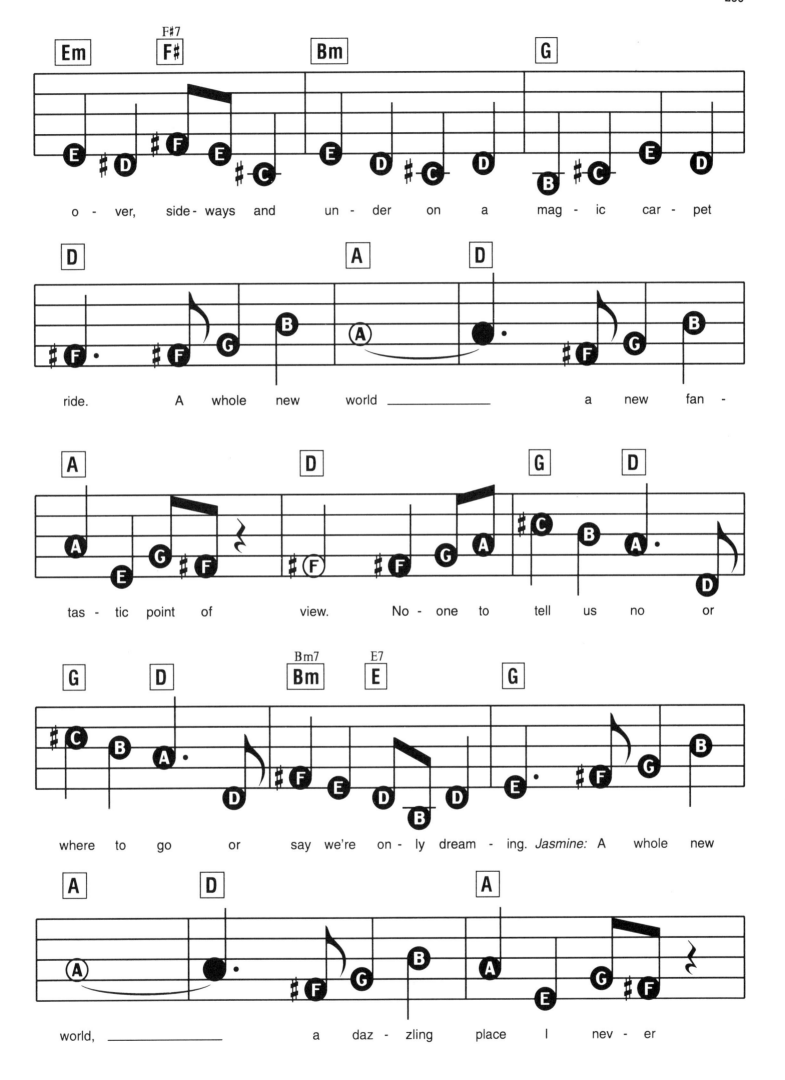

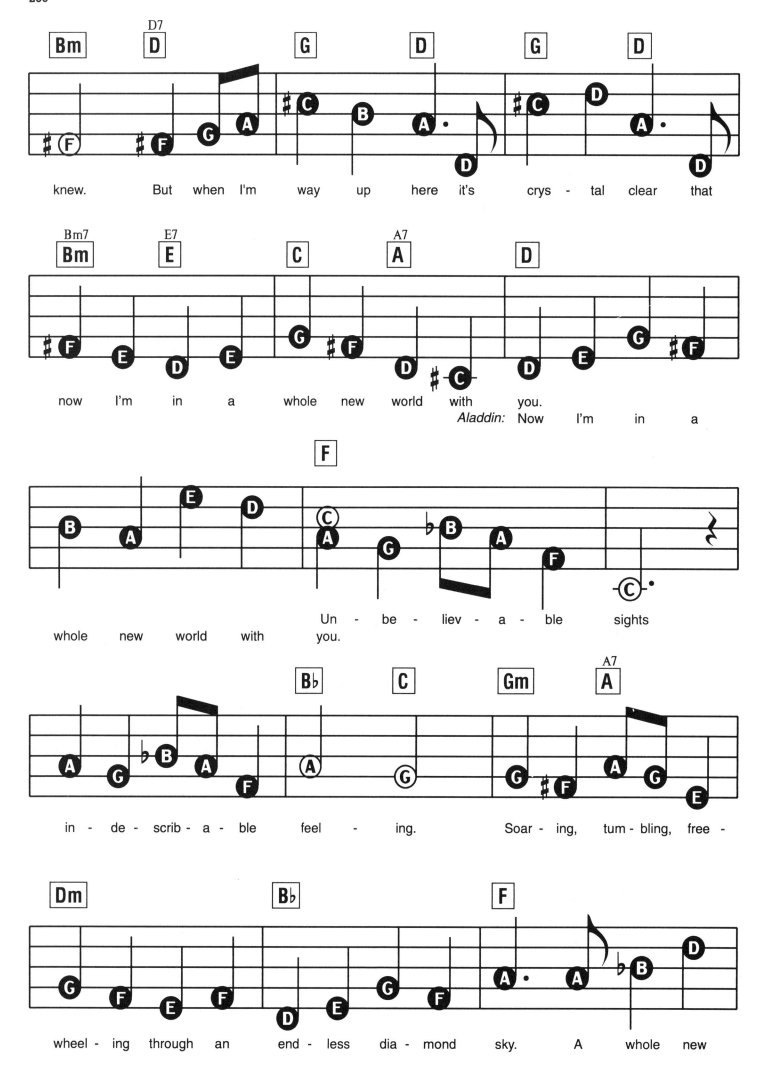

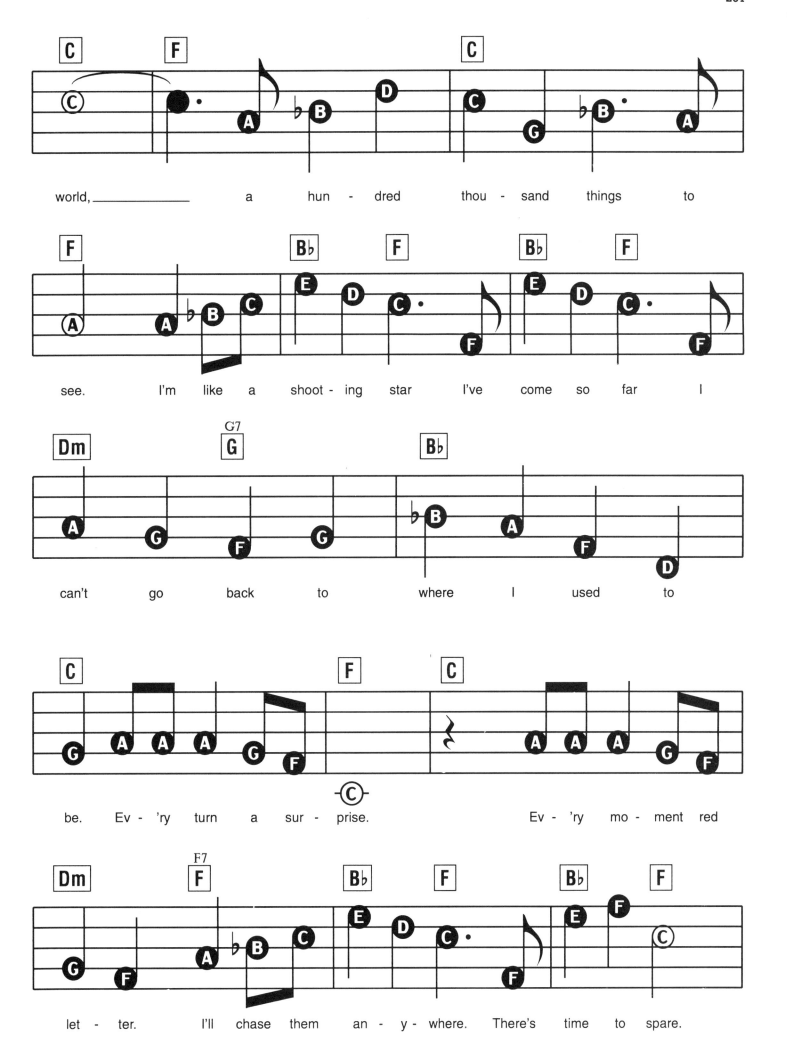

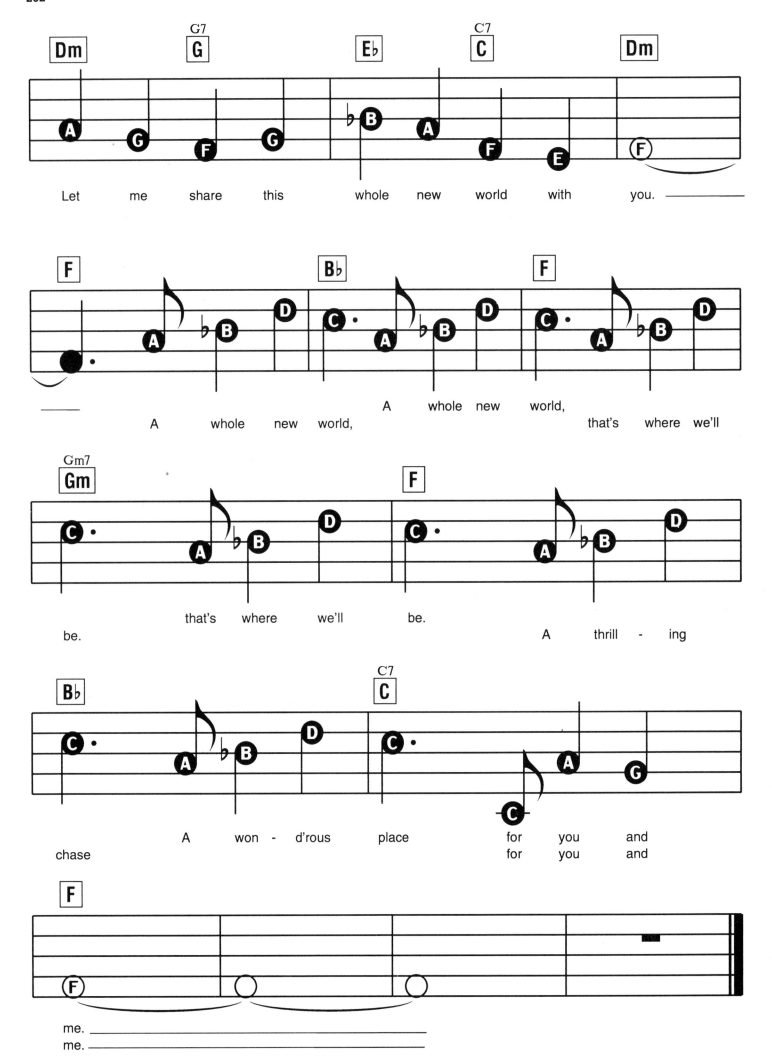

1994
The Power of Love

Registration 4
Rhythm: Rock or 8 Beat

Words by Mary Susan Applegate and Jennifer Rush
Music by Candy Derouge and Gunther Mende

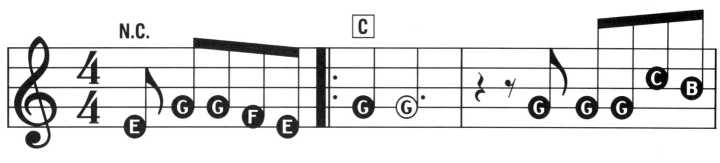

The whis-pers in the morn-ing of lov-ers sleep-ing
feel-ing ly-ing in your

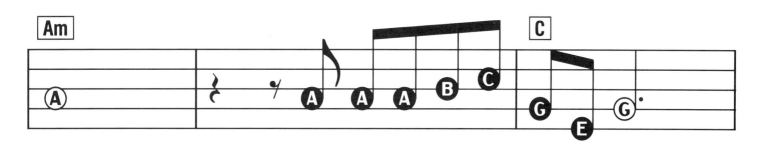

tight
arms.

are roll-ing by like thun-der now
When the world out-side's too much to take

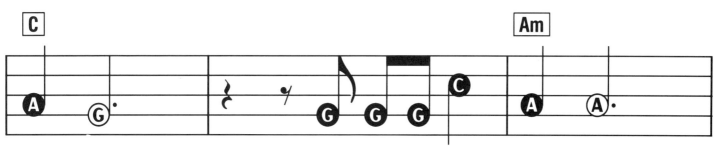

that all
as I look in your eyes.
ends when I'm with you.

I hold on-to your
Even though there may be

bod-y
times_____

and feel each move you make.
it seems I'm far a-way.

264

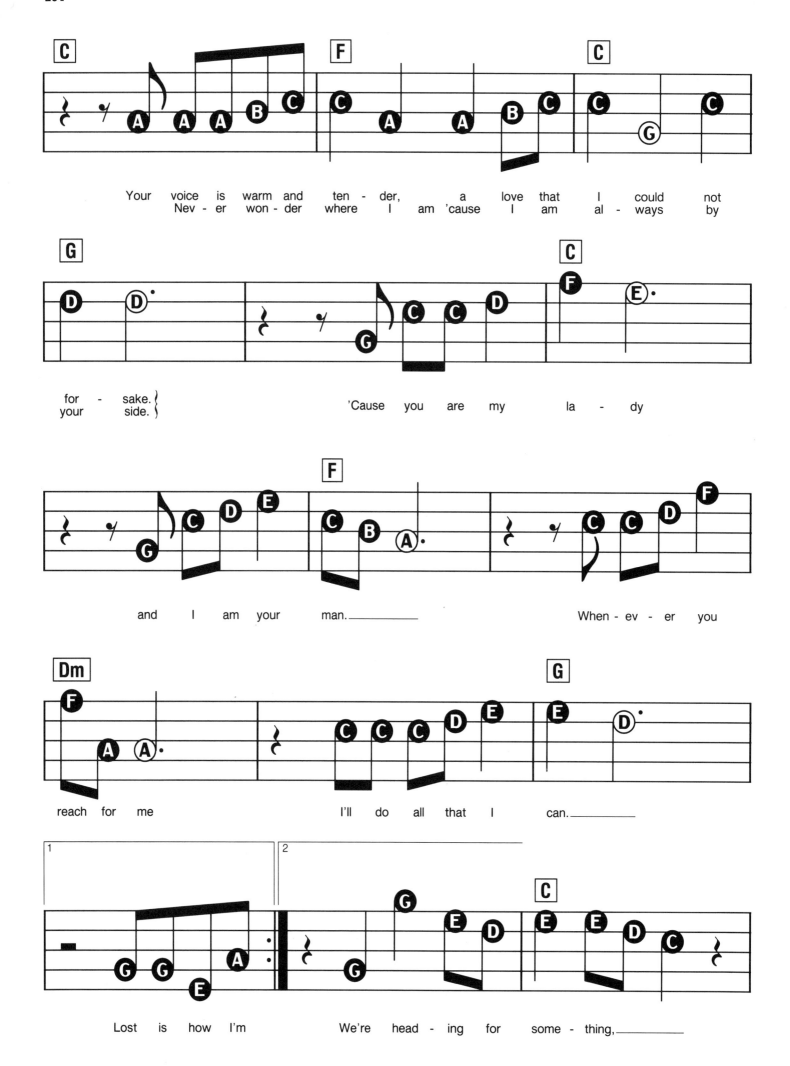

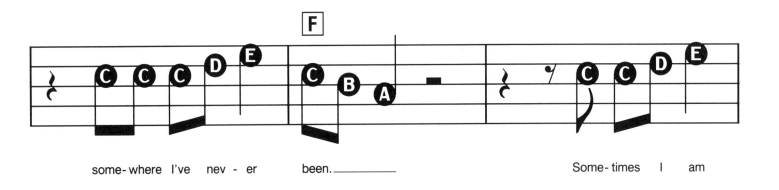

some-where I've nev - er been.___ Some-times I am

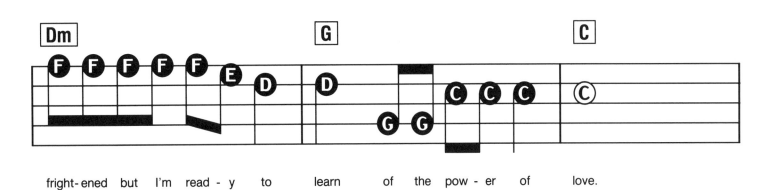

fright-ened but I'm read - y to learn of the pow - er of love.

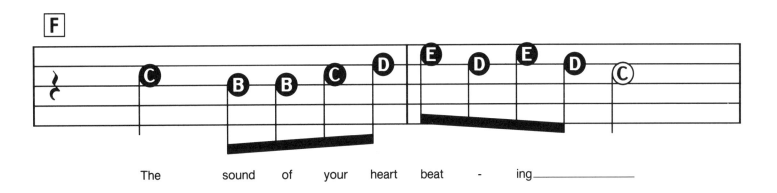

The sound of your heart beat - ing___

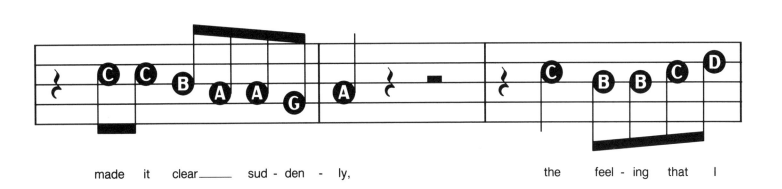

made it clear___ sud - den - ly, the feel - ing that I

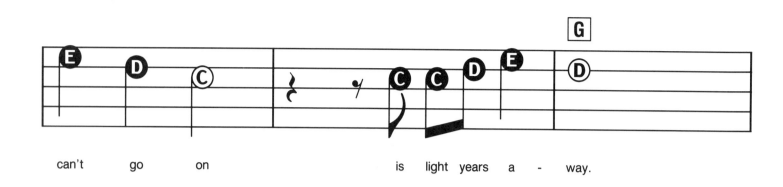

can't go on   is light years a - way.

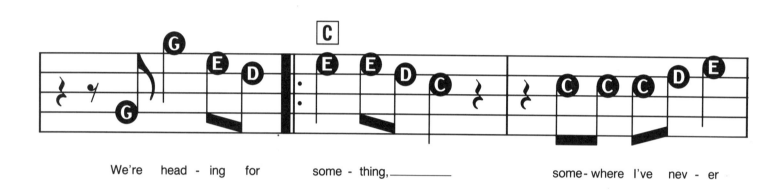

We're head - ing for   some - thing, _____   some - where I've nev - er

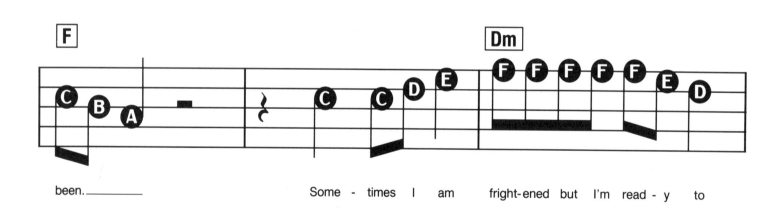

been. _____   Some - times I am   fright-ened but I'm read - y to

Repeat and Fade

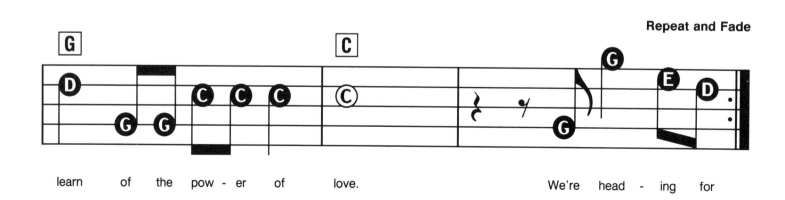

learn   of the pow - er   of love.   We're head - ing for

1995
One Sweet Day

Registration 4
Rhythm: 8 Beat or Rock

Words and Music by Mariah Carey, Walter Afanasieff, Shawn Stockman,
Michael McCary, Nathan Morris and Wanya Morris

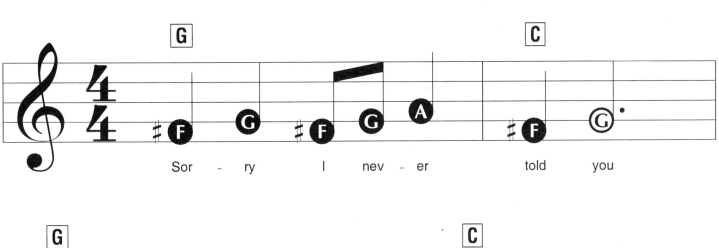

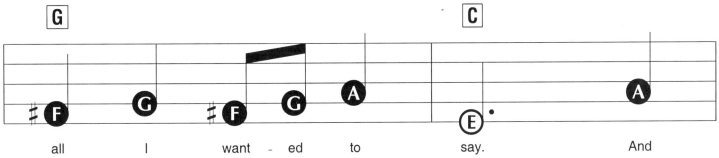

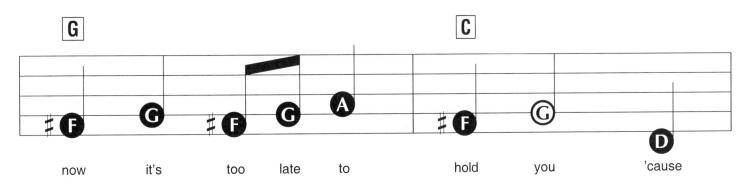

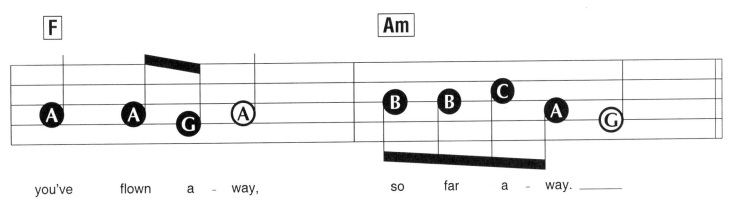

268

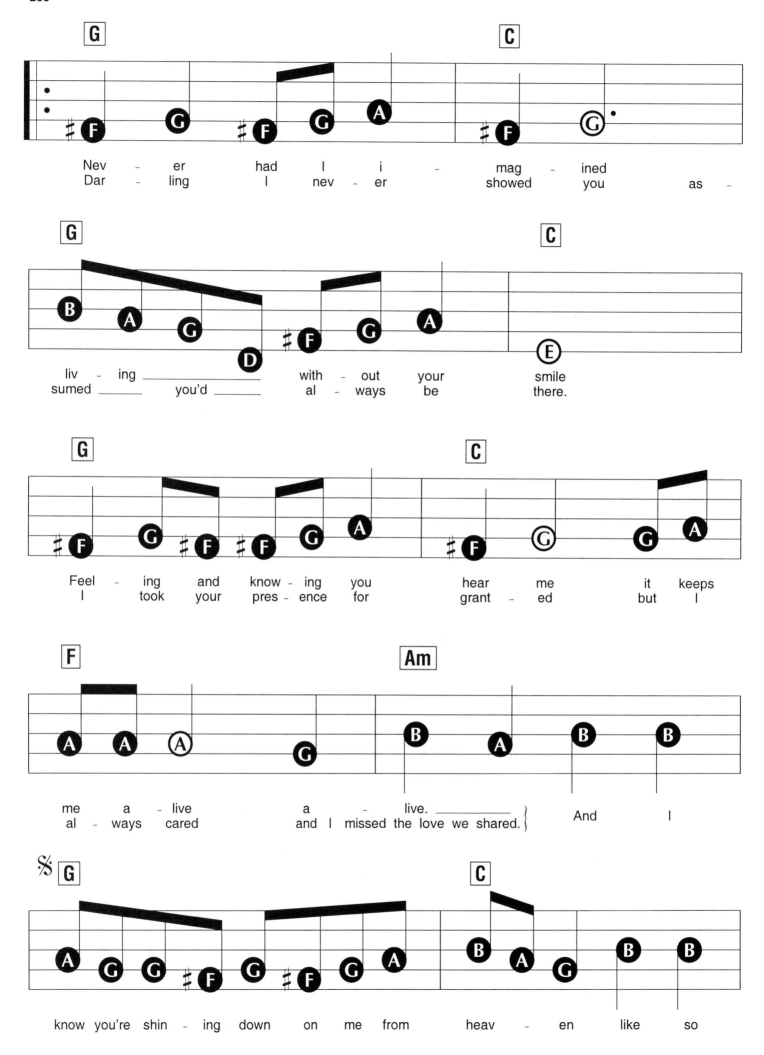

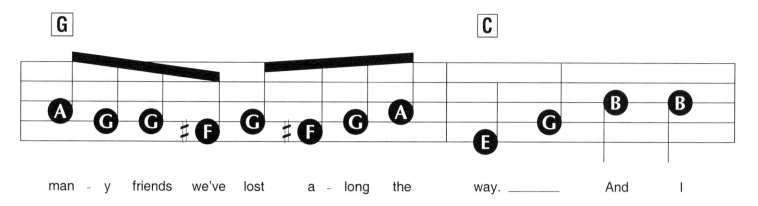

man – y friends we've lost a – long the way. _____ And I

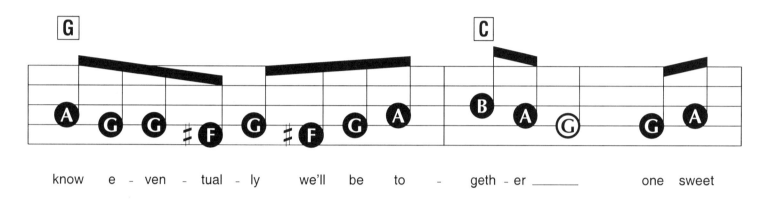

know e – ven – tual – ly we'll be to – geth – er _____ one sweet

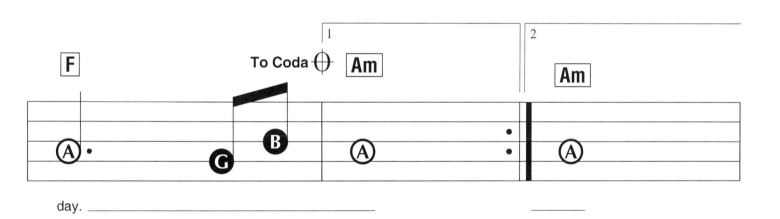

day. _____   _____

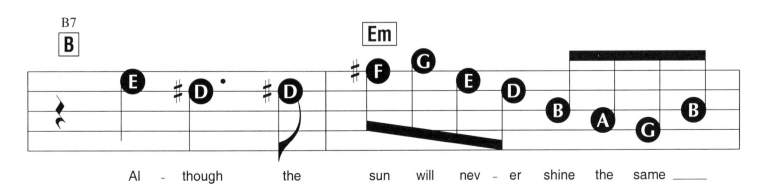

Al – though the sun will nev – er shine the same _____

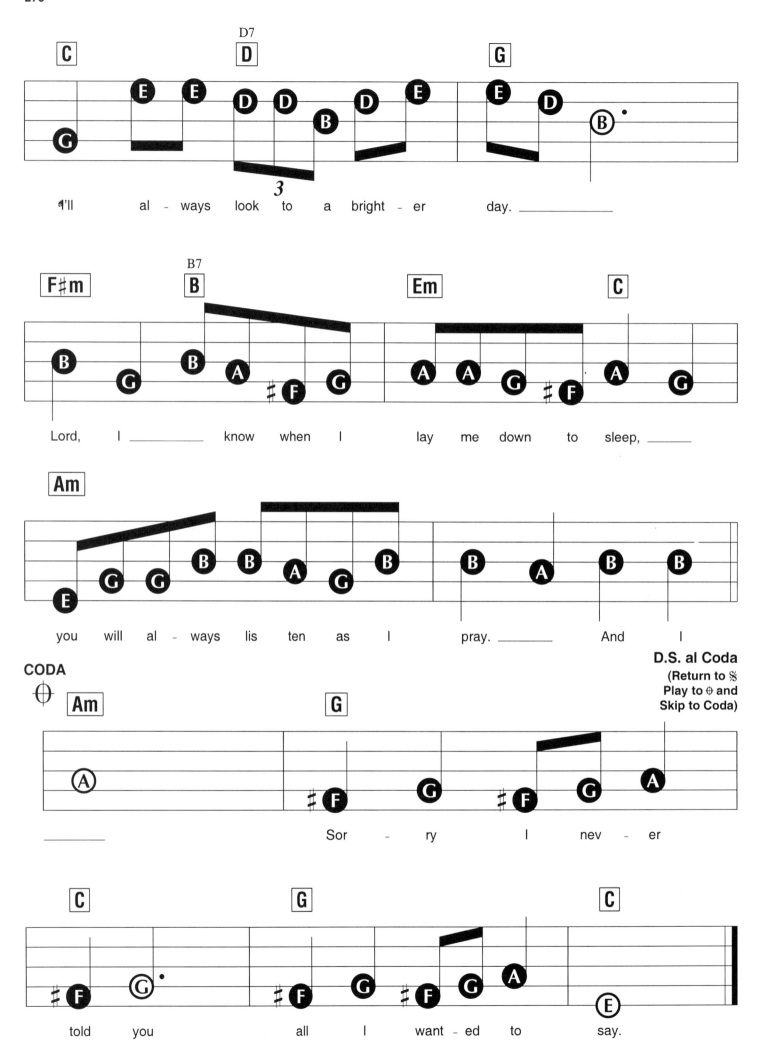

1996
I Believe in You and Me
from the Touchstone Motion Picture THE PREACHER'S WIFE

Registration 7
Rhythm: Rock or 8 Beat

Words and Music by David Wolfert
and Sandy Linzer

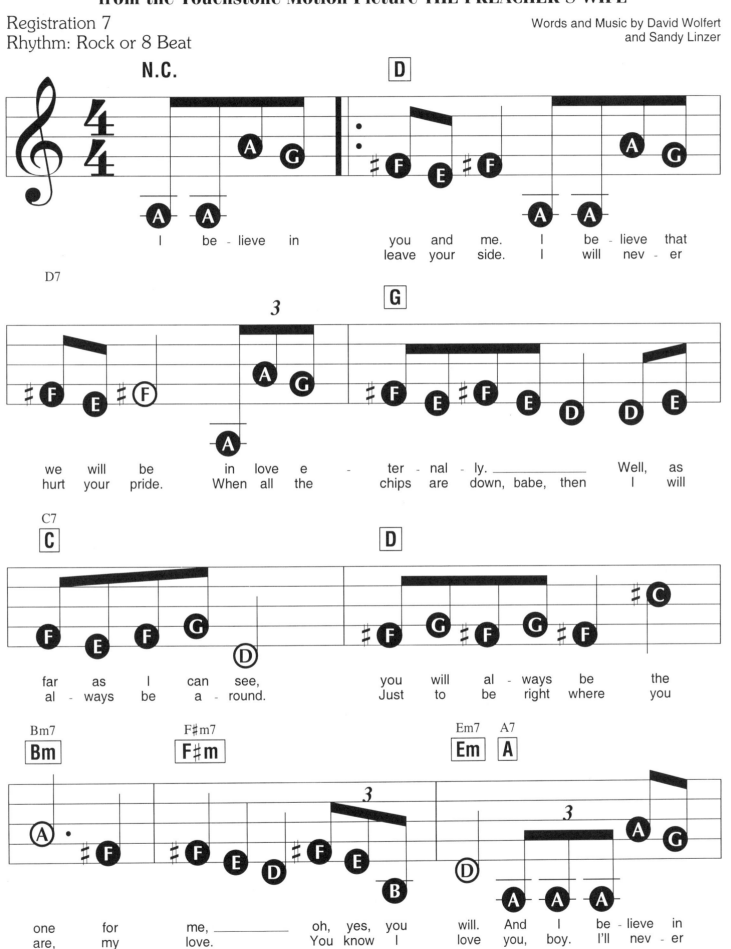

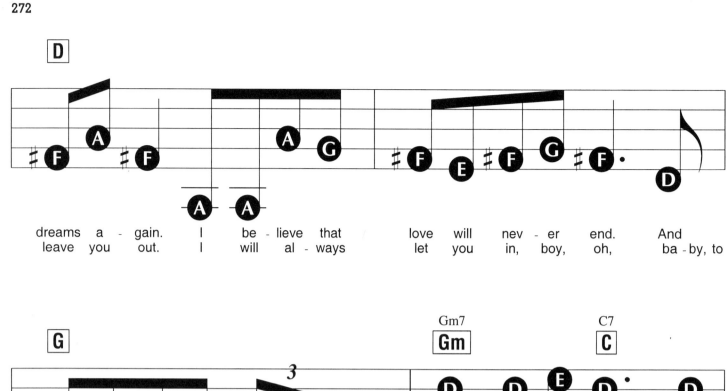

dreams a - gain. I be - lieve that love will nev - er end. And
leave you out. I will al - ways let you in, boy, oh, ba - by, to

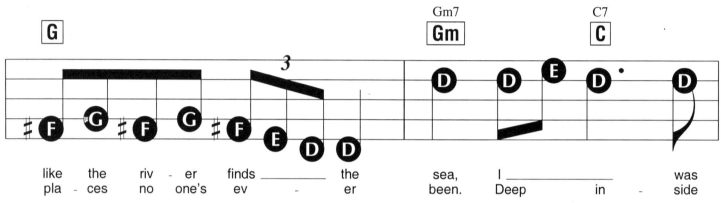

like the riv - er finds _____ the sea, I _____ was
pla - ces no one's ev - er been. Deep in - side

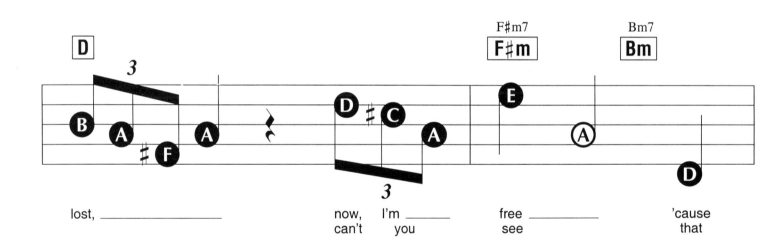

lost, _____ now, I'm _____ free _____ 'cause
can't you see that

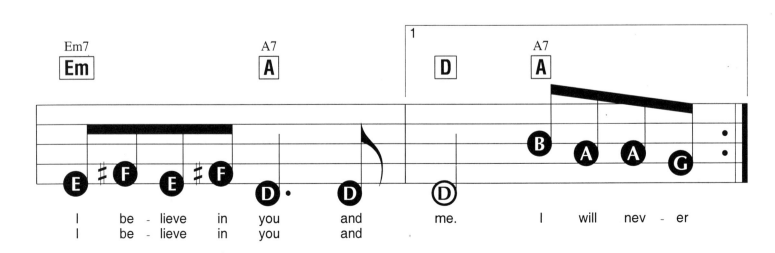

I be - lieve in you and me. I will nev - er
I be - lieve in you and

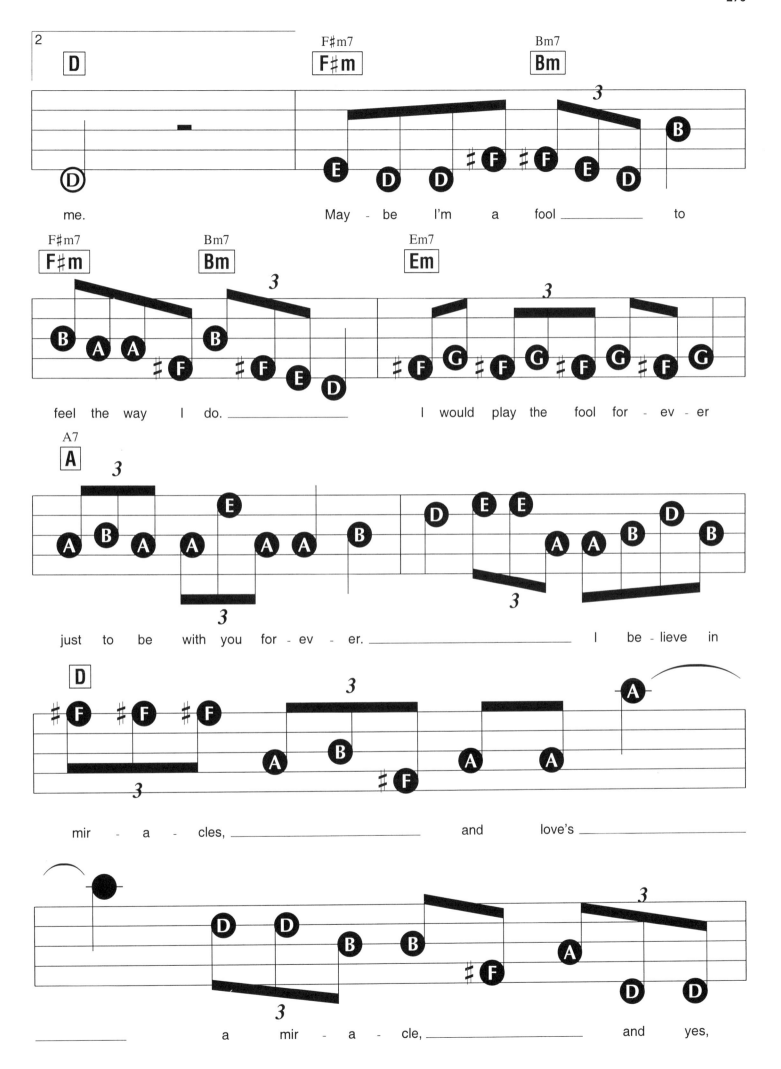

274

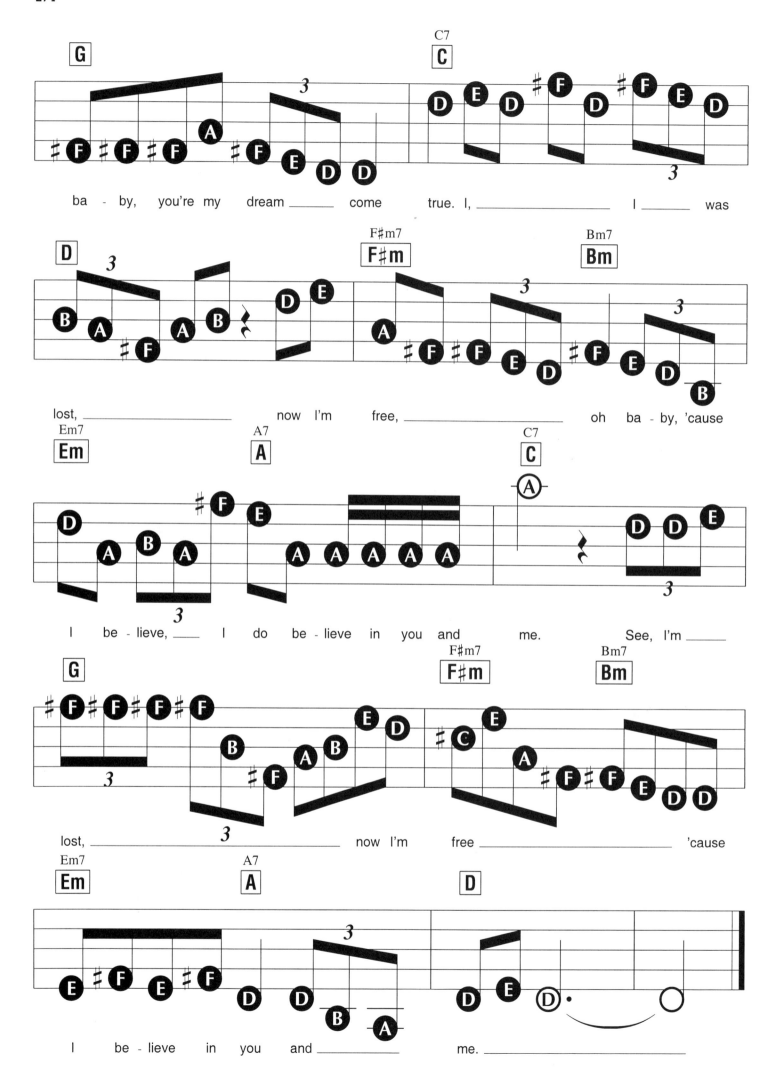

1997
Candle in the Wind 1997

Registration 1
Rhythm: Rock or Pops

Music by Elton John
Words by Bernie Taupin

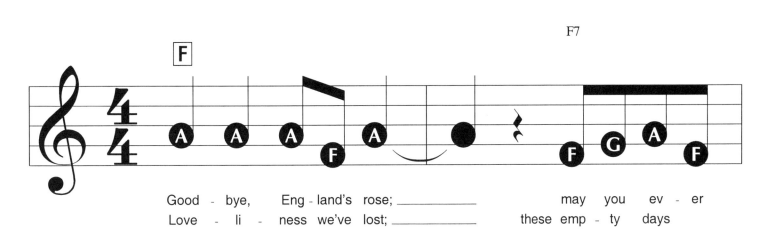

Good - bye, Eng - land's rose; _____ may you ev - er
Love - li - ness we've lost; _____ these emp - ty days

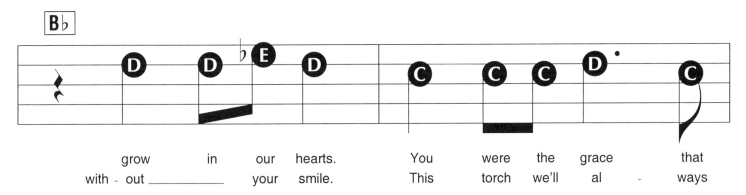

grow in our hearts. You were the grace that
with - out _____ your smile. This torch we'll al - ways

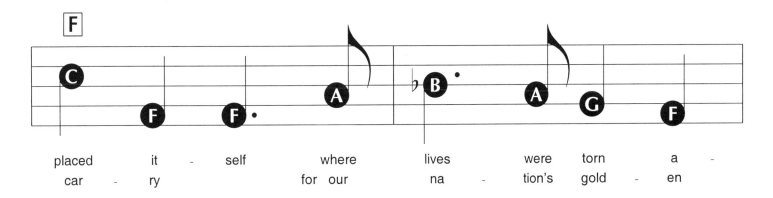

placed it - self where lives were torn a -
car - ry for our na - tion's gold - en

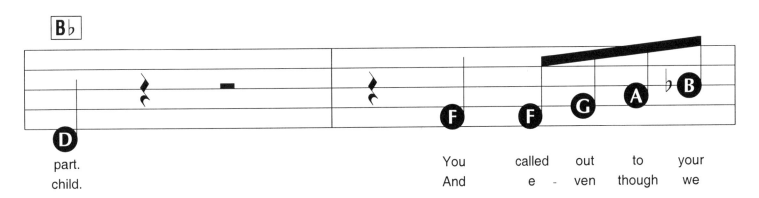

part. You called out to your
child. And e - ven though we

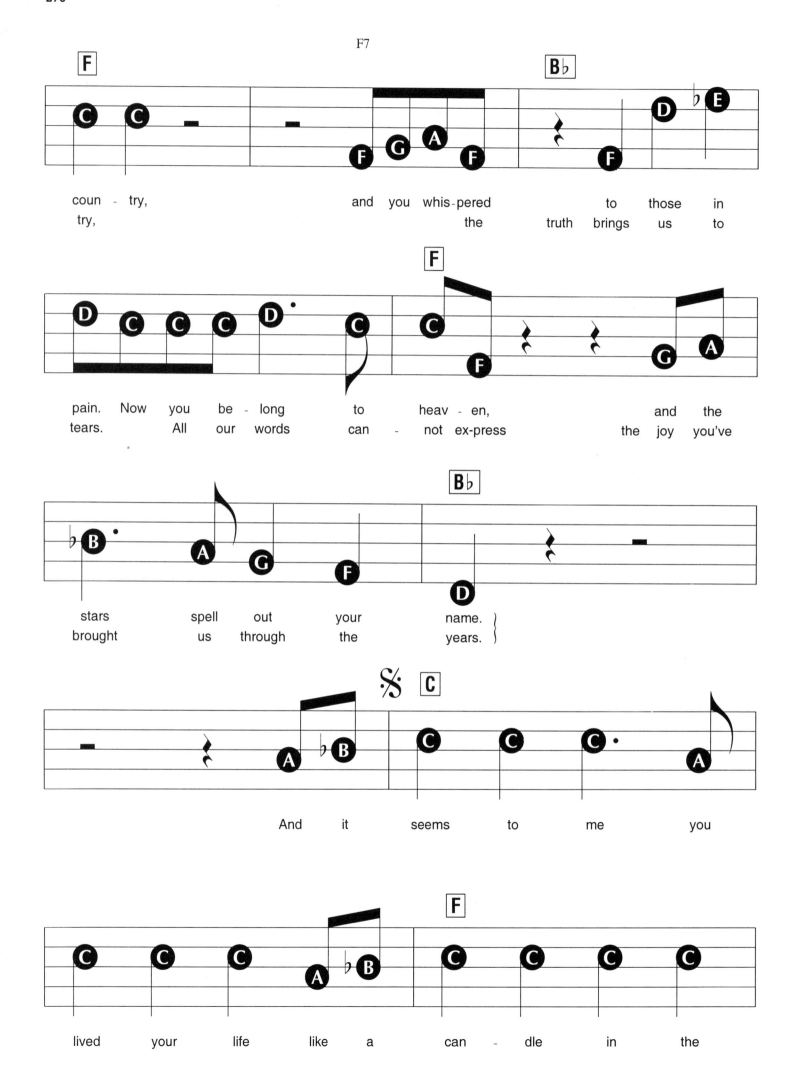

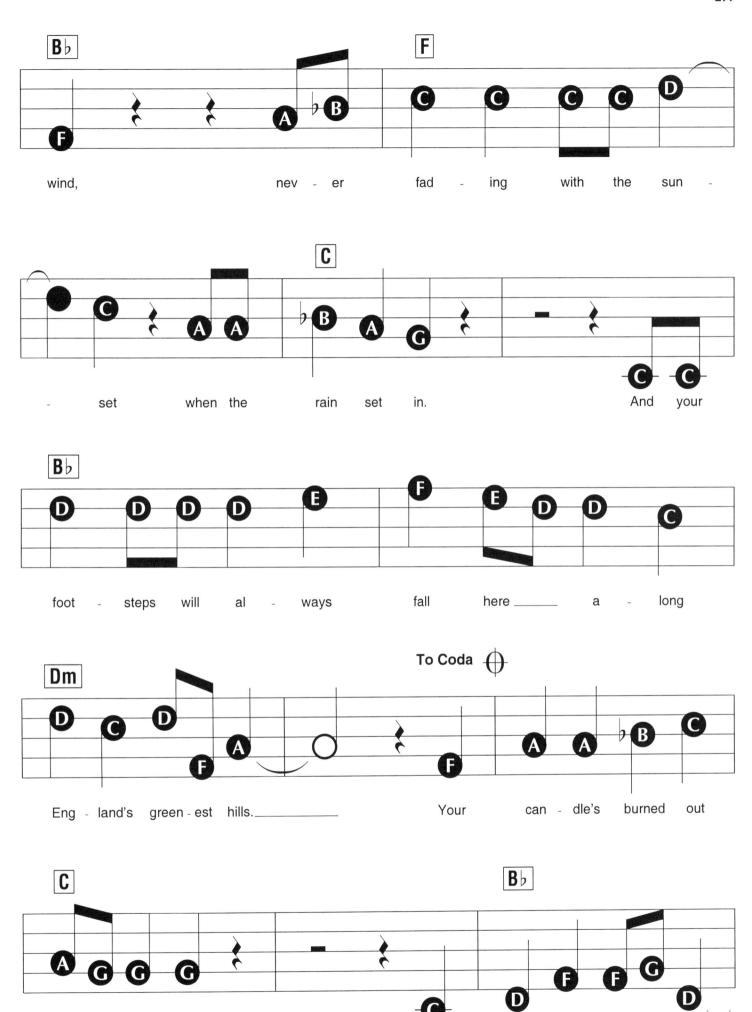

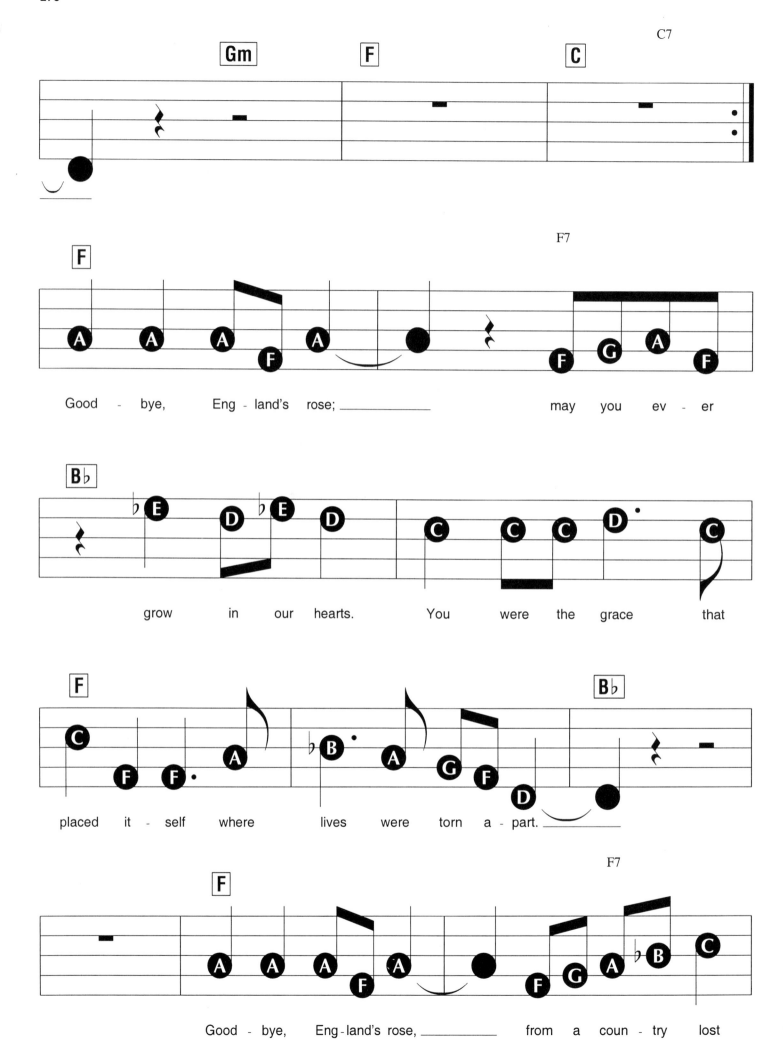

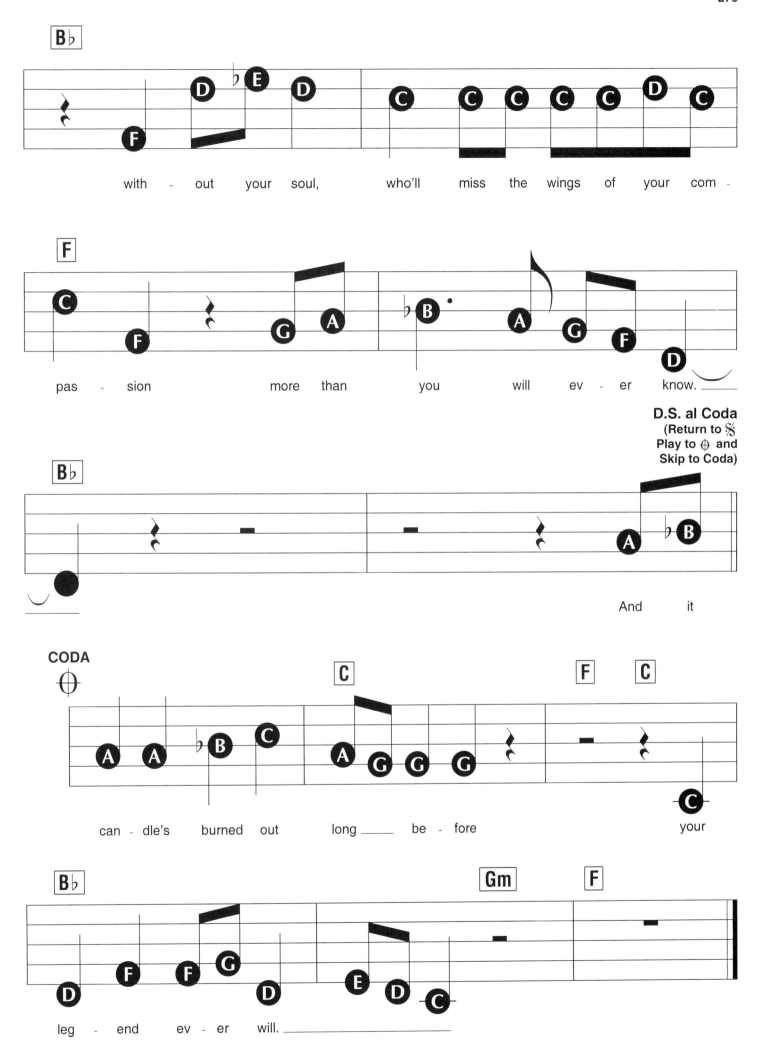

1998
My Heart Will Go On
(Love Theme from 'Titanic')
from the Paramount and Twentieth Century Fox Motion Picture TITANIC

Registration 8
Rhythm: Ballad

Music by James Horner
Lyric by Will Jennings

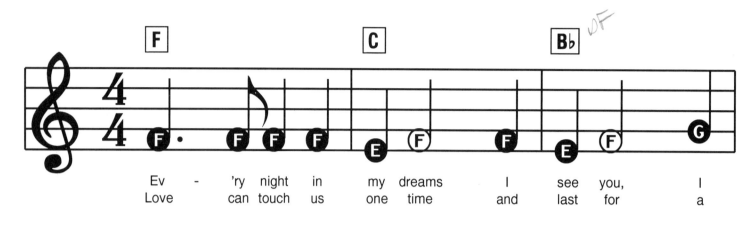

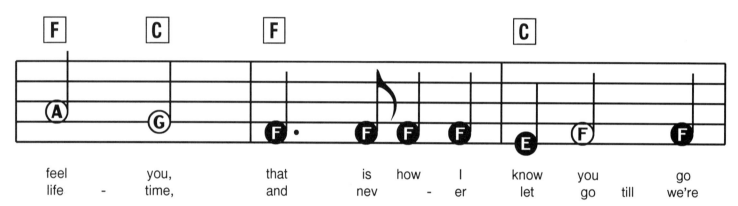

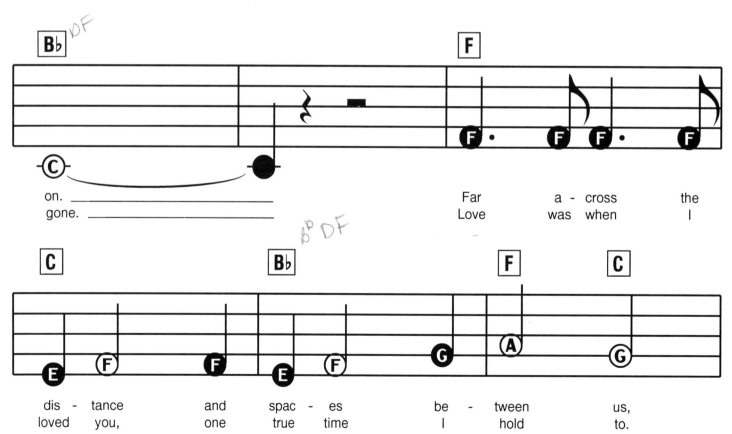

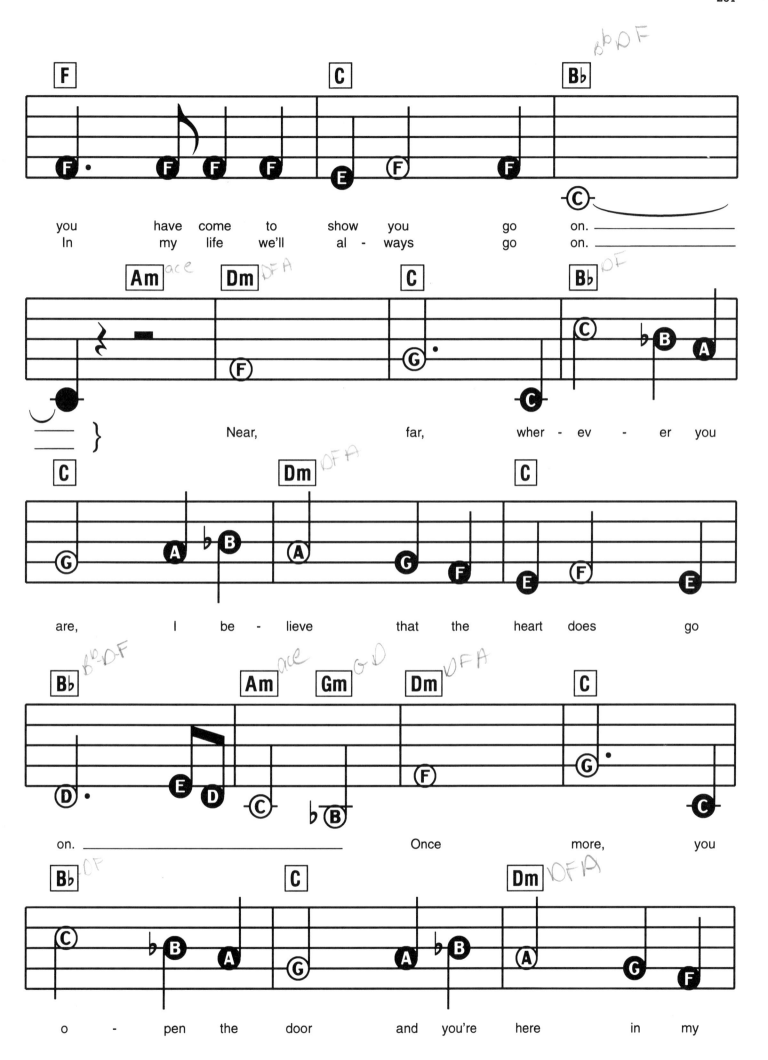

282

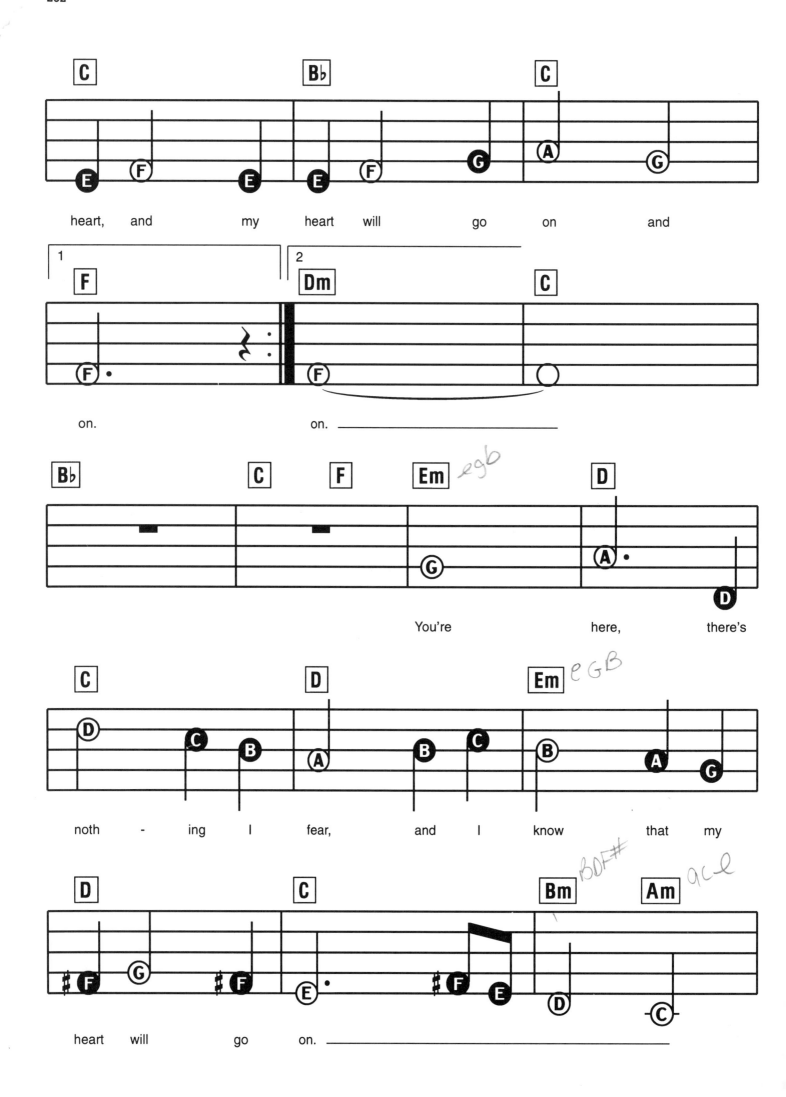

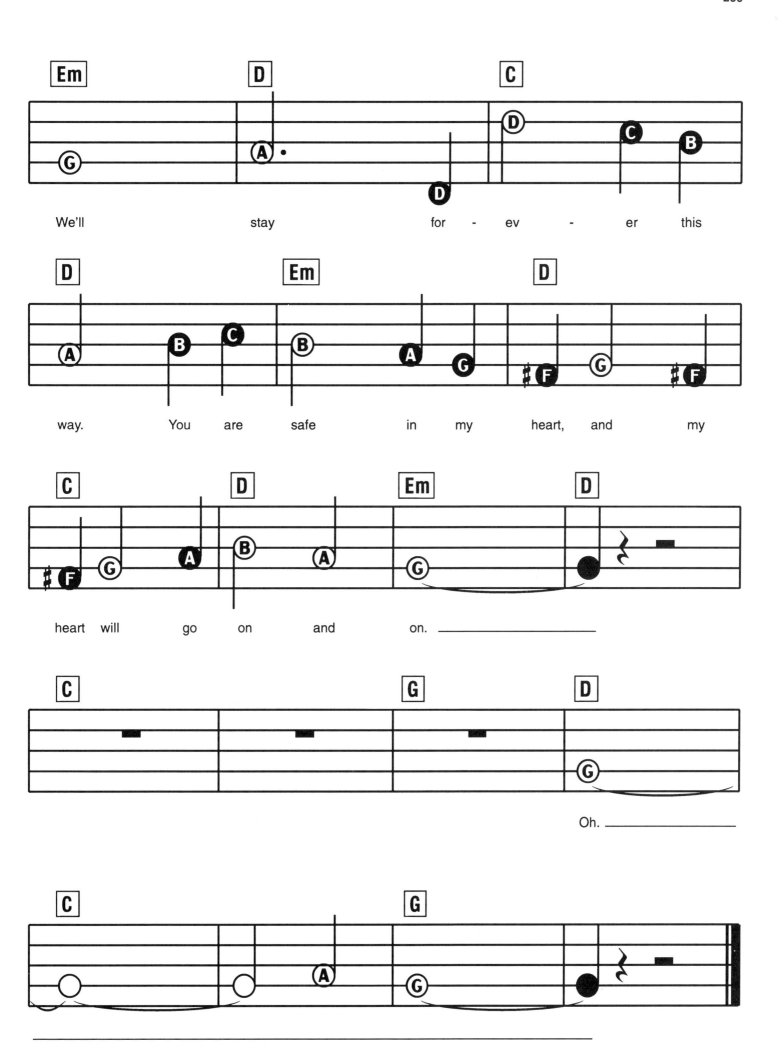

1999
Angel

Registration 8
Rhythm: Waltz

Words and Music by
Sarah McLachlan

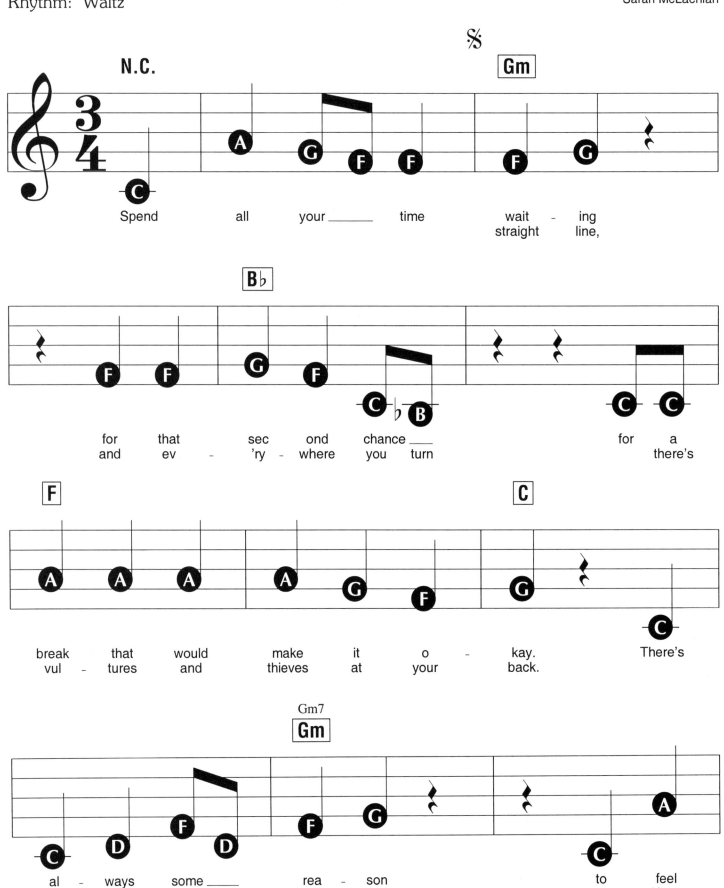

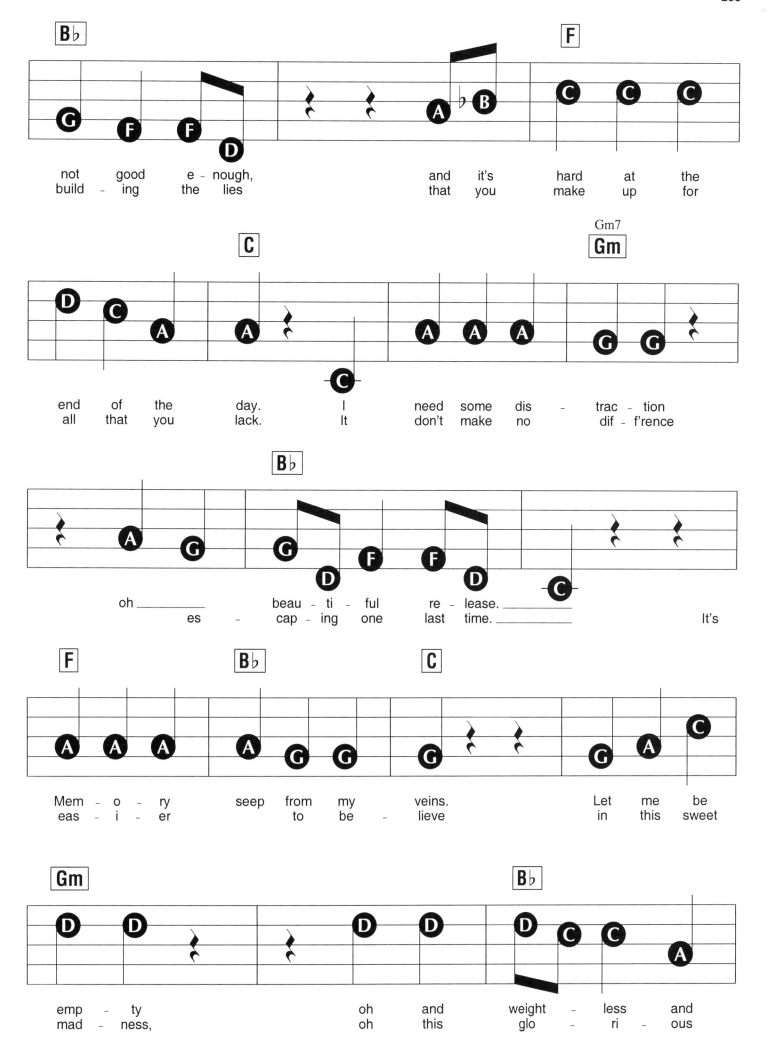

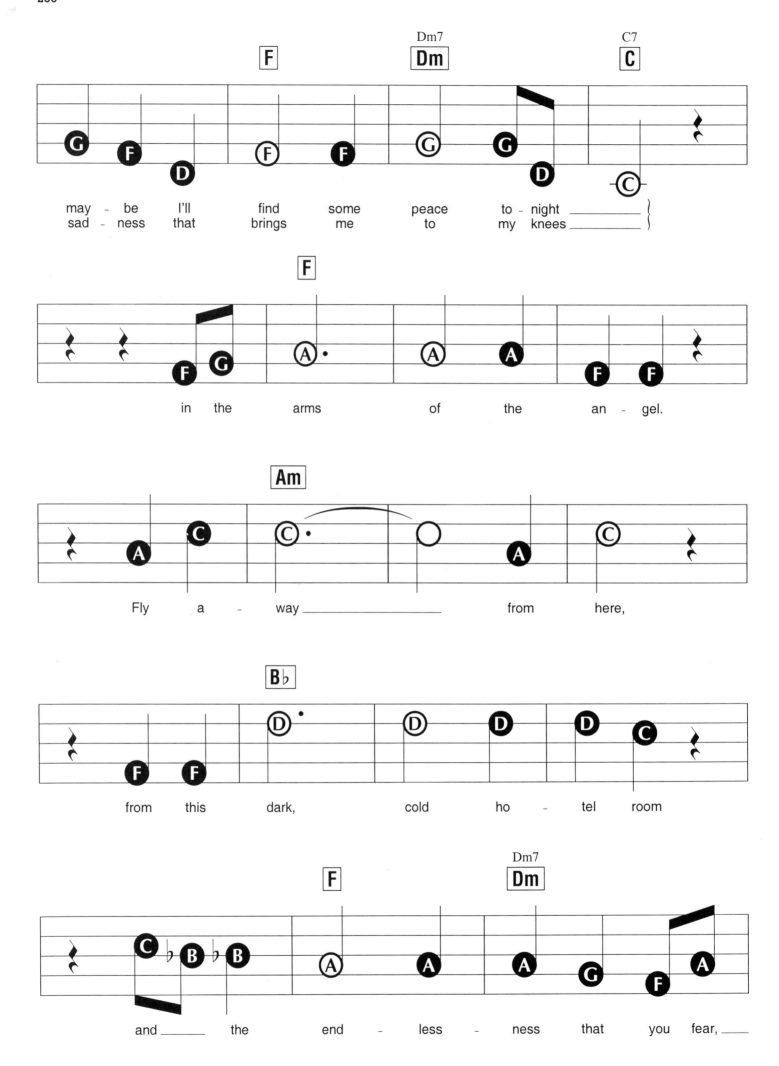

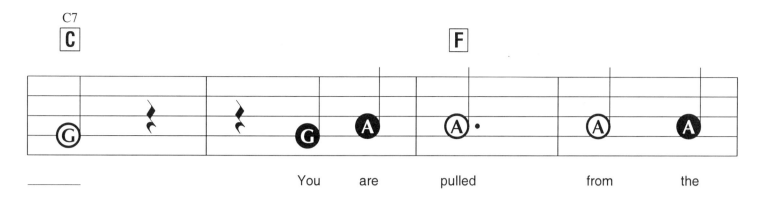

You are pulled from the

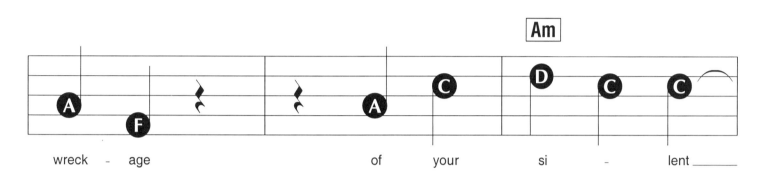

wreck - age of your si - lent _____

_____ rev - er - ie. _____ You're in the

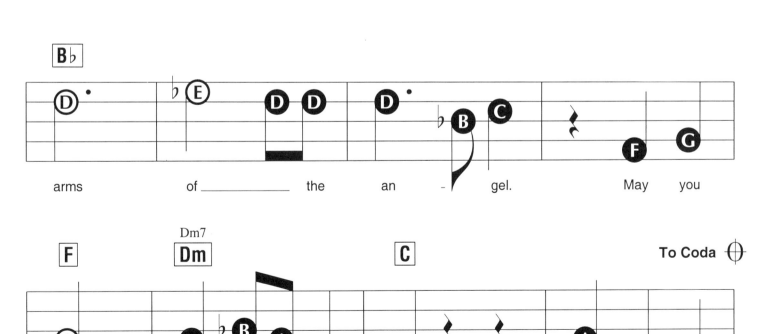

arms of _____ the an - gel. May you

find _____ some com - fort _____

288

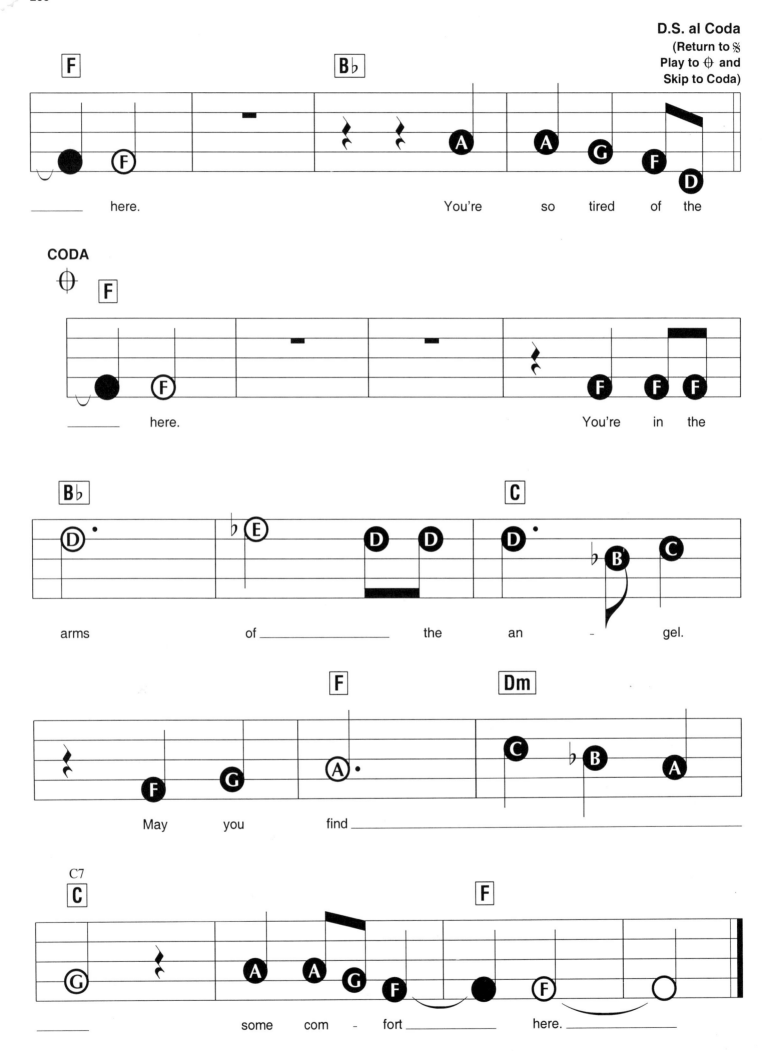

D.S. al Coda
(Return to %
Play to ⊕ and
Skip to Coda)